# kare kano

## his and her circumstances

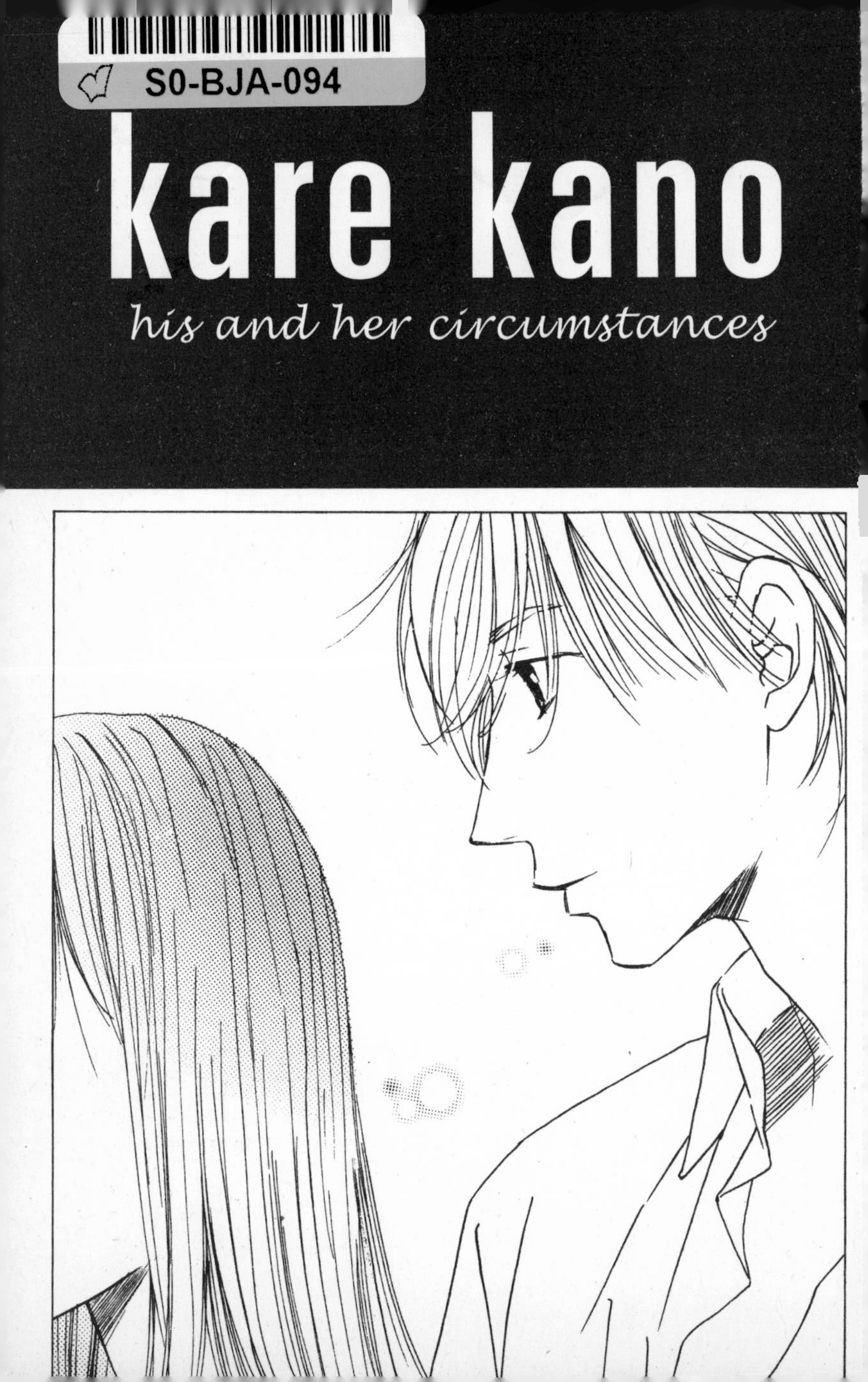

## *Kare Kano Vol. 21*
### Created by Masami Tsuda

Translation - Michelle Kobayashi
English Adaption - Darcy Lockman
Layout and Lettering - Star Print Brokers
Production Artist - Kimie Kim
Graphic Designer - Jose Macasocol, Jr.

Editor - Carol Fox
Digital Imaging Manager - Chris Buford
Pre-Production Supervisor - Erika Terriquez
Art Director - Anne Marie Horne
Production Manager - Elisabeth Brizzi
VP of Production - Ron Klamert
Editor-in-Chief - Rob Tokar
Publisher - Mike Kiley
President and C.O.O. - John Parker
C.E.O. and Chief Creative Officer - Stuart Levy

A  Manga

TOKYOPOP and 🐱 are trademarks or registered trademarks of TOKYOPOP Inc.

TOKYOPOP Inc.
5900 Wilshire Blvd. Suite 2000
Los Angeles, CA 90036

E-mail: info@TOKYOPOP.com
Come visit us online at www.TOKYOPOP.com

KARESHI KANOJO NO JIJOU by Masami Tsuda.
© 2005 Masami Tsuda. All Rights Reserved.
First published in Japan in 2005 by HAKUSENSHA, INC. Tokyo.
English language translation rights in the United States of
America and Canada arranged with HAKUSENSHA, INC., Tokyo
through Tuttle-Mori Agency Inc., Tokyo.
English text copyright © 2007 TOKYOPOP Inc.

ISBN: 978-1-59816-840-2

First TOKYOPOP printing: January 2007
10  9  8  7  6  5  4  3  2  1
Printed in the USA

# kare kano

*his and her circumstances*

## volume twenty-one

**by Masami Tsuda**

HAMBURG // LONDON // LOS ANGELES // TOKYO

# KARE KANO: THE STORY SO FAR

Yukino Miyazawa seemed like the perfect student: kind, athletic and smart. But in actuality, she was the self-professed "queen of vanity"--her only goal was to win the praise and admiration of others, and her sacred duty was to look and act perfect during school hours. Only at home would she let down her guard and let her true self show.

But when Yukino entered high school, she met her match: Soichiro Arima, a handsome, popular, ultra-intelligent guy. At first when he stole the top seat in class from her, Yukino saw him as a bitter rival. But over time, she learned that she and Soichiro had more in common than she had ever imagined. As their love blossomed, the two made a vow to finally stop pretending to be perfect and simply be true to themselves.

Still, they had plenty of obstacles. Jealous classmates tried to break them up, and so did teachers when their grades began to suffer as a result of the relationship. Yet somehow Yukino and Soichiro's love managed to persevere. But their greatest challenge was yet to come.

For although Soichiro's life seemed perfect, he'd endured a very traumatic childhood...and the ghosts were coming back to haunt him. His father left him early, and his mother was so abusive that his uncle adopted him and raised him as his own. But when Soichiro started to get nationwide attention for his high school achievements, his birth mother resurfaced, hoping to cash in. Soichiro met with her a few times to learn more about the family that abandoned him...until he realized she had nothing for him but more abuse and lies. With that (and a little help from his friends), he severed contact.

Soichiro had been keeping his family drama secret from Yukino, afraid it would destroy everything they'd worked to achieve. But she finally broke down his walls and made him tell her everything. Then, Soichiro's father Reiji returned to Japan, and as the son and father spent time together, all the painful details of the circle of birth, violence, and suffering in three generations of Soichiro's family came out.

After Reiji returns to New York, Yukino tells Soichiro the secret she's been hiding: she's pregnant. Soichiro is able to accept the prospect of becoming a father, and the two happily share the news with their families. They've even got a plan for the future: Yukino will go to medical school while Soichiro pursues his dream of becoming a cop. Will this be happily ever after...?

kare kano
volume twenty-one

# TABLE OF CONTENTS

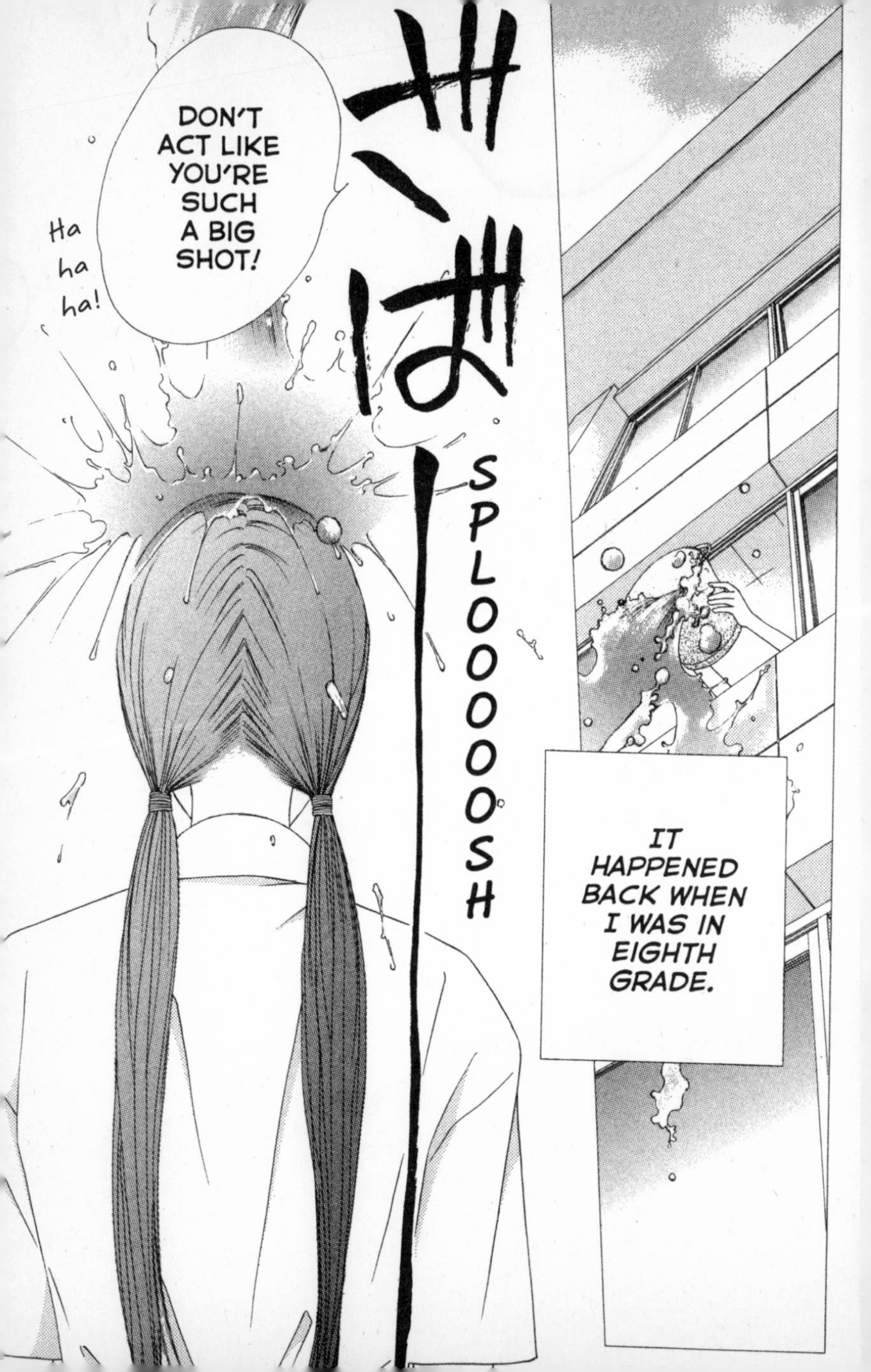
IT HAPPENED BACK WHEN I WAS IN EIGHTH GRADE.
SPLOOOOOOSH
DON'T ACT LIKE YOU'RE SUCH A BIG SHOT!
Ha ha ha!

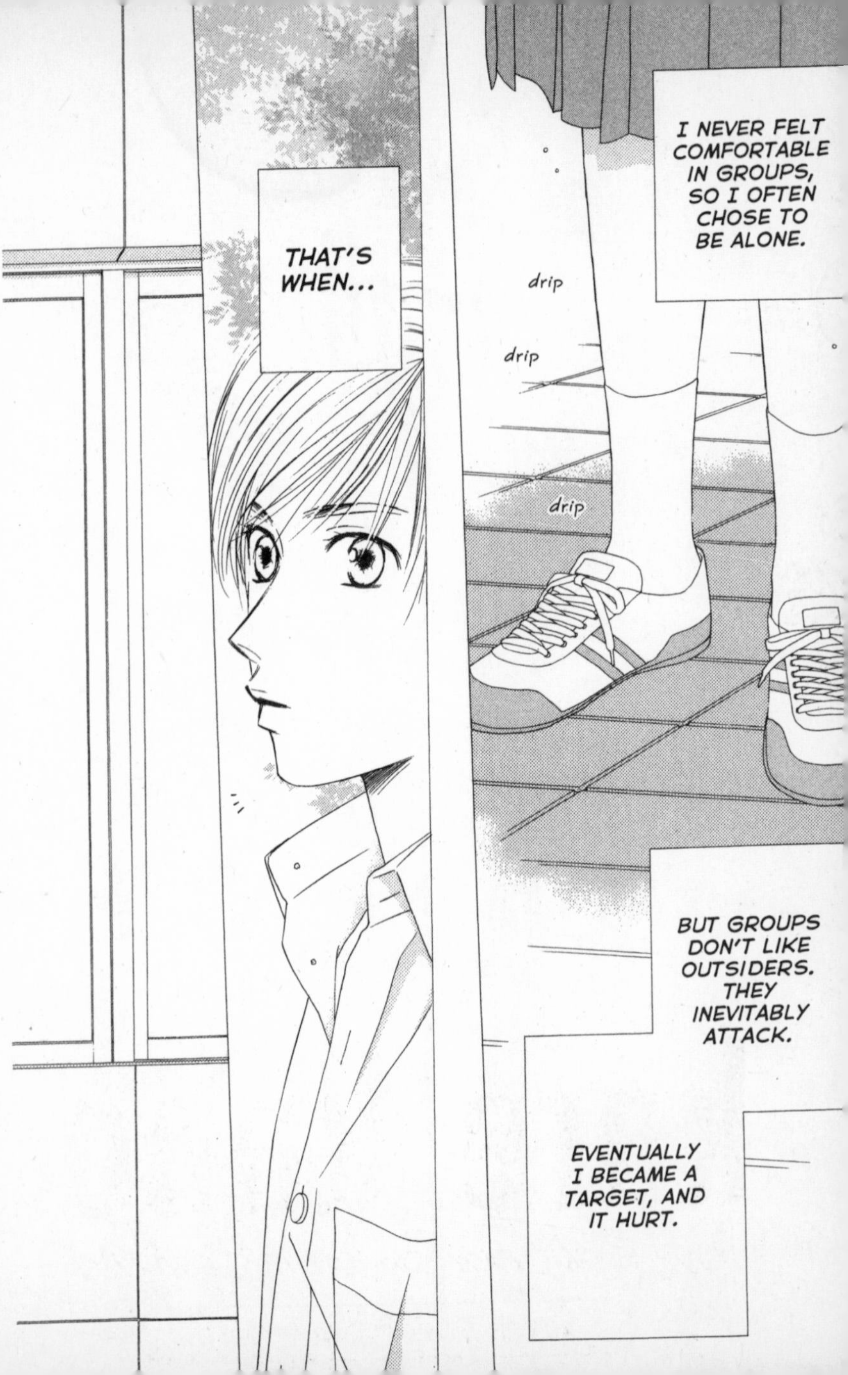
I NEVER FELT COMFORTABLE IN GROUPS, SO I OFTEN CHOSE TO BE ALONE.
drip
drip
drip
BUT GROUPS DON'T LIKE OUTSIDERS. THEY INEVITABLY ATTACK.
EVENTUALLY I BECAME A TARGET, AND IT HURT.
THAT'S WHEN...

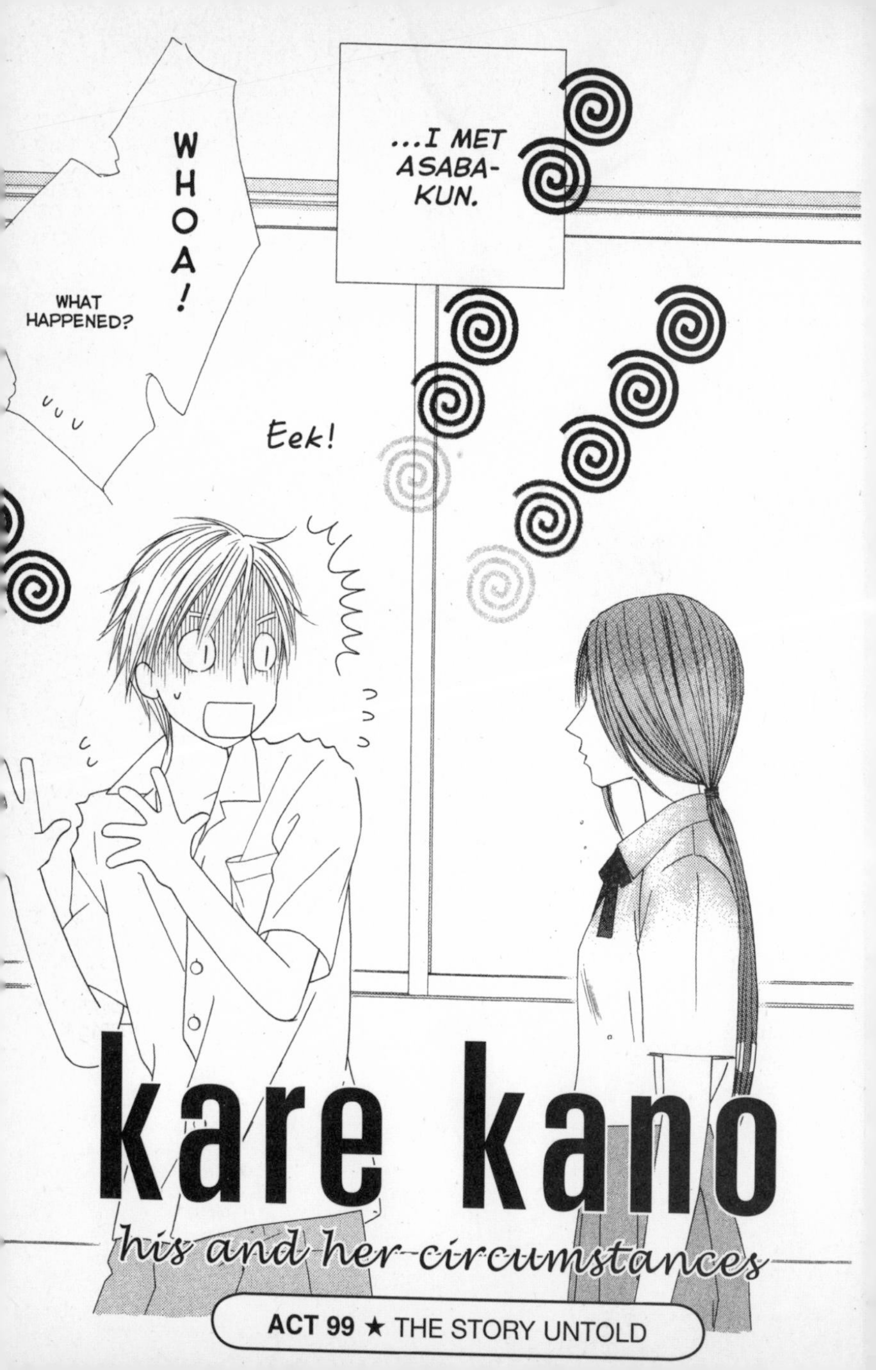
...I MET ASABA-KUN.
WHOA!
WHAT HAPPENED?
Eek!
kare kano
his and her circumstances
ACT 99 ★ THE STORY UNTOLD

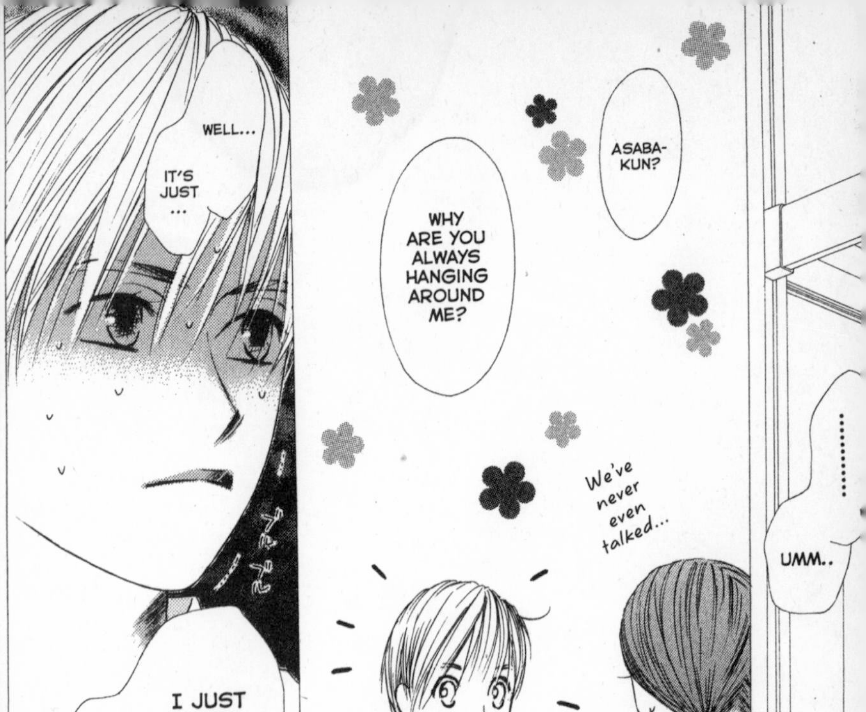
ASABA-KUN?
WHY ARE YOU ALWAYS HANGING AROUND ME?
......
UMM..
We've never even talked...
WELL...
IT'S JUST ...
I JUST HATE SEEING YOU BULLIED.
I REALLY CAN'T STAND IT!

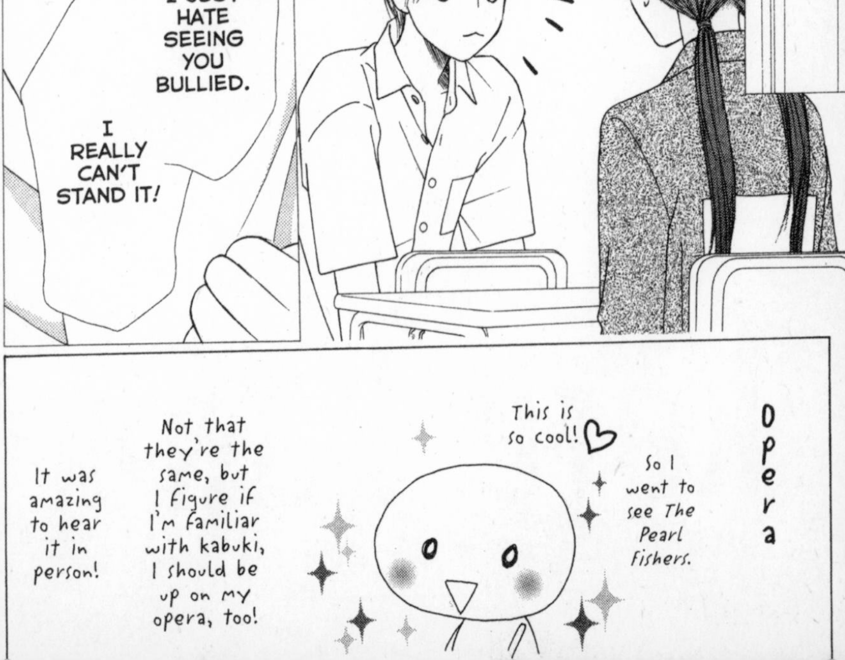
Opera
So I went to see The Pearl Fishers.
This is so cool!
Not that they're the same, but I figure if I'm familiar with kabuki, I should be up on my opera, too!
It was amazing to hear it in person!

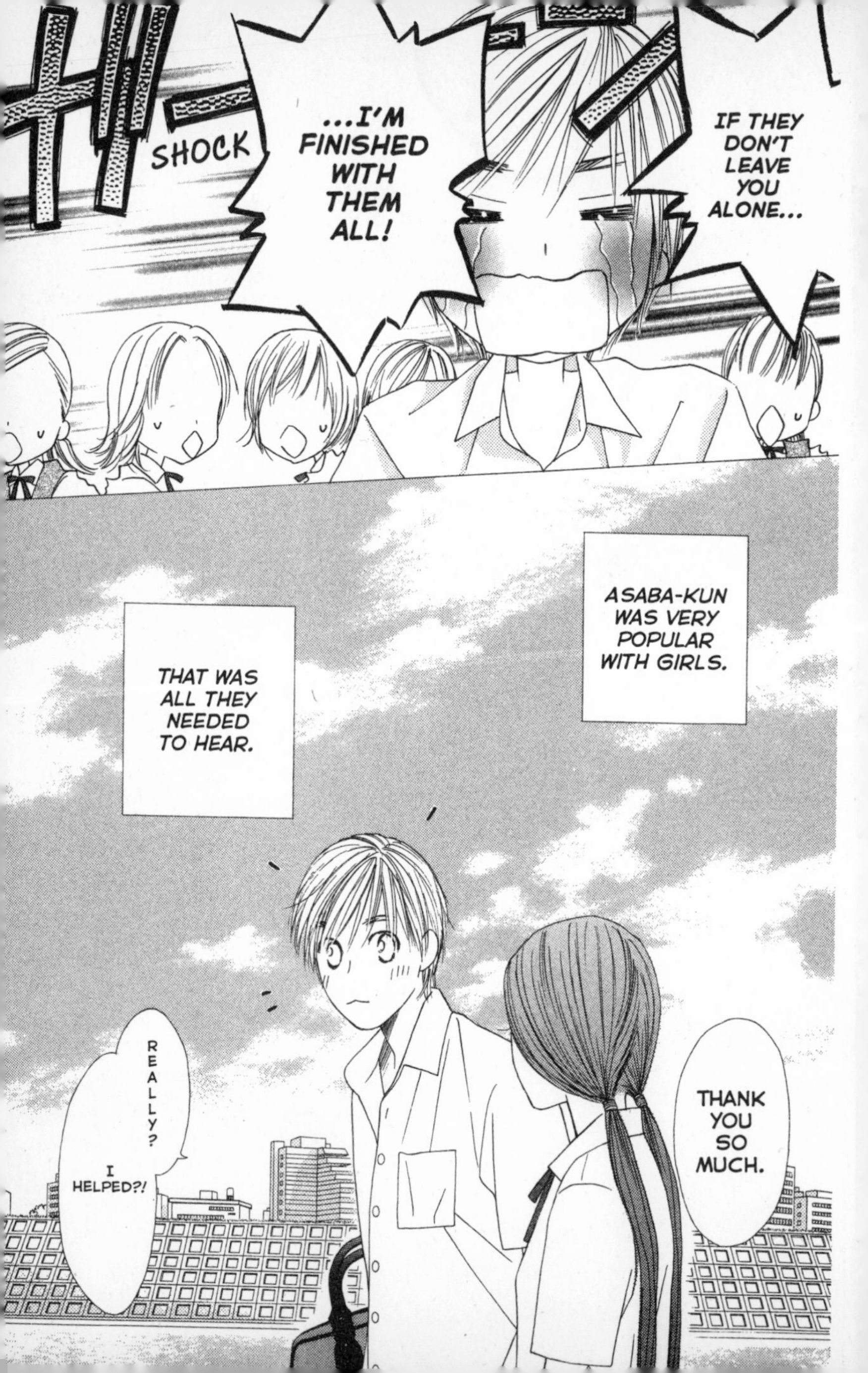
IF THEY DON'T LEAVE YOU ALONE...
...I'M FINISHED WITH THEM ALL!
SHOCK
ASABA-KUN WAS VERY POPULAR WITH GIRLS.
THAT WAS ALL THEY NEEDED TO HEAR.
THANK YOU SO MUCH.
REALLY? I HELPED?!

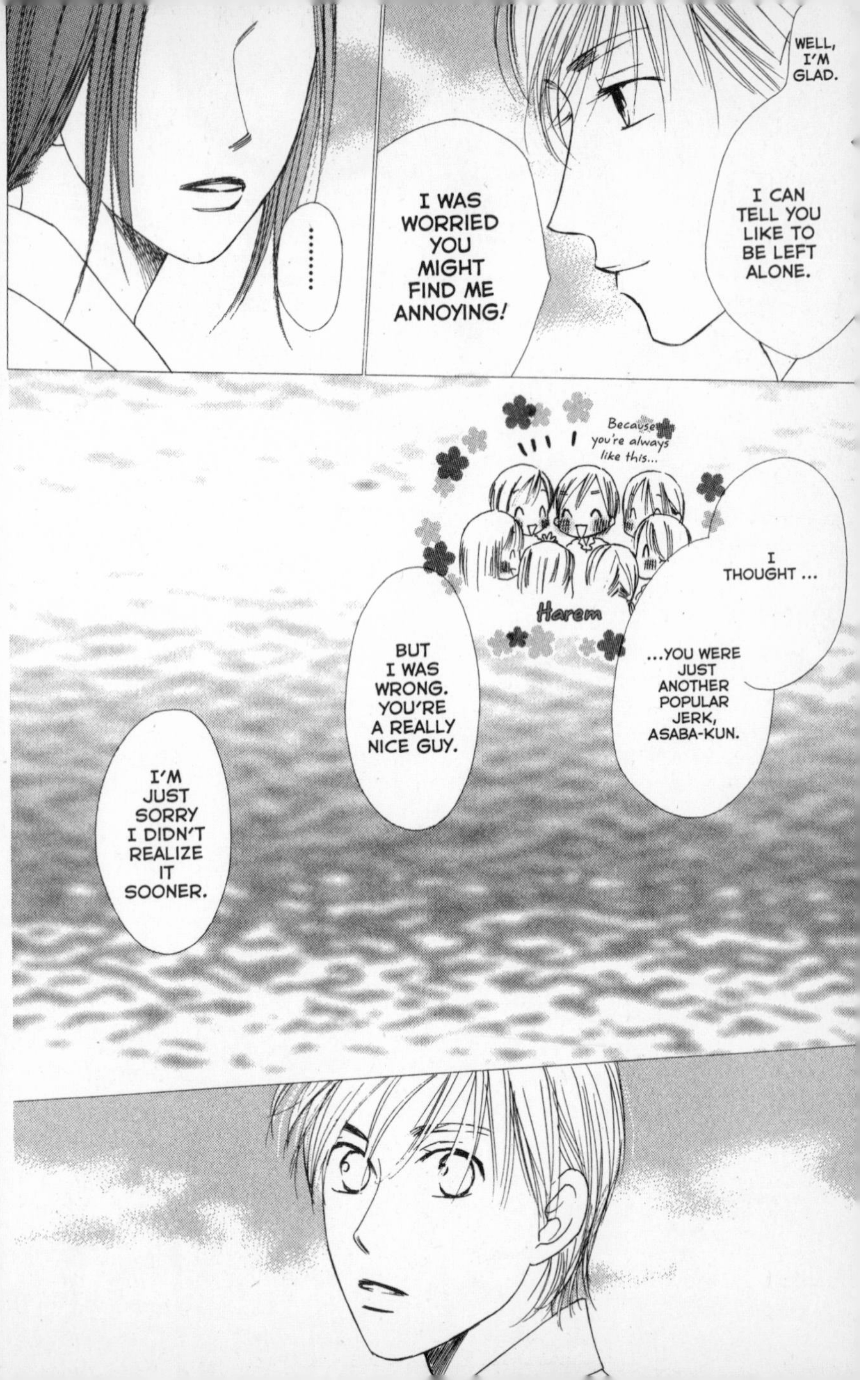
WELL, I'M GLAD.
I CAN TELL YOU LIKE TO BE LEFT ALONE.
I WAS WORRIED YOU MIGHT FIND ME ANNOYING!
.........
I THOUGHT ...
...YOU WERE JUST ANOTHER POPULAR JERK, ASABA-KUN.
Because you're always like this...
Harem
BUT I WAS WRONG. YOU'RE A REALLY NICE GUY.
I'M JUST SORRY I DIDN'T REALIZE IT SOONER.

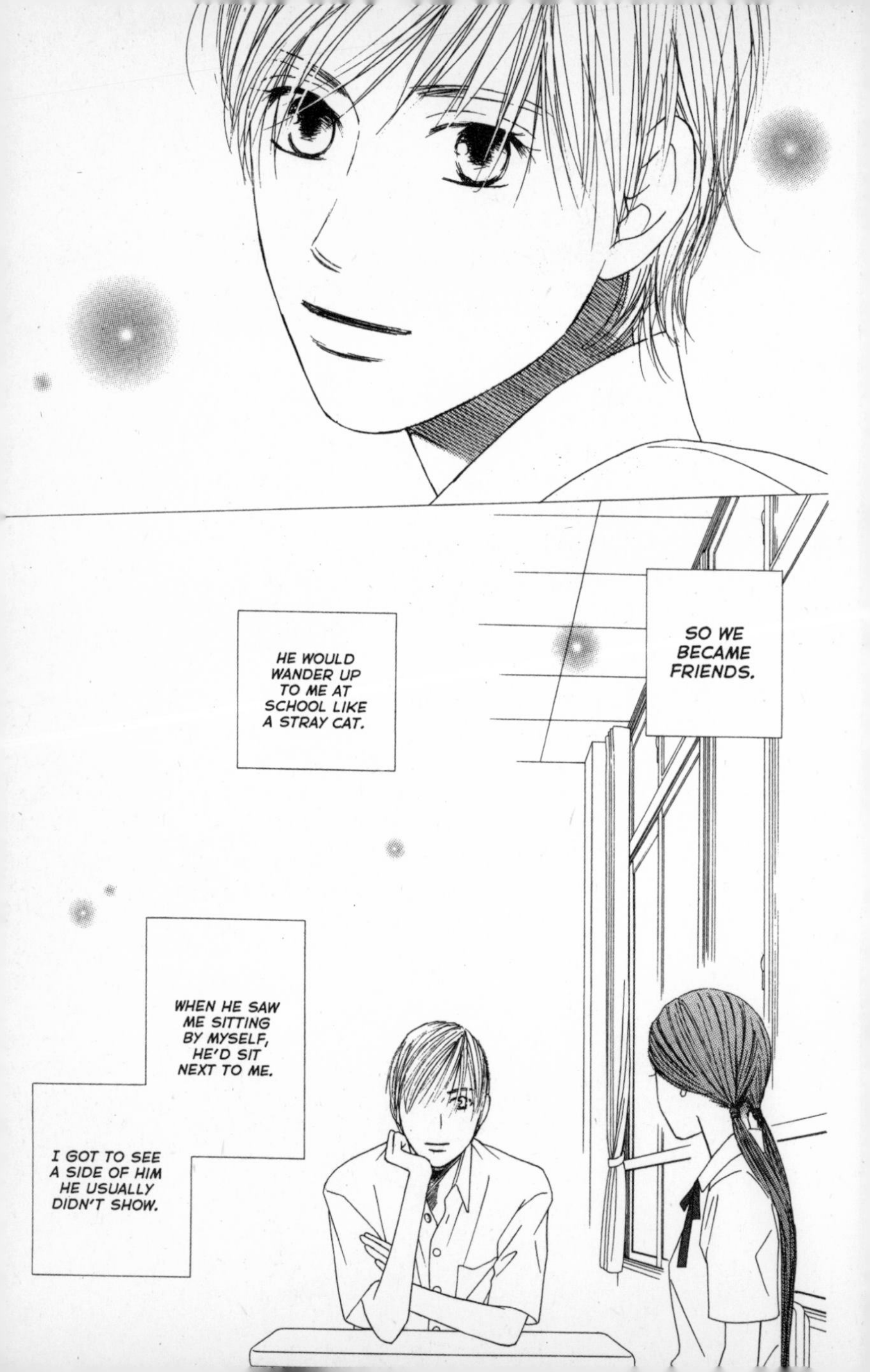
SO WE BECAME FRIENDS.
HE WOULD WANDER UP TO ME AT SCHOOL LIKE A STRAY CAT.
WHEN HE SAW ME SITTING BY MYSELF, HE'D SIT NEXT TO ME.
I GOT TO SEE A SIDE OF HIM HE USUALLY DIDN'T SHOW.

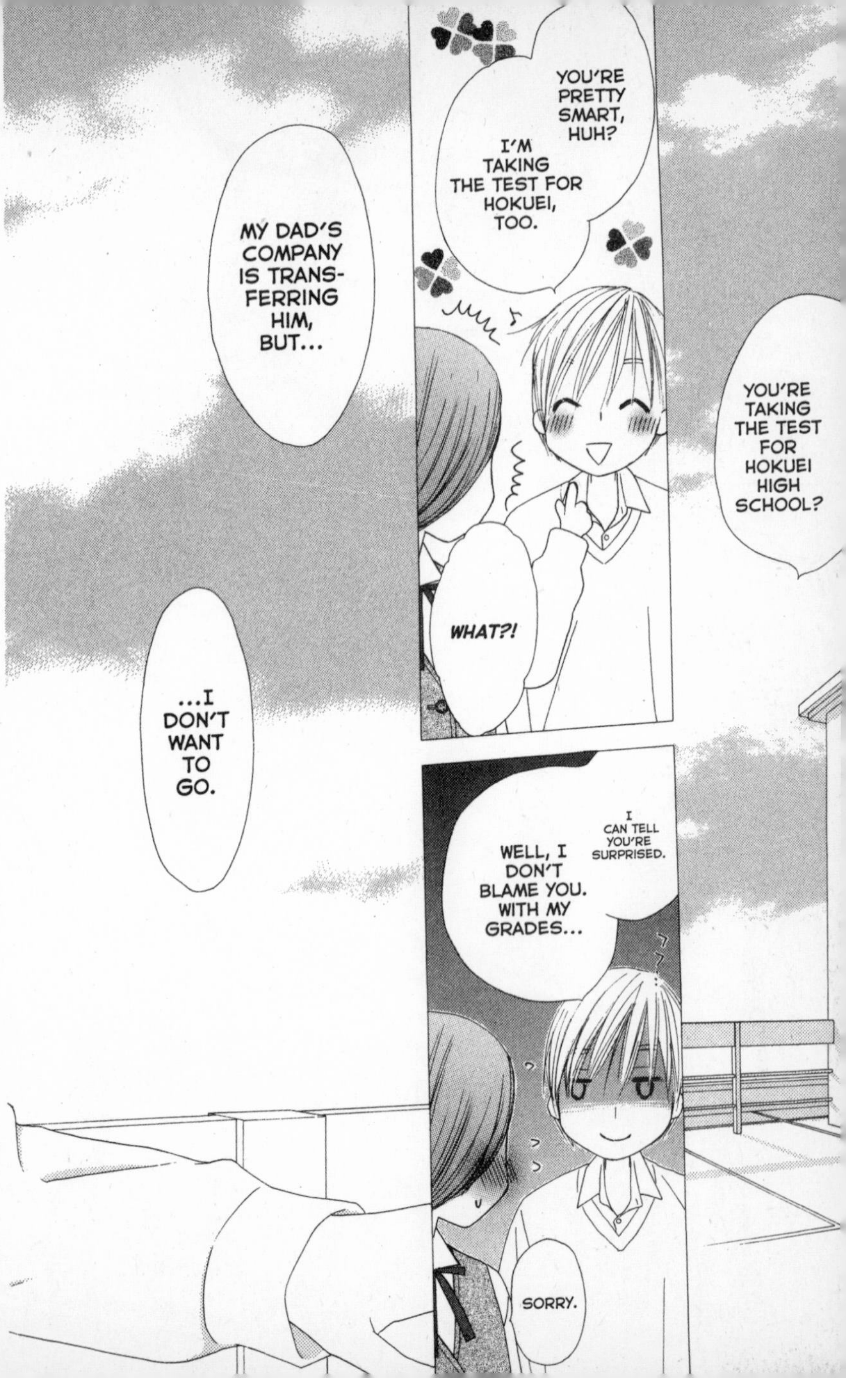

YOU'RE TAKING THE TEST FOR HOKUEI HIGH SCHOOL?
YOU'RE PRETTY SMART, HUH?
I'M TAKING THE TEST FOR HOKUEI, TOO.
WHAT?!
I CAN TELL YOU'RE SURPRISED.
WELL, I DON'T BLAME YOU. WITH MY GRADES...
SORRY.
MY DAD'S COMPANY IS TRANS-FERRING HIM, BUT...
...I DON'T WANT TO GO.

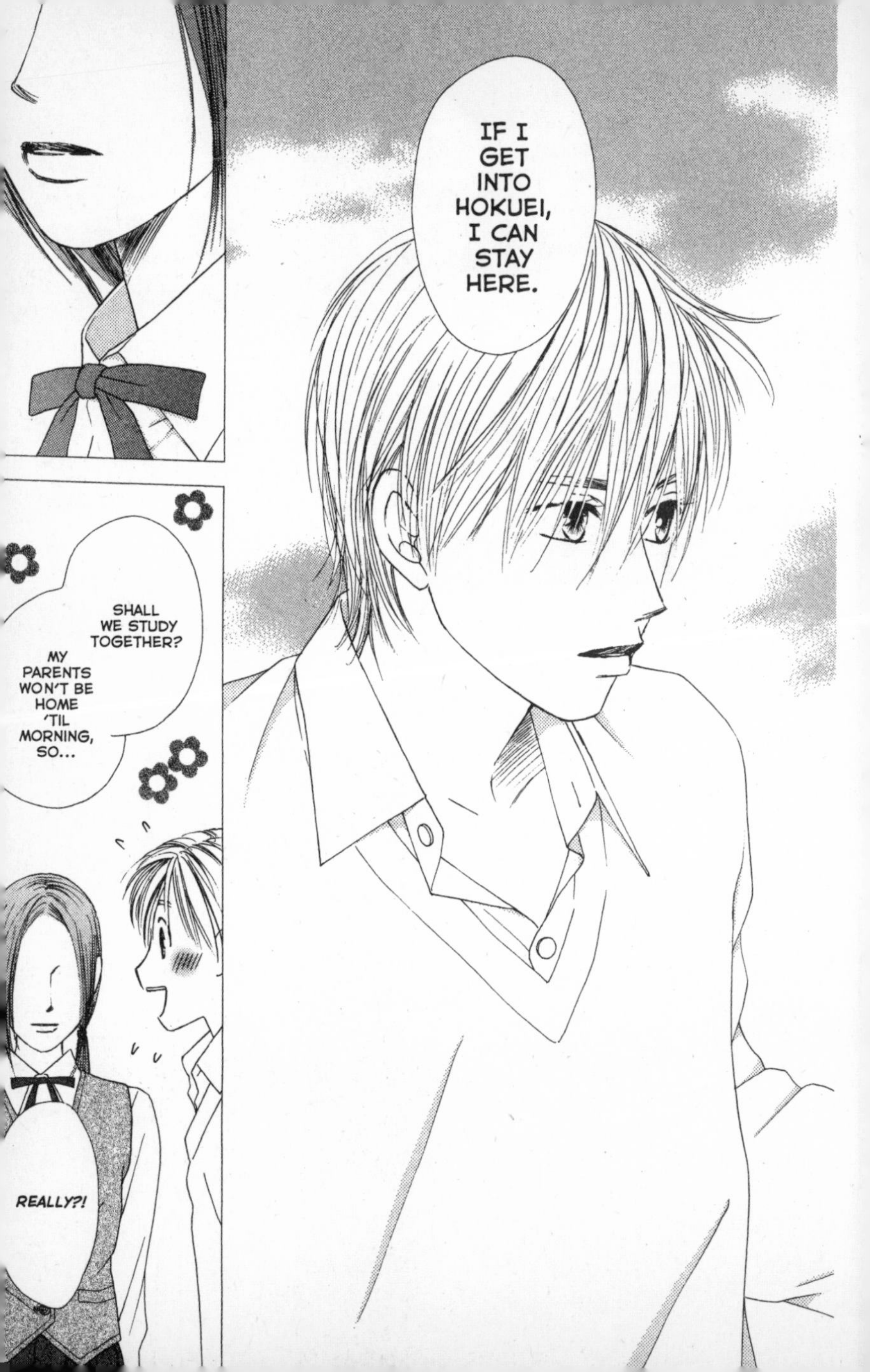
IF I GET INTO HOKUEI, I CAN STAY HERE.
SHALL WE STUDY TOGETHER?
MY PARENTS WON'T BE HOME 'TIL MORNING, SO...
REALLY?!

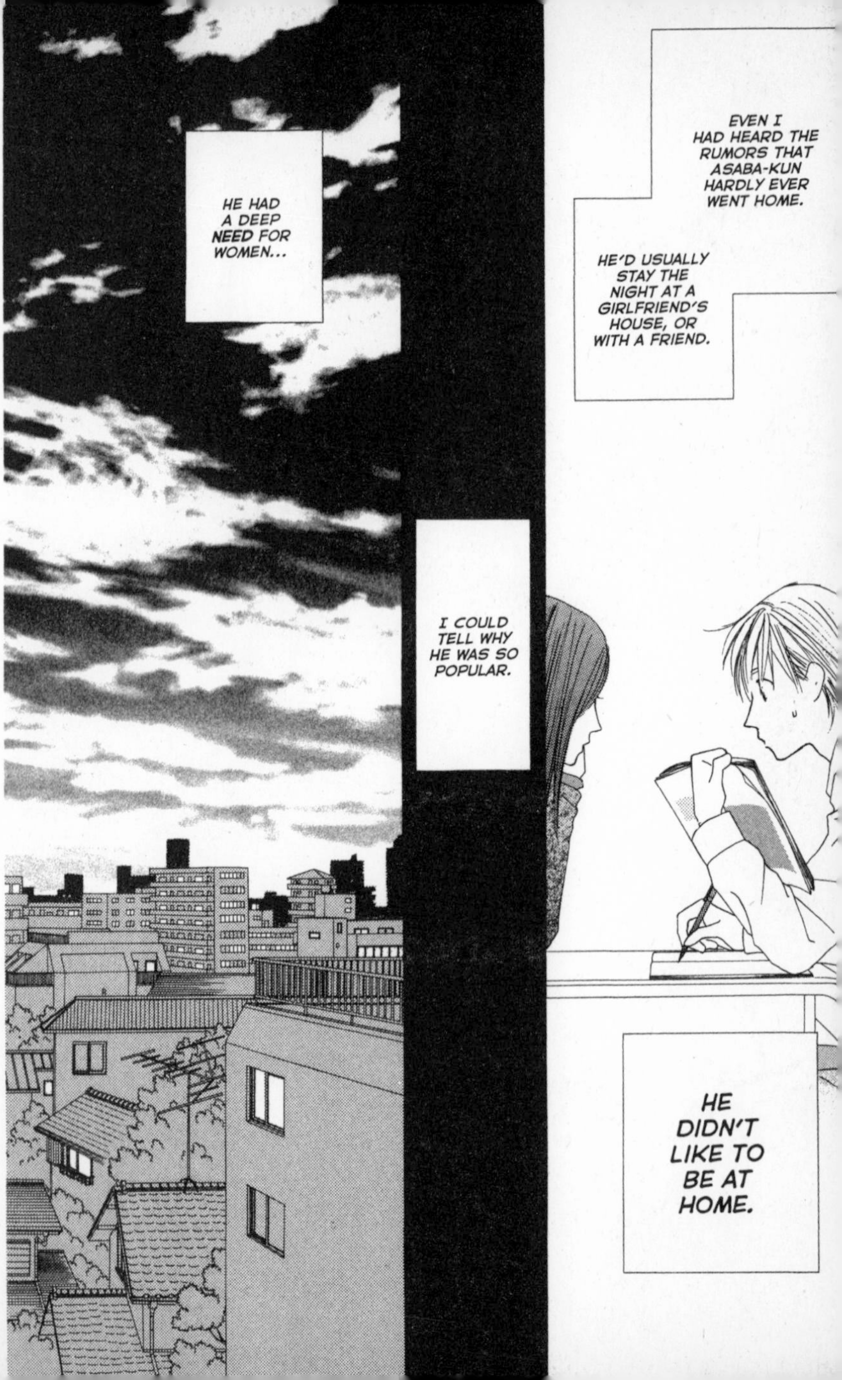
EVEN I HAD HEARD THE RUMORS THAT ASABA-KUN HARDLY EVER WENT HOME.
HE'D USUALLY STAY THE NIGHT AT A GIRLFRIEND'S HOUSE, OR WITH A FRIEND.
HE DIDN'T LIKE TO BE AT HOME.
I COULD TELL WHY HE WAS SO POPULAR.
HE HAD A DEEP NEED FOR WOMEN...

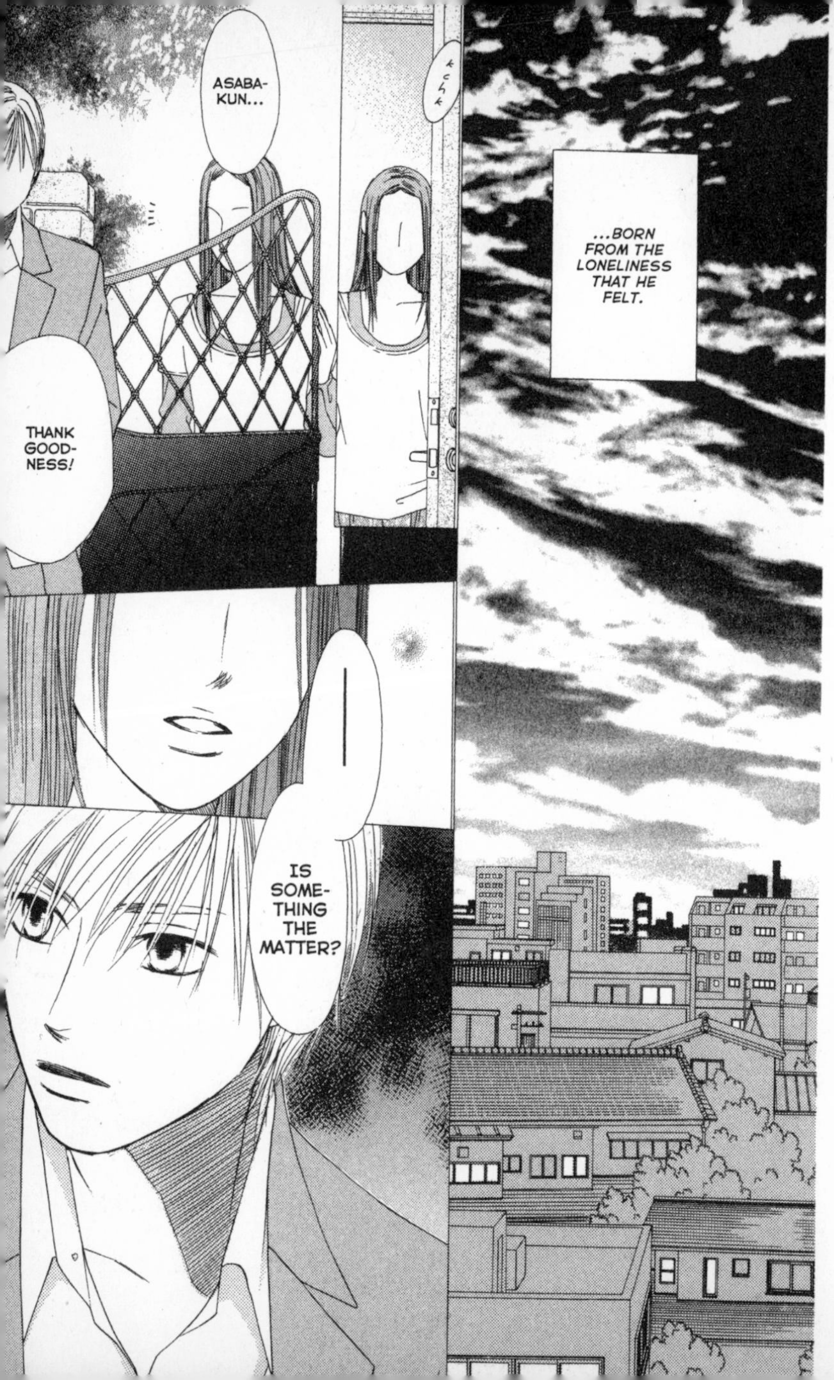
...BORN FROM THE LONELINESS THAT HE FELT.
kchk
ASABA-KUN...
THANK GOOD-NESS!
—
IS SOME-THING THE MATTER?

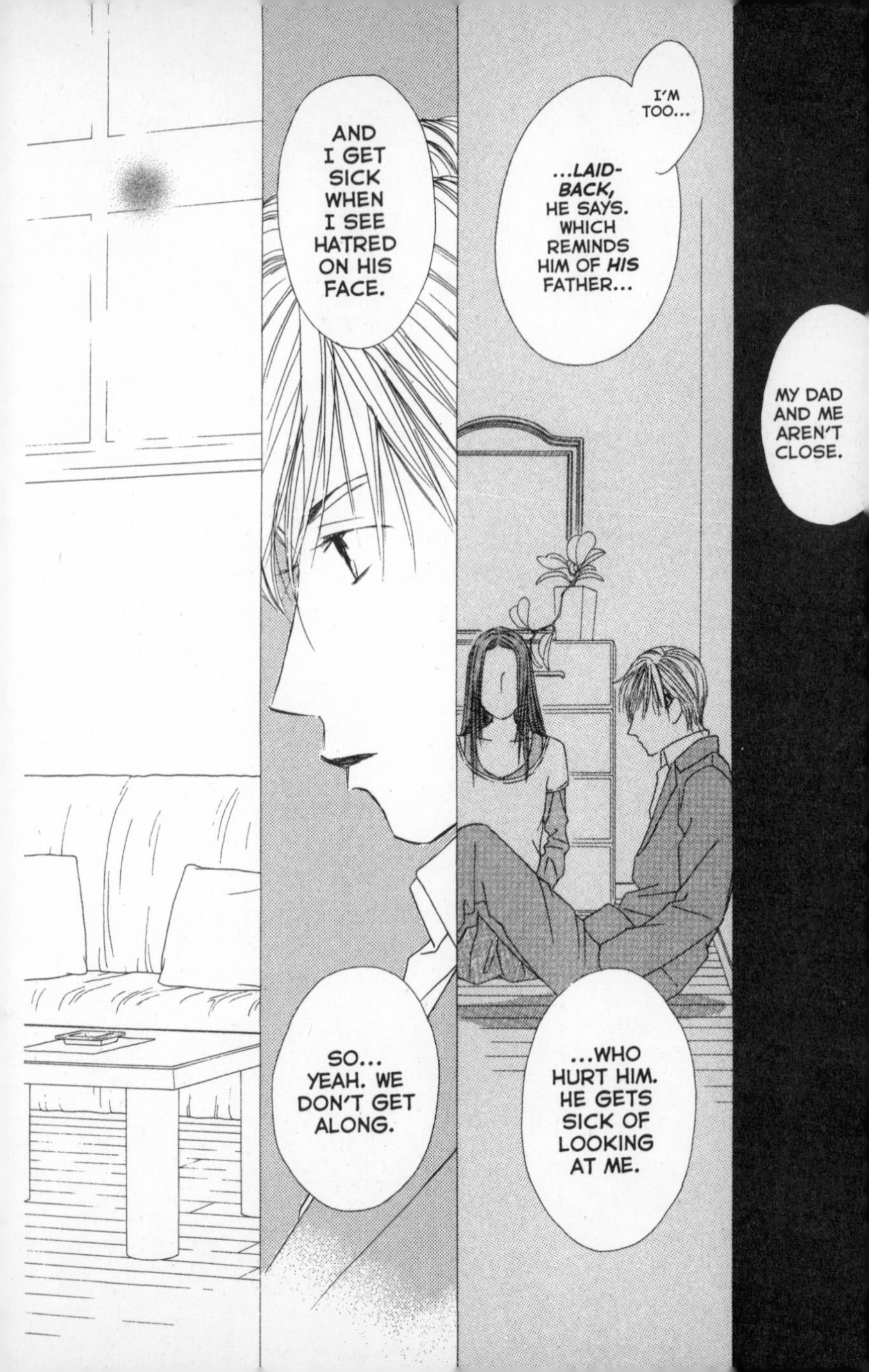
MY DAD AND ME AREN'T CLOSE.
I'M TOO...
...*LAID-BACK,* HE SAYS. WHICH REMINDS HIM OF *HIS* FATHER...
...WHO HURT HIM. HE GETS SICK OF LOOKING AT ME.
AND I GET SICK WHEN I SEE HATRED ON HIS FACE.
SO... YEAH. WE DON'T GET ALONG.

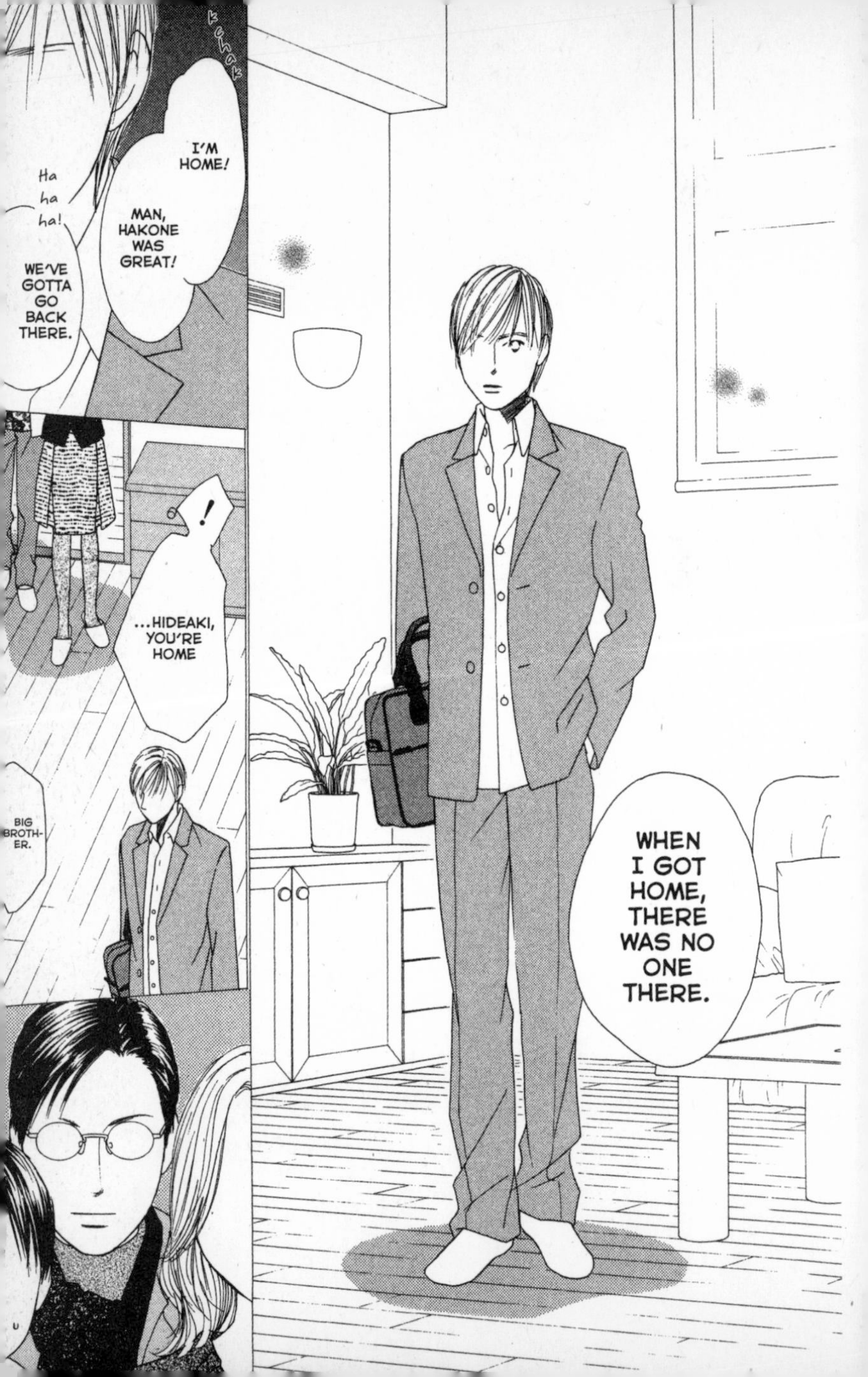
WHEN I GOT HOME, THERE WAS NO ONE THERE.
kchak
I'M HOME!
MAN, HAKONE WAS GREAT!
Ha ha ha!
WE'VE GOTTA GO BACK THERE.
!
...HIDEAKI, YOU'RE HOME
BIG BROTH-ER.

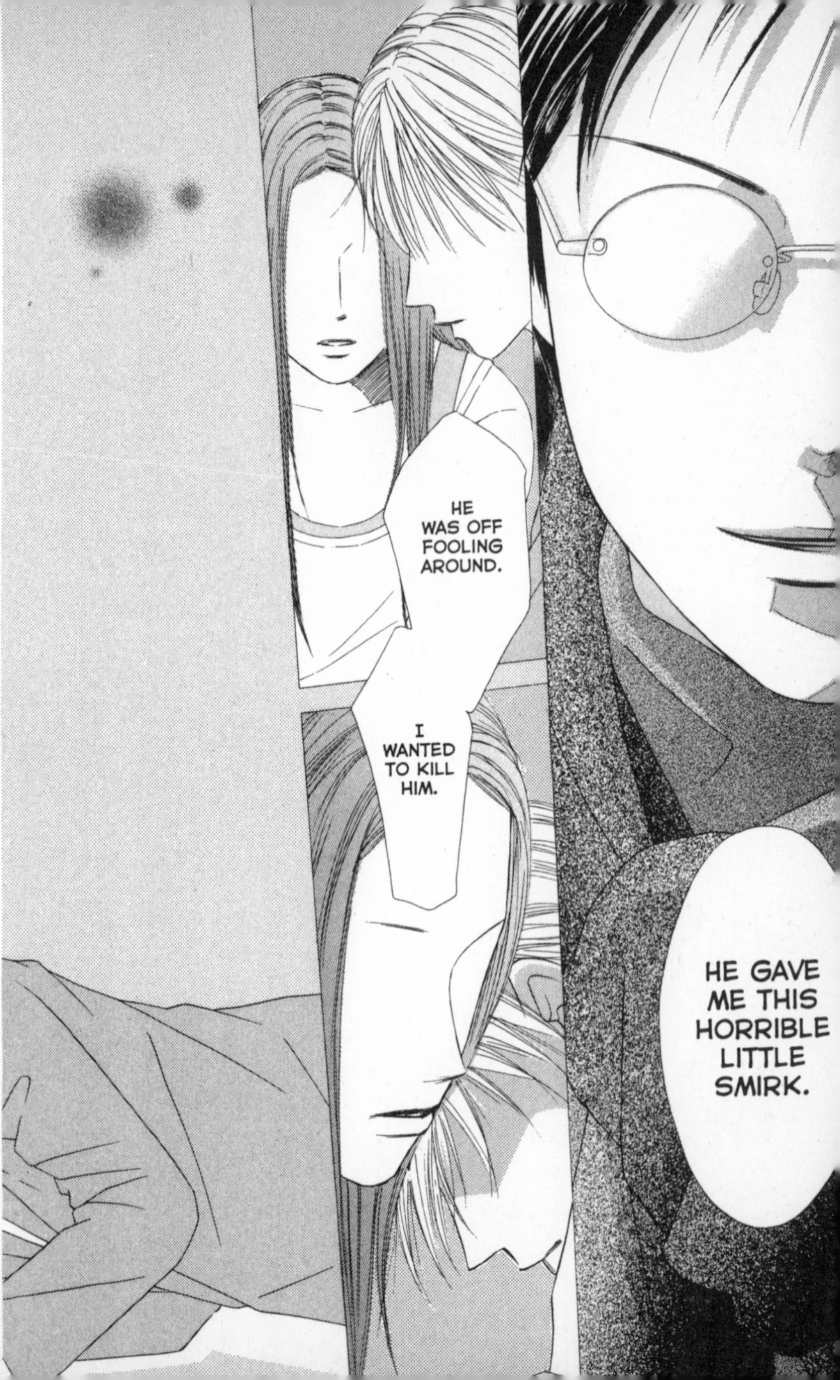
HE GAVE ME THIS HORRIBLE LITTLE SMIRK.
HE WAS OFF FOOLING AROUND.
I WANTED TO KILL HIM.

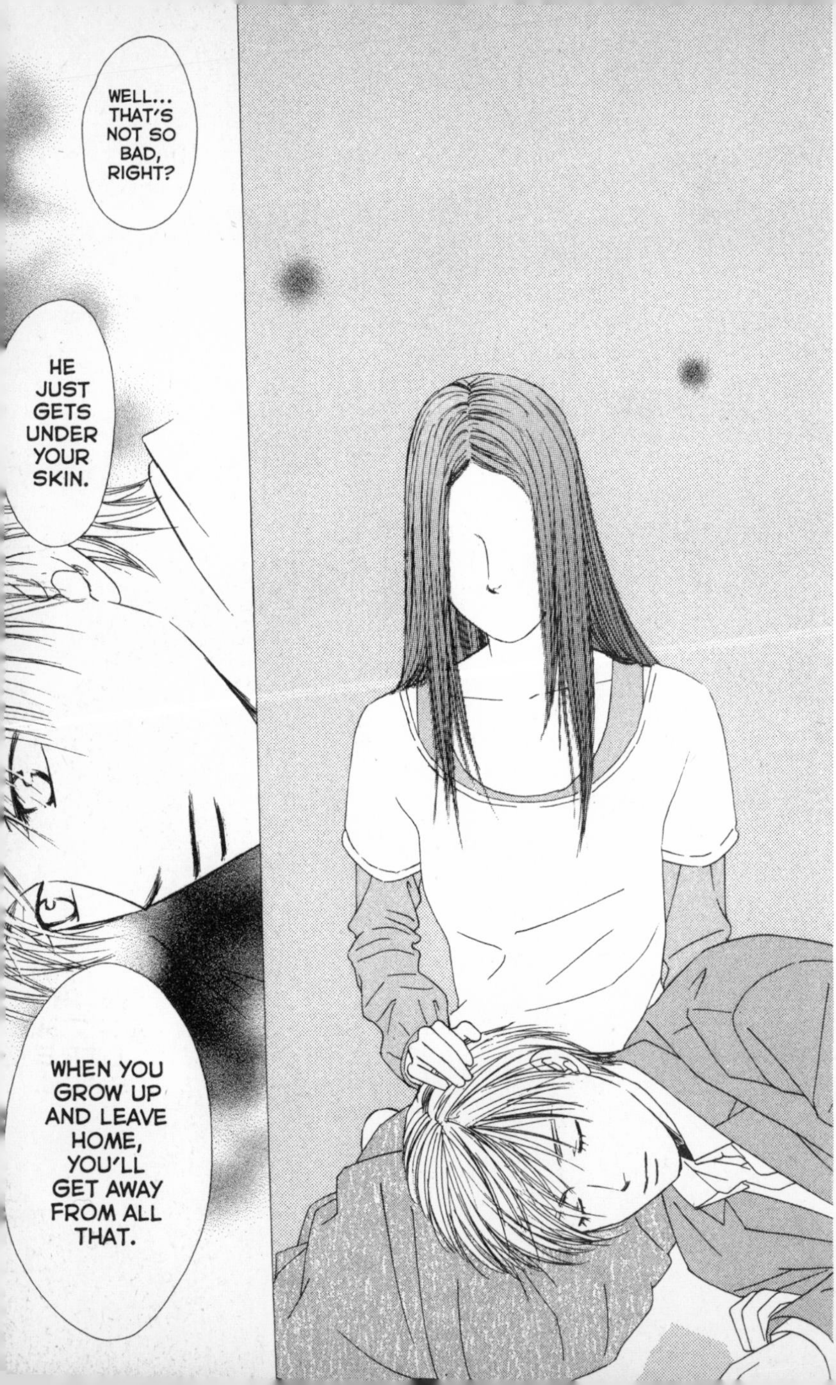
WELL... THAT'S NOT SO BAD, RIGHT?
HE JUST GETS UNDER YOUR SKIN.
WHEN YOU GROW UP AND LEAVE HOME, YOU'LL GET AWAY FROM ALL THAT.

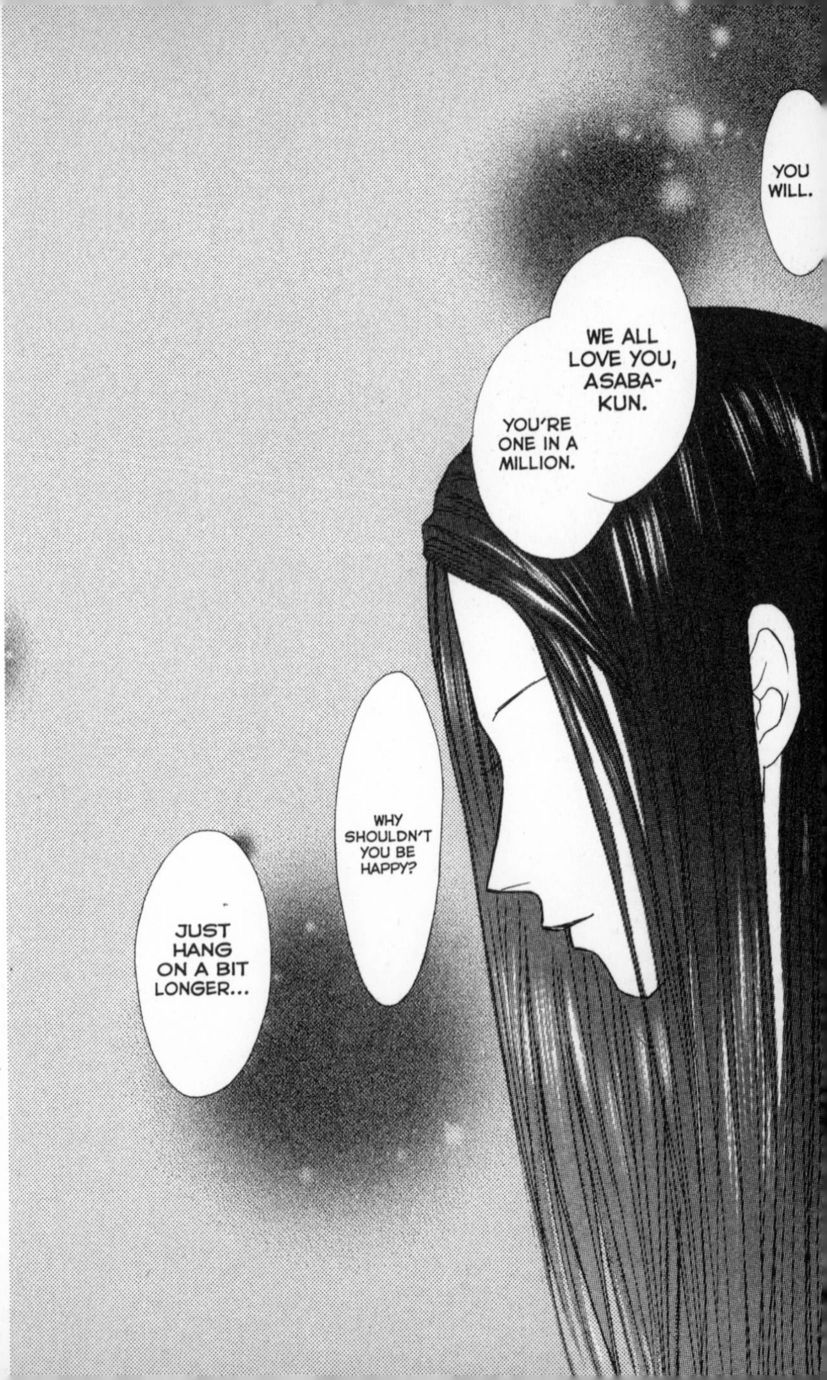
YOU WILL.
WE ALL LOVE YOU, ASABA-KUN.
YOU'RE ONE IN A MILLION.
WHY SHOULDN'T YOU BE HAPPY?
JUST HANG ON A BIT LONGER...

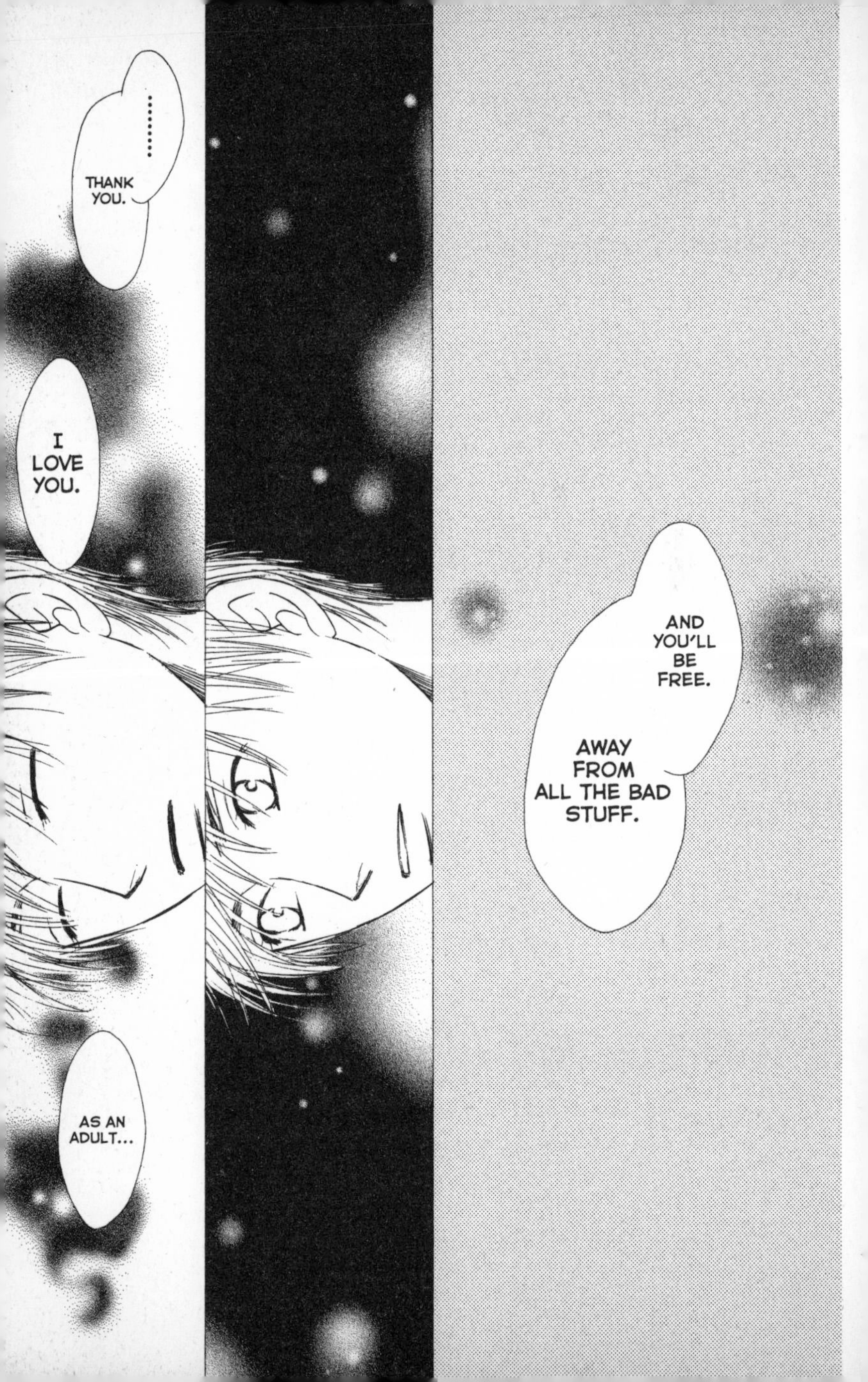
AND YOU'LL BE FREE.
AWAY FROM ALL THE BAD STUFF.
......
THANK YOU.
I LOVE YOU.
AS AN ADULT...

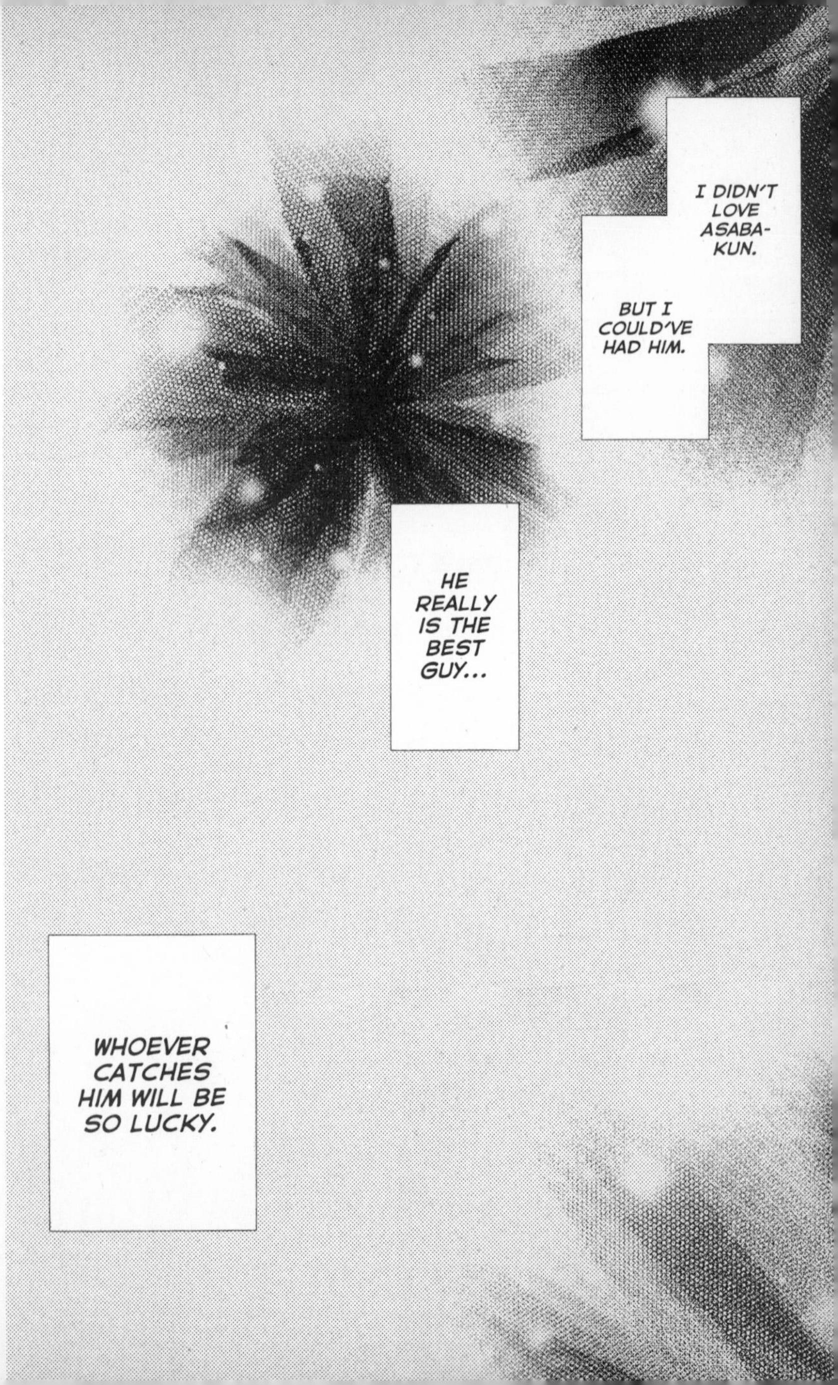
I DIDN'T LOVE ASABA-KUN.
BUT I COULD'VE HAD HIM.
HE REALLY IS THE BEST GUY...
WHOEVER CATCHES HIM WILL BE SO LUCKY.

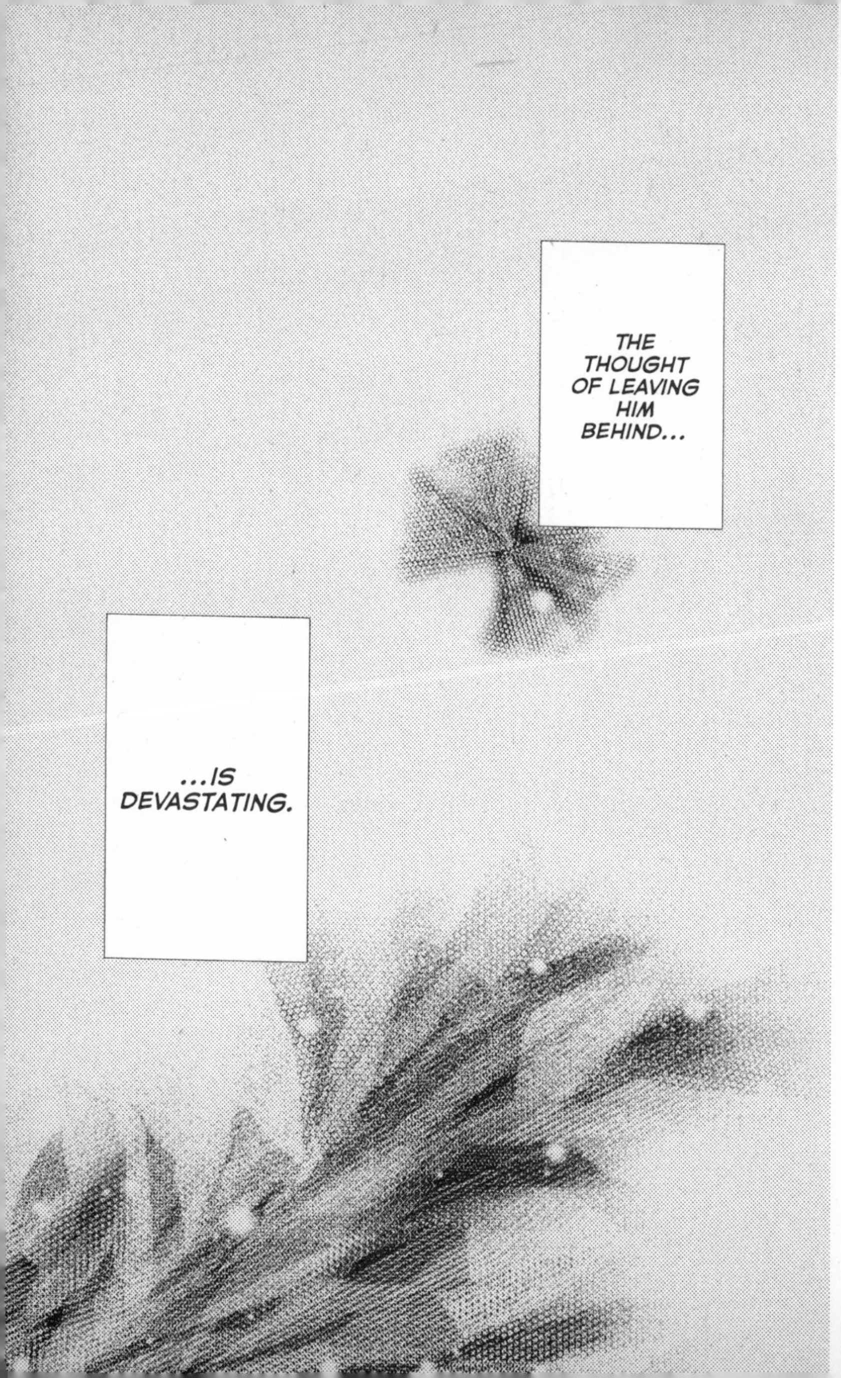
THE THOUGHT OF LEAVING HIM BEHIND...
...IS DEVASTATING.

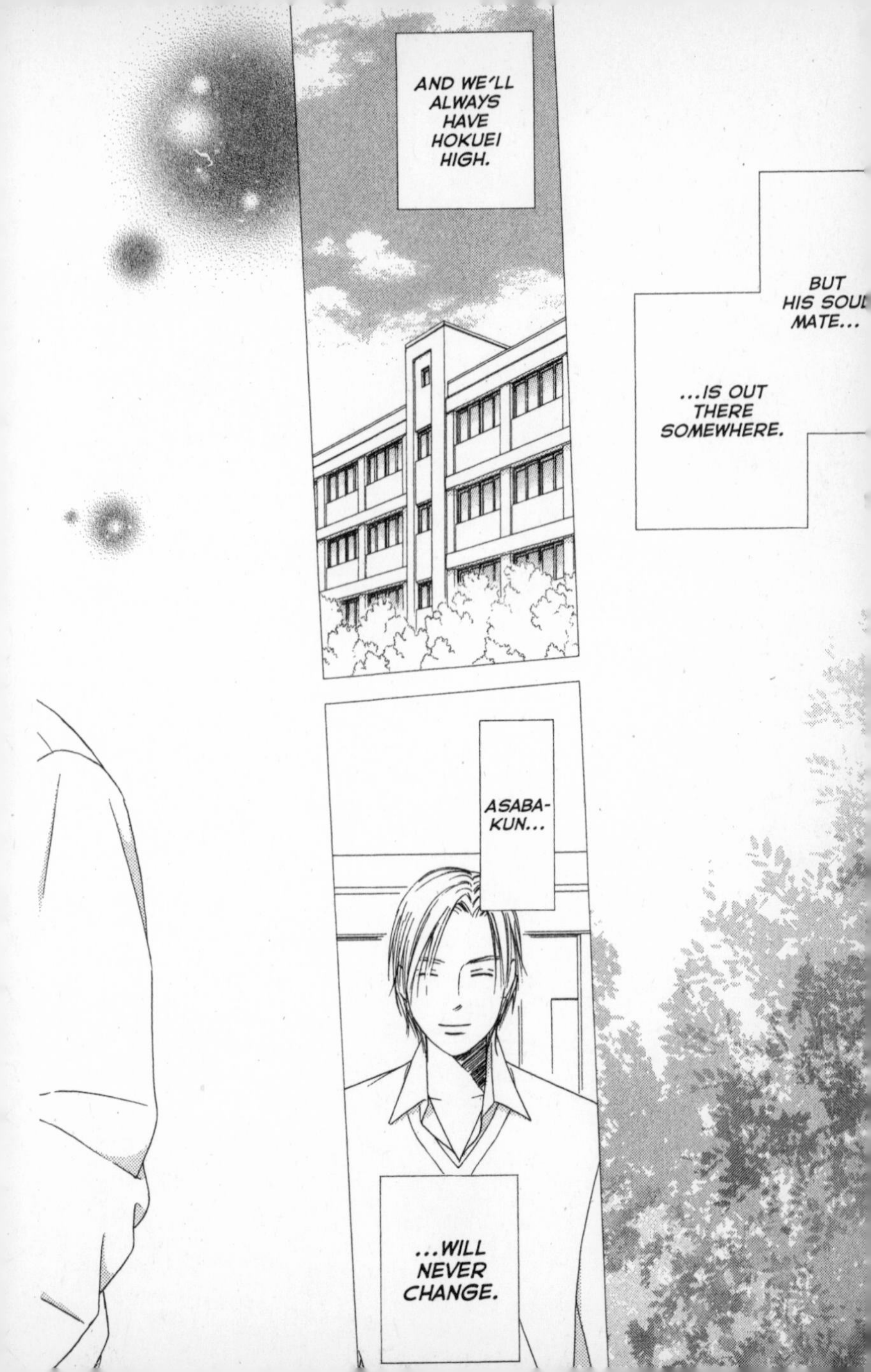
BUT HIS SOUL MATE...
...IS OUT THERE SOMEWHERE.
AND WE'LL ALWAYS HAVE HOKUEI HIGH.
ASABA-KUN...
...WILL NEVER CHANGE.

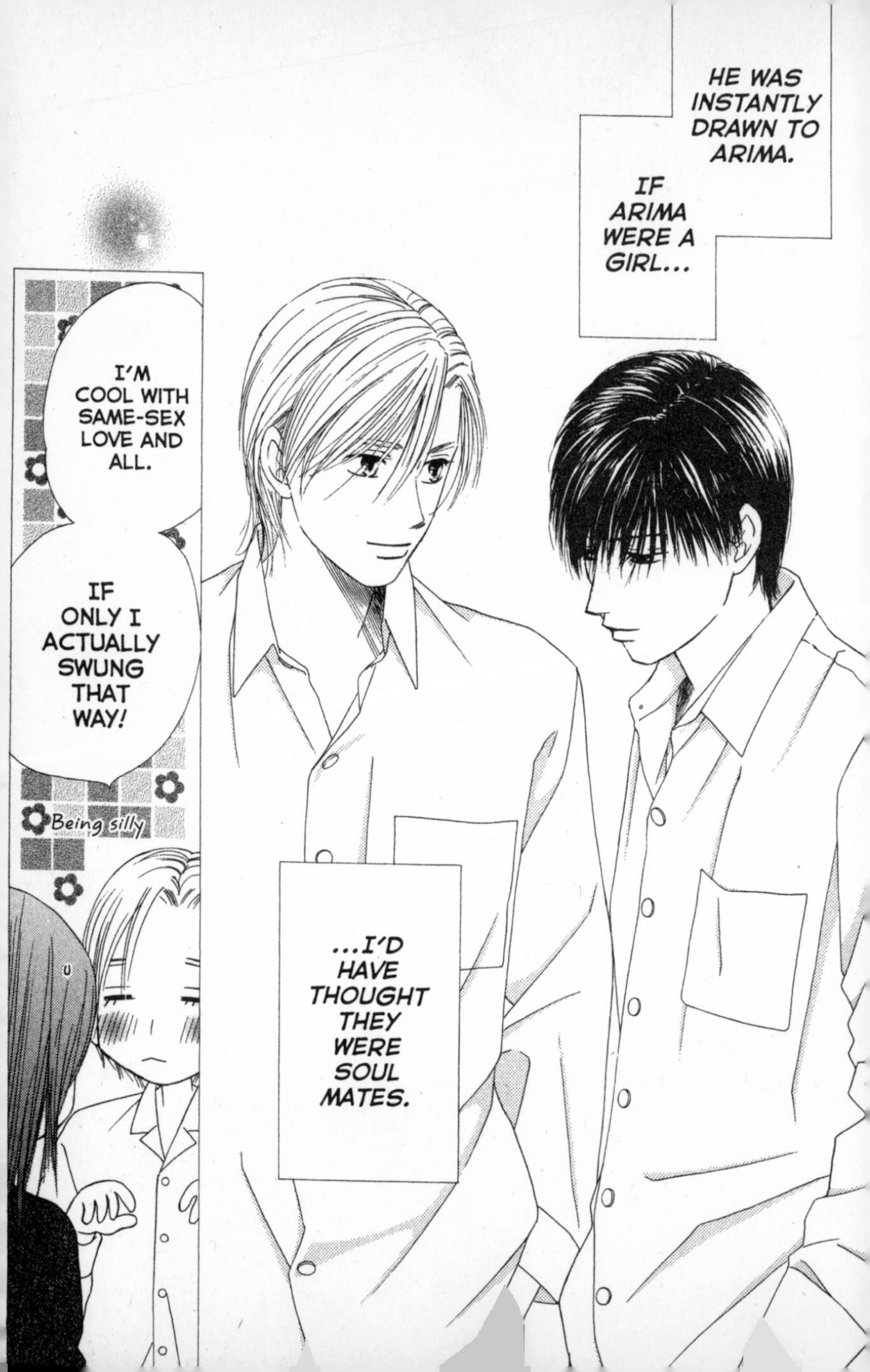
HE WAS INSTANTLY DRAWN TO ARIMA.
IF ARIMA WERE A GIRL...
...I'D HAVE THOUGHT THEY WERE SOUL MATES.
I'M COOL WITH SAME-SEX LOVE AND ALL.
IF ONLY I ACTUALLY SWUNG THAT WAY!
Being silly

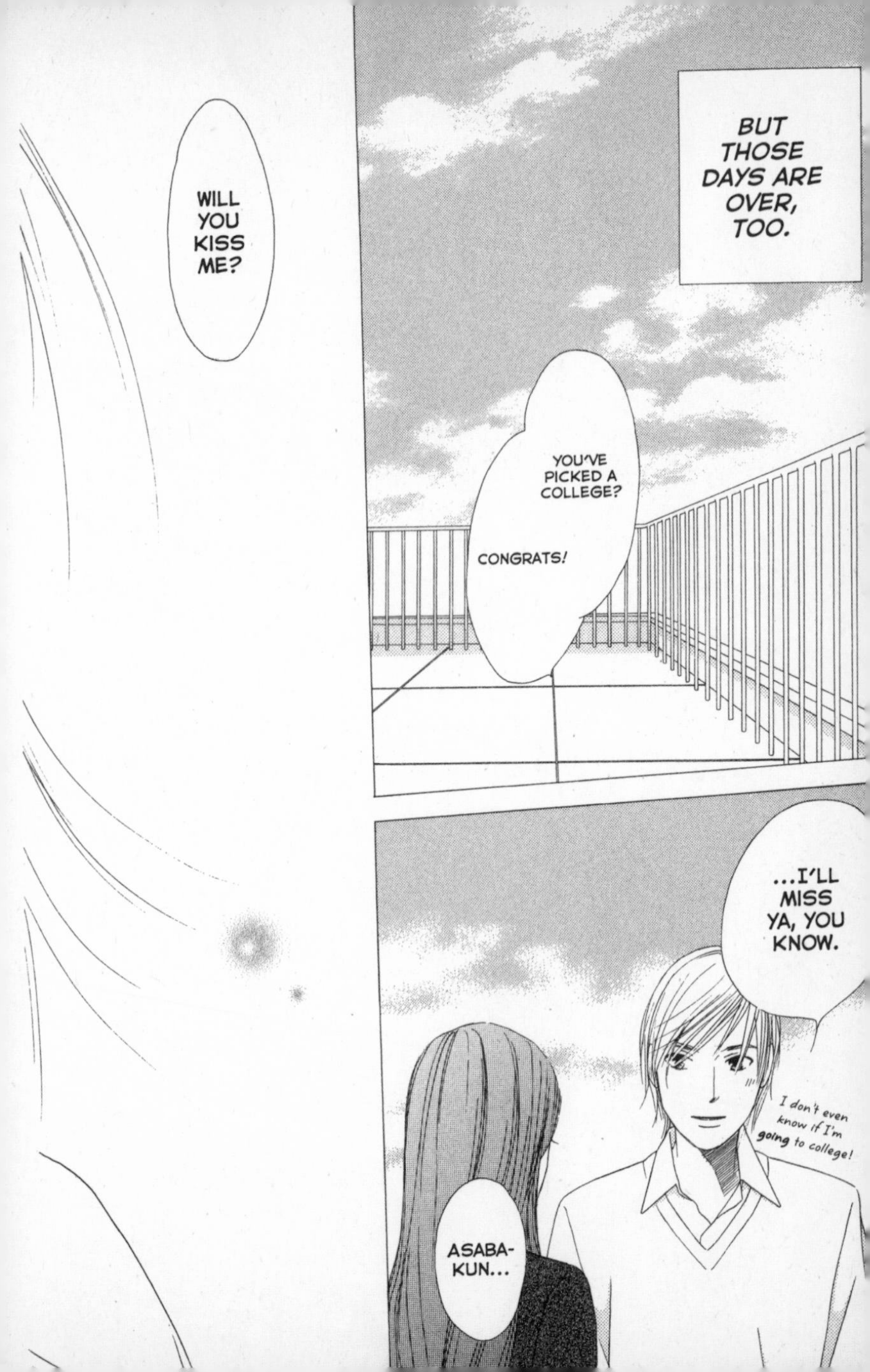
BUT THOSE DAYS ARE OVER, TOO.
YOU'VE PICKED A COLLEGE?
CONGRATS!
...I'LL MISS YA, YOU KNOW.
I don't even know if I'm going to college!
ASABA-KUN...
WILL YOU KISS ME?

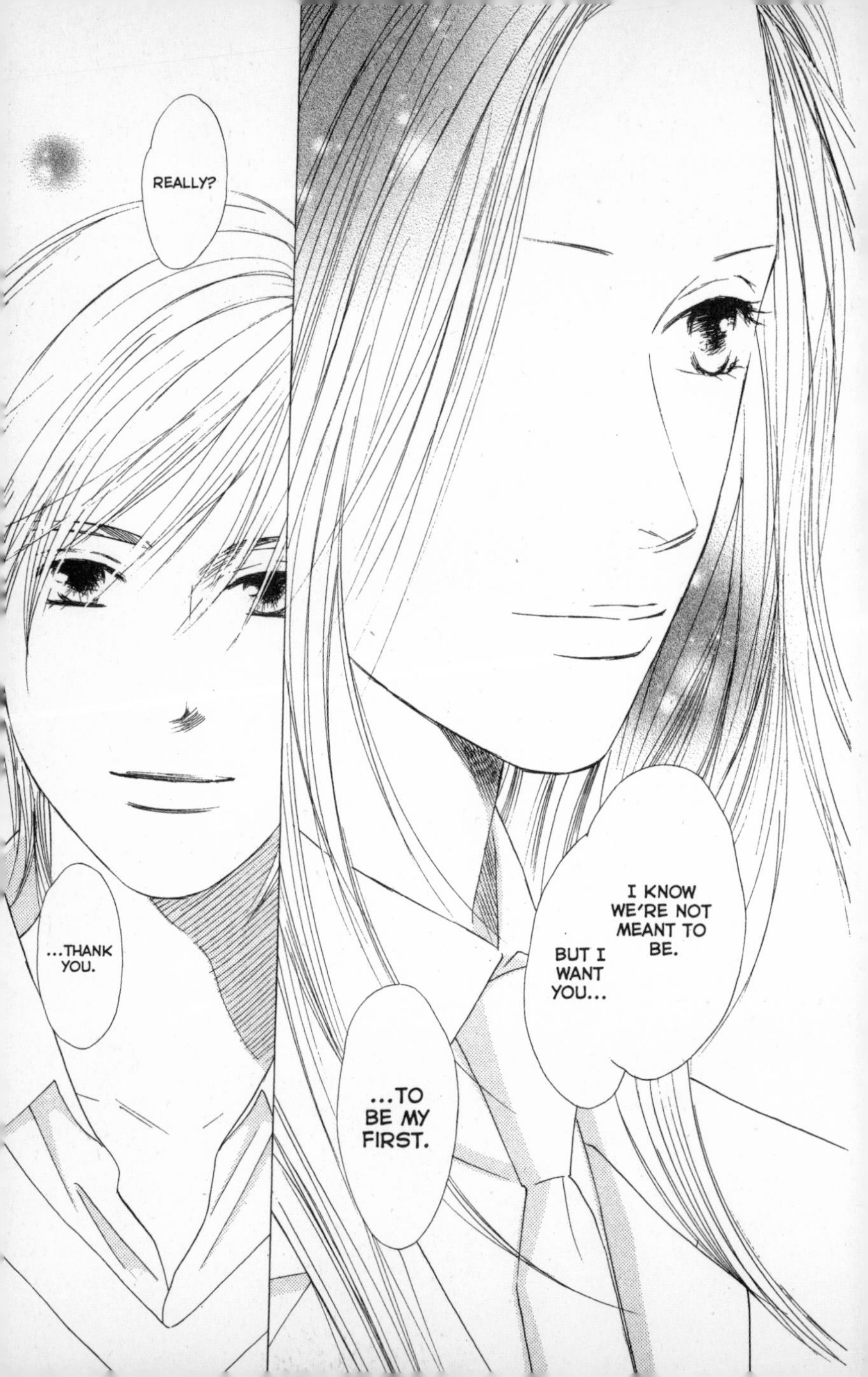
I KNOW WE'RE NOT MEANT TO BE.
BUT I WANT YOU...
...TO BE MY FIRST.
REALLY?
...THANK YOU.

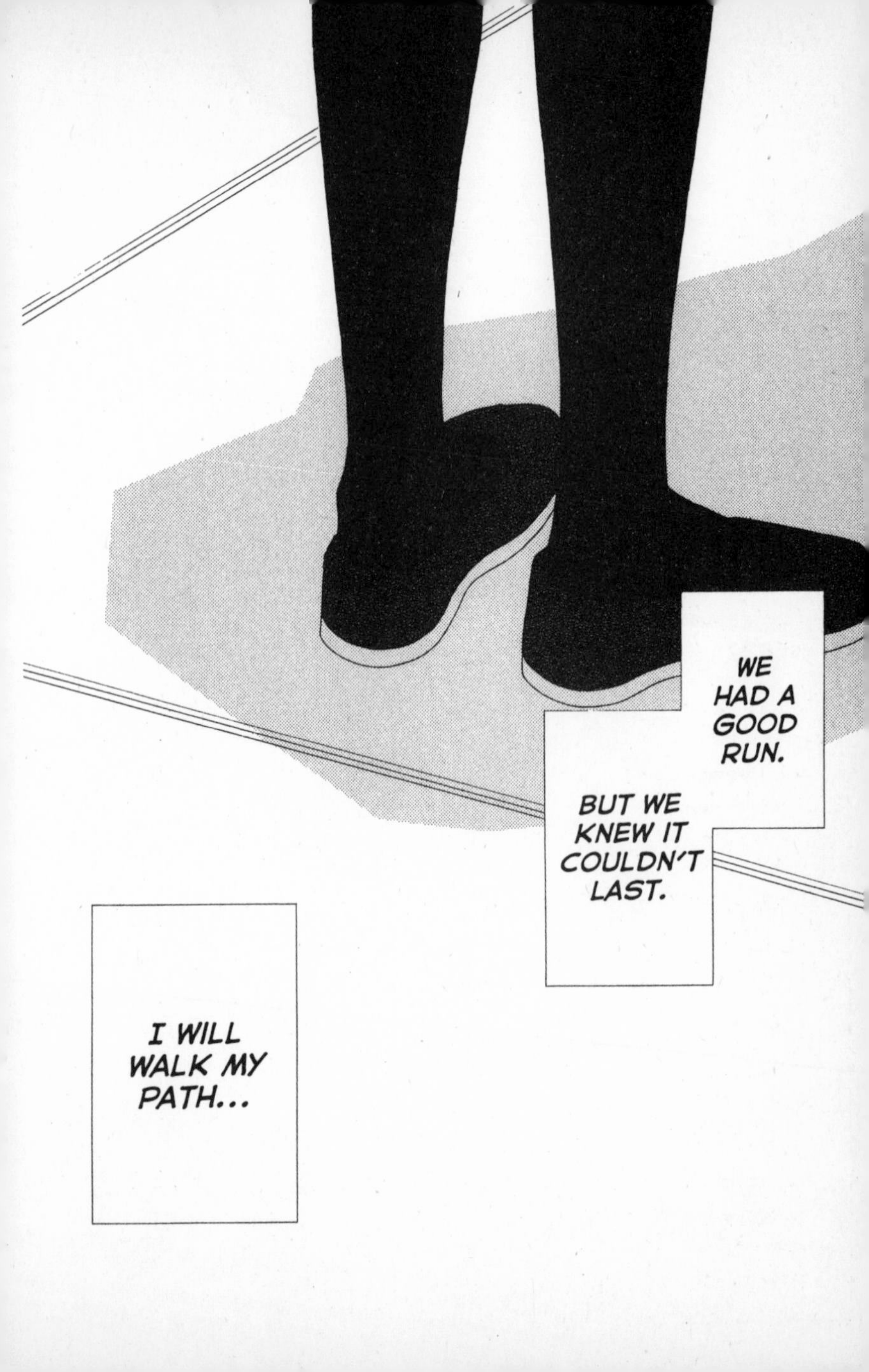
WE HAD A GOOD RUN.
BUT WE KNEW IT COULDN'T LAST.
I WILL WALK MY PATH...

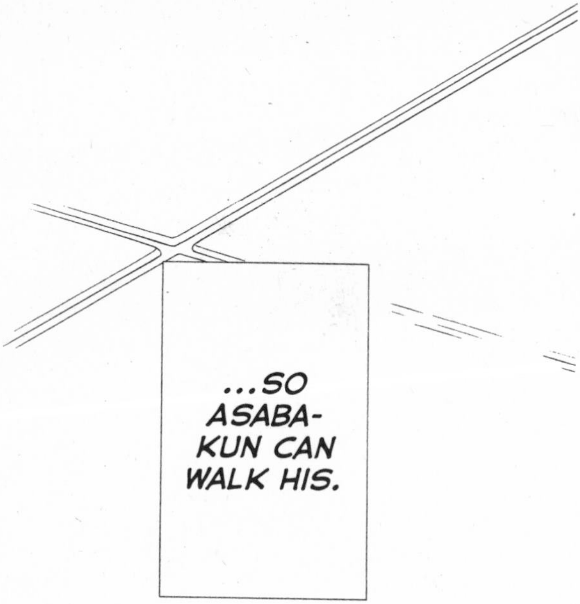
...SO ASABA-KUN CAN WALK HIS.

1

Hello! This is my 25th comic, *Kare Kano 21*... **THE LAST VOLUME!**

It's over... I'm so busy right now. Everything is happening so fast, and my mind is a complete blur.

It still hasn't hit me that it's actually over. I haven't even gotten any responses from my readers yet!

In denial...

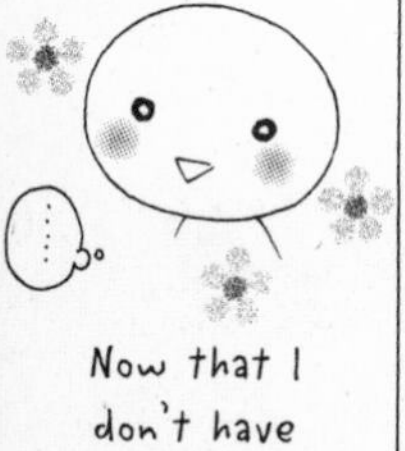

Now that I don't have deadlines, I never think about manga.

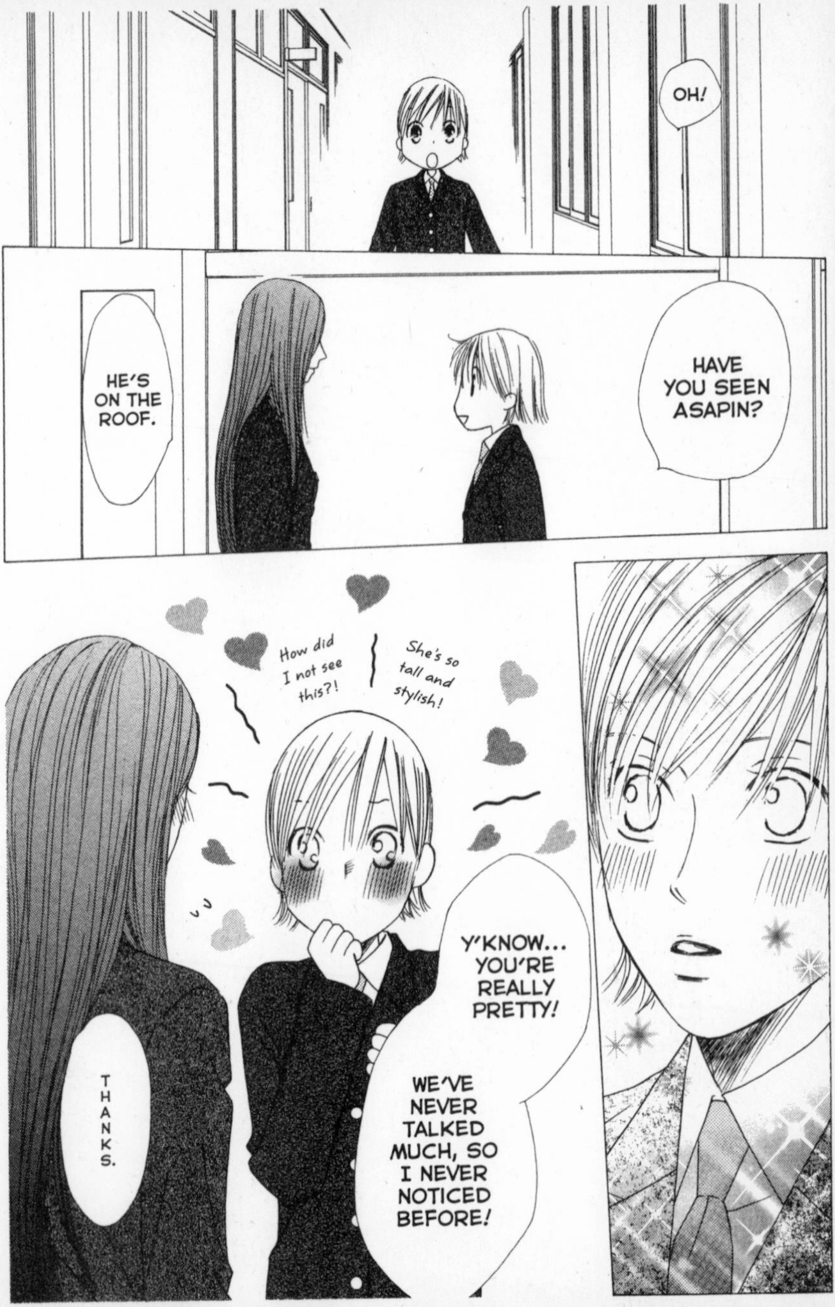
OH!
HAVE YOU SEEN ASAPIN?
HE'S ON THE ROOF.
She's so tall and stylish!
How did I not see this?!
Y'KNOW... YOU'RE REALLY PRETTY!
WE'VE NEVER TALKED MUCH, SO I NEVER NOTICED BEFORE!
THANKS.

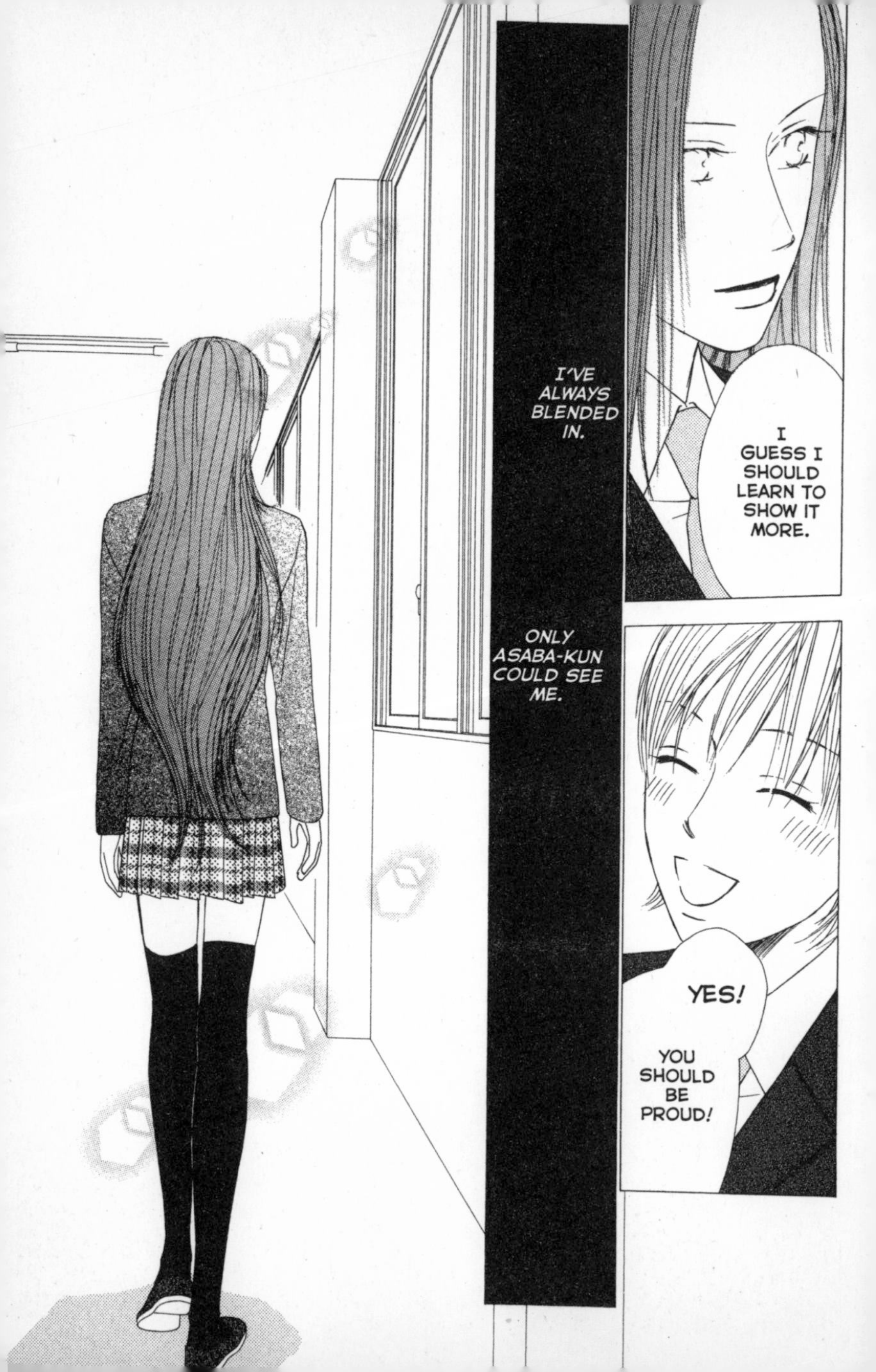
I GUESS I SHOULD LEARN TO SHOW IT MORE.
YES!
YOU SHOULD BE PROUD!
I'VE ALWAYS BLENDED IN.
ONLY ASABA-KUN COULD SEE ME.

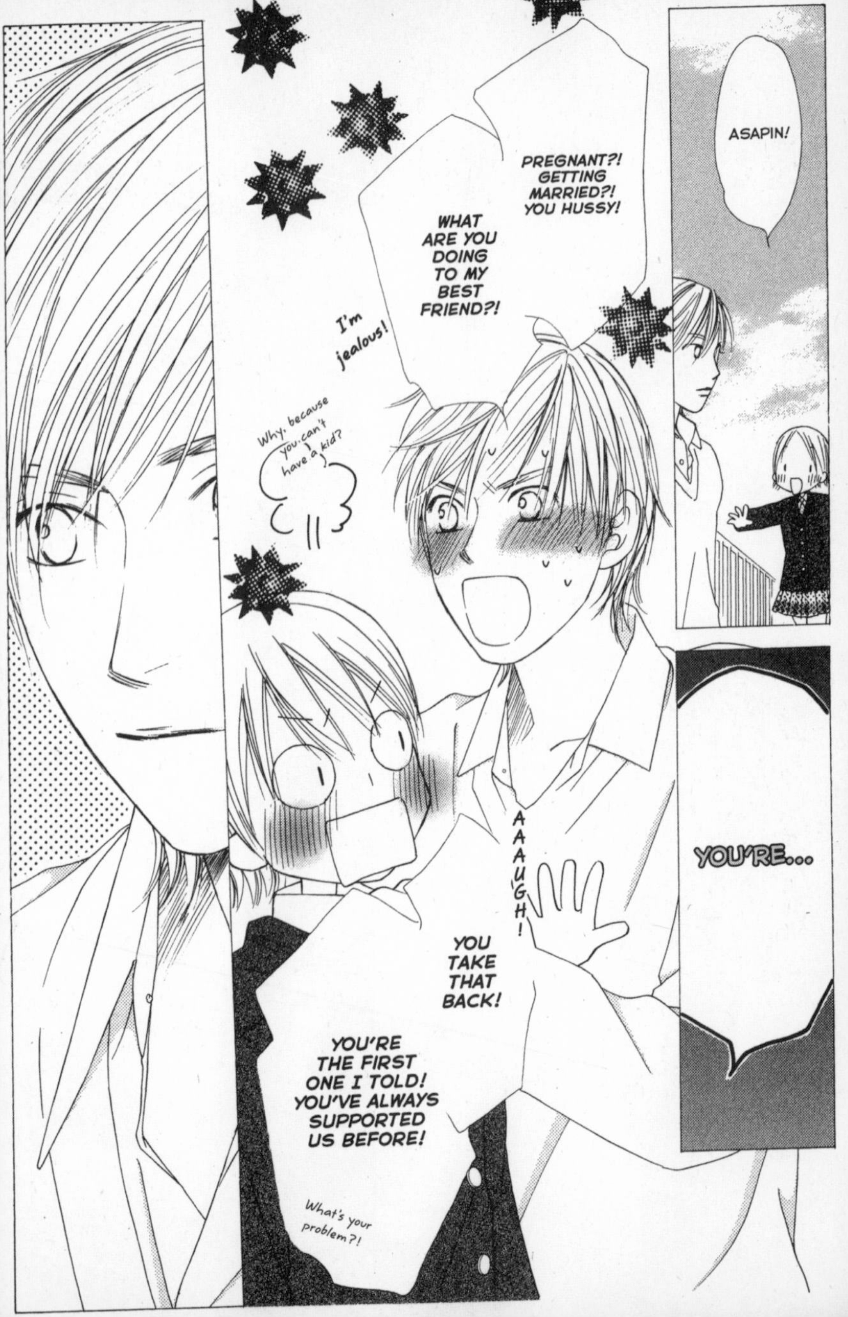
ASAPIN!
YOU'RE...
PREGNANT?! GETTING MARRIED?! YOU HUSSY!
WHAT ARE YOU DOING TO MY BEST FRIEND?!
I'm jealous!
Why, because you can't have a kid?
AAAUGH!
YOU TAKE THAT BACK!
YOU'RE THE FIRST ONE I TOLD! YOU'VE ALWAYS SUPPORTED US BEFORE!
What's your problem?!

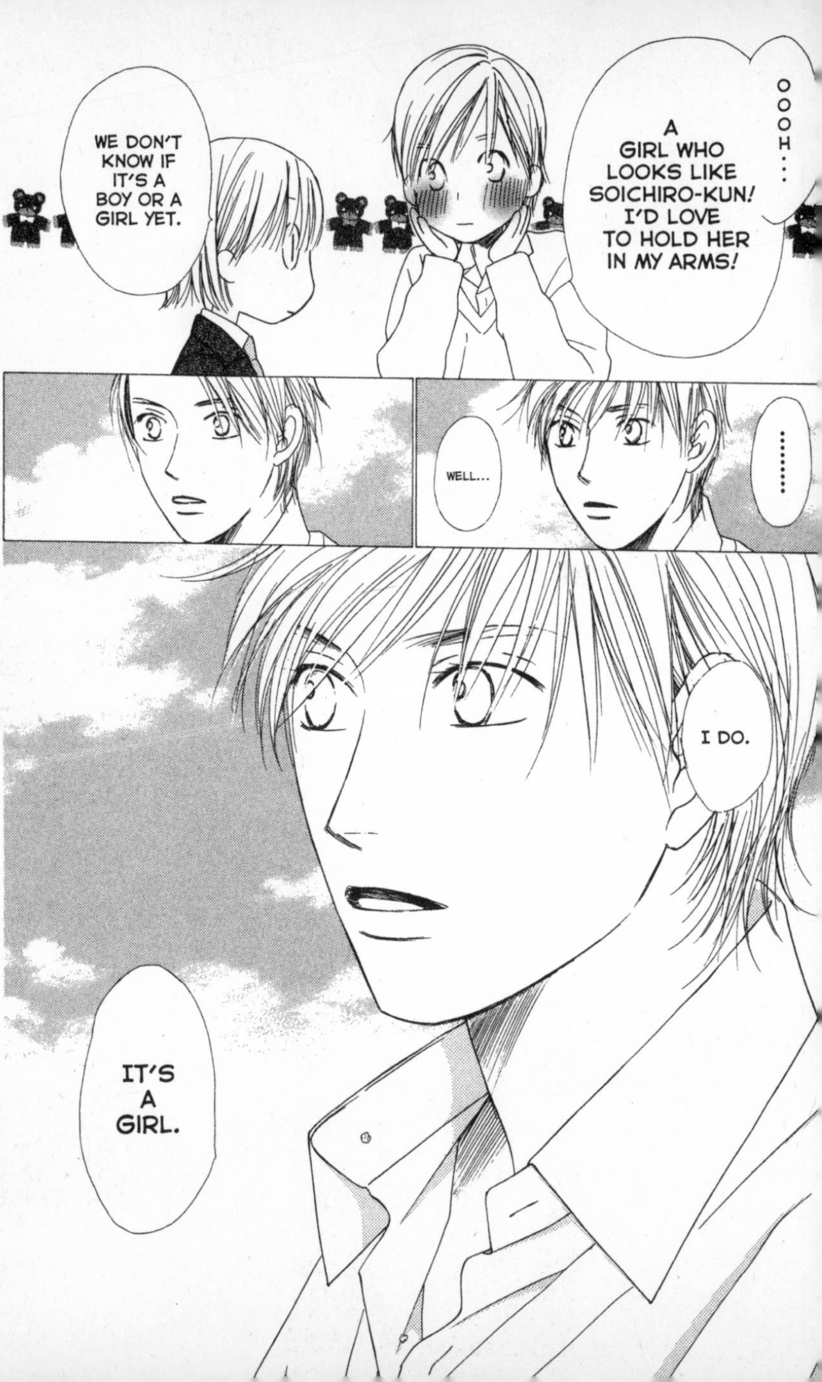
OOOH...
A GIRL WHO LOOKS LIKE SOICHIRO-KUN! I'D LOVE TO HOLD HER IN MY ARMS!
WE DON'T KNOW IF IT'S A BOY OR A GIRL YET.
.........
WELL...
I DO.
IT'S A GIRL.

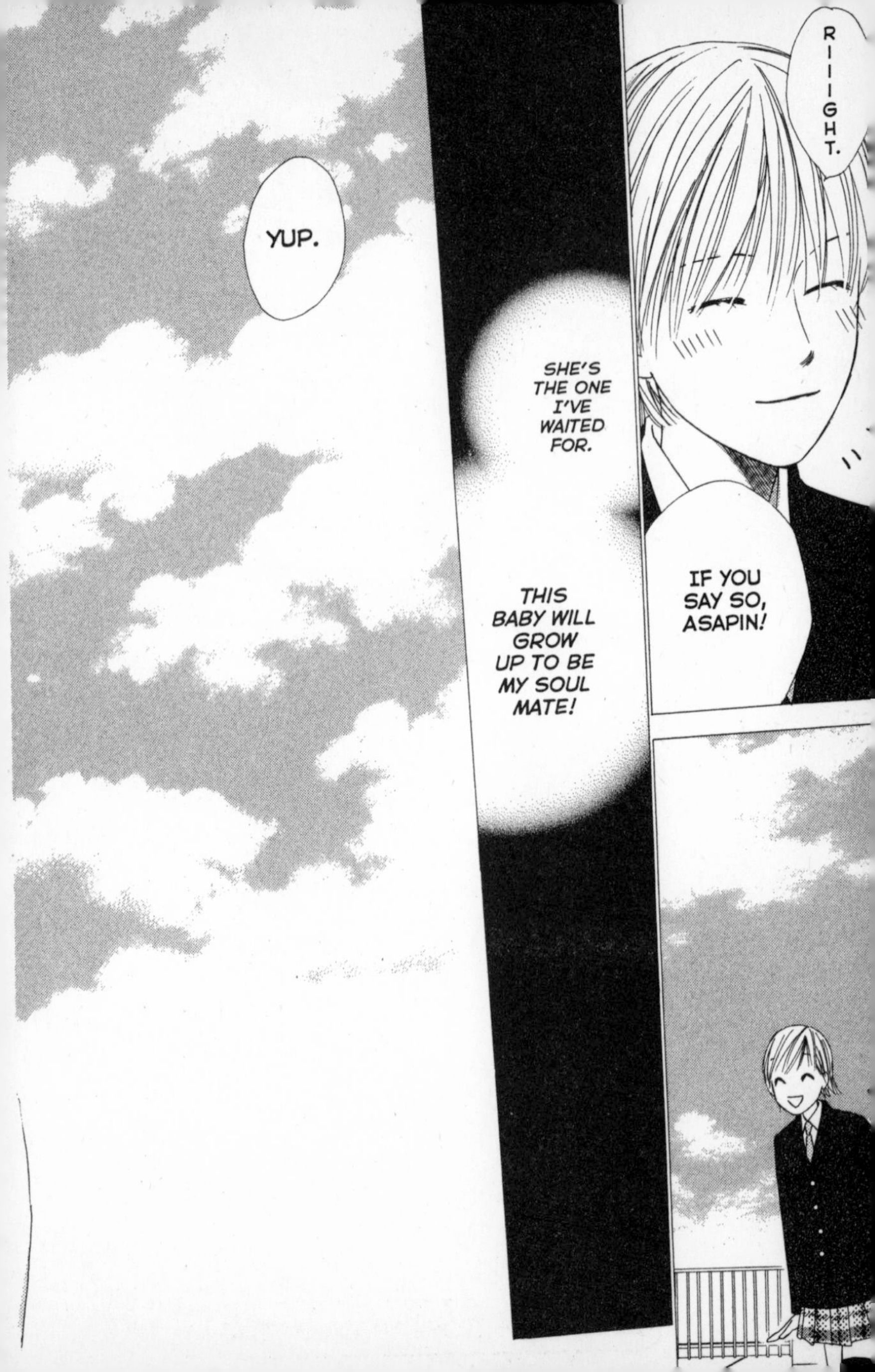
RIIIGHT.
IF YOU SAY SO, ASAPIN!
SHE'S THE ONE I'VE WAITED FOR.
THIS BABY WILL GROW UP TO BE MY SOUL MATE!
YUP.

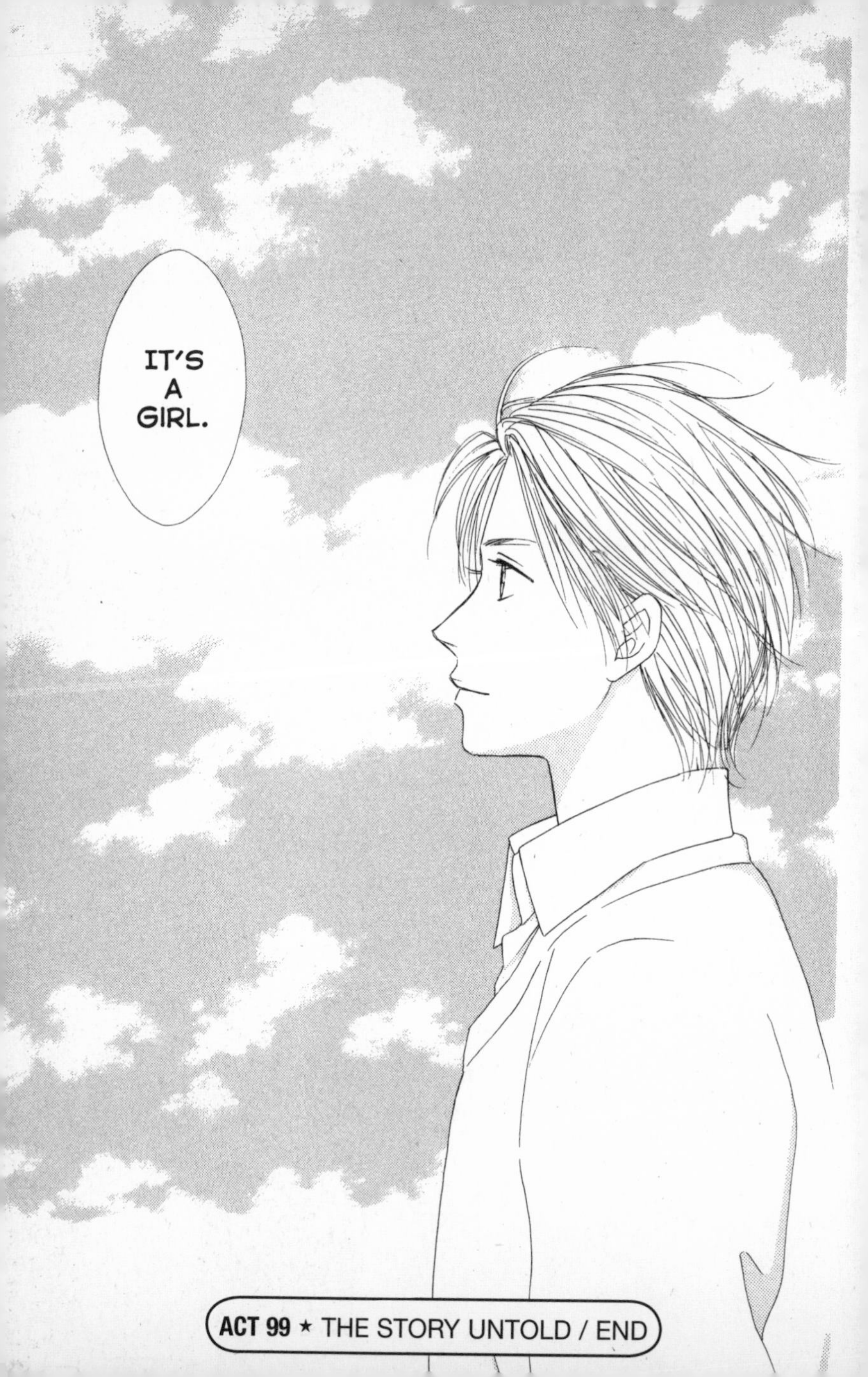
IT'S A GIRL.
ACT 99 ★ THE STORY UNTOLD / END

# kare kano

*his and her circumstances*

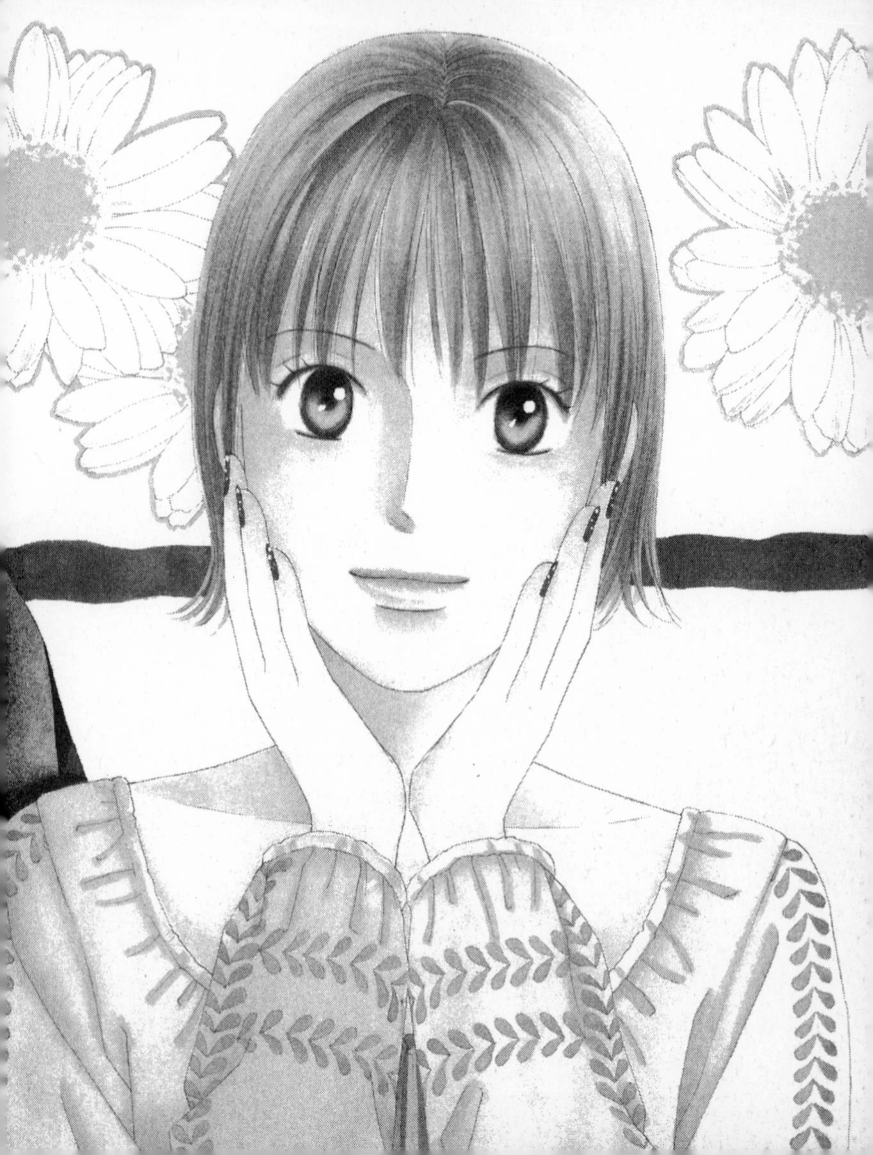

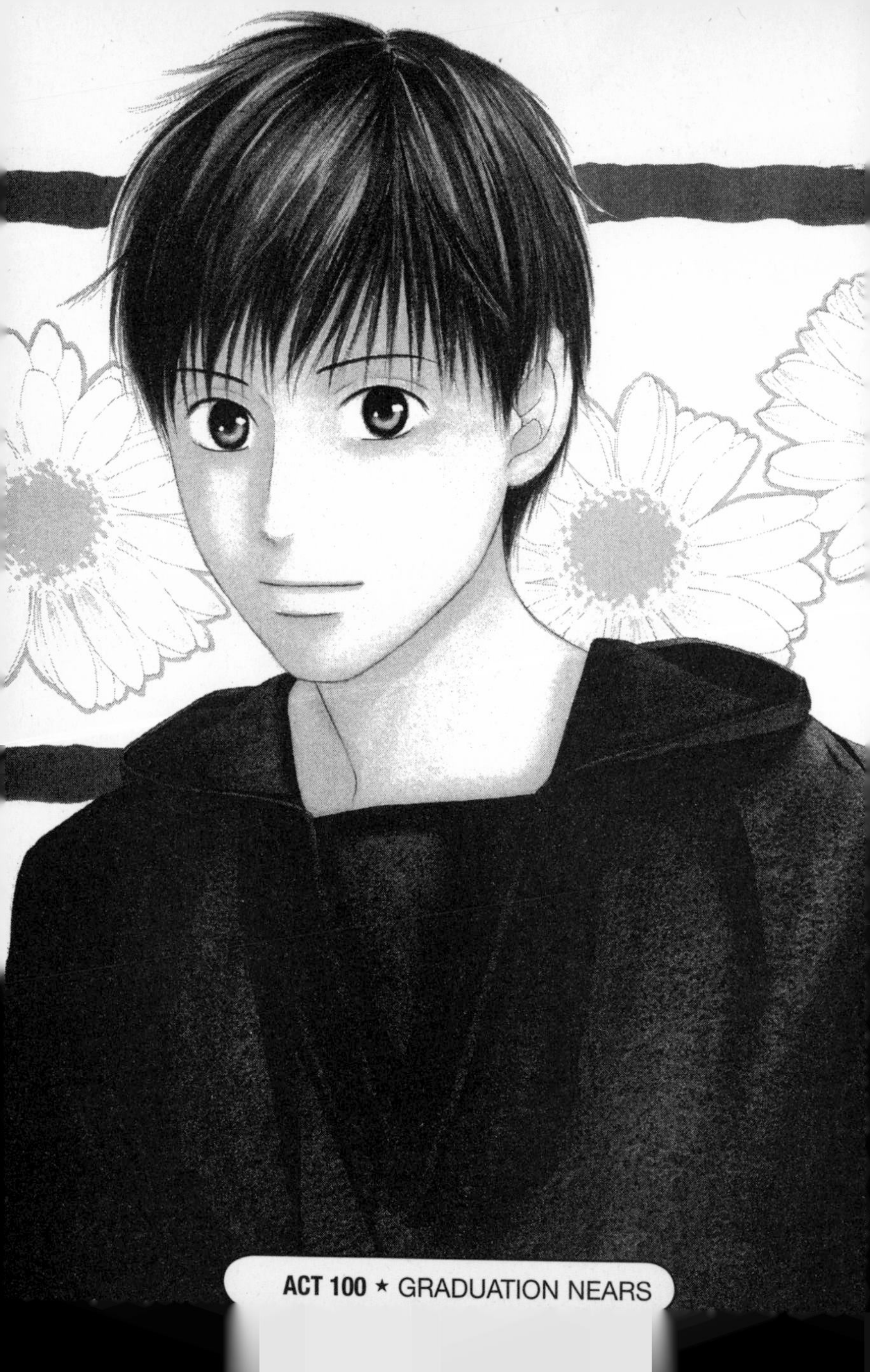

## ACT 100 ★ GRADUATION NEARS

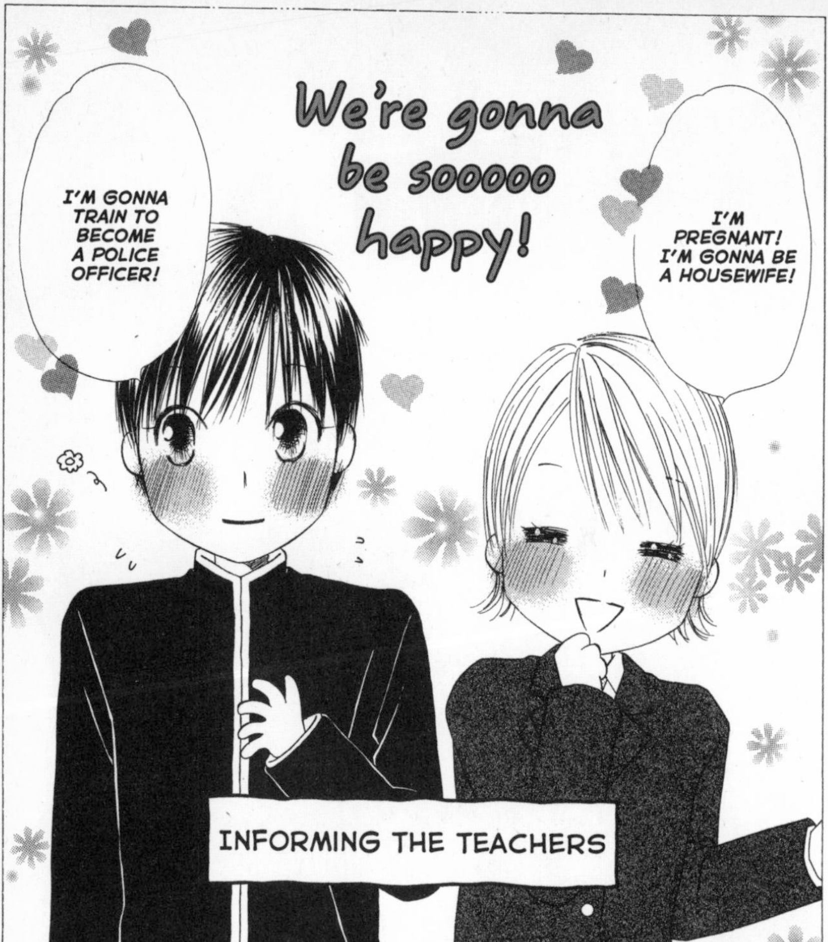
I'M PREGNANT! I'M GONNA BE A HOUSEWIFE!
We're gonna be sooooo happy!
I'M GONNA TRAIN TO BECOME A POLICE OFFICER!
INFORMING THE TEACHERS

Captain
A baseball anime

I'm not a hardcore anime or game fan, but a while ago I asked myself, "What are my favorite animes?" The two answers were Akage no Anne (Anne of Green Gables) and Captain. Really old series, but GREAT!

Just hearing their theme songs makes me feel warm...

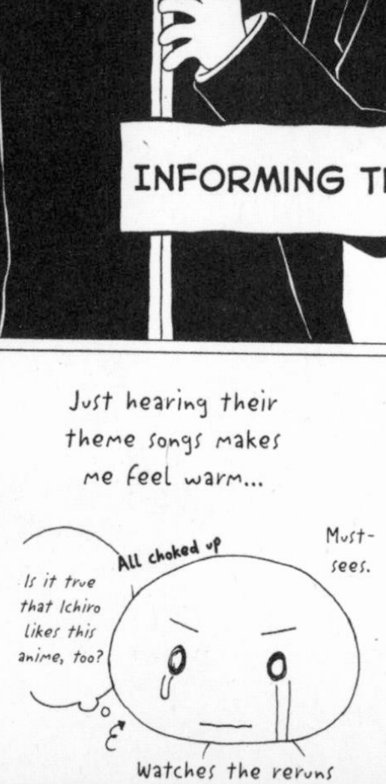
Must-sees.
All choked up
Is it true that Ichiro likes this anime, too?
Watches the reruns

I barely remember the stories, though. Maybe I'll buy them, if they come out on DVD...

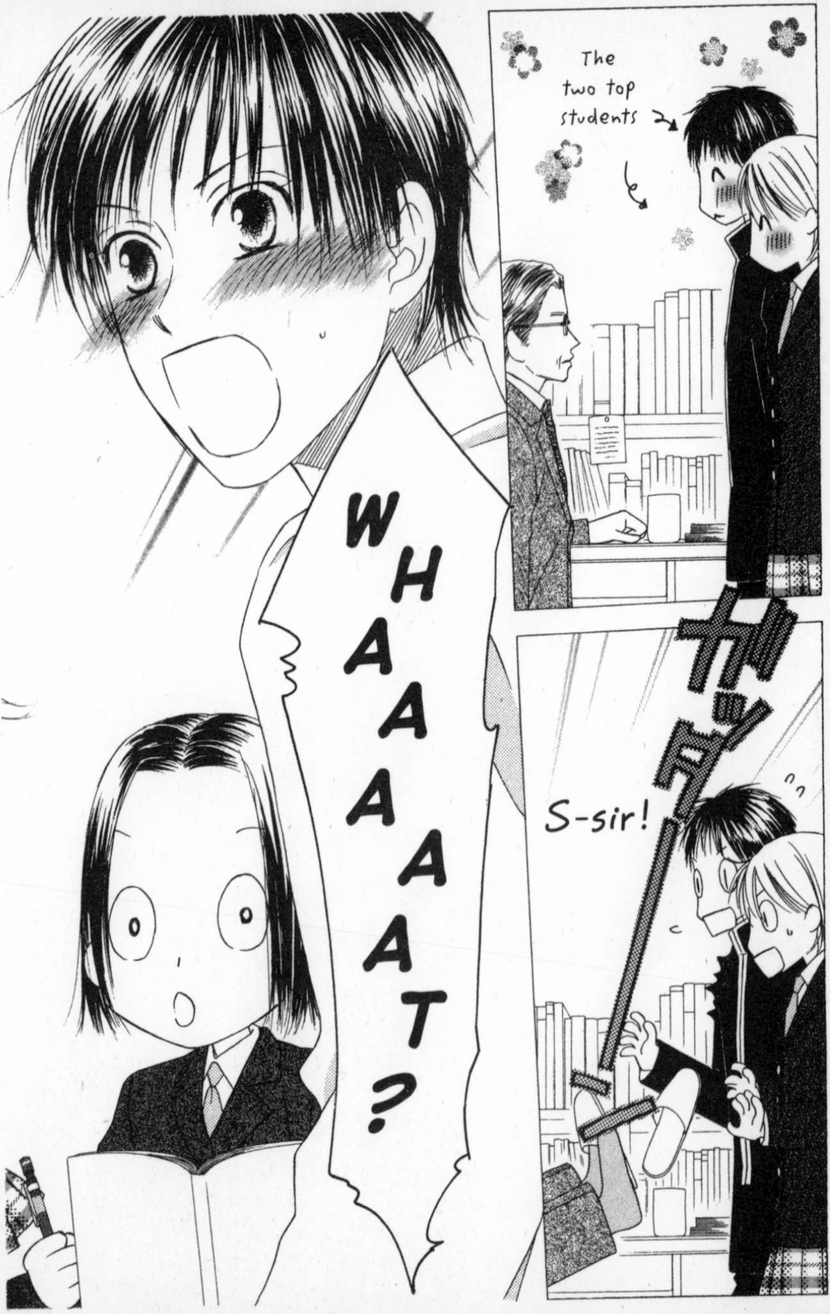
The two top students
S-sir!
WHAAAAT?

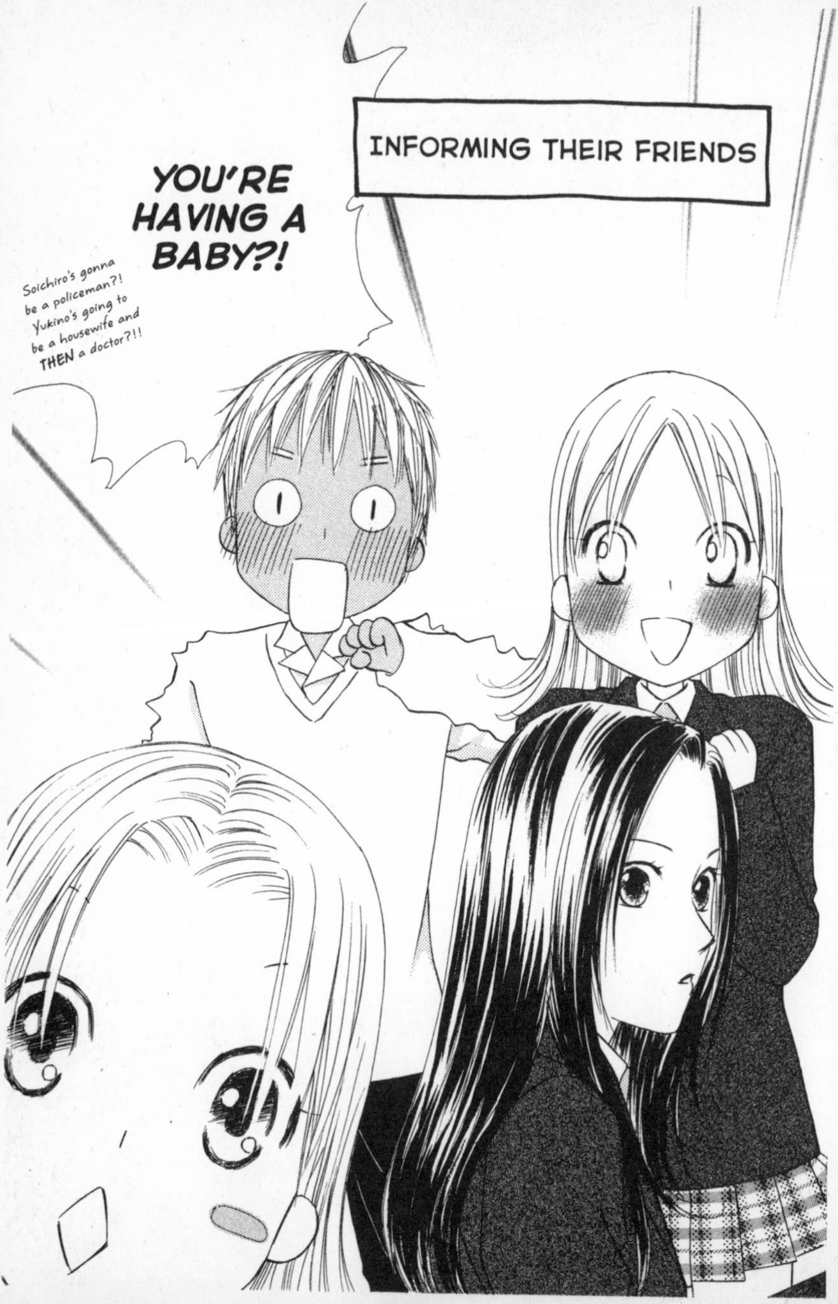
INFORMING THEIR FRIENDS
YOU'RE HAVING A BABY?!
Soichiro's gonna be a policeman?! Yukino's going to be a housewife and THEN a doctor?!!

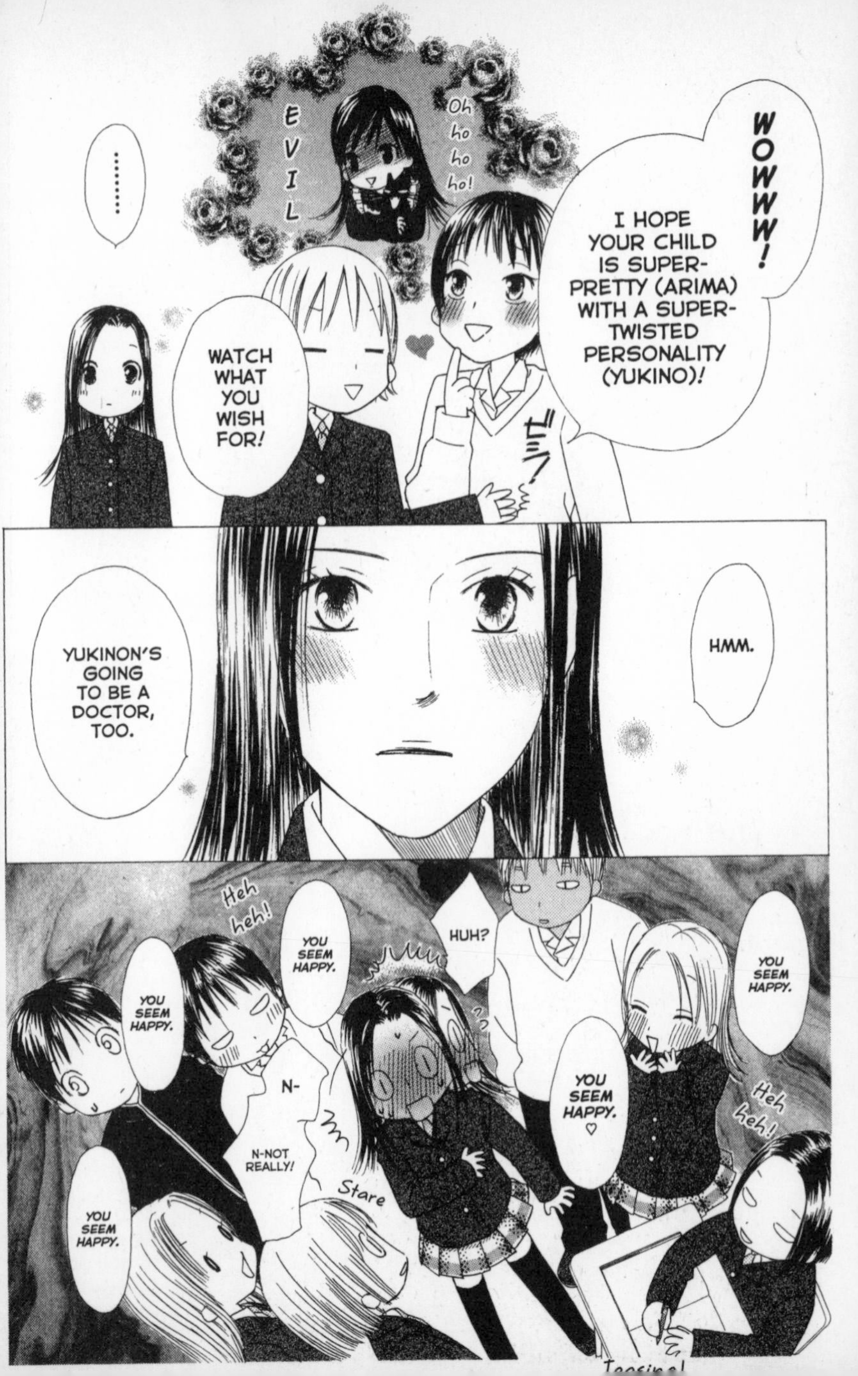
WOWWW!
I HOPE YOUR CHILD IS SUPER-PRETTY (ARIMA) WITH A SUPER-TWISTED PERSONALITY (YUKINO)!
Oh ho ho ho!
EVIL
.........
WATCH WHAT YOU WISH FOR!
HMM.
YUKINON'S GOING TO BE A DOCTOR, TOO.
YOU SEEM HAPPY.
Heh heh!
HUH?
YOU SEEM HAPPY. ♡
YOU SEEM HAPPY.
Heh heh!
YOU SEEM HAPPY.
N-
N-NOT REALLY!
Stare
YOU SEEM HAPPY.

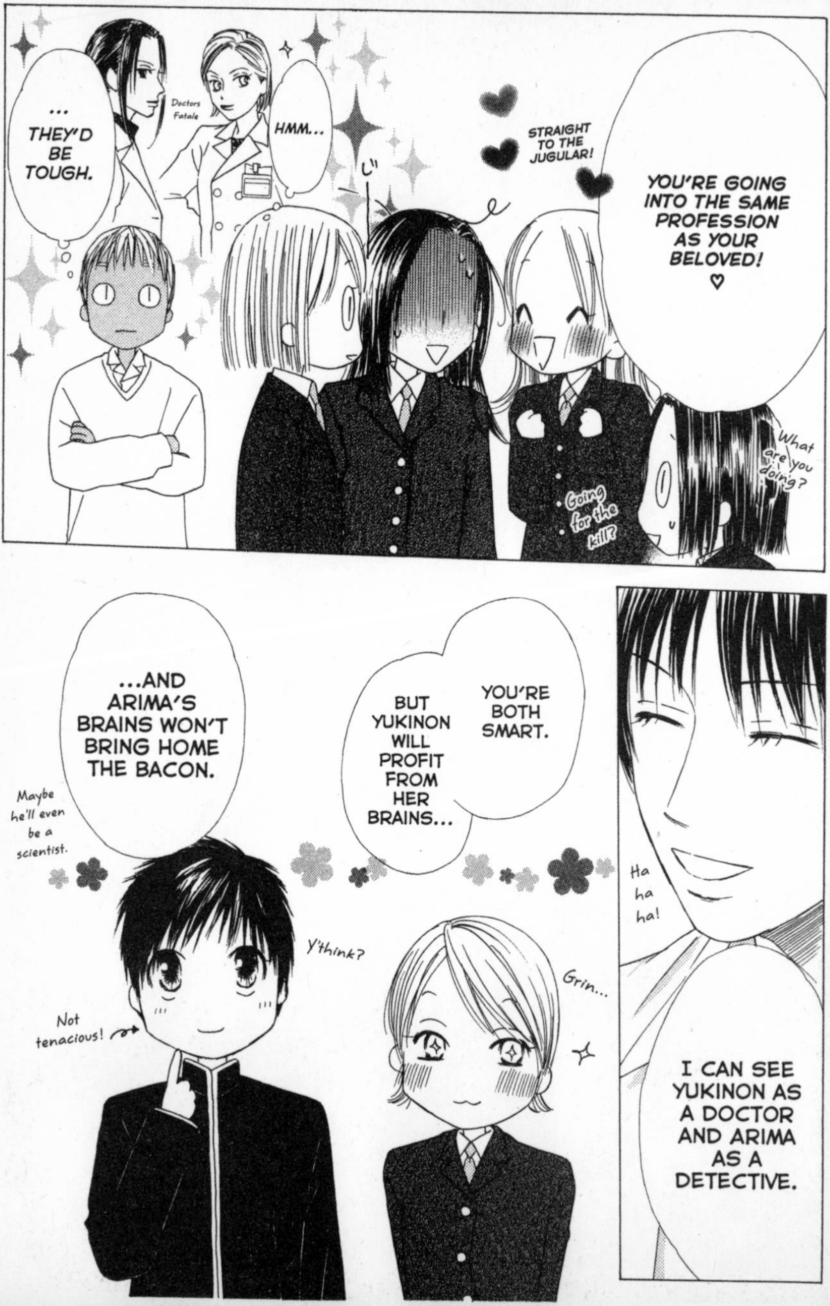
YOU'RE GOING INTO THE SAME PROFESSION AS YOUR BELOVED! ♡
What are you doing?
STRAIGHT TO THE JUGULAR!
Going for the kill?
じ
HMM...
Doctors Fatale
... THEY'D BE TOUGH.
I CAN SEE YUKINON AS A DOCTOR AND ARIMA AS A DETECTIVE.
Ha ha ha!
YOU'RE BOTH SMART.
BUT YUKINON WILL PROFIT FROM HER BRAINS...
...AND ARIMA'S BRAINS WON'T BRING HOME THE BACON.
Grin...
Y'think?
Maybe he'll even be a scientist.
Not tenacious!

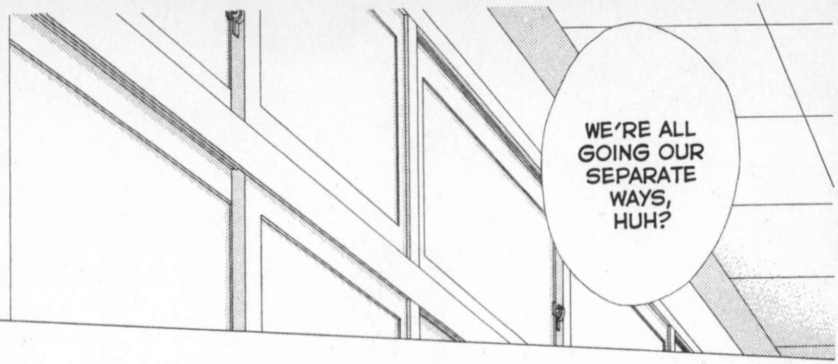
WE'RE ALL GOING OUR SEPARATE WAYS, HUH?

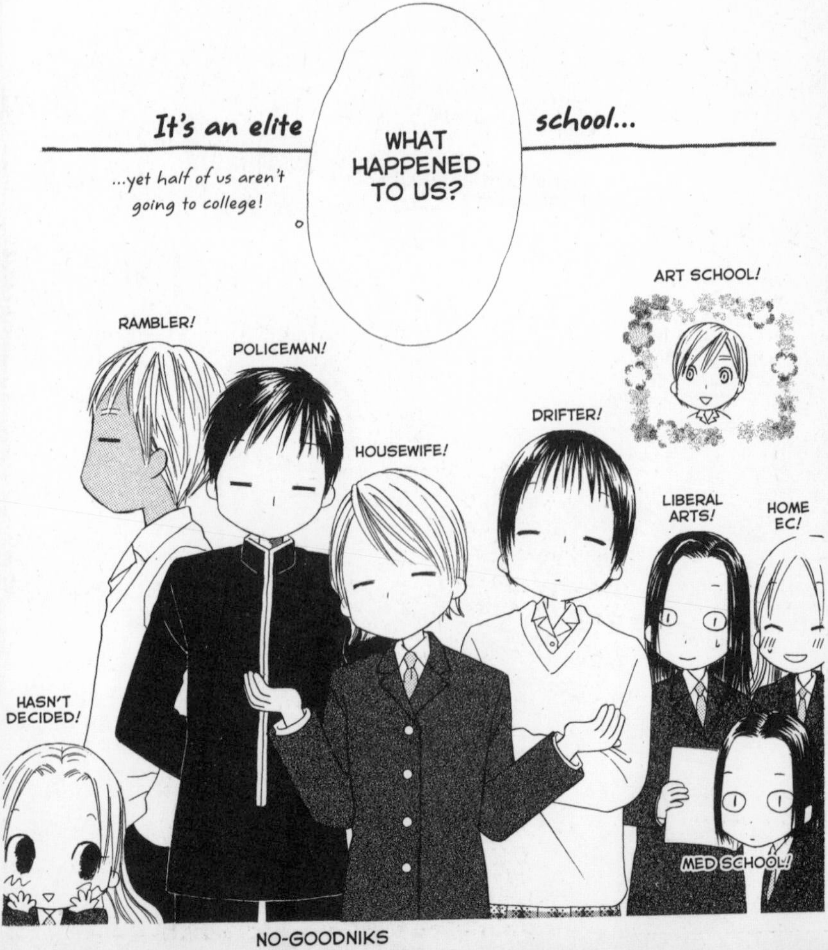
WHAT HAPPENED TO US?
It's an elite school...
...yet half of us aren't going to college!
ART SCHOOL!
HOME EC!
LIBERAL ARTS!
MED SCHOOL!
DRIFTER!
HOUSEWIFE!
POLICEMAN!
RAMBLER!
HASN'T DECIDED!
NO-GOODNIKS

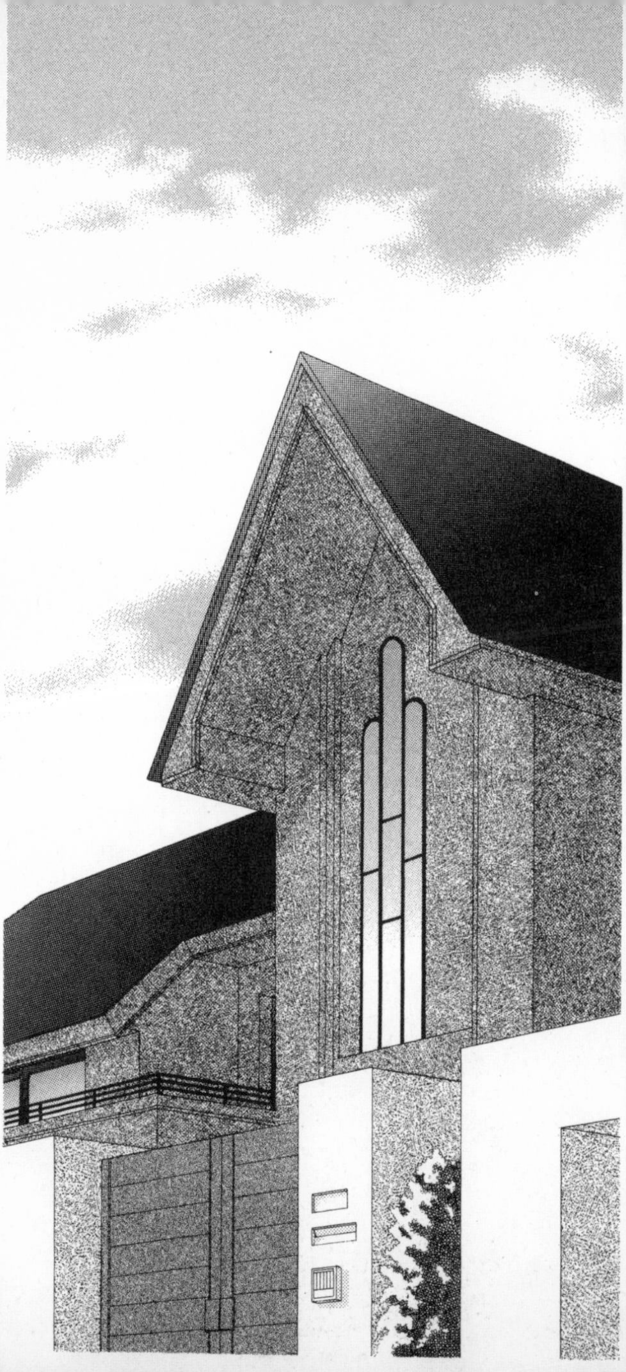

2

Last time, I wrote that this year's theme would be "beautiful," and I'm sticking to it...for now!

Who will be the muse for her new spring and summer look??

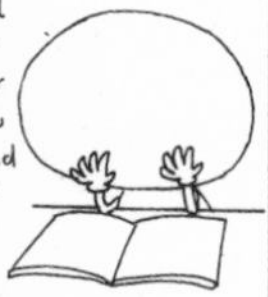

Why "for now"? Well, keeping my room clean is hard. It's both my home and my office. I thought, "Once *Kare Kano* is over, I'll clean this whole place up in one shot!" But it's hard to get rid of so much stuff!

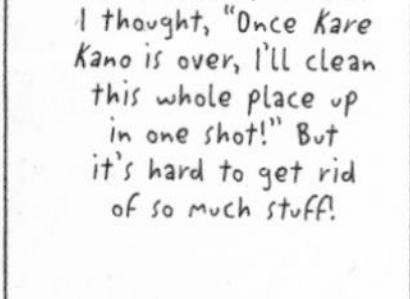

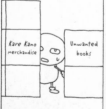

*Kare Kano* merchandise
Unwanted books


But once I sort through all the stuff I've hoarded and open up some space, it sure will be a relief! ♡

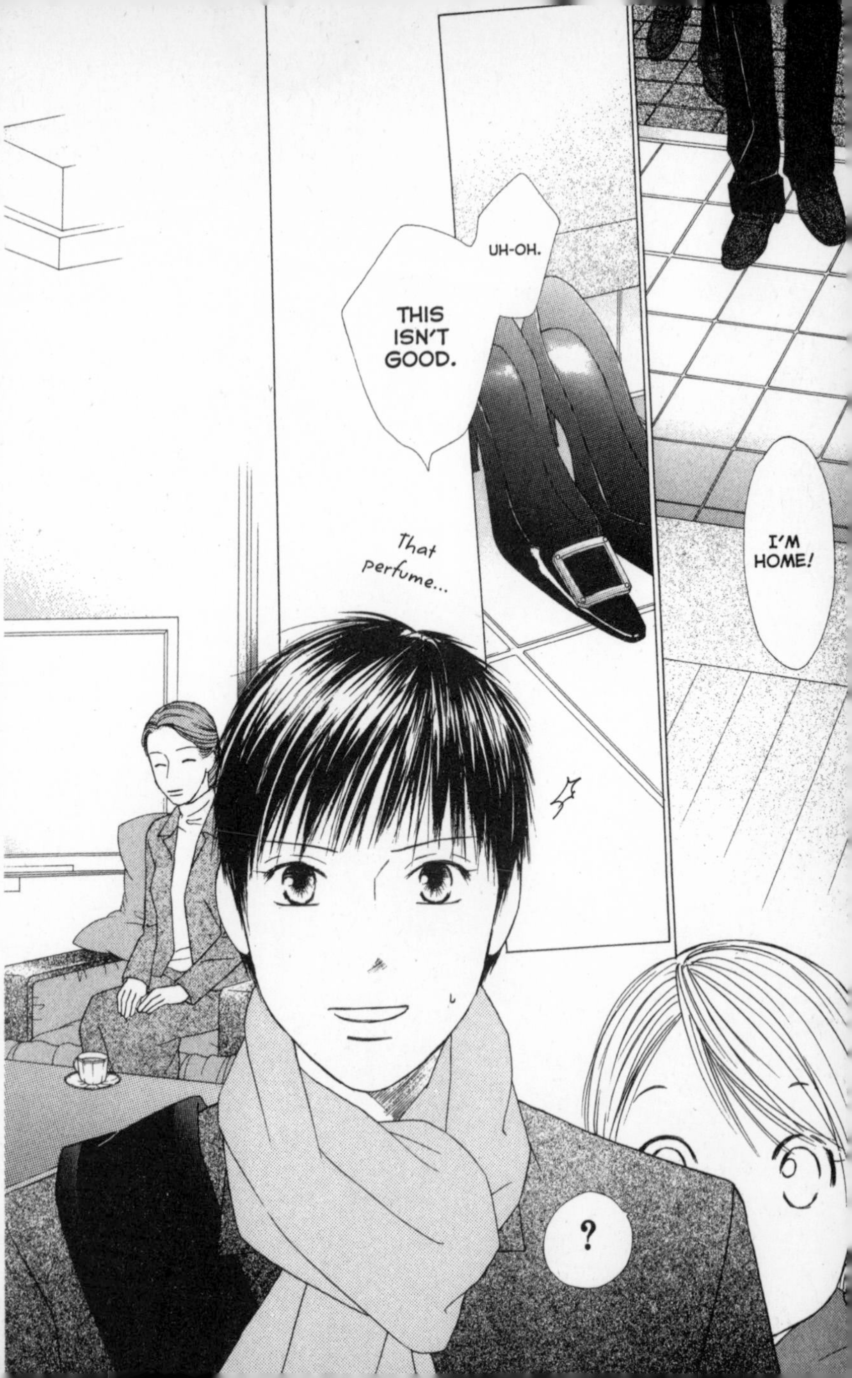
I'M HOME!
UH-OH.
THIS ISN'T GOOD.
That perfume...
?

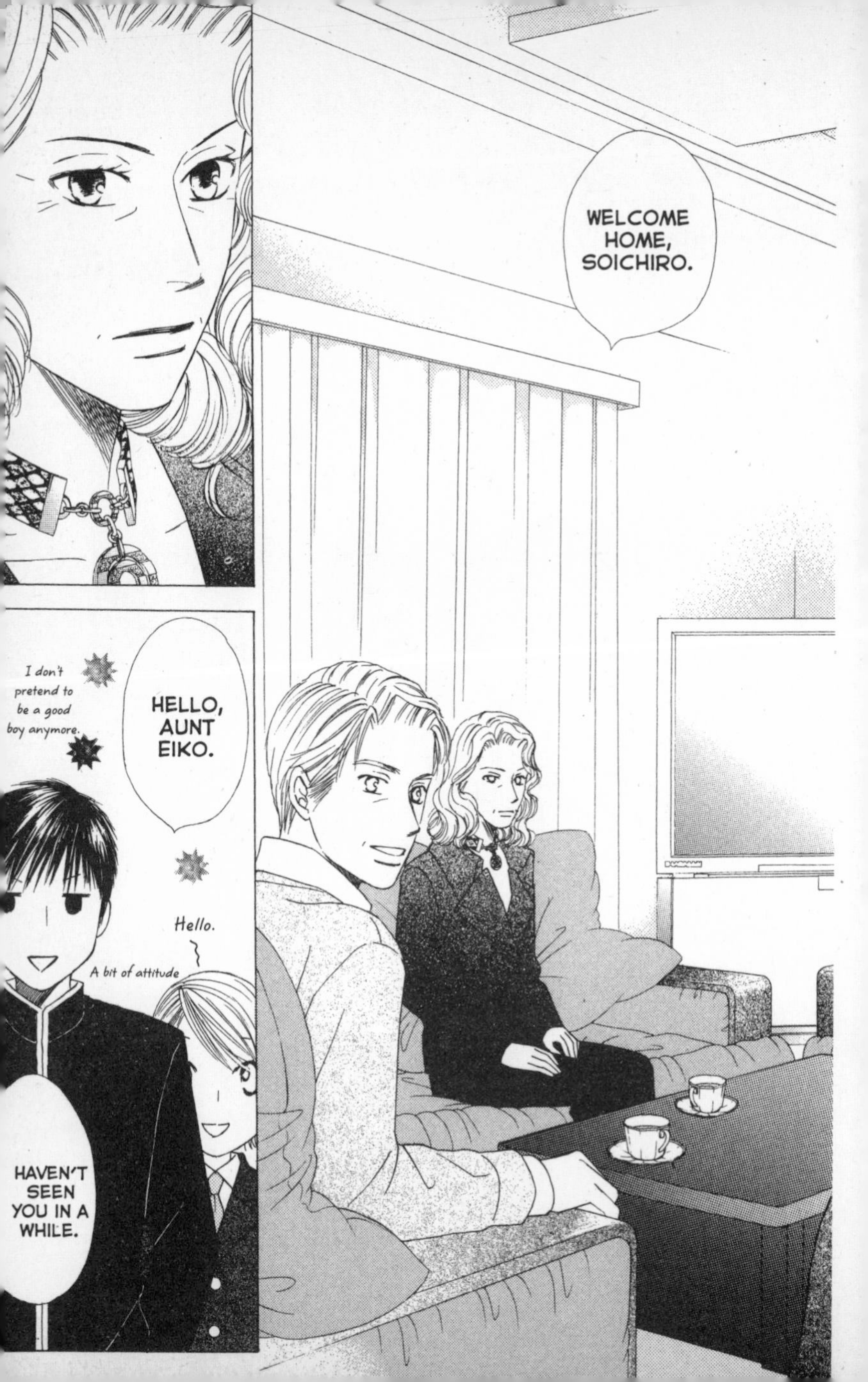
WELCOME HOME, SOICHIRO.
HELLO, AUNT EIKO.
I don't pretend to be a good boy anymore.
Hello.
A bit of attitude
HAVEN'T SEEN YOU IN A WHILE.

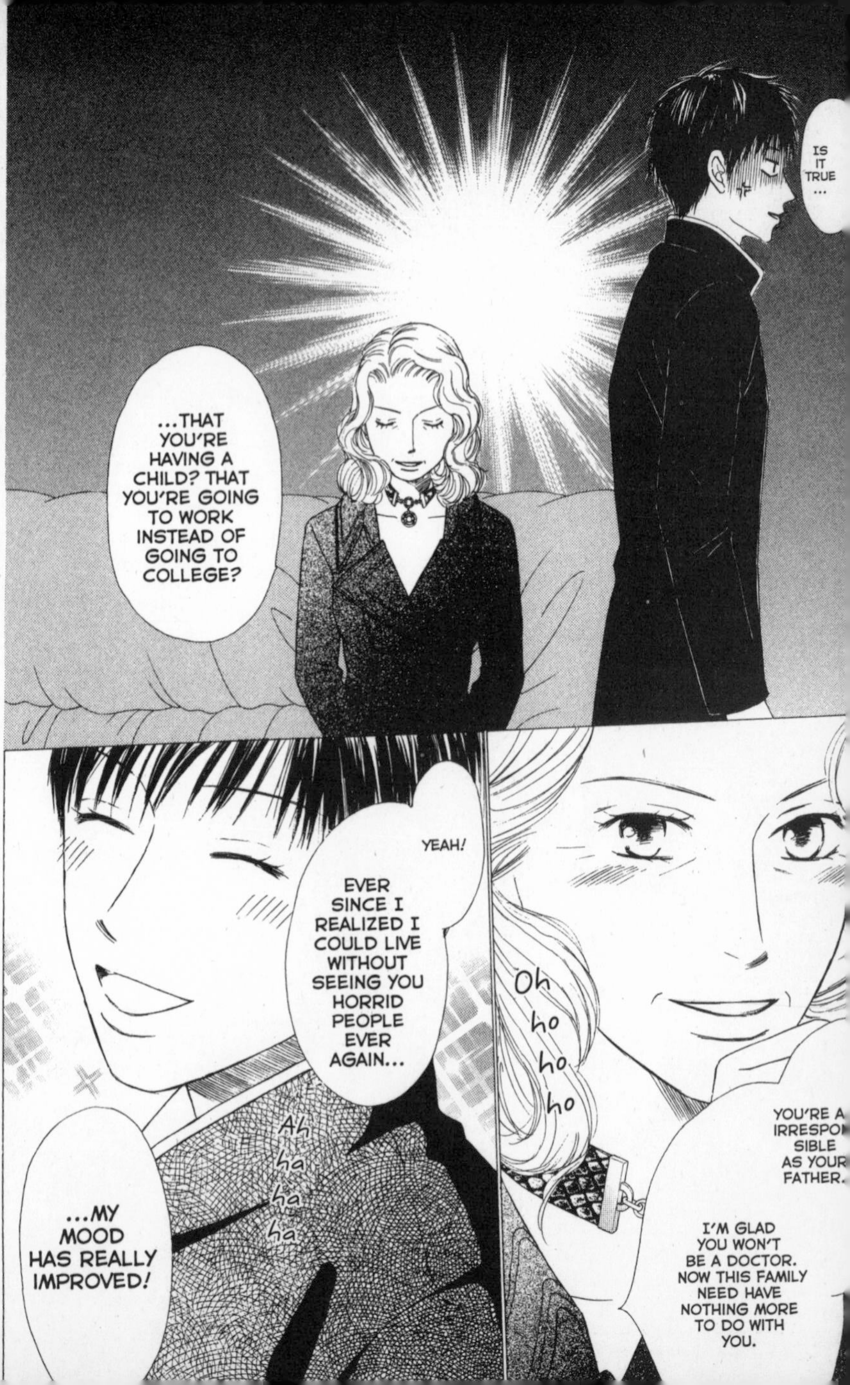
IS IT TRUE...
...THAT YOU'RE HAVING A CHILD? THAT YOU'RE GOING TO WORK INSTEAD OF GOING TO COLLEGE?
Oh ho ho ho
YOU'RE A IRRESPO SIBLE AS YOUR FATHER.
I'M GLAD YOU WON'T BE A DOCTOR. NOW THIS FAMILY NEED HAVE NOTHING MORE TO DO WITH YOU.
YEAH!
EVER SINCE I REALIZED I COULD LIVE WITHOUT SEEING YOU HORRID PEOPLE EVER AGAIN...
Ah ha ha ha
...MY MOOD HAS REALLY IMPROVED!

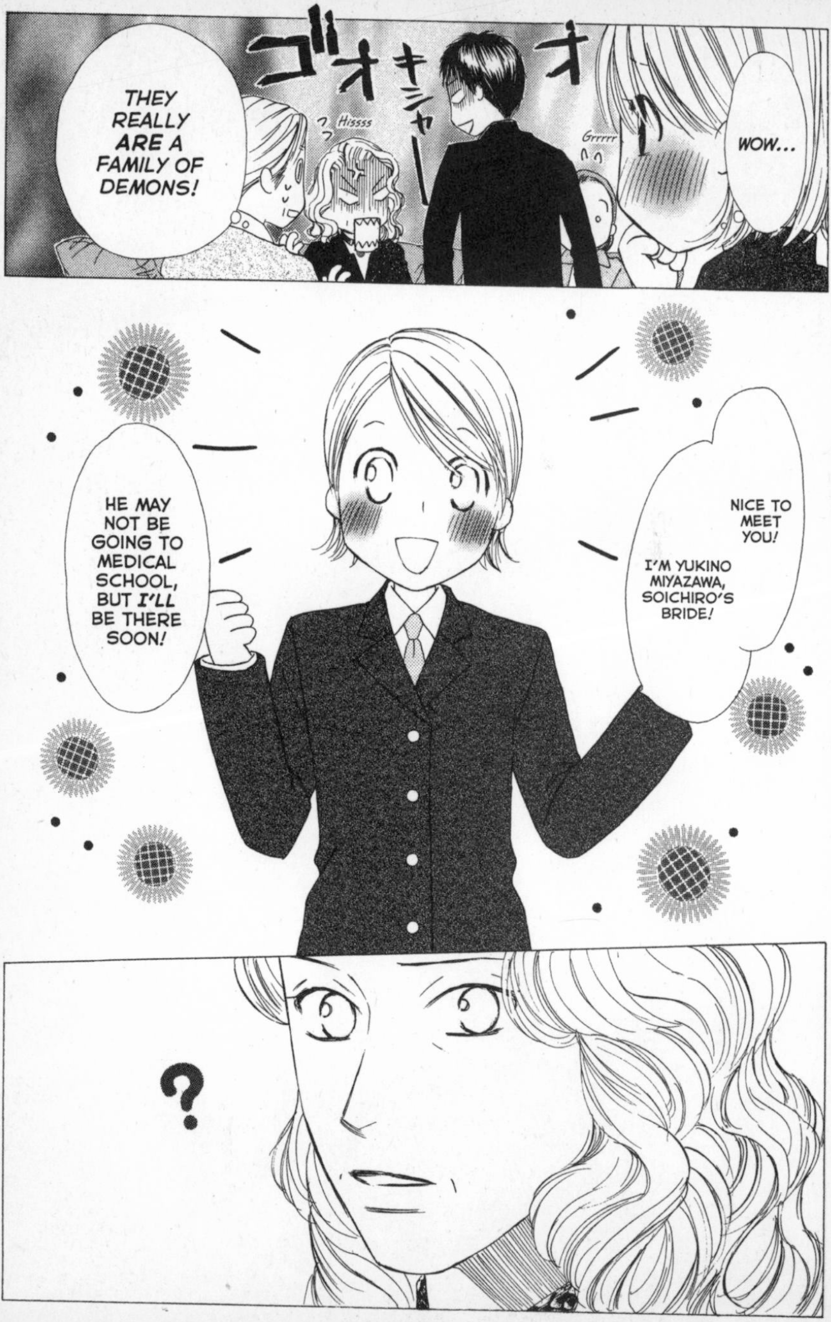
WOW...
Grrrrr
Hissss
THEY REALLY ARE A FAMILY OF DEMONS!
NICE TO MEET YOU!
I'M YUKINO MIYAZAWA, SOICHIRO'S BRIDE!
HE MAY NOT BE GOING TO MEDICAL SCHOOL, BUT I'LL BE THERE SOON!
?

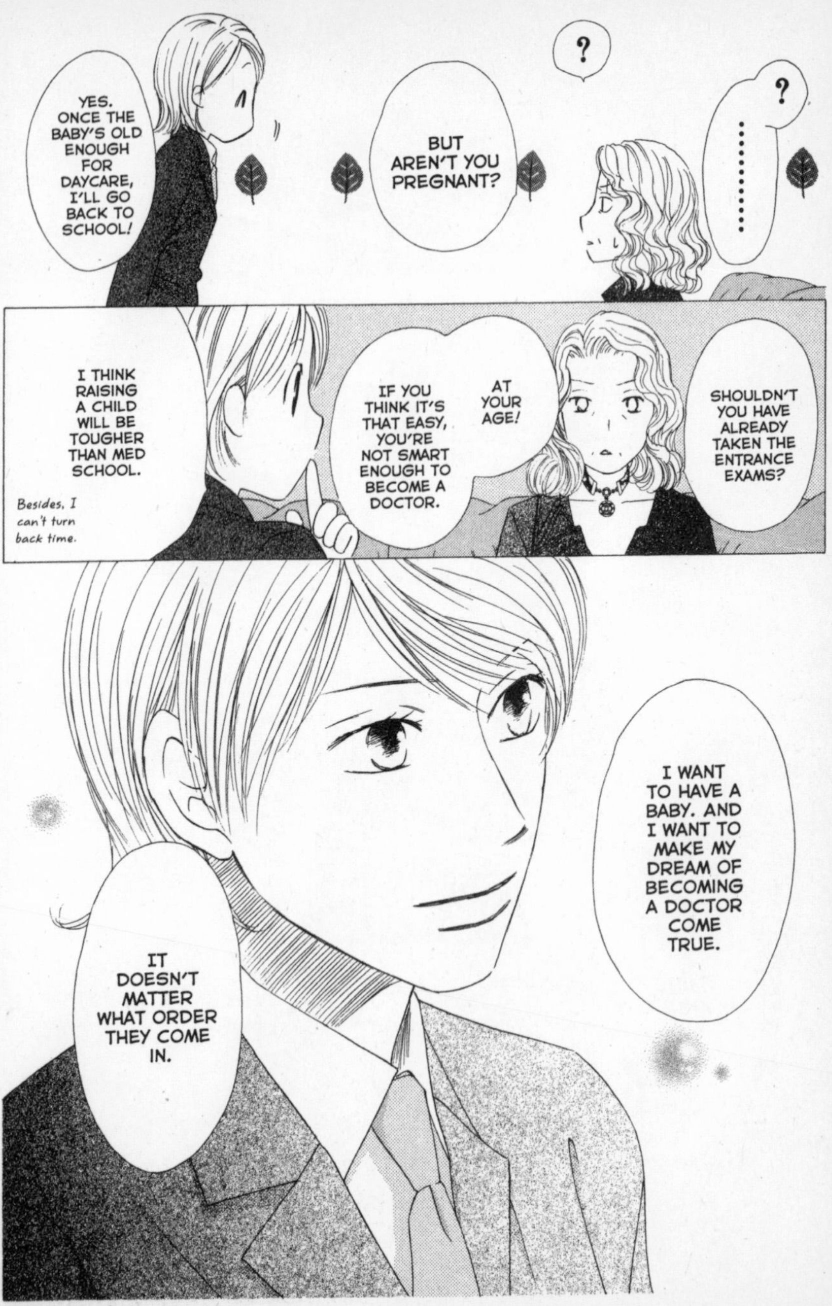
?
......
?
BUT AREN'T YOU PREGNANT?
YES. ONCE THE BABY'S OLD ENOUGH FOR DAYCARE, I'LL GO BACK TO SCHOOL!
SHOULDN'T YOU HAVE ALREADY TAKEN THE ENTRANCE EXAMS?
AT YOUR AGE!
IF YOU THINK IT'S THAT EASY, YOU'RE NOT SMART ENOUGH TO BECOME A DOCTOR.
I THINK RAISING A CHILD WILL BE TOUGHER THAN MED SCHOOL.
Besides, I can't turn back time.
I WANT TO HAVE A BABY. AND I WANT TO MAKE MY DREAM OF BECOMING A DOCTOR COME TRUE.
IT DOESN'T MATTER WHAT ORDER THEY COME IN.

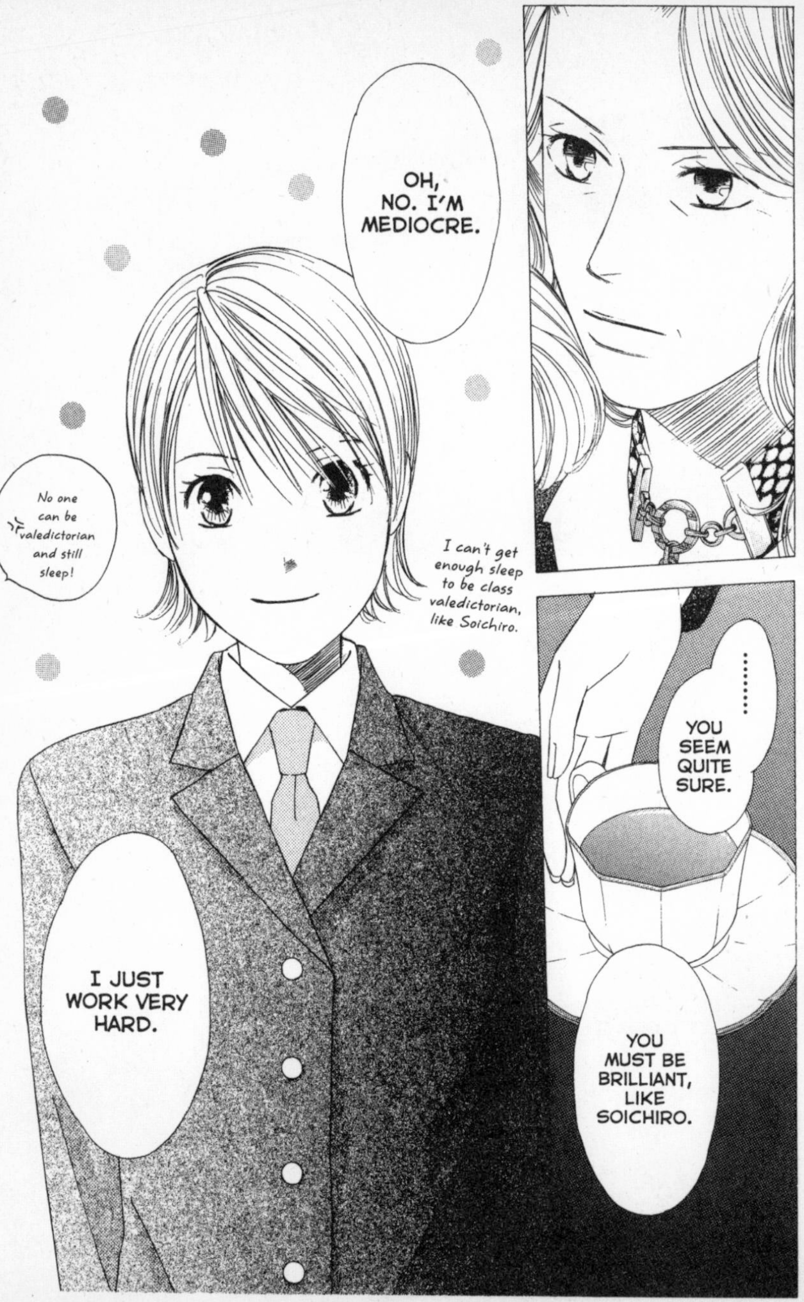
......
YOU SEEM QUITE SURE.
YOU MUST BE BRILLIANT, LIKE SOICHIRO.
OH, NO. I'M MEDIOCRE.
I can't get enough sleep to be class valedictorian, like Soichiro.
No one can be valedictorian and still sleep!
I JUST WORK VERY HARD.

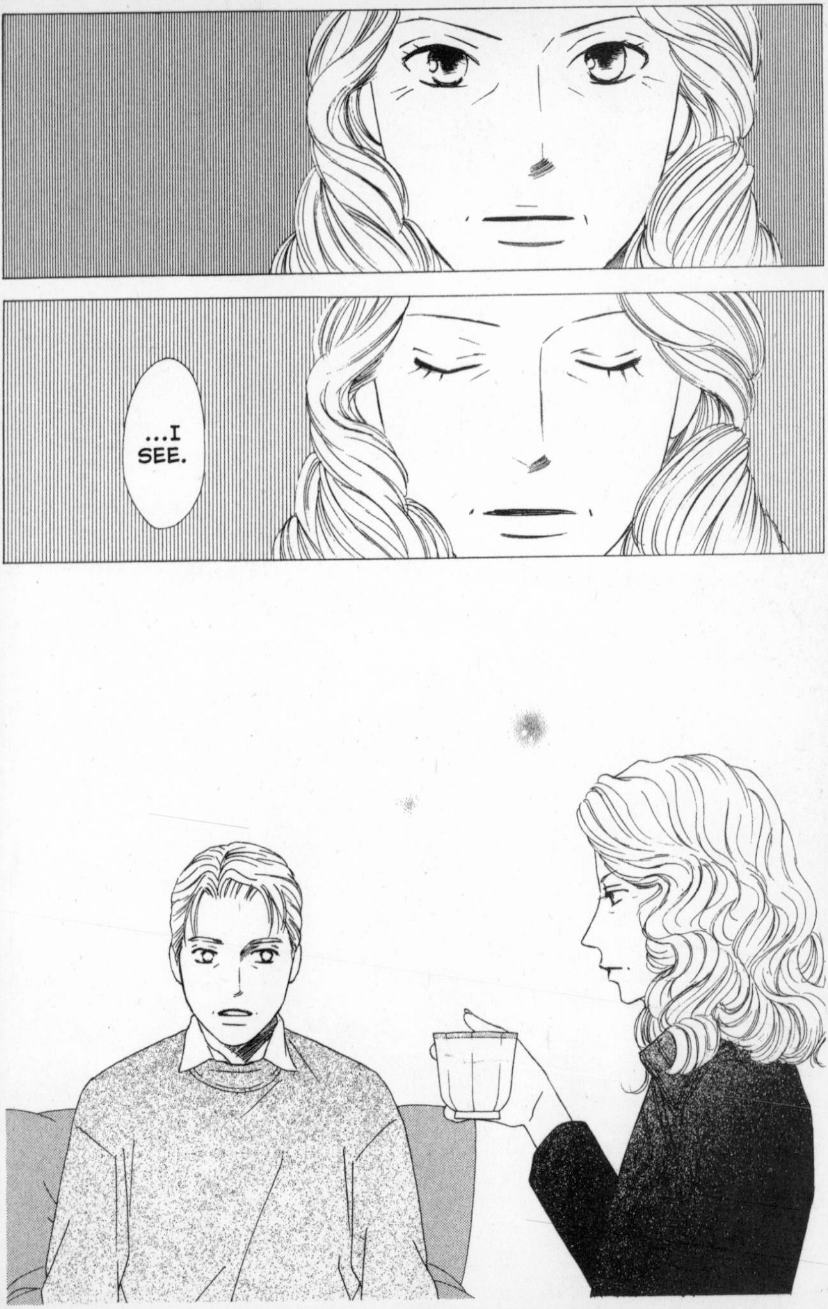
...I SEE.

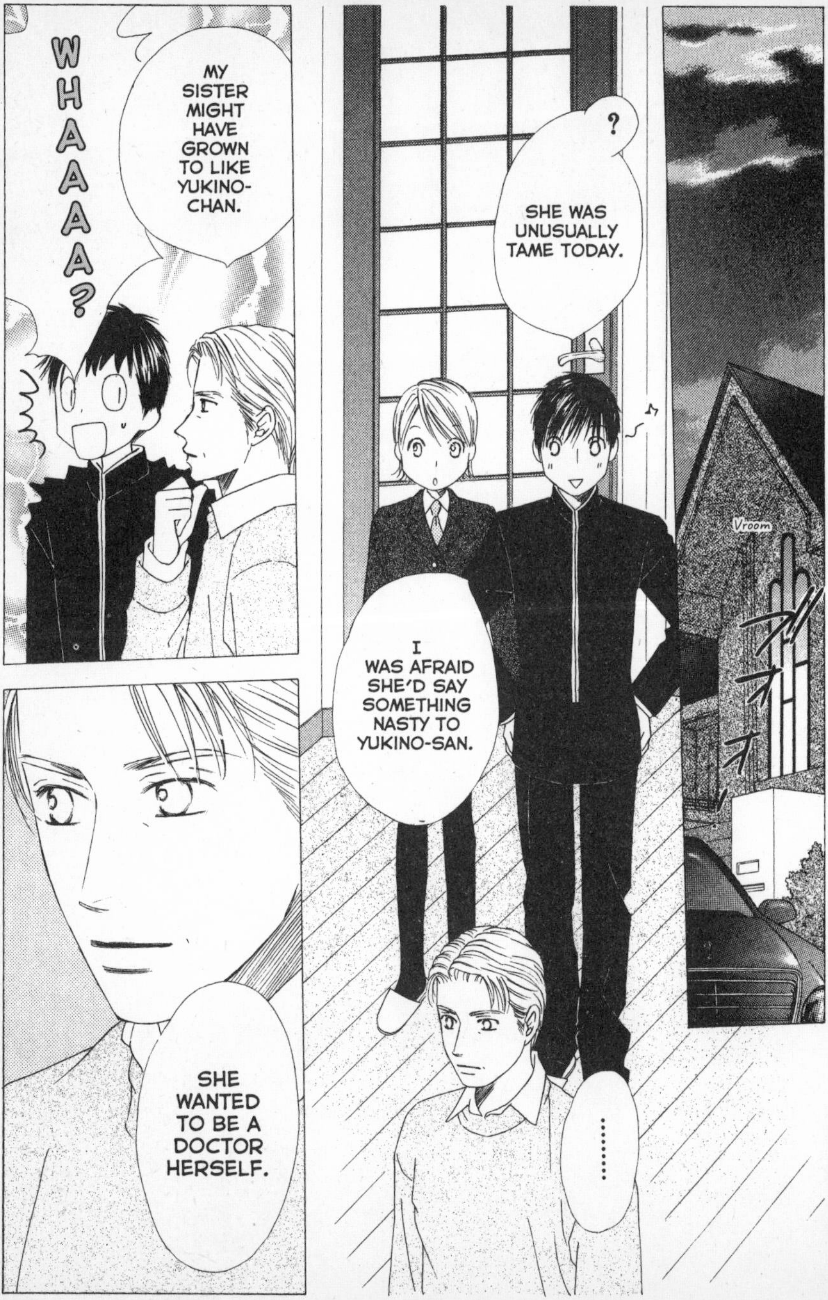
Vroom
?
SHE WAS UNUSUALLY TAME TODAY.
I WAS AFRAID SHE'D SAY SOMETHING NASTY TO YUKINO-SAN.
......
MY SISTER MIGHT HAVE GROWN TO LIKE YUKINO-CHAN.
WHAAAA?
SHE WANTED TO BE A DOCTOR HERSELF.

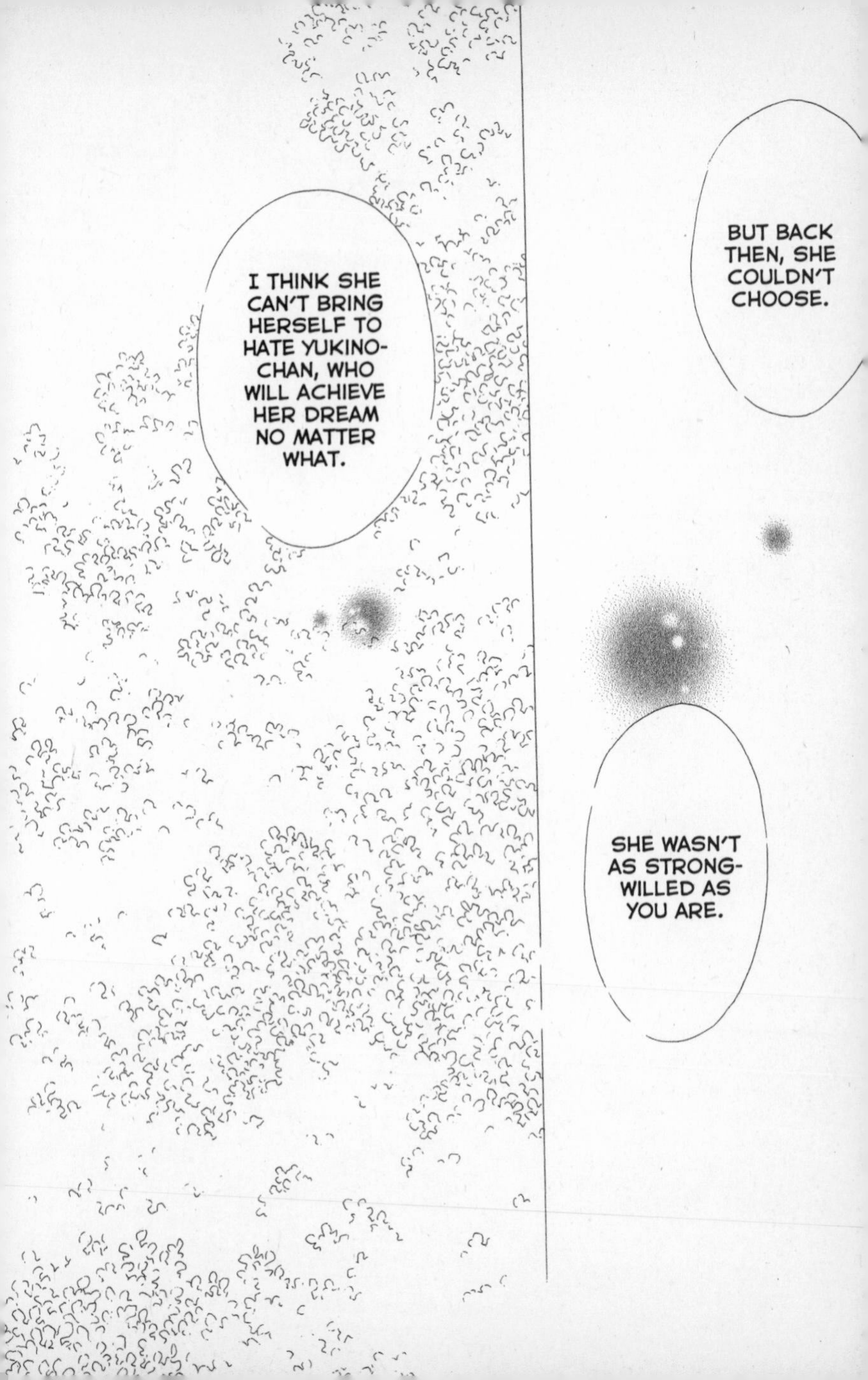
BUT BACK THEN, SHE COULDN'T CHOOSE.
SHE WASN'T AS STRONG-WILLED AS YOU ARE.
I THINK SHE CAN'T BRING HERSELF TO HATE YUKINO-CHAN, WHO WILL ACHIEVE HER DREAM NO MATTER WHAT.

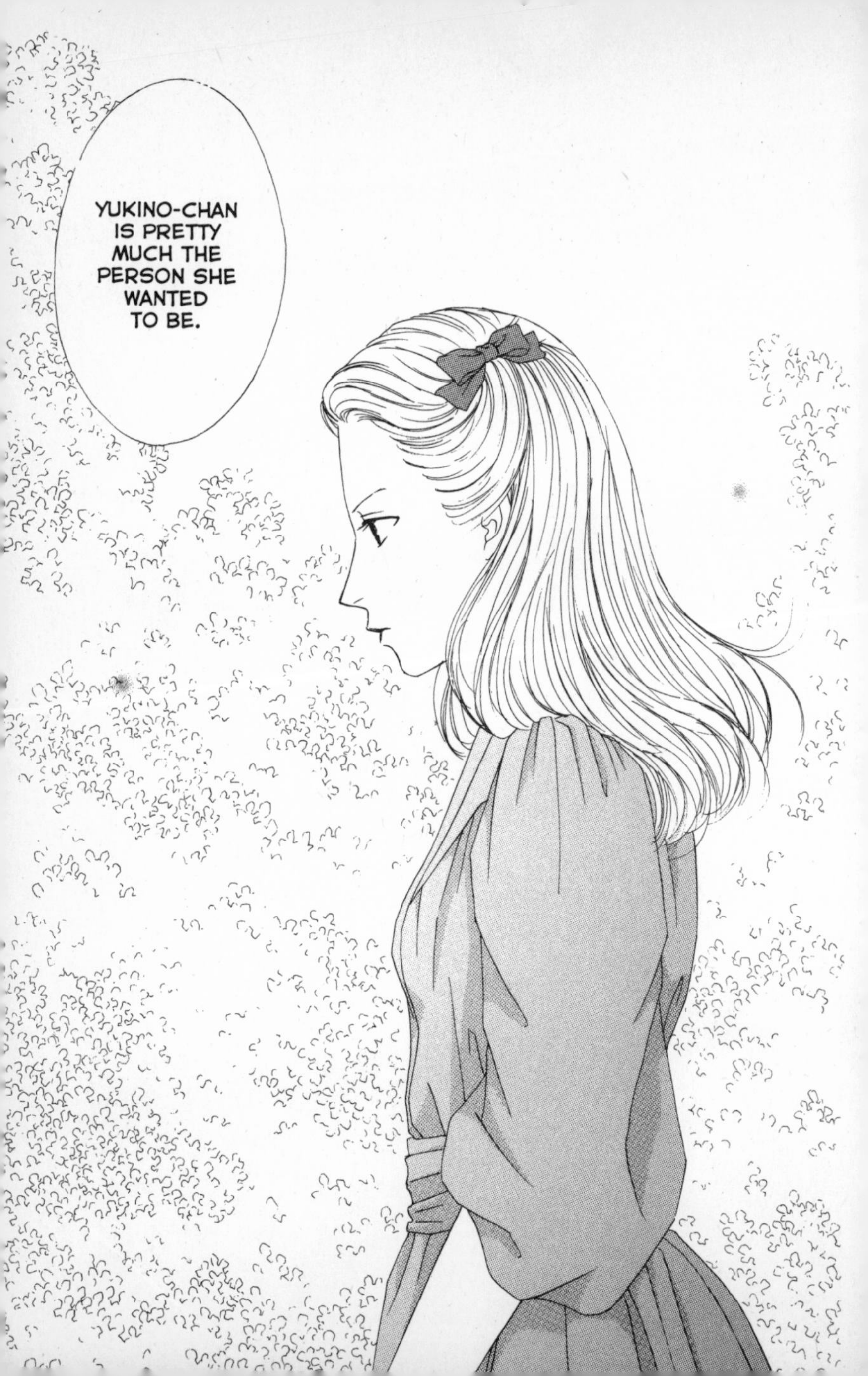
YUKINO-CHAN IS PRETTY MUCH THE PERSON SHE WANTED TO BE.

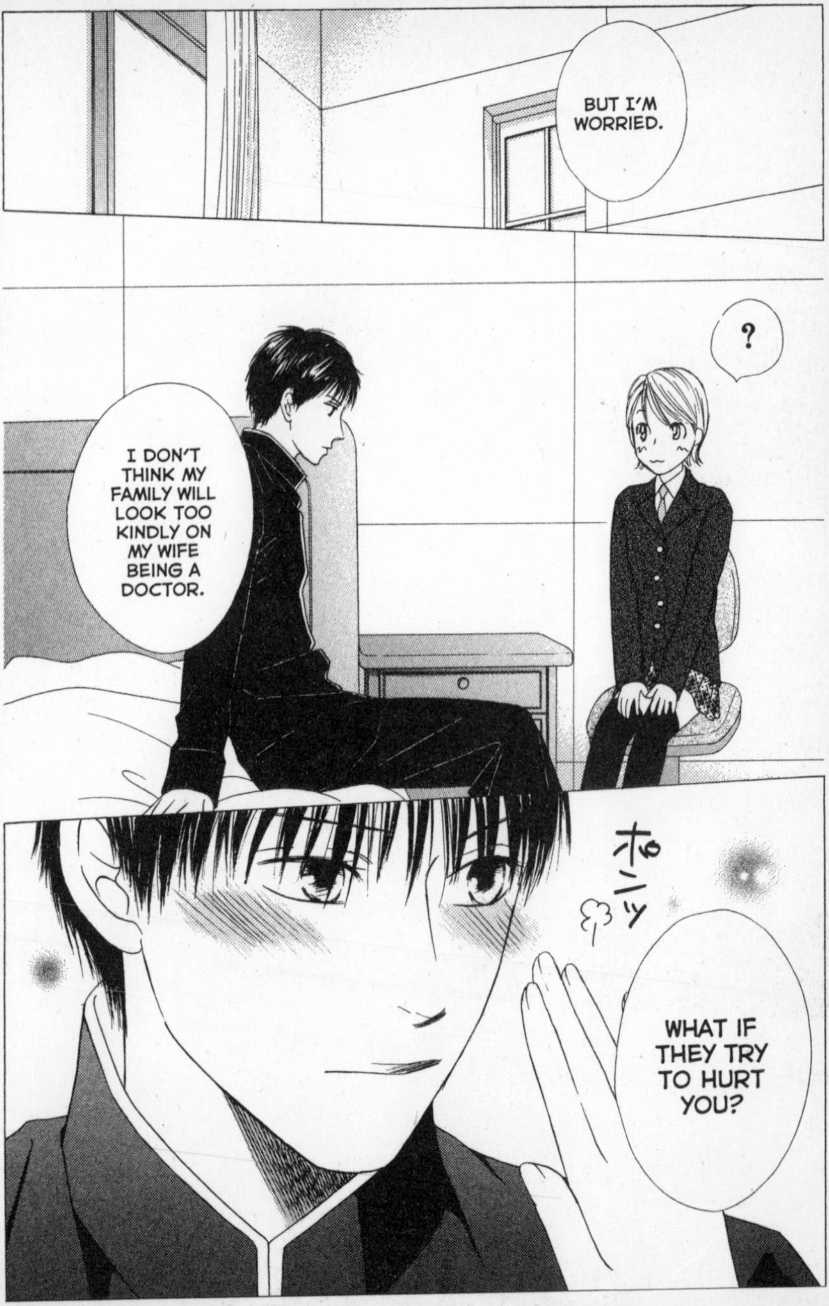
BUT I'M WORRIED.
?
I DON'T THINK MY FAMILY WILL LOOK TOO KINDLY ON MY WIFE BEING A DOCTOR.
ポンッ
WHAT IF THEY TRY TO HURT YOU?

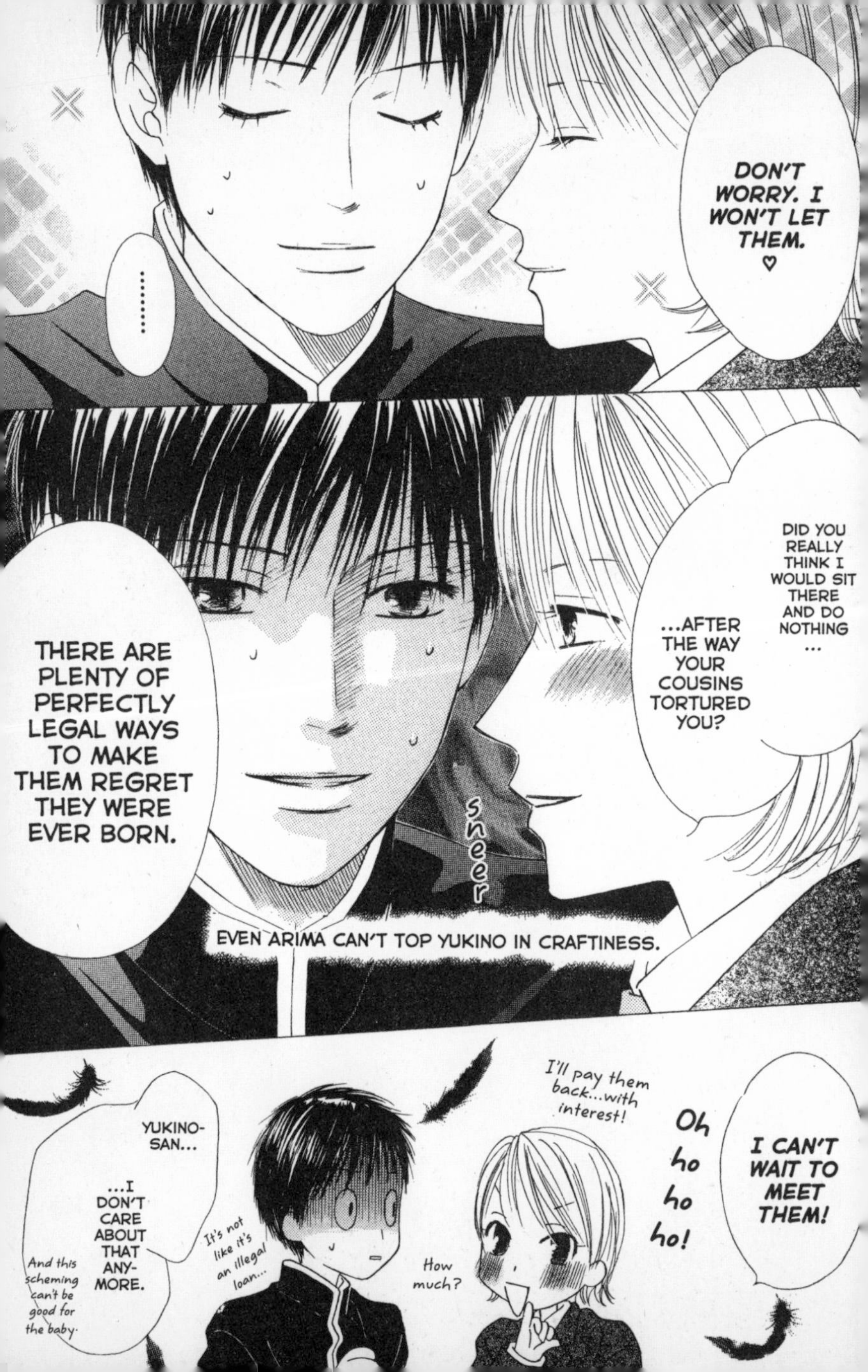
DON'T WORRY. I WON'T LET THEM. ♡
......
DID YOU REALLY THINK I WOULD SIT THERE AND DO NOTHING ...
...AFTER THE WAY YOUR COUSINS TORTURED YOU?
sneer
THERE ARE PLENTY OF PERFECTLY LEGAL WAYS TO MAKE THEM REGRET THEY WERE EVER BORN.
EVEN ARIMA CAN'T TOP YUKINO IN CRAFTINESS.
I CAN'T WAIT TO MEET THEM!
Oh ho ho ho!
I'll pay them back...with interest!
How much?
It's not like it's an illegal loan...
YUKINO-SAN...
...I DON'T CARE ABOUT THAT ANYMORE.
And this scheming can't be good for the baby.

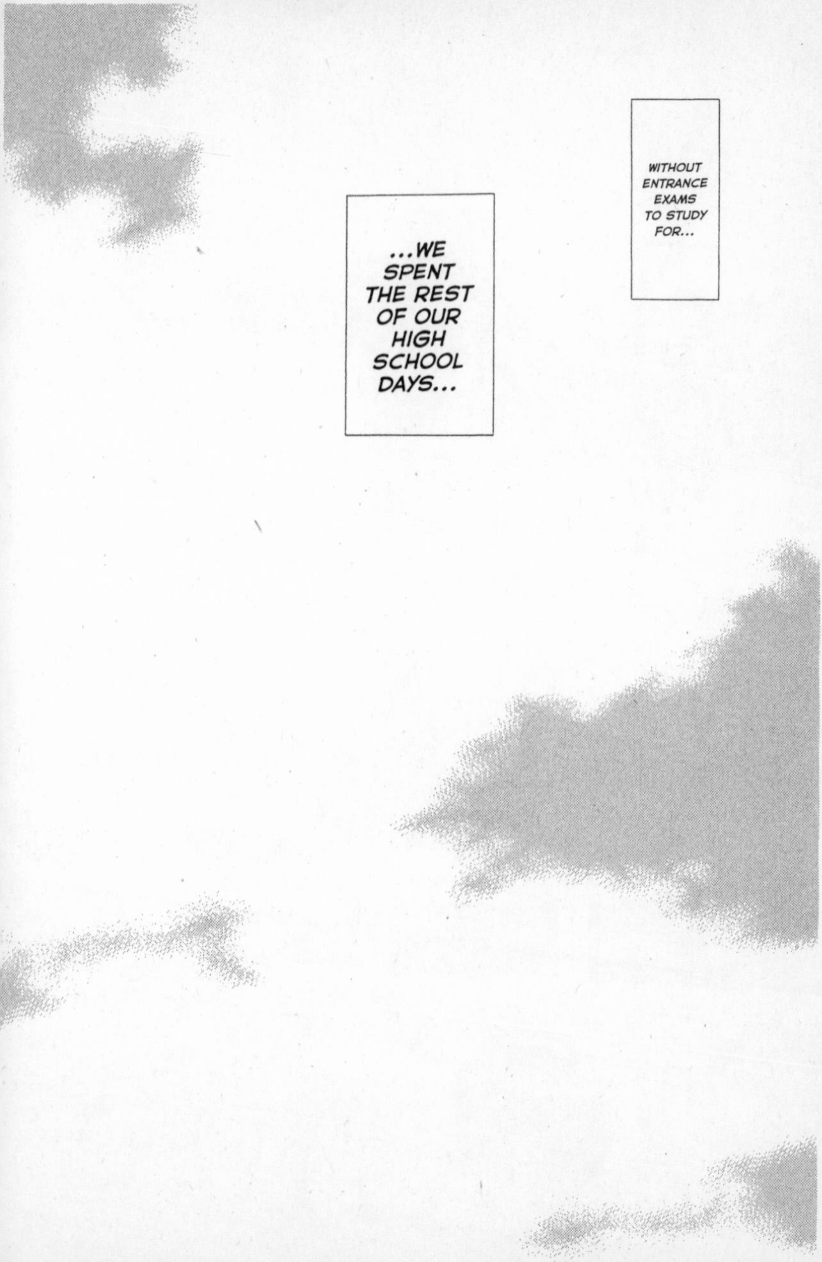
WITHOUT ENTRANCE EXAMS TO STUDY FOR...
...WE SPENT THE REST OF OUR HIGH SCHOOL DAYS...

...CARE-
FREE.

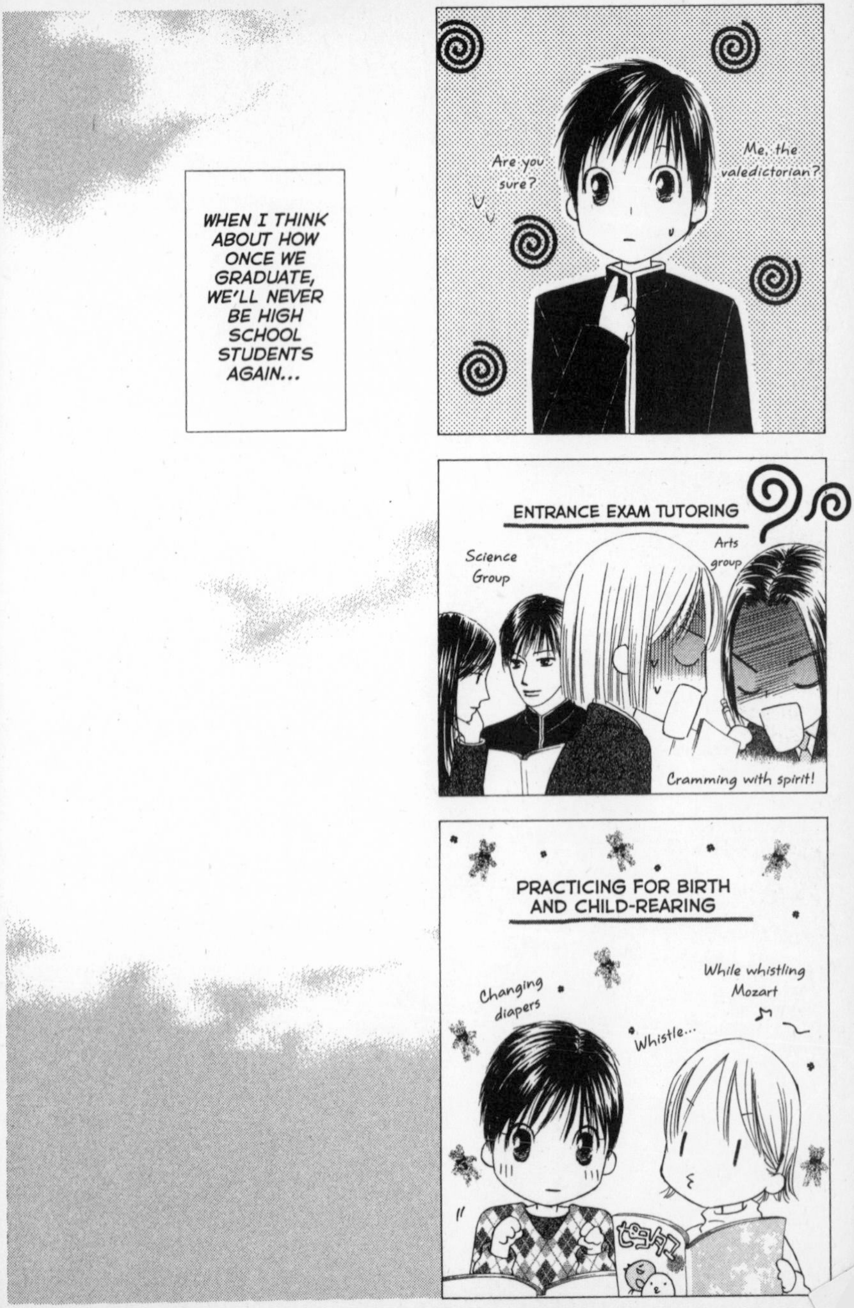
Me, the valedictorian?
Are you sure?
ENTRANCE EXAM TUTORING
Arts group
Science Group
Cramming with spirit!
PRACTICING FOR BIRTH AND CHILD-REARING
While whistling Mozart
Changing diapers
Whistle...
WHEN I THINK ABOUT HOW ONCE WE GRADUATE, WE'LL NEVER BE HIGH SCHOOL STUDENTS AGAIN...

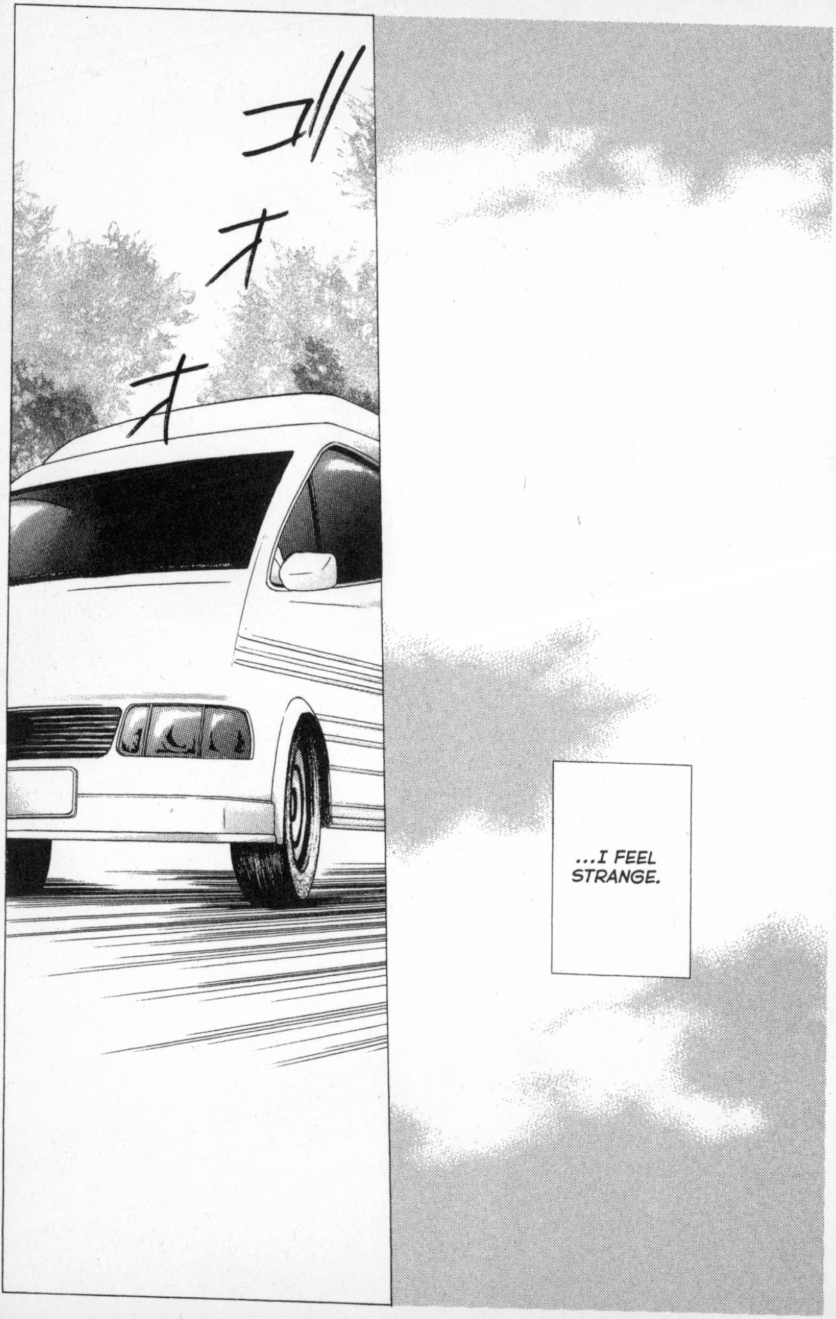
...I FEEL STRANGE.
ゴオオ

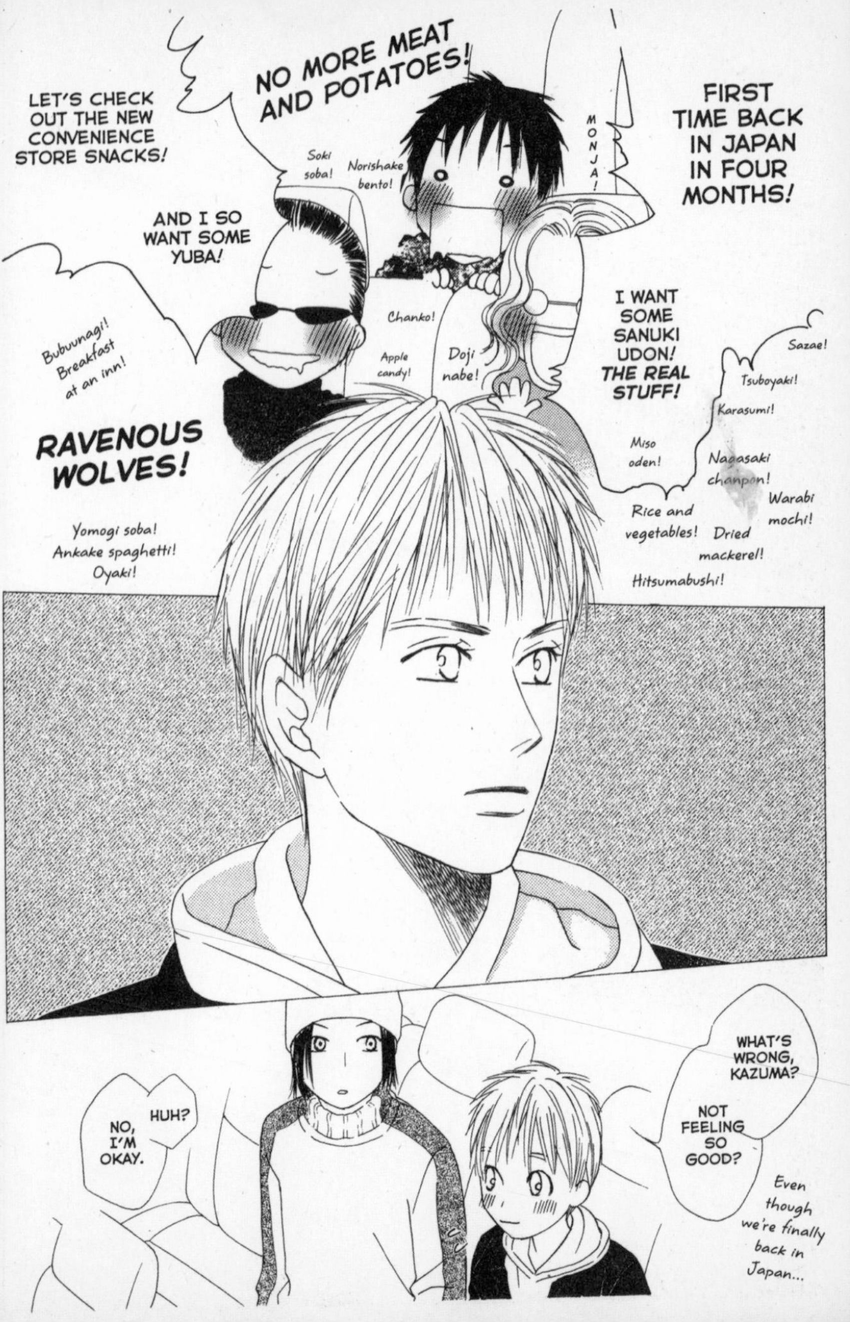
FIRST TIME BACK IN JAPAN IN FOUR MONTHS!
MONJA!
NO MORE MEAT AND POTATOES!
Norishake bento!
Soki soba!
LET'S CHECK OUT THE NEW CONVENIENCE STORE SNACKS!
I WANT SOME SANUKI UDON! THE REAL STUFF!
Sazae!
Tsuboyaki!
Karasumi!
Nagasaki chanpon!
Miso oden!
Warabi mochi!
Dried mackerel!
Rice and vegetables!
Hitsumabushi!
Doji nabe!
Chanko!
Apple candy!
AND I SO WANT SOME YUBA!
Bubuunagi! Breakfast at an inn!
RAVENOUS WOLVES!
Yomogi soba! Ankake spaghetti! Oyaki!
WHAT'S WRONG, KAZUMA?
NOT FEELING SO GOOD?
Even though we're finally back in Japan...
HUH?
NO, I'M OKAY.

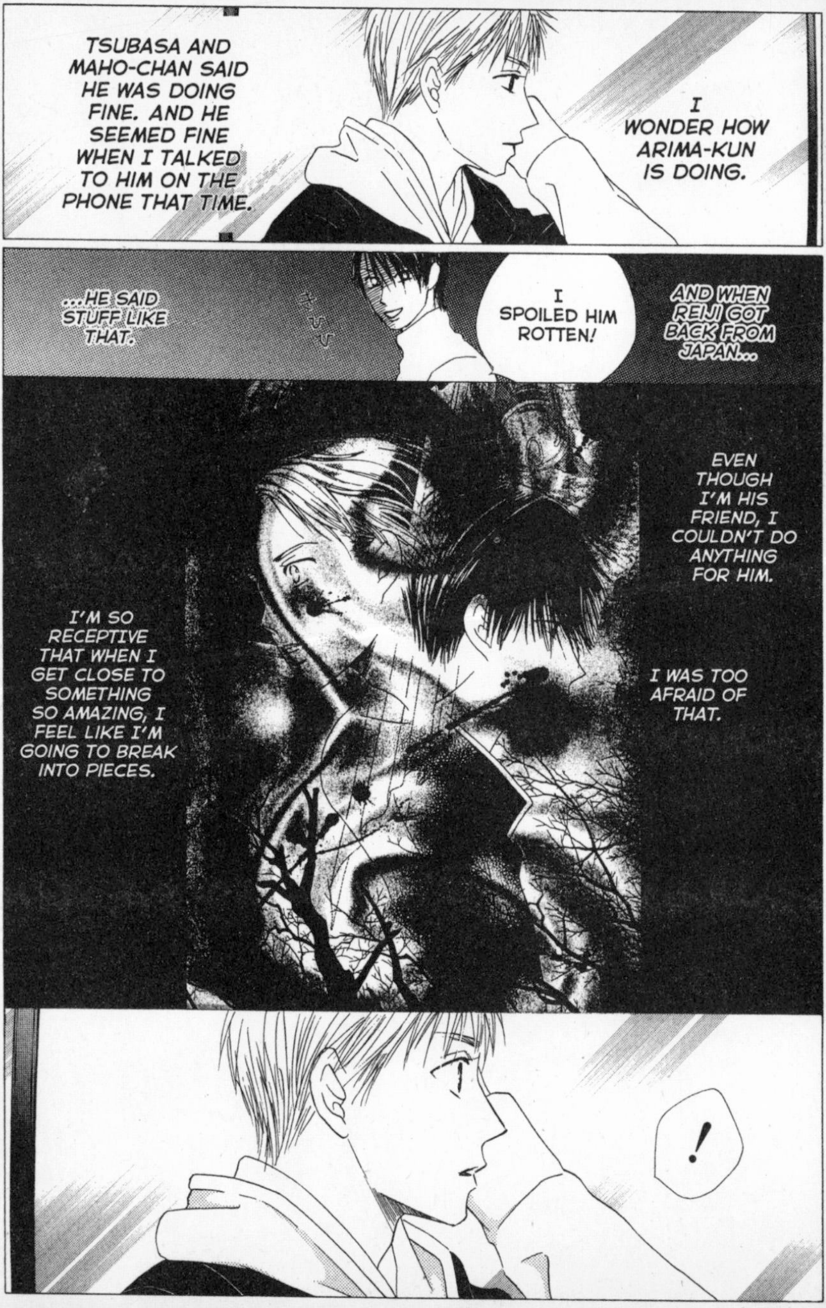
I WONDER HOW ARIMA-KUN IS DOING.
TSUBASA AND MAHO-CHAN SAID HE WAS DOING FINE. AND HE SEEMED FINE WHEN I TALKED TO HIM ON THE PHONE THAT TIME.
AND WHEN REIJI GOT BACK FROM JAPAN...
I SPOILED HIM ROTTEN!
...HE SAID STUFF LIKE THAT.
EVEN THOUGH I'M HIS FRIEND, I COULDN'T DO ANYTHING FOR HIM.
I WAS TOO AFRAID OF THAT.
I'M SO RECEPTIVE THAT WHEN I GET CLOSE TO SOMETHING SO AMAZING, I FEEL LIKE I'M GOING TO BREAK INTO PIECES.
!

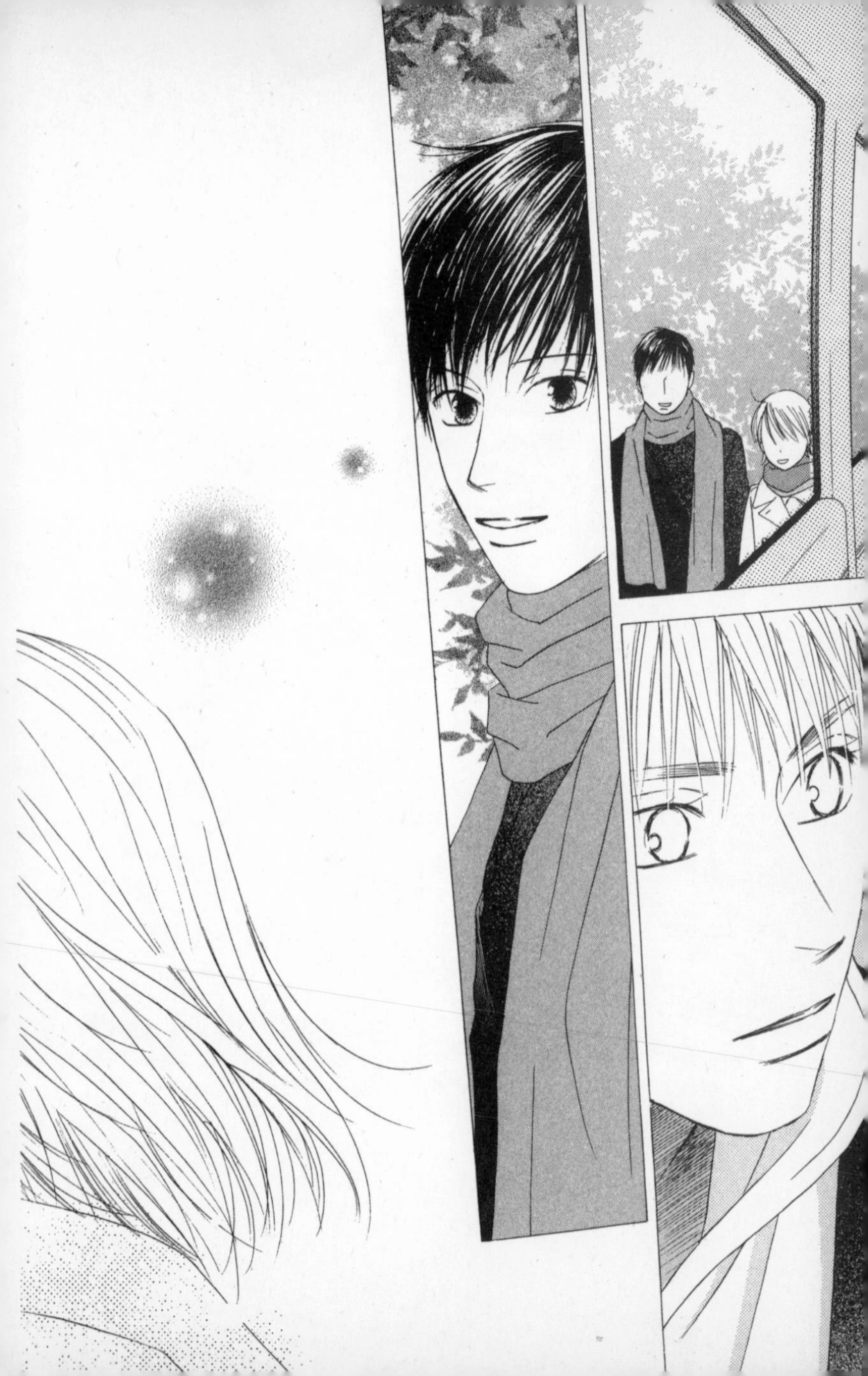

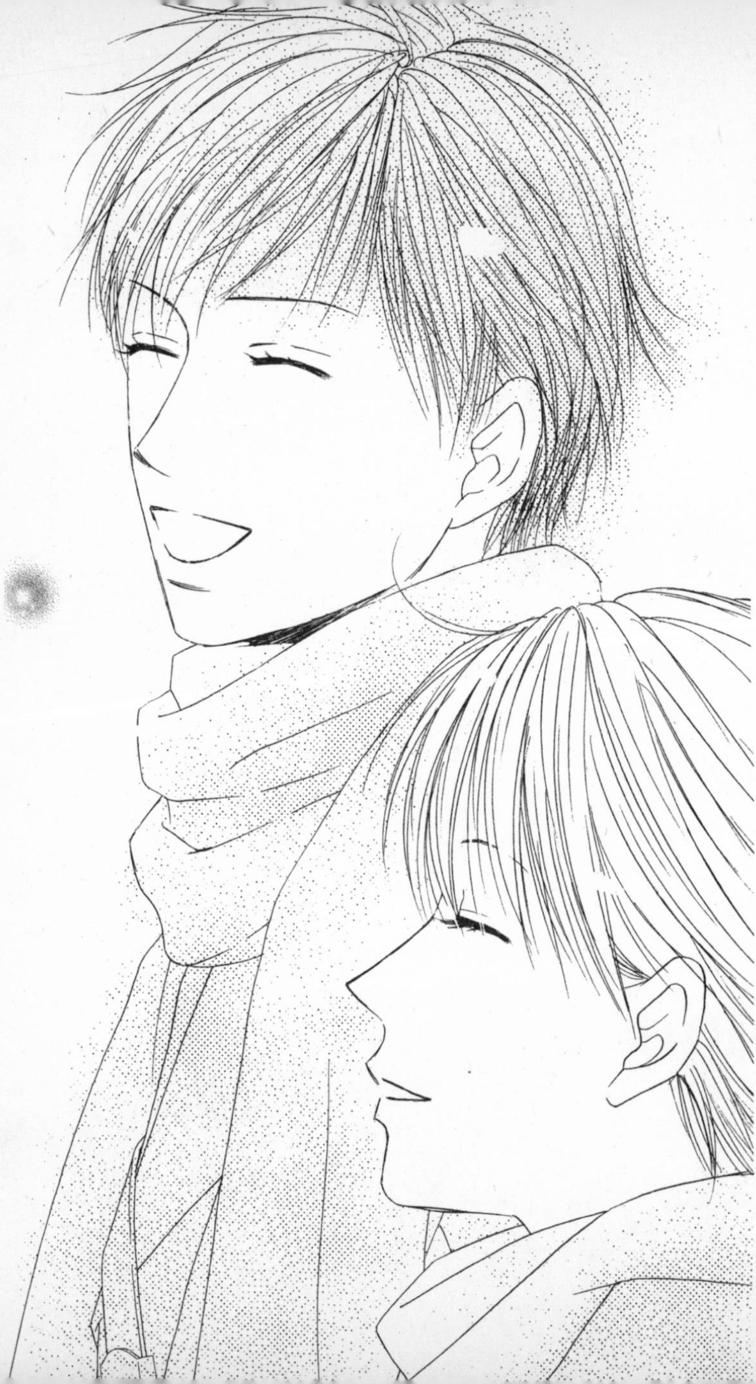

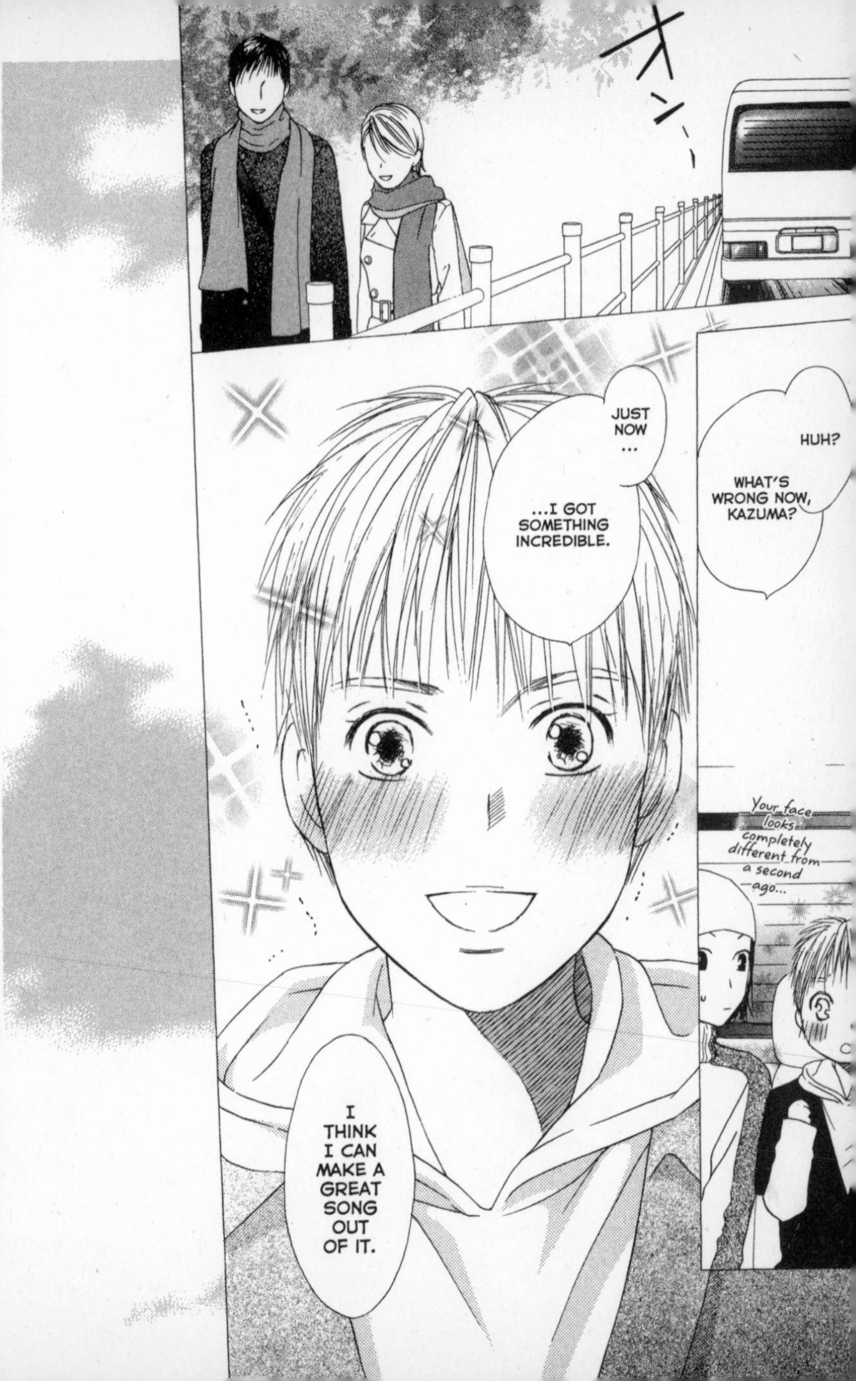
HUH?
WHAT'S WRONG NOW, KAZUMA?
Your face looks completely different from a second ago...
JUST NOW ...
...I GOT SOMETHING INCREDIBLE.
I THINK I CAN MAKE A GREAT SONG OUT OF IT.

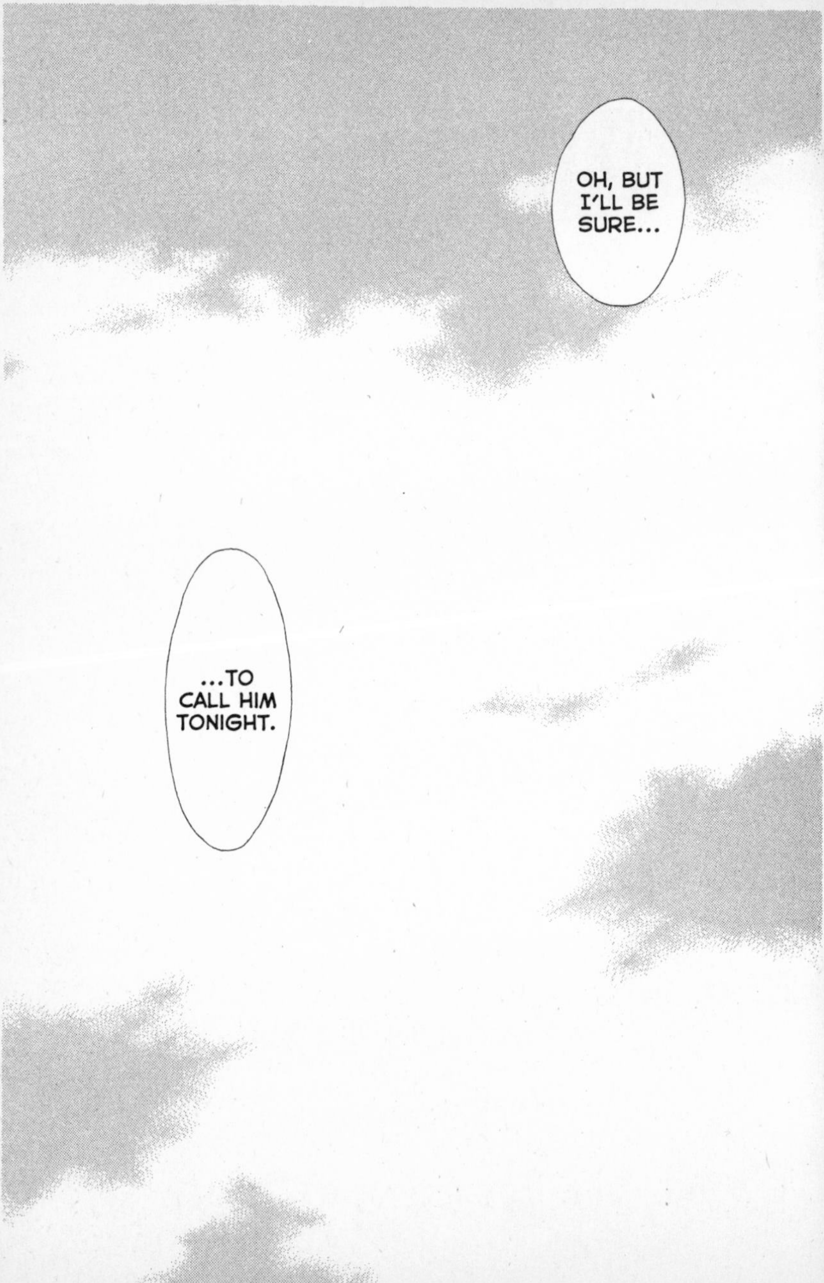
OH, BUT I'LL BE SURE...
...TO CALL HIM TONIGHT.

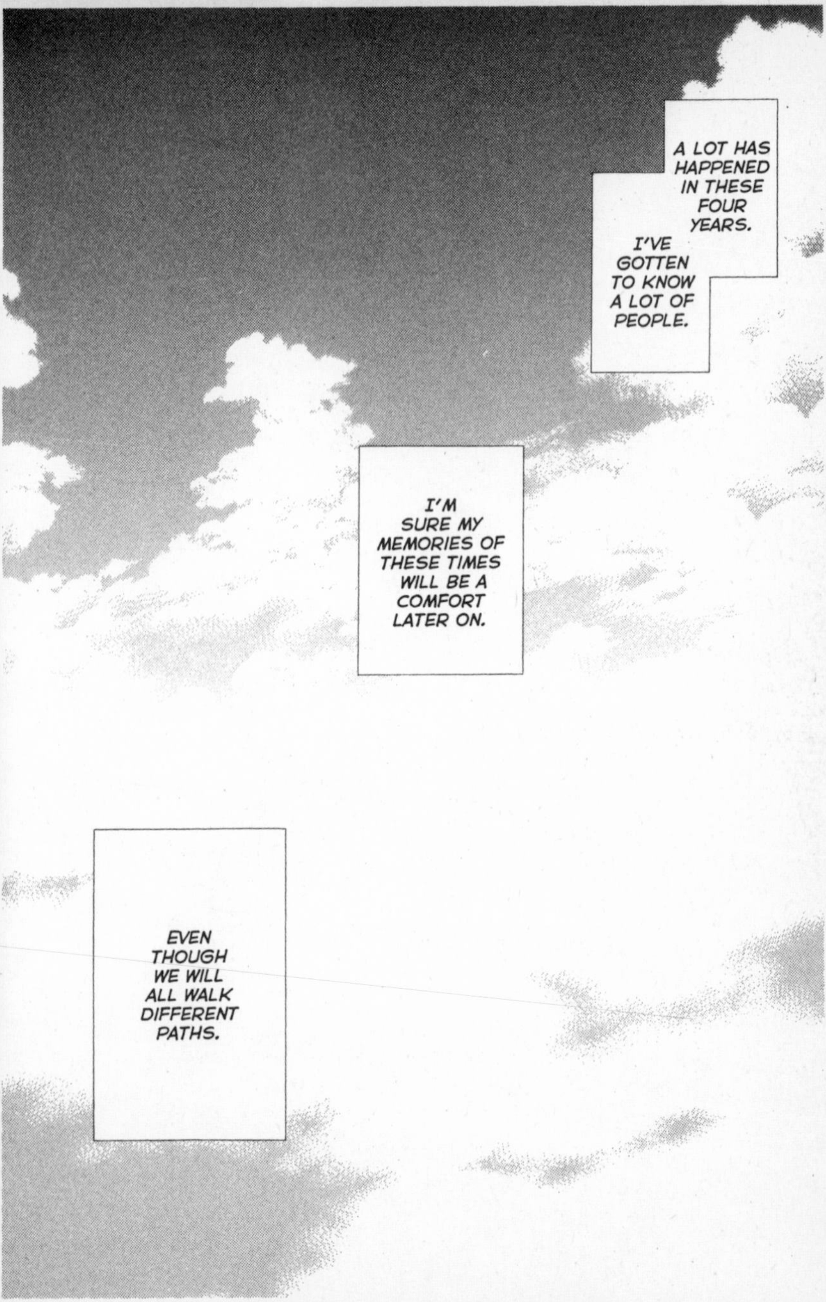
A LOT HAS HAPPENED IN THESE FOUR YEARS.
I'VE GOTTEN TO KNOW A LOT OF PEOPLE.
I'M SURE MY MEMORIES OF THESE TIMES WILL BE A COMFORT LATER ON.
EVEN THOUGH WE WILL ALL WALK DIFFERENT PATHS.

**ACT 100** ★ GRADUATION NEARS / END

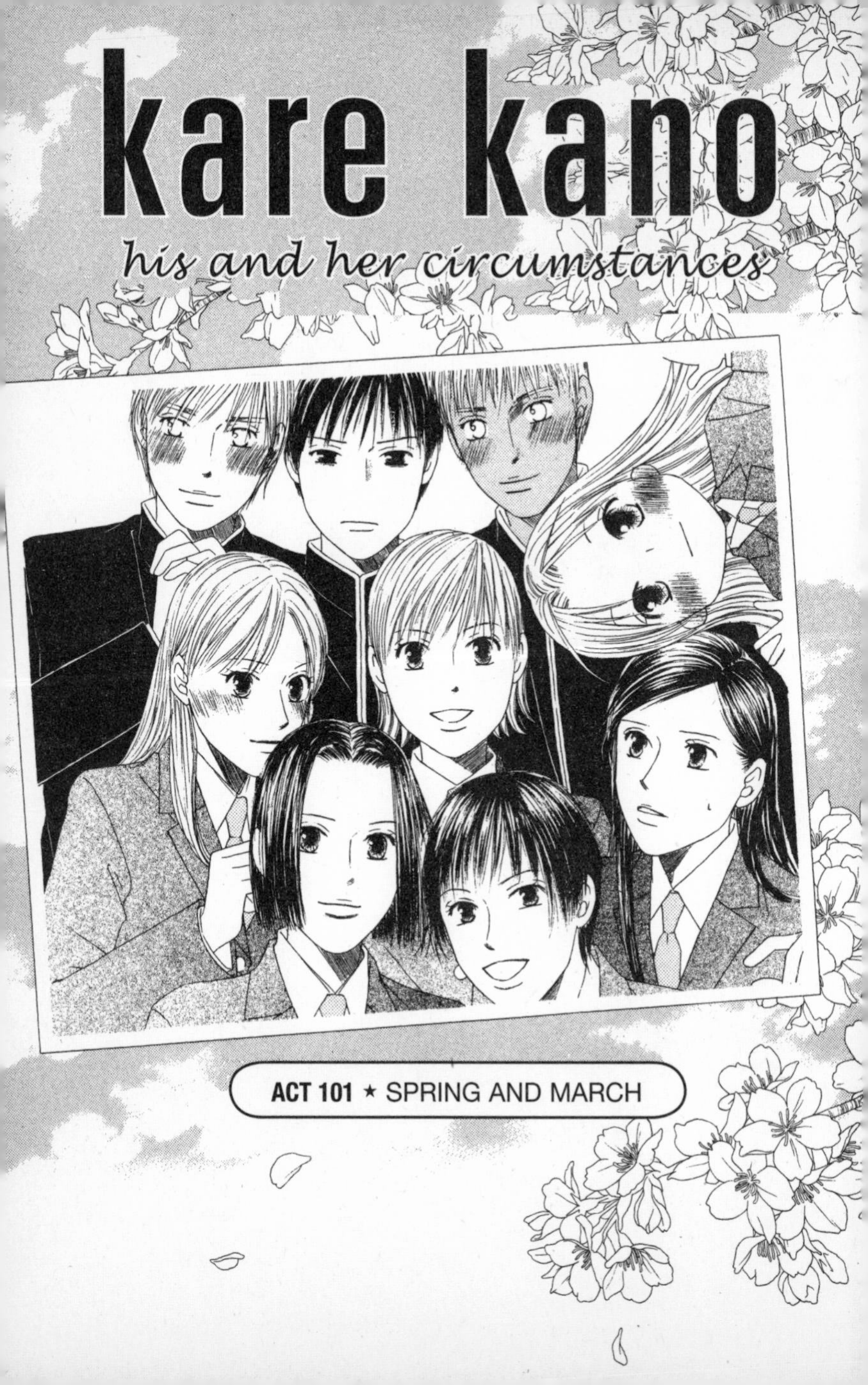
kare kano
his and her circumstances
ACT 101 ★ SPRING AND MARCH

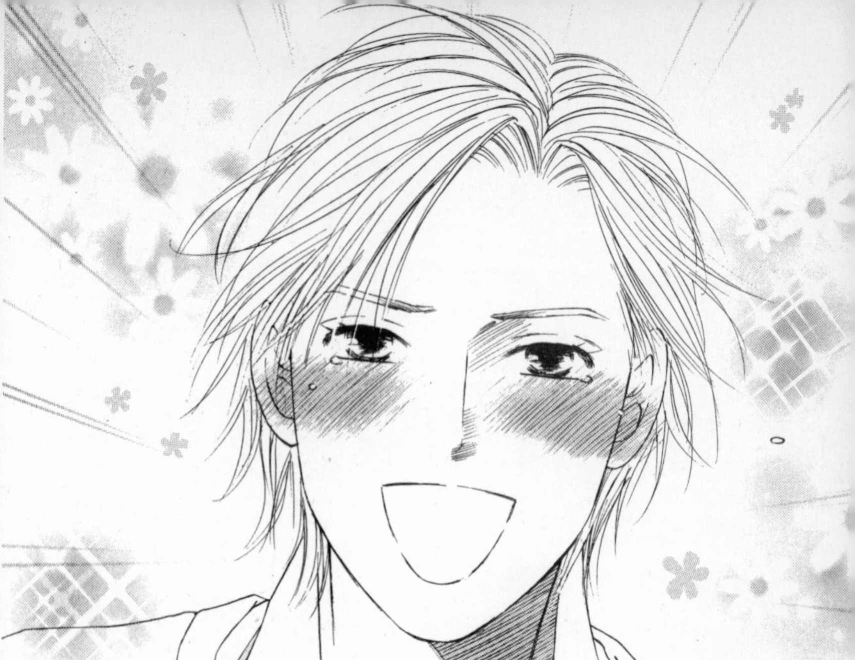

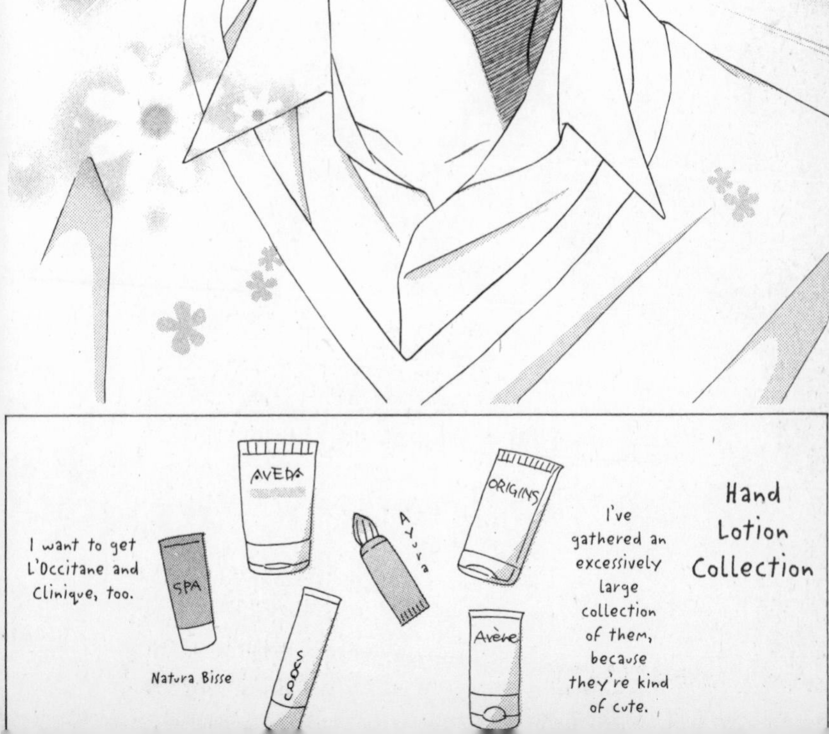

Hand Lotion Collection
I've gathered an excessively large collection of them, because they're kind of cute.
ORIGINS
Avène
AVEDA
Ayura
SPA
Natura Bisse
I want to get L'Occitane and Clinique, too.

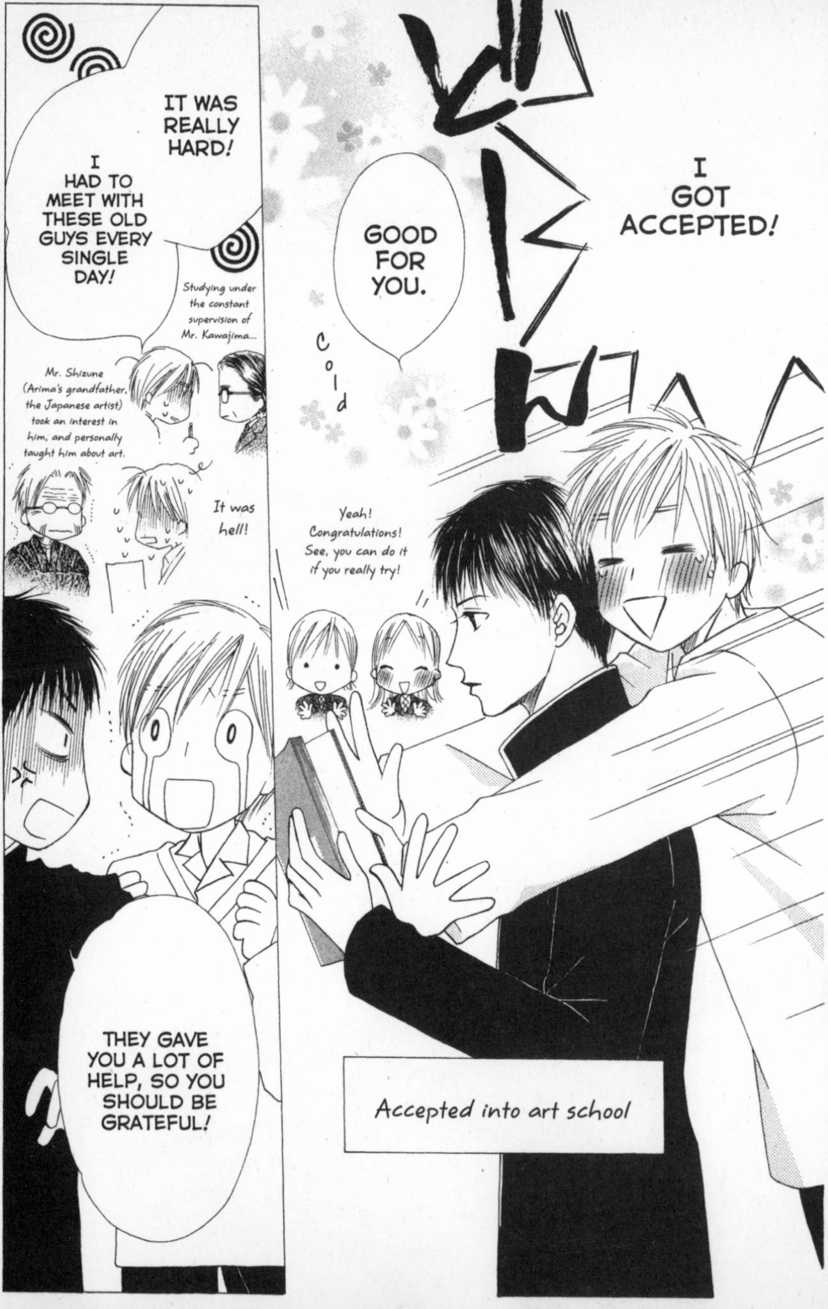
I GOT ACCEPTED!
GOOD FOR YOU.
Cold
Yeah! Congratulations! See, you can do it if you really try!
Accepted into art school
IT WAS REALLY HARD!
I HAD TO MEET WITH THESE OLD GUYS EVERY SINGLE DAY!
Studying under the constant supervision of Mr. Kawajima...
Mr. Shizune (Arima's grandfather, the Japanese artist) took an interest in him, and personally taught him about art.
It was hell!
THEY GAVE YOU A LOT OF HELP, SO YOU SHOULD BE GRATEFUL!

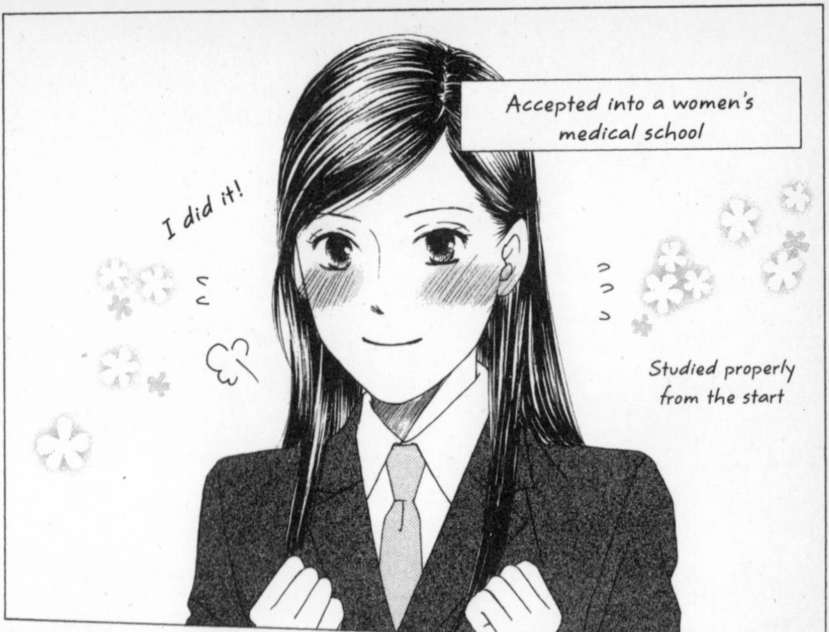
Accepted into a women's medical school
I did it!
Studied properly from the start

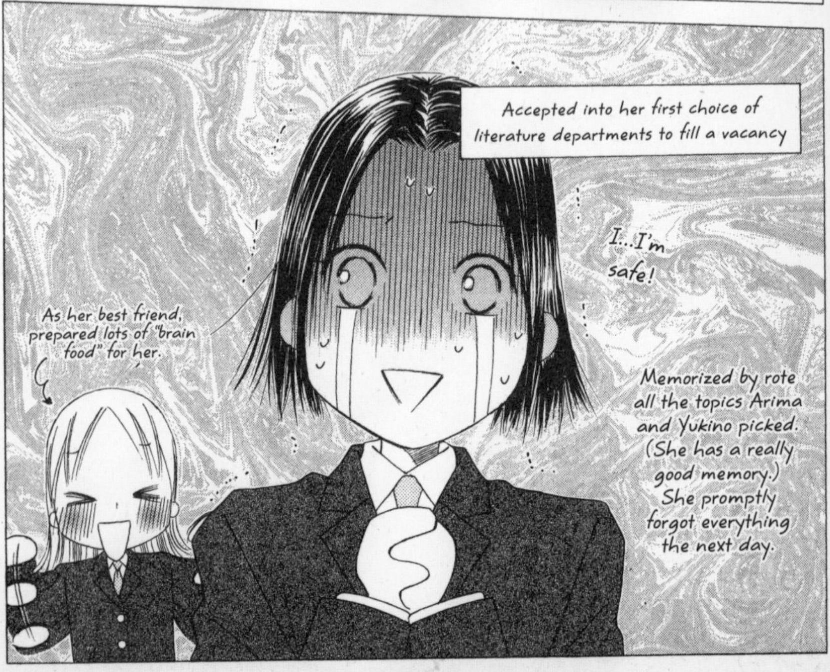
Accepted into her first choice of literature departments to fill a vacancy
I...I'm safe!
Memorized by rote all the topics Arima and Yukino picked. (She has a really good memory.) She promptly forgot everything the next day.
As her best friend, prepared lots of "brain food" for her.

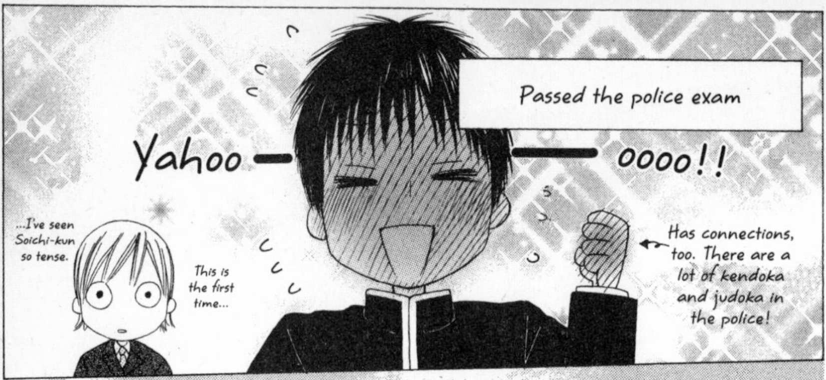
Passed the police exam
Yahoo—————oooo!!
Has connections, too. There are a lot of kendoka and judoka in the police!
This is the first time...
...I've seen Soichi-kun so tense.
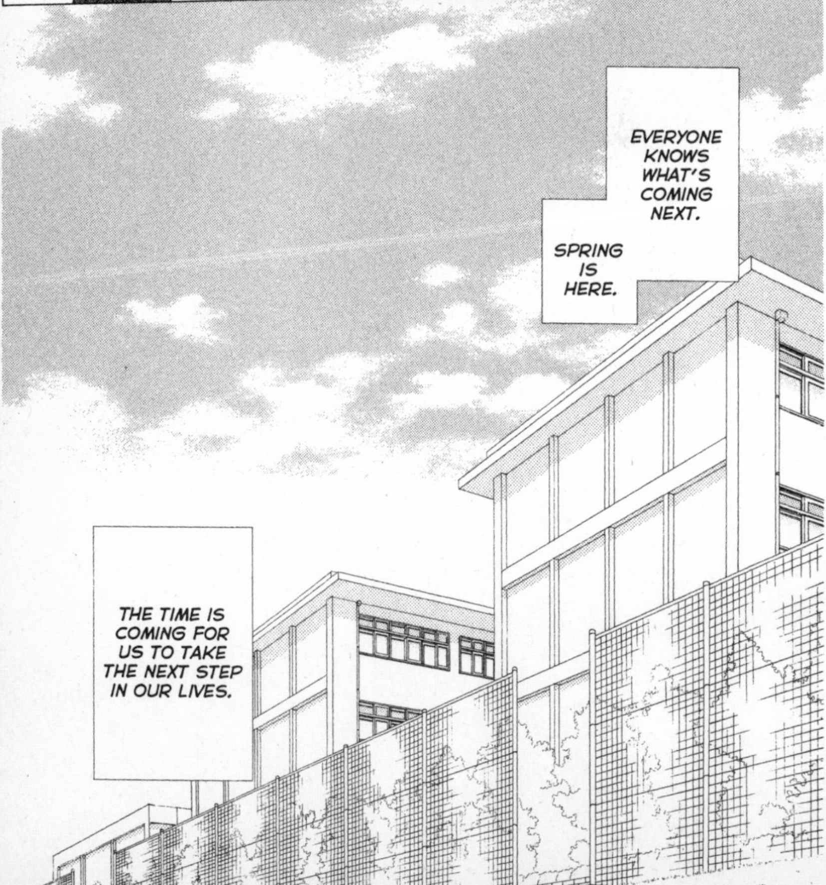
EVERYONE KNOWS WHAT'S COMING NEXT.
SPRING IS HERE.
THE TIME IS COMING FOR US TO TAKE THE NEXT STEP IN OUR LIVES.

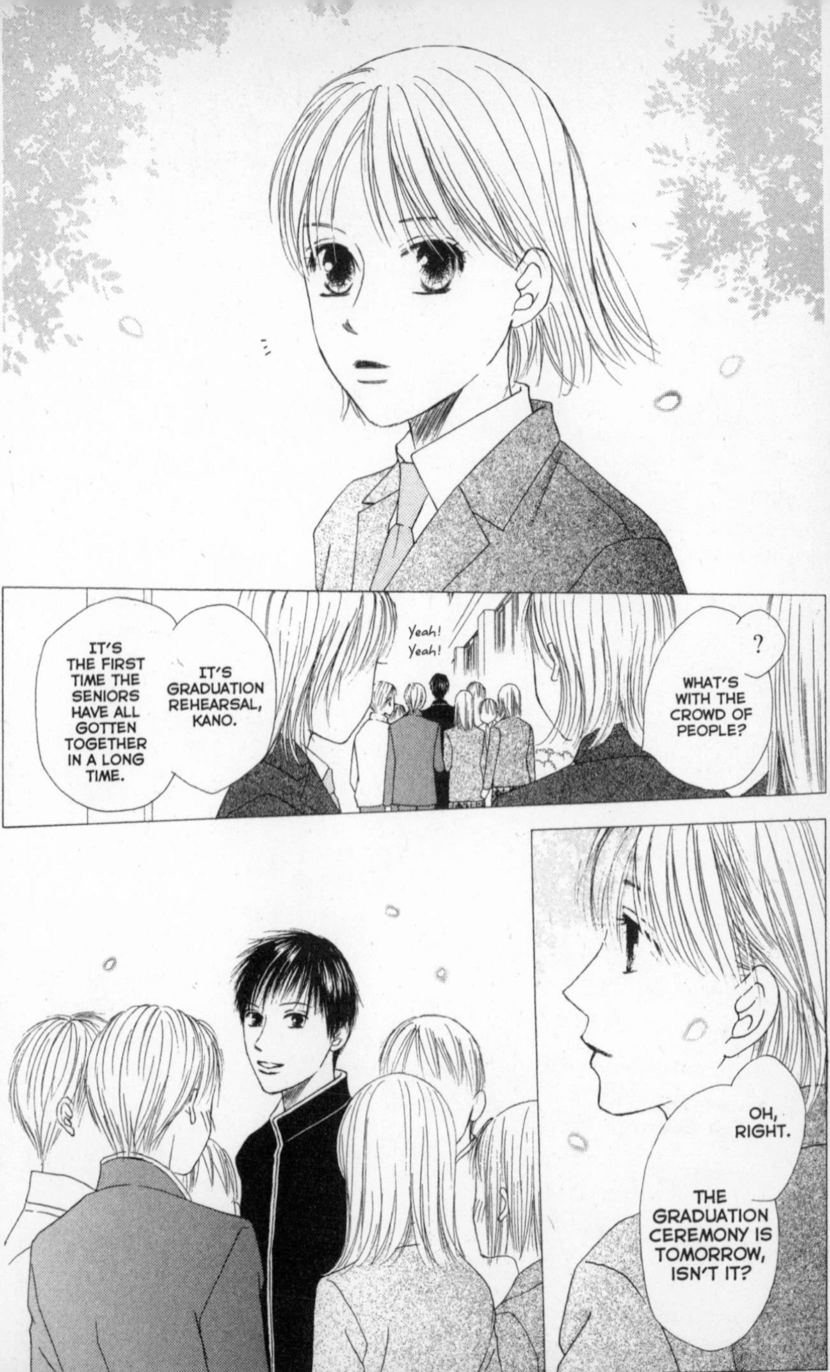
?
WHAT'S WITH THE CROWD OF PEOPLE?
Yeah! Yeah!
IT'S GRADUATION REHEARSAL, KANO.
IT'S THE FIRST TIME THE SENIORS HAVE ALL GOTTEN TOGETHER IN A LONG TIME.
OH, RIGHT.
THE GRADUATION CEREMONY IS TOMORROW, ISN'T IT?

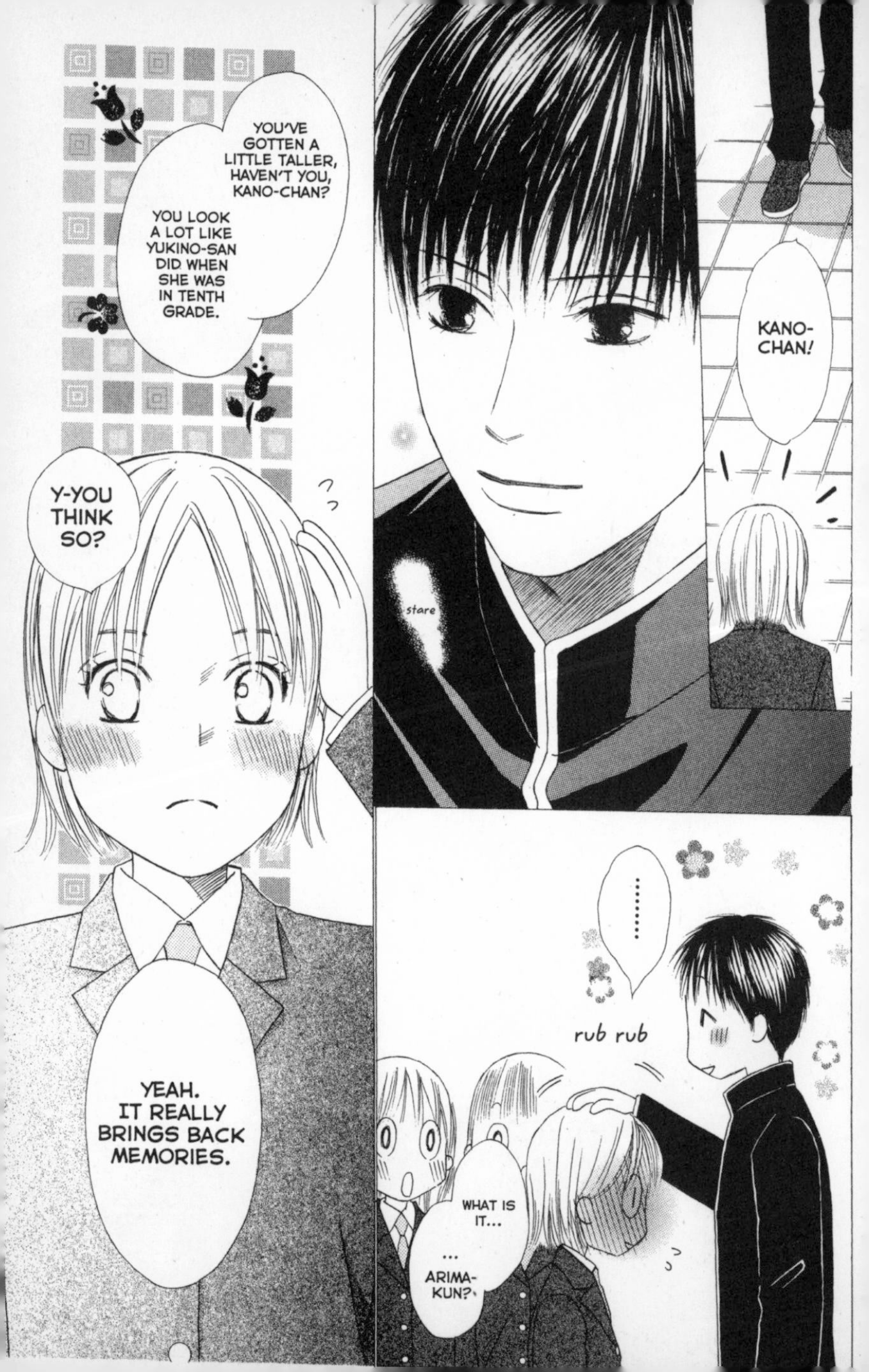
KANO-CHAN!
stare
......
rub rub
WHAT IS IT...
...ARIMA-KUN?
YOU'VE GOTTEN A LITTLE TALLER, HAVEN'T YOU, KANO-CHAN?
YOU LOOK A LOT LIKE YUKINO-SAN DID WHEN SHE WAS IN TENTH GRADE.
Y-YOU THINK SO?
YEAH. IT REALLY BRINGS BACK MEMORIES.

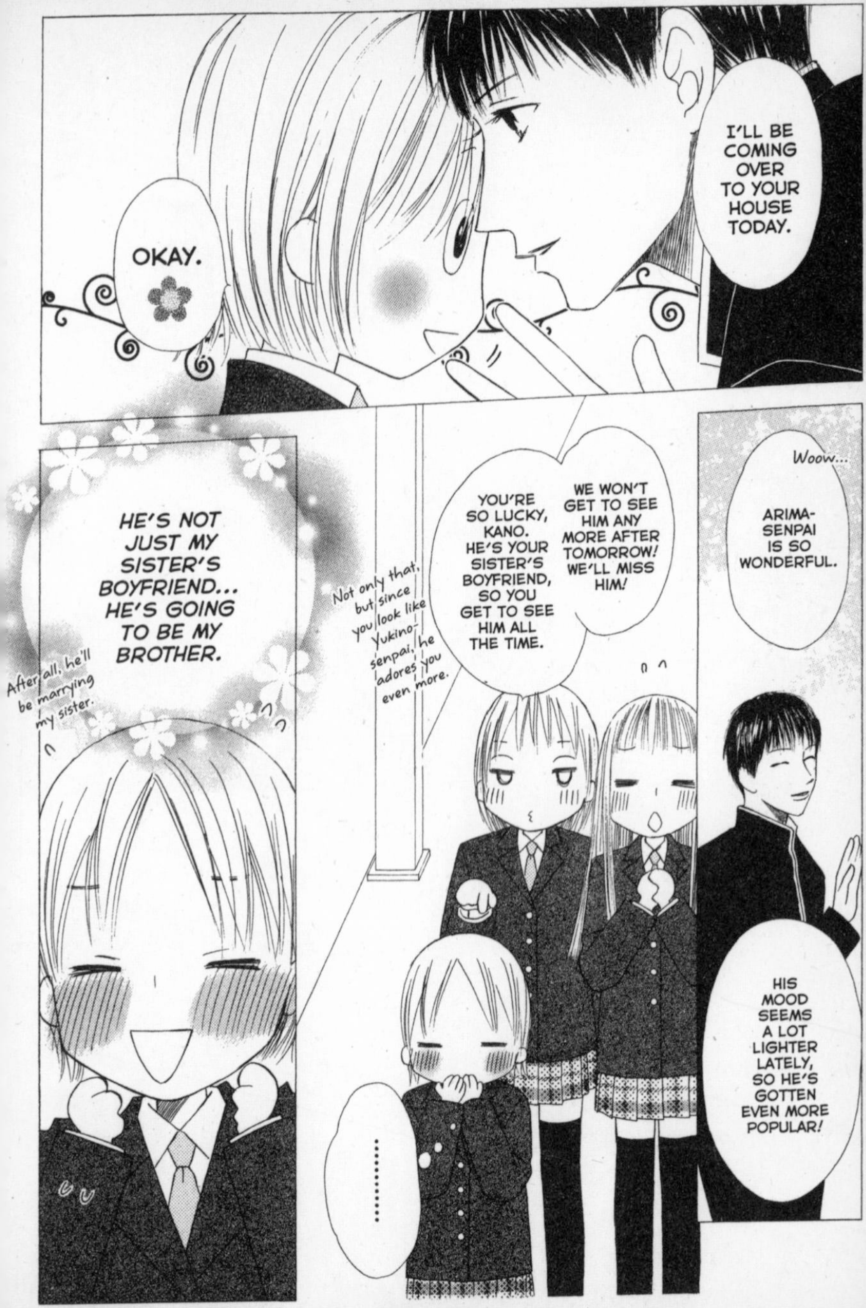
I'LL BE COMING OVER TO YOUR HOUSE TODAY.
OKAY.
Woow...
ARIMA-SENPAI IS SO WONDERFUL.
HIS MOOD SEEMS A LOT LIGHTER LATELY, SO HE'S GOTTEN EVEN MORE POPULAR!
WE WON'T GET TO SEE HIM ANY MORE AFTER TOMORROW! WE'LL MISS HIM!
YOU'RE SO LUCKY, KANO. HE'S YOUR SISTER'S BOYFRIEND, SO YOU GET TO SEE HIM ALL THE TIME.
Not only that, but since you look like Yukino-senpai, he adores you even more.
......
HE'S NOT JUST MY SISTER'S BOYFRIEND... HE'S GOING TO BE MY BROTHER.
After all, he'll be marrying my sister.

STILL ON THE DOWN-LOW

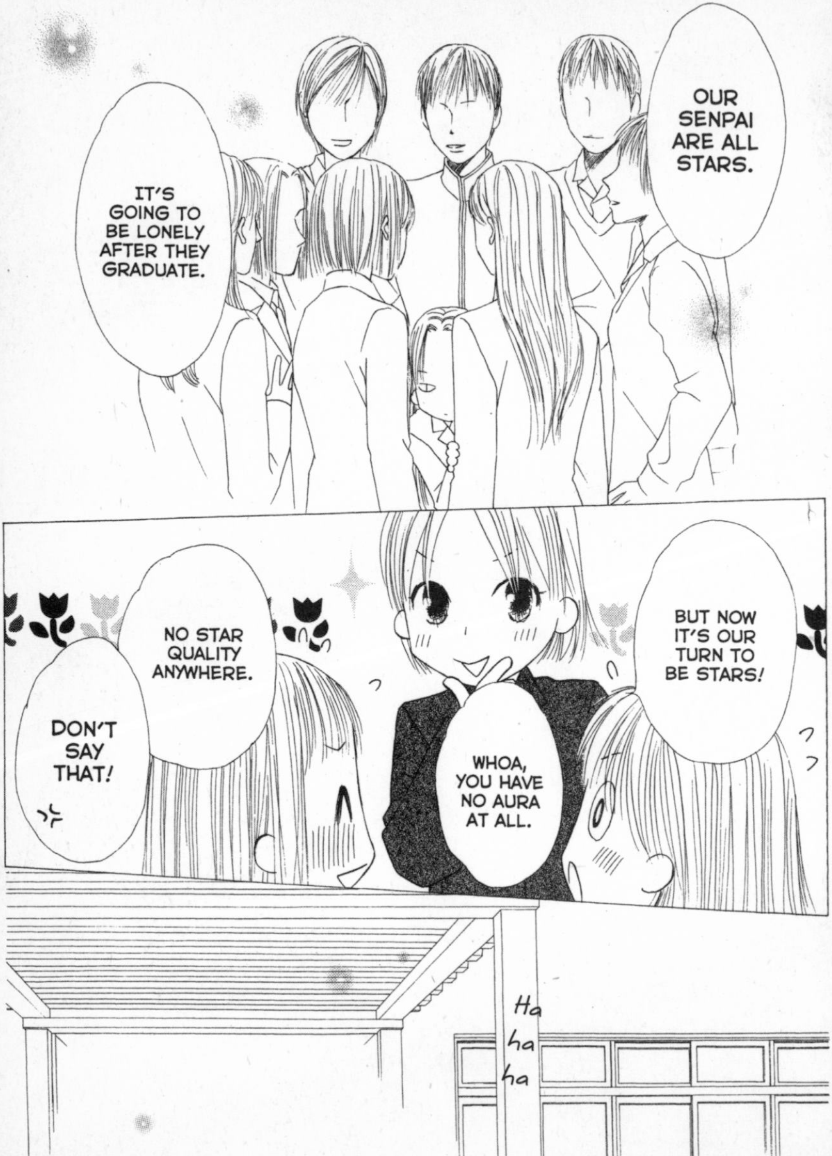
OUR SENPAI ARE ALL STARS.
IT'S GOING TO BE LONELY AFTER THEY GRADUATE.
BUT NOW IT'S OUR TURN TO BE STARS!
WHOA, YOU HAVE NO AURA AT ALL.
NO STAR QUALITY ANYWHERE.
DON'T SAY THAT!
Ha ha ha

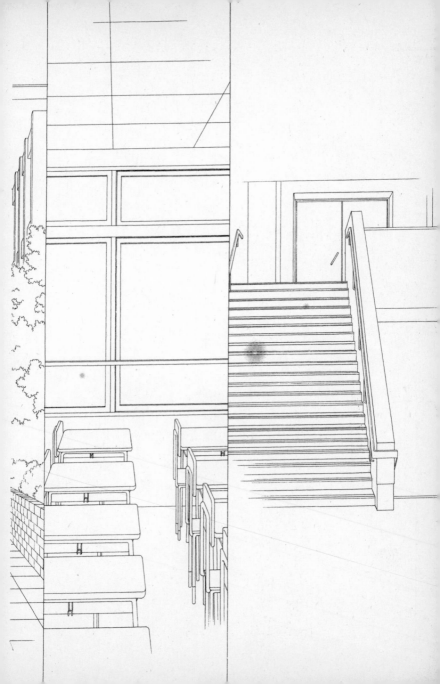

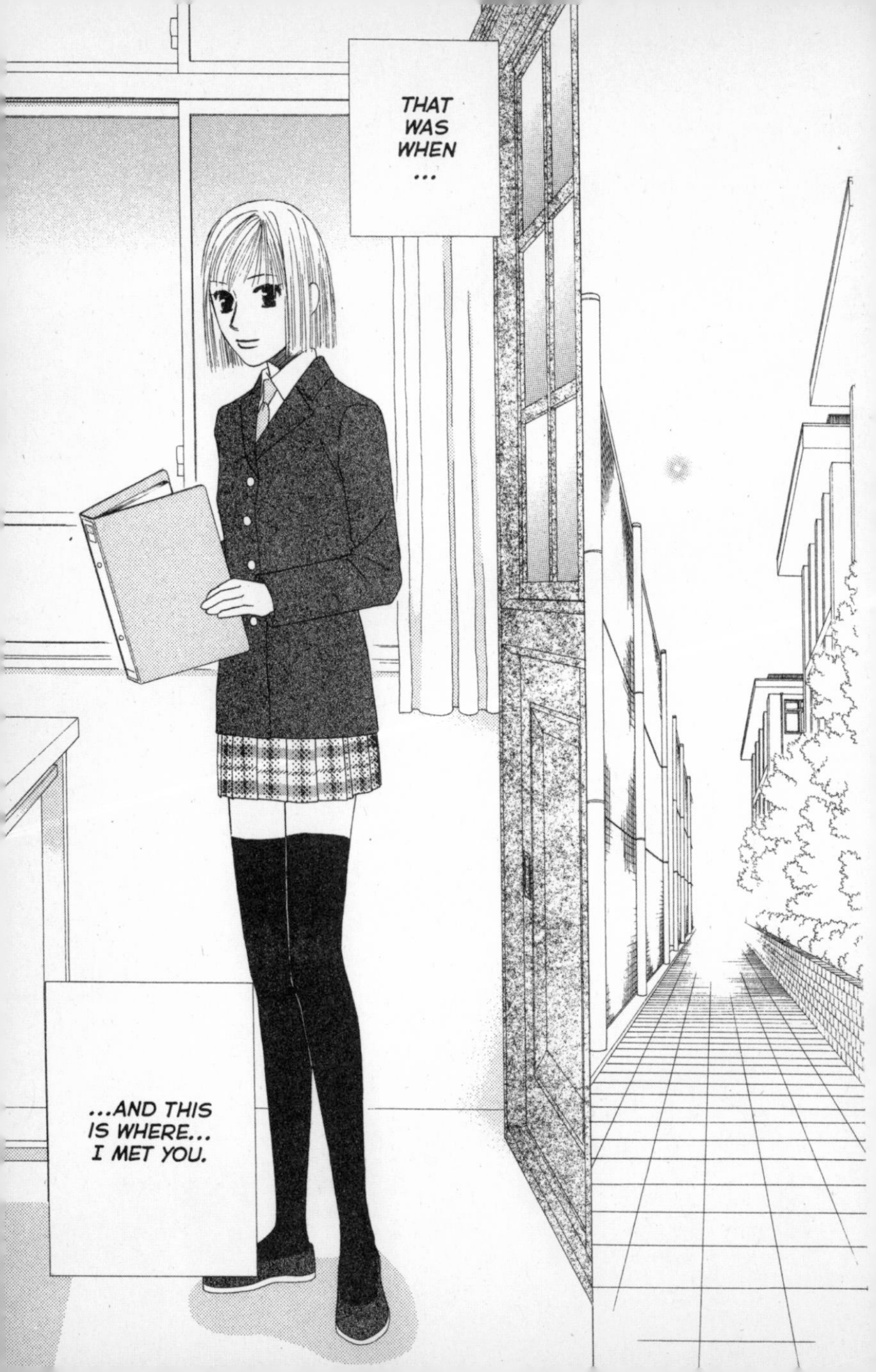
THAT WAS WHEN ...
...AND THIS IS WHERE... I MET YOU.

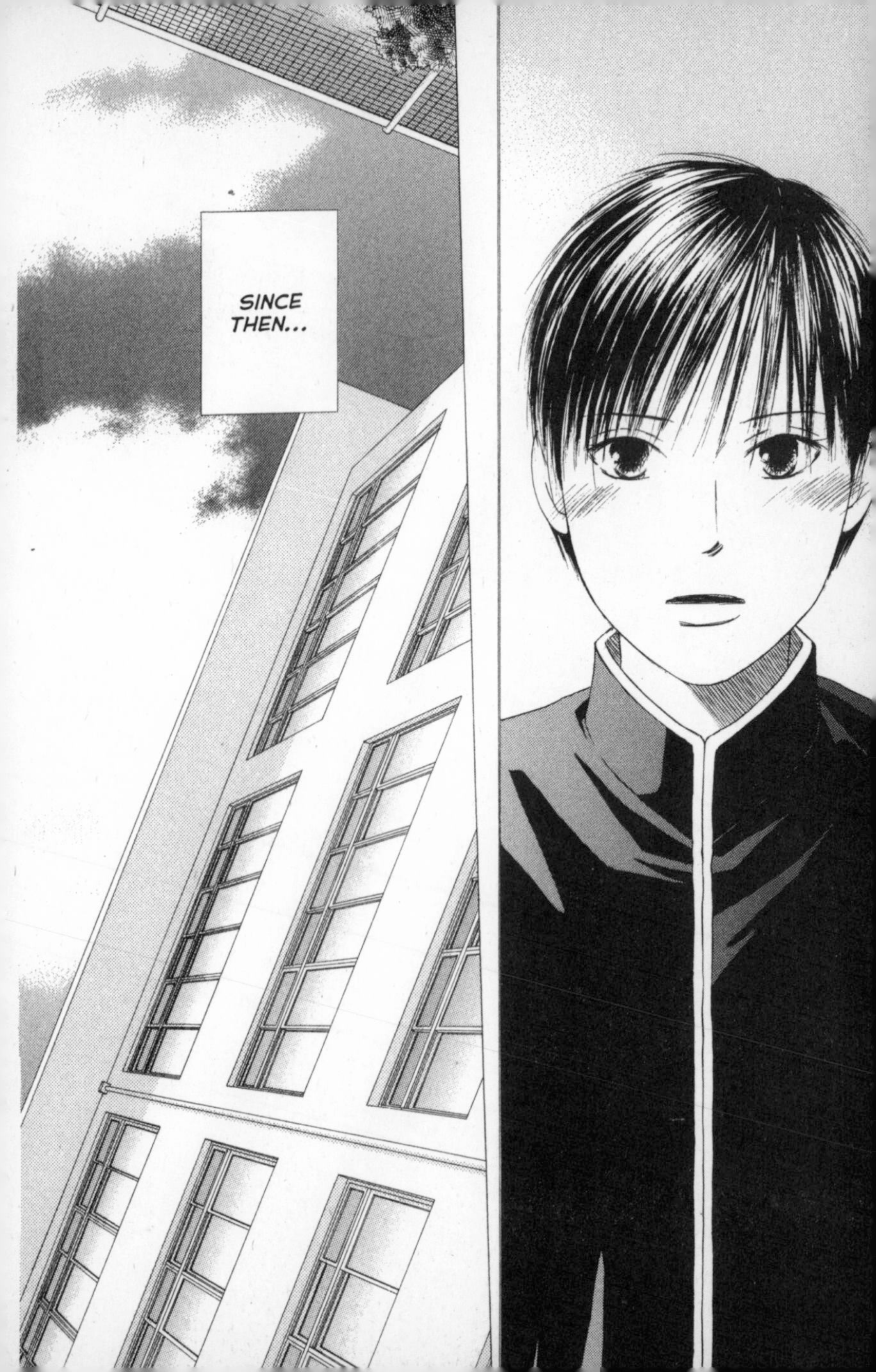
SINCE THEN...

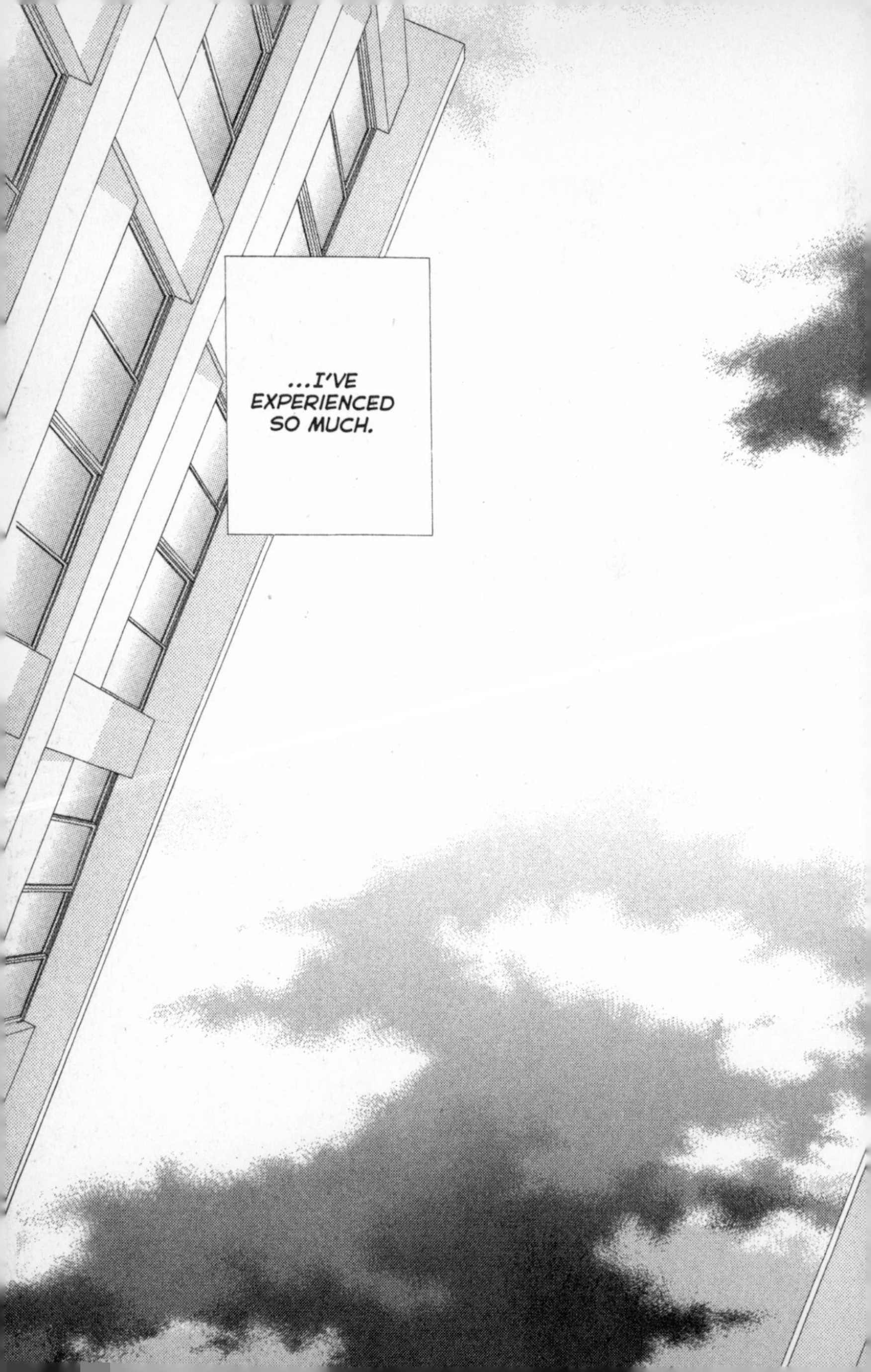
...I'VE EXPERIENCED SO MUCH.

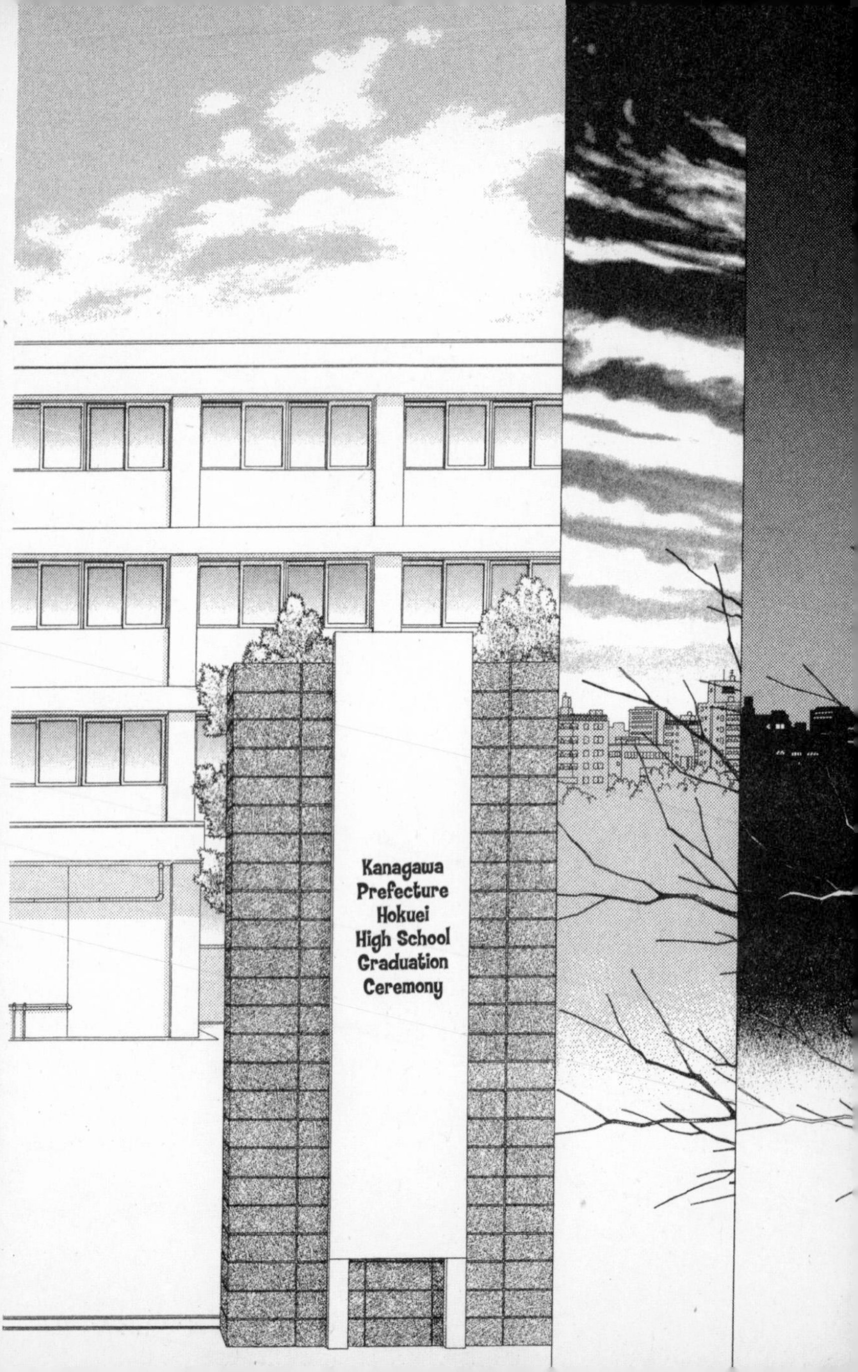
Kanagawa Prefecture Hokuei High School Graduation Ceremony

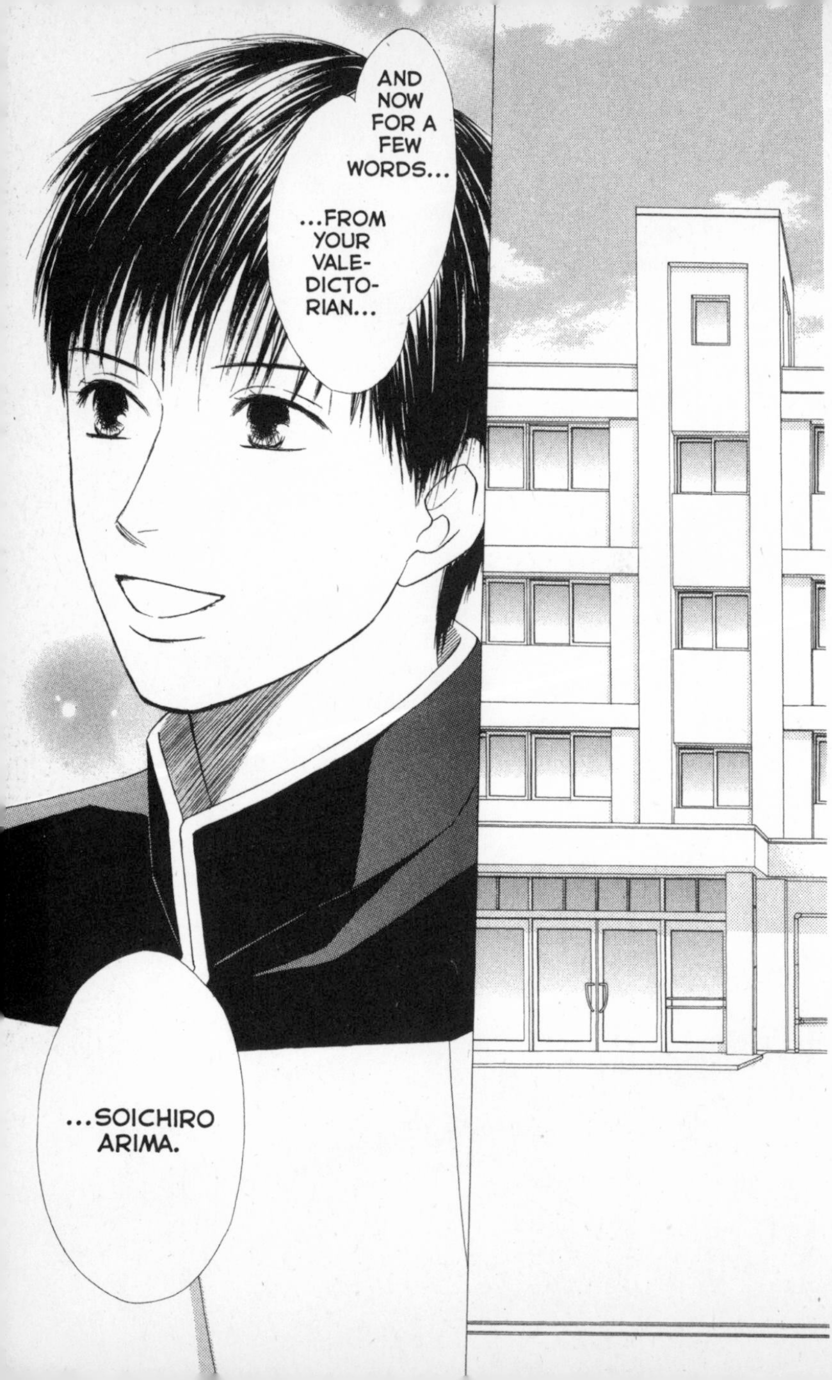
AND NOW FOR A FEW WORDS...
...FROM YOUR VALE-DICTO-RIAN...
...SOICHIRO ARIMA.

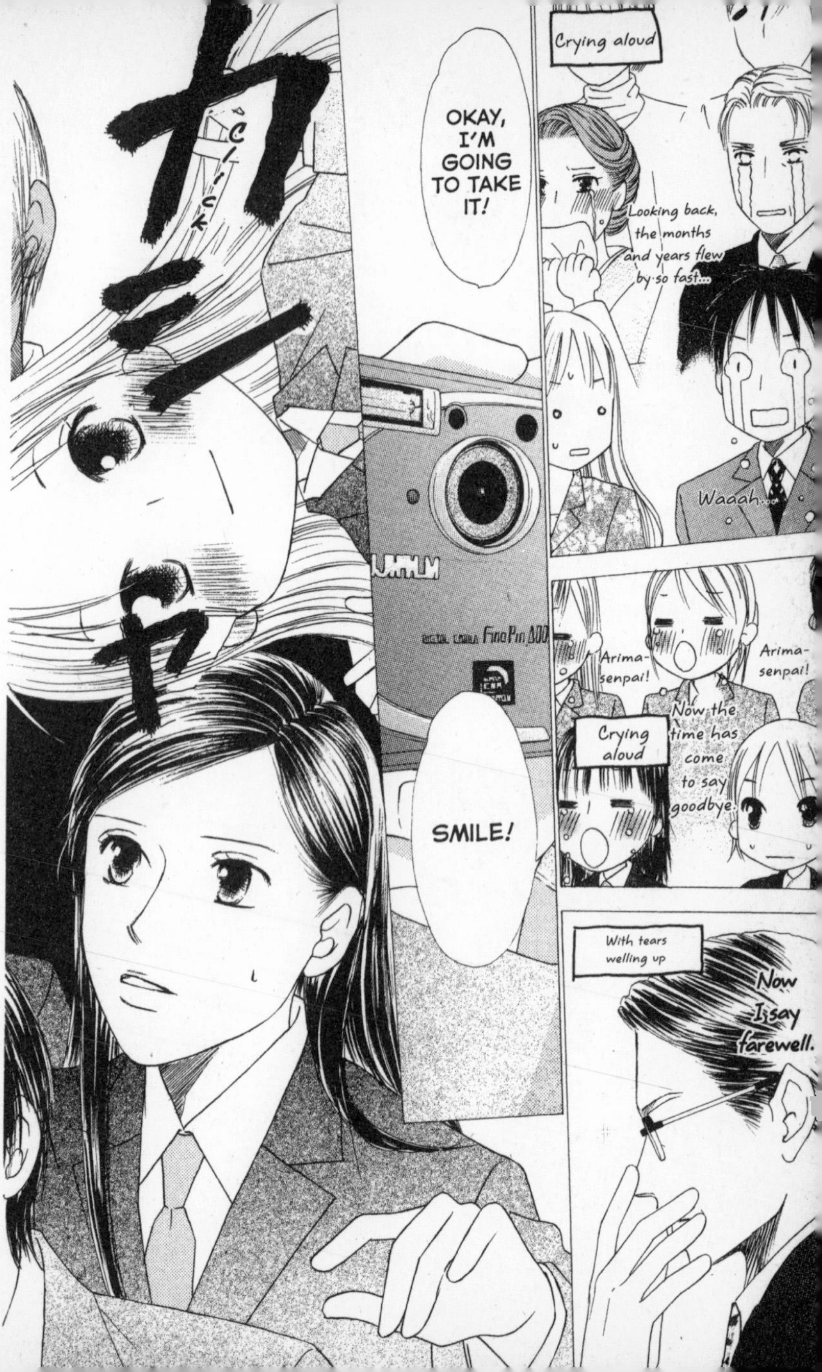
Crying aloud
Looking back, the months and years flew by so fast...
Waaah...
Arima-senpai!
Arima-senpai!
Crying aloud
Now the time has come to say goodbye.
With tears welling up
Now I say farewell.
OKAY, I'M GOING TO TAKE IT!
SMILE!
Click

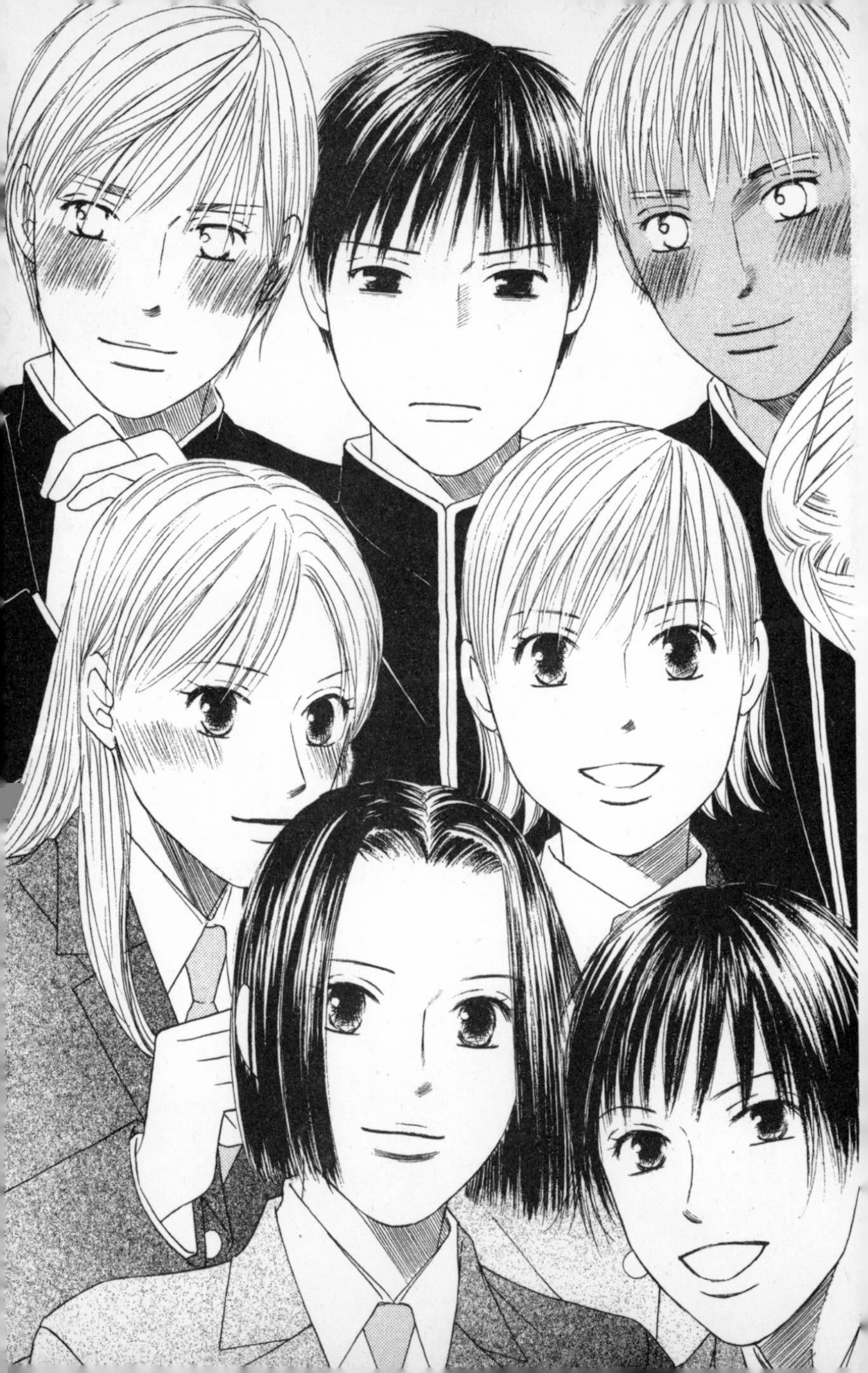

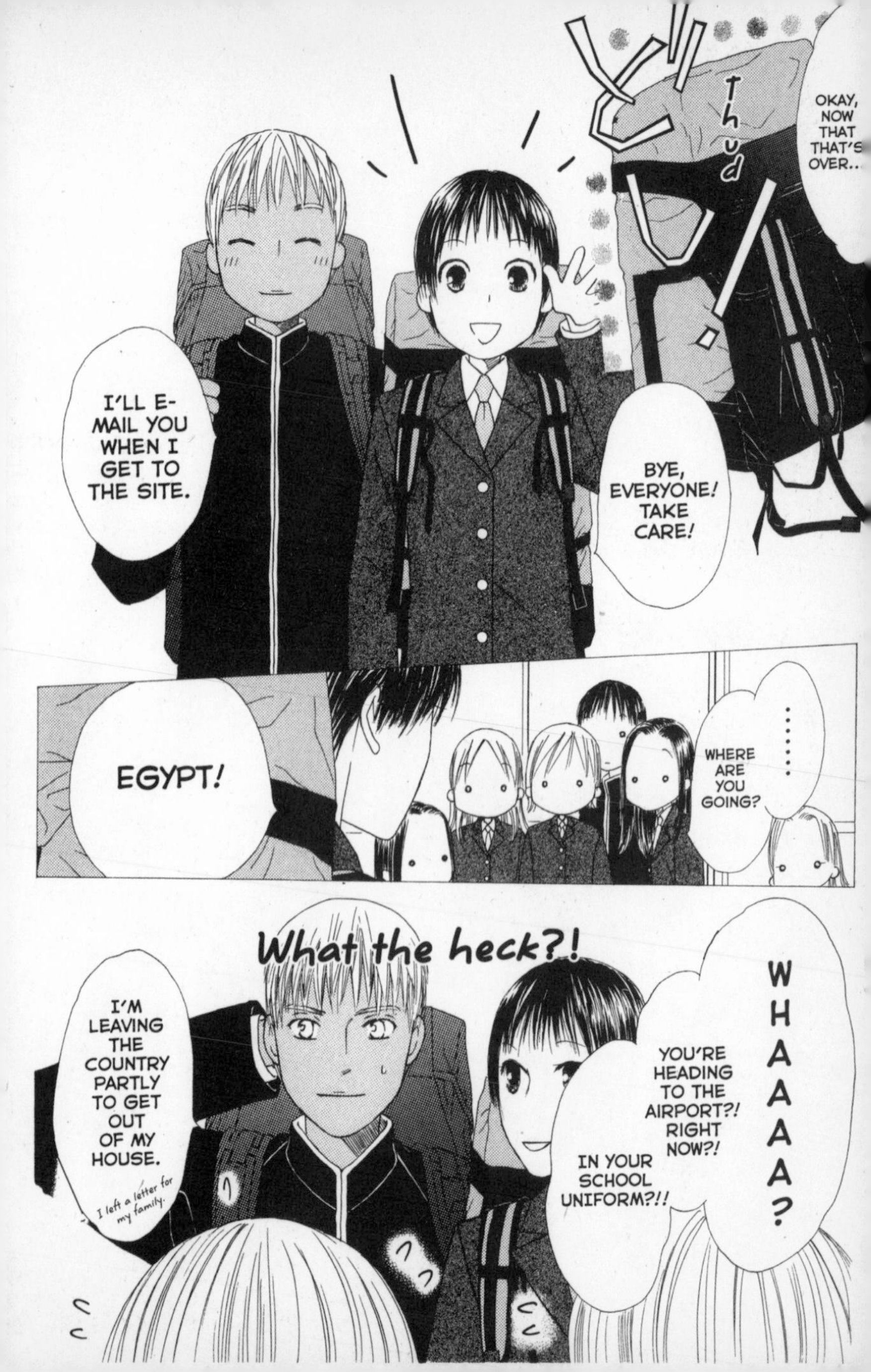
Thud
OKAY, NOW THAT THAT'S OVER..
BYE, EVERYONE! TAKE CARE!
I'LL E-MAIL YOU WHEN I GET TO THE SITE.
......
WHERE ARE YOU GOING?
EGYPT!
WHAAAAA?
YOU'RE HEADING TO THE AIRPORT?! RIGHT NOW?!
IN YOUR SCHOOL UNIFORM?!!
What the heck?!
I'M LEAVING THE COUNTRY PARTLY TO GET OUT OF MY HOUSE.
I left a letter for my family.

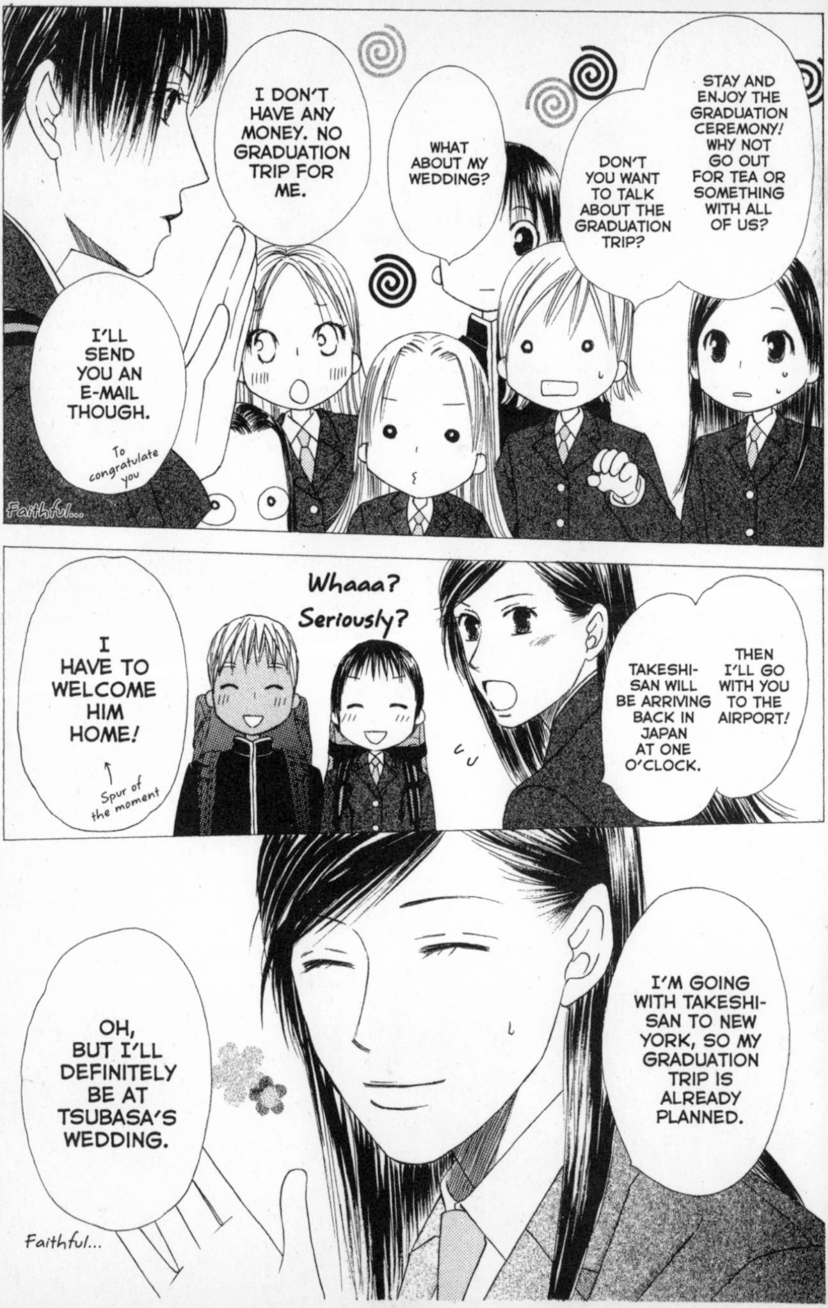
STAY AND ENJOY THE GRADUATION CEREMONY! WHY NOT GO OUT FOR TEA OR SOMETHING WITH ALL OF US?
DON'T YOU WANT TO TALK ABOUT THE GRADUATION TRIP?
WHAT ABOUT MY WEDDING?
I DON'T HAVE ANY MONEY. NO GRADUATION TRIP FOR ME.
I'LL SEND YOU AN E-MAIL THOUGH.
To congratulate you
Faithful...
THEN I'LL GO WITH YOU TO THE AIRPORT!
TAKESHI-SAN WILL BE ARRIVING BACK IN JAPAN AT ONE O'CLOCK.
Whaaa? Seriously?
I HAVE TO WELCOME HIM HOME!
Spur of the moment
I'M GOING WITH TAKESHI-SAN TO NEW YORK, SO MY GRADUATION TRIP IS ALREADY PLANNED.
OH, BUT I'LL DEFINITELY BE AT TSUBASA'S WEDDING.
Faithful...

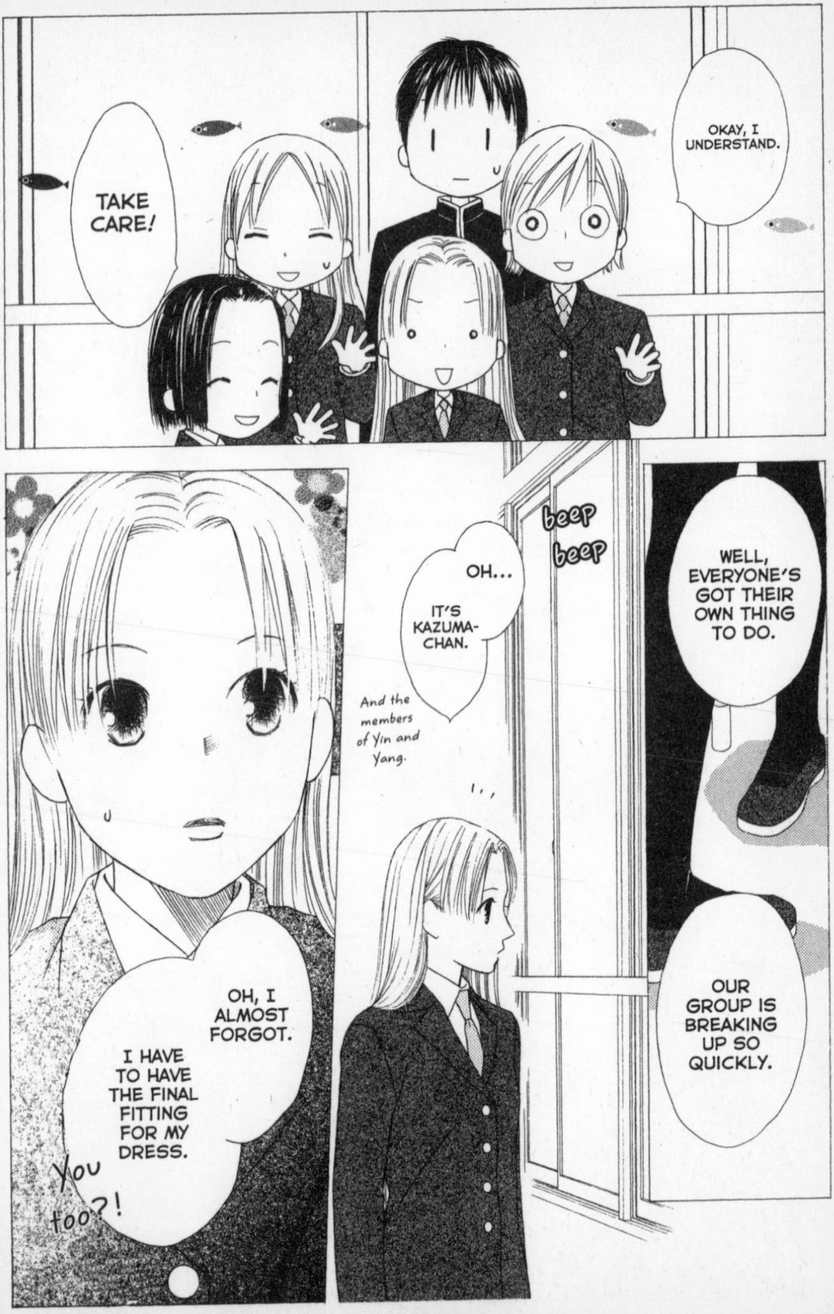
OKAY, I UNDERSTAND.
TAKE CARE!
WELL, EVERYONE'S GOT THEIR OWN THING TO DO.
OUR GROUP IS BREAKING UP SO QUICKLY.
beep beep
OH...
IT'S KAZUMA-CHAN.
And the members of Yin and Yang.
OH, I ALMOST FORGOT.
I HAVE TO HAVE THE FINAL FITTING FOR MY DRESS.
You too?!

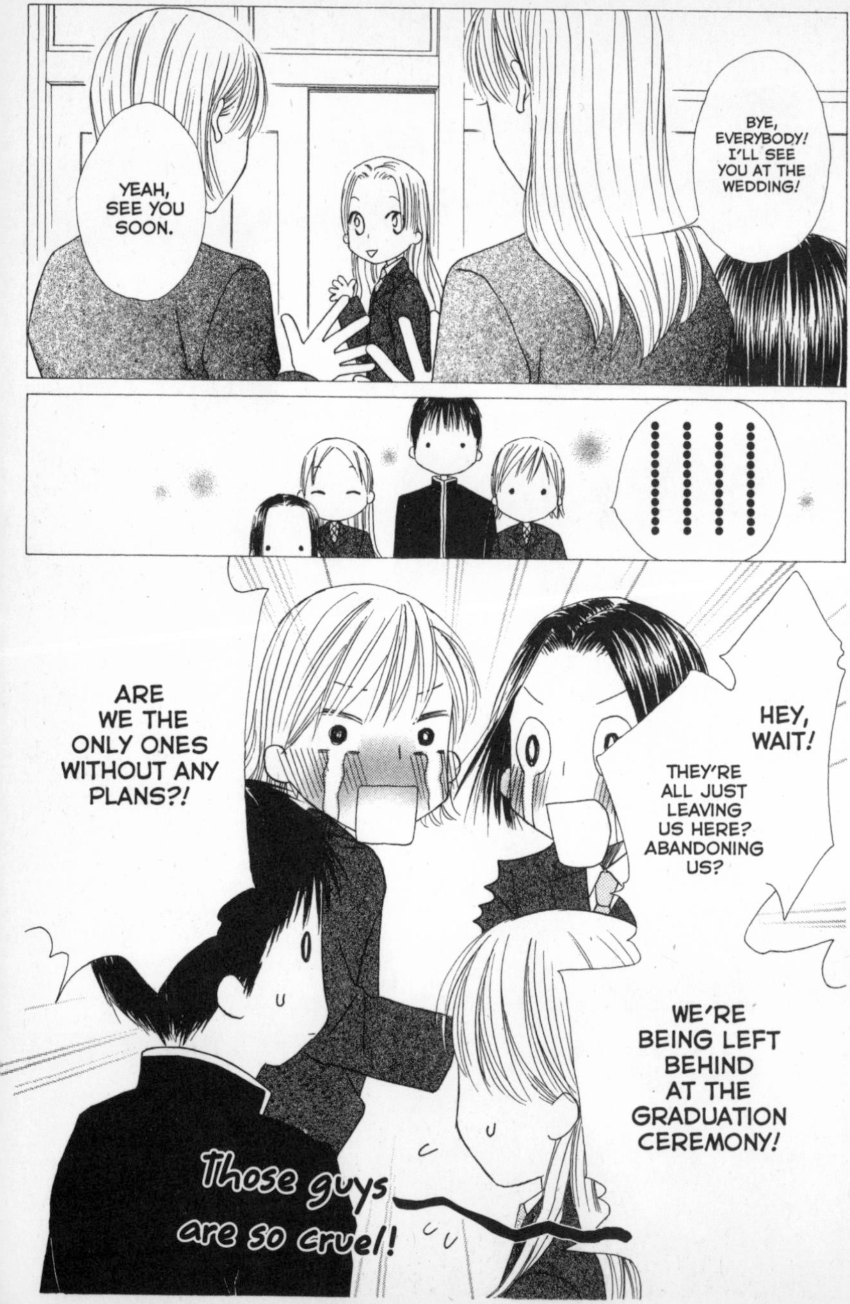
BYE, EVERYBODY! I'LL SEE YOU AT THE WEDDING!
YEAH, SEE YOU SOON.
........
HEY, WAIT!
THEY'RE ALL JUST LEAVING US HERE? ABANDONING US?
ARE WE THE ONLY ONES WITHOUT ANY PLANS?!
WE'RE BEING LEFT BEHIND AT THE GRADUATION CEREMONY!
Those guys are so cruel!

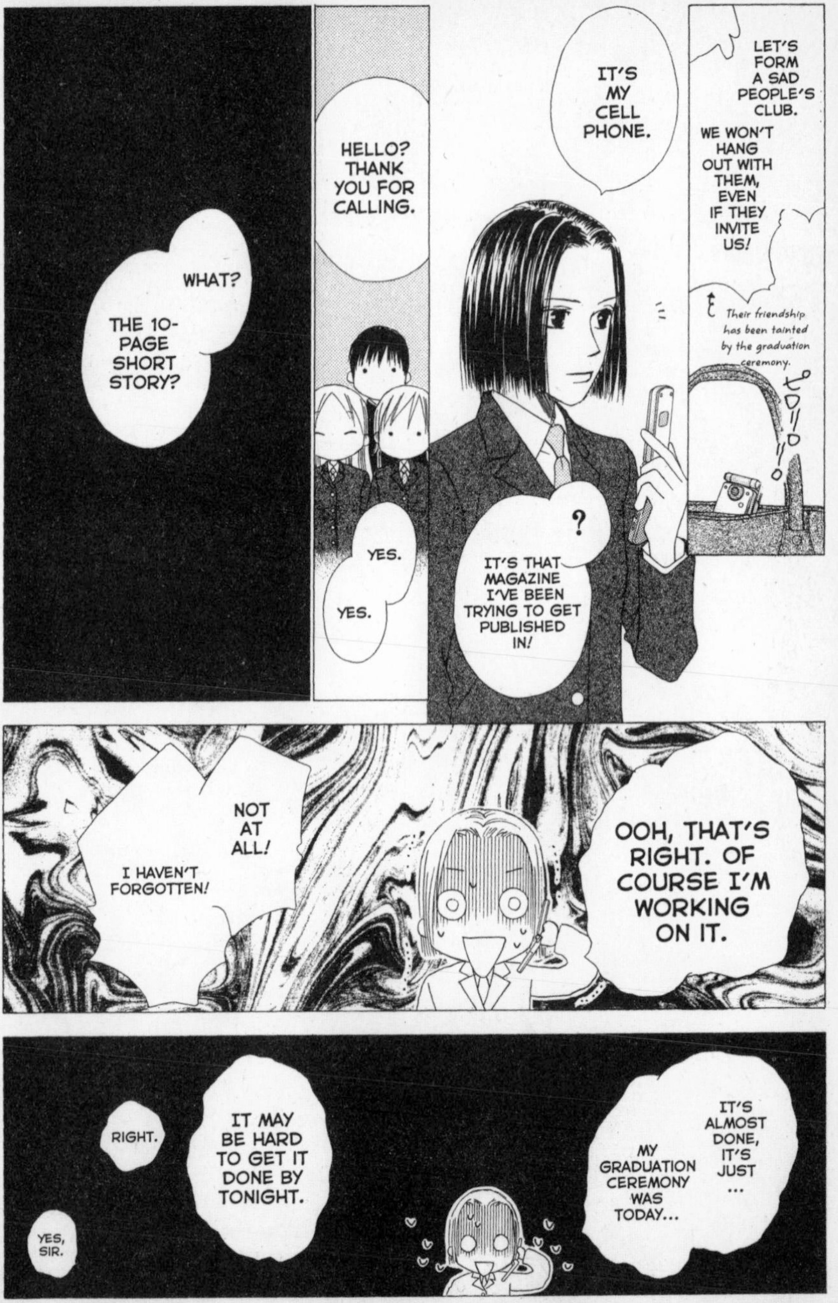
LET'S FORM A SAD PEOPLE'S CLUB.
WE WON'T HANG OUT WITH THEM, EVEN IF THEY INVITE US!
Their friendship has been tainted by the graduation ceremony.
IT'S MY CELL PHONE.
?
IT'S THAT MAGAZINE I'VE BEEN TRYING TO GET PUBLISHED IN!
HELLO? THANK YOU FOR CALLING.
YES.
YES.
WHAT?
THE 10-PAGE SHORT STORY?
OOH, THAT'S RIGHT. OF COURSE I'M WORKING ON IT.
NOT AT ALL!
I HAVEN'T FORGOTTEN!
IT'S ALMOST DONE, IT'S JUST ...
MY GRADUATION CEREMONY WAS TODAY...
IT MAY BE HARD TO GET IT DONE BY TONIGHT.
RIGHT.
YES, SIR.

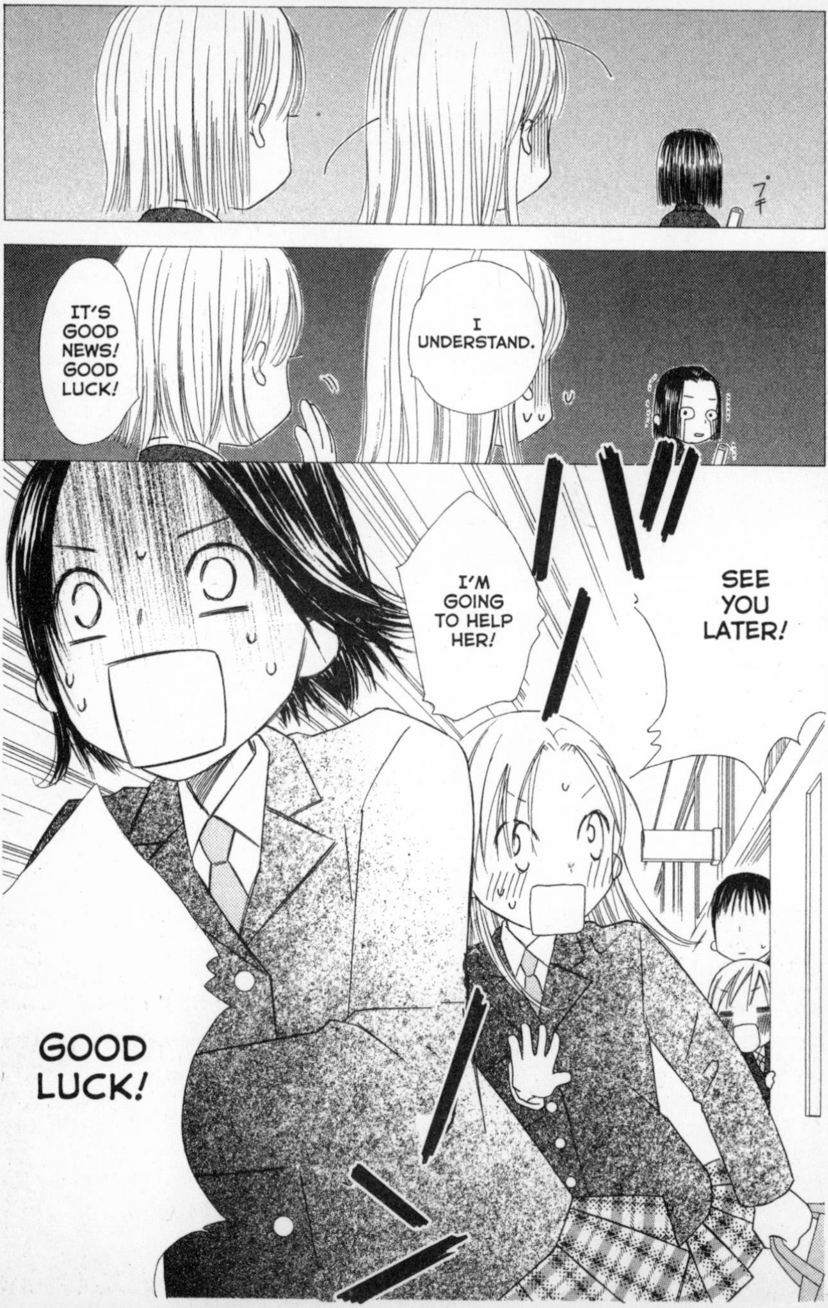
I UNDERSTAND.
IT'S GOOD NEWS! GOOD LUCK!
SEE YOU LATER!
I'M GOING TO HELP HER!
GOOD LUCK!

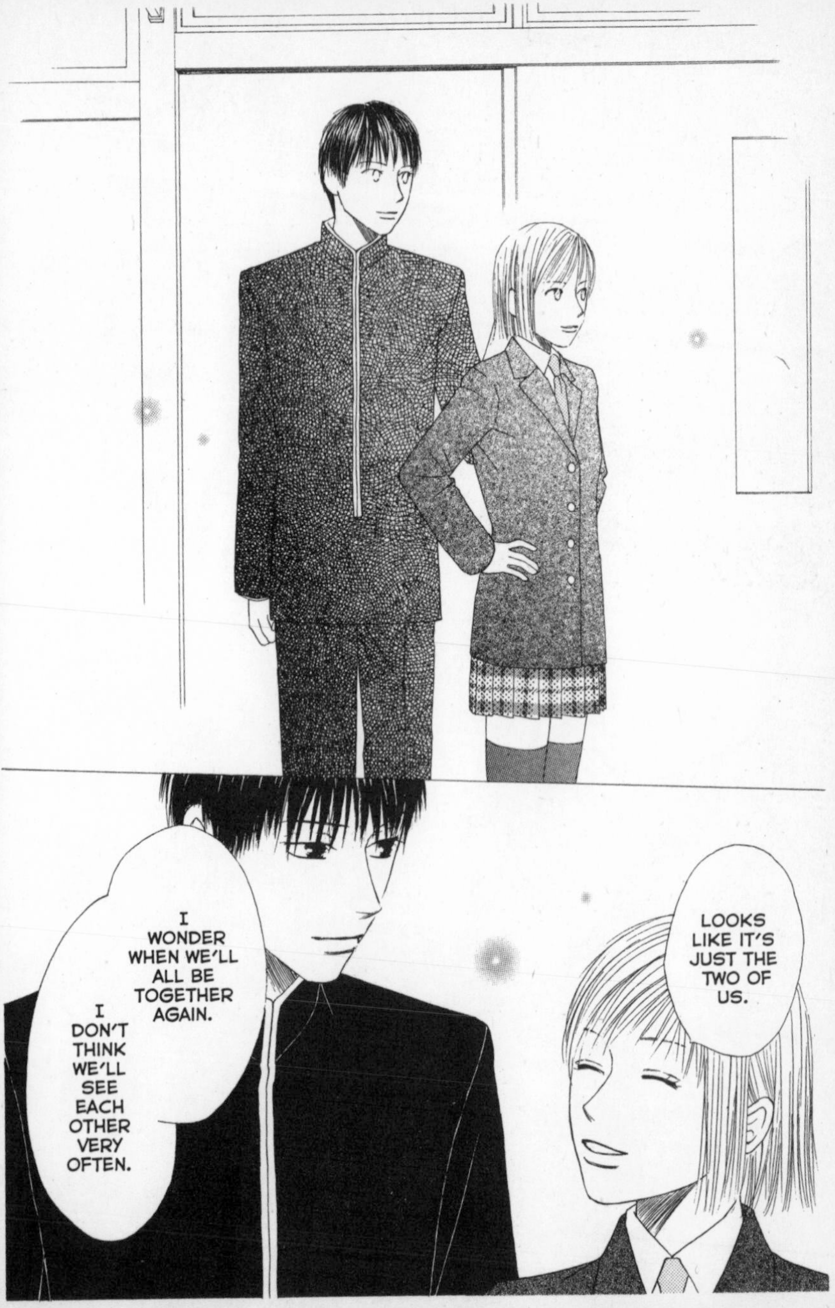
LOOKS LIKE IT'S JUST THE TWO OF US.
I WONDER WHEN WE'LL ALL BE TOGETHER AGAIN.
I DON'T THINK WE'LL SEE EACH OTHER VERY OFTEN.

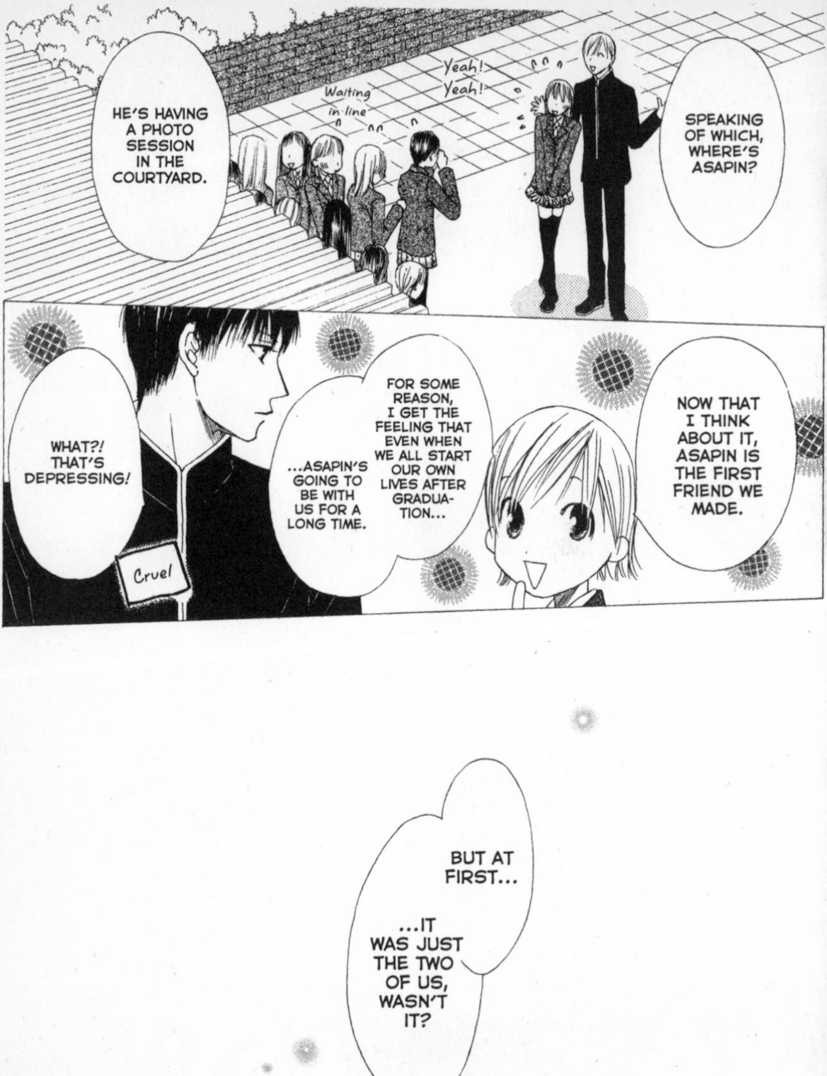
SPEAKING OF WHICH, WHERE'S ASAPIN?
Yeah! Yeah!
Waiting in line
HE'S HAVING A PHOTO SESSION IN THE COURTYARD.
NOW THAT I THINK ABOUT IT, ASAPIN IS THE FIRST FRIEND WE MADE.
FOR SOME REASON, I GET THE FEELING THAT EVEN WHEN WE ALL START OUR OWN LIVES AFTER GRADUATION...
...ASAPIN'S GOING TO BE WITH US FOR A LONG TIME.
WHAT?! THAT'S DEPRESSING!
Cruel
BUT AT FIRST...
...IT WAS JUST THE TWO OF US, WASN'T IT?

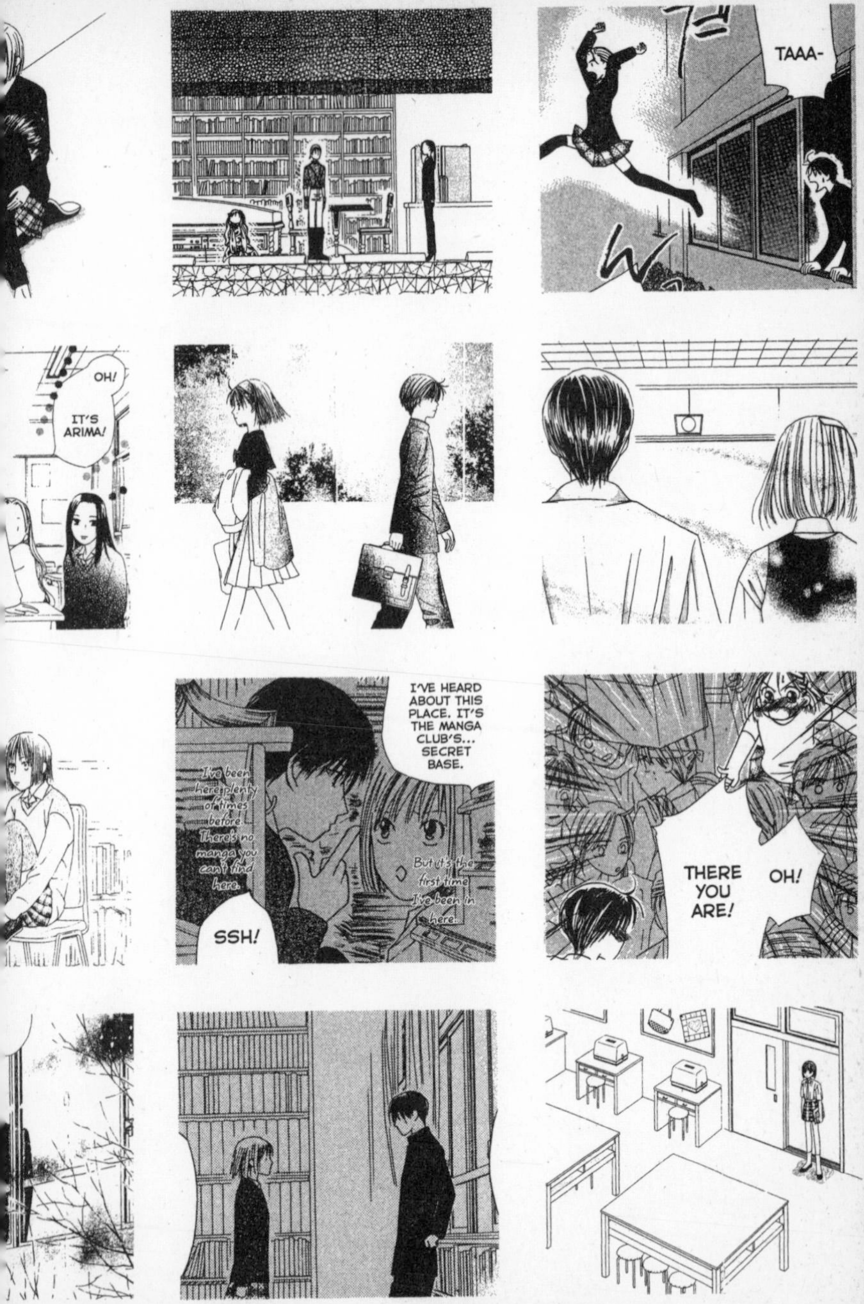
TAAA-
OH!
IT'S ARIMA!
OH!
THERE YOU ARE!
I'VE HEARD ABOUT THIS PLACE. IT'S THE MANGA CLUB'S... SECRET BASE.
But it's the first time I've been in here..
I've been here plenty of times before. There's no manga you can't find here.
SSH!

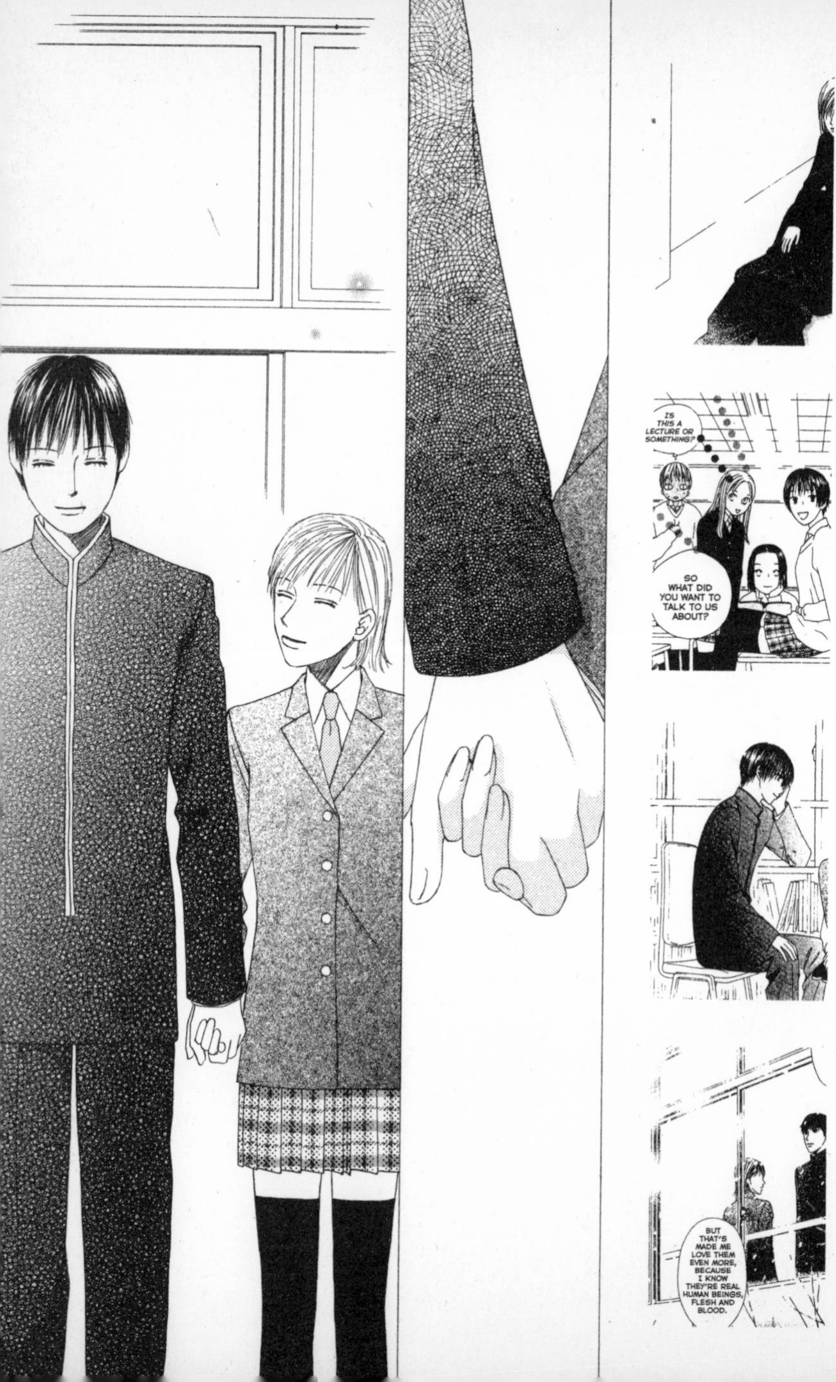
IS THIS A LECTURE OR SOMETHING?
SO WHAT DID YOU WANT TO TALK TO US ABOUT?
BUT THAT'S MADE ME LOVE THEM EVEN MORE, BECAUSE I KNOW THEY'RE REAL HUMAN BEINGS, FLESH AND BLOOD.

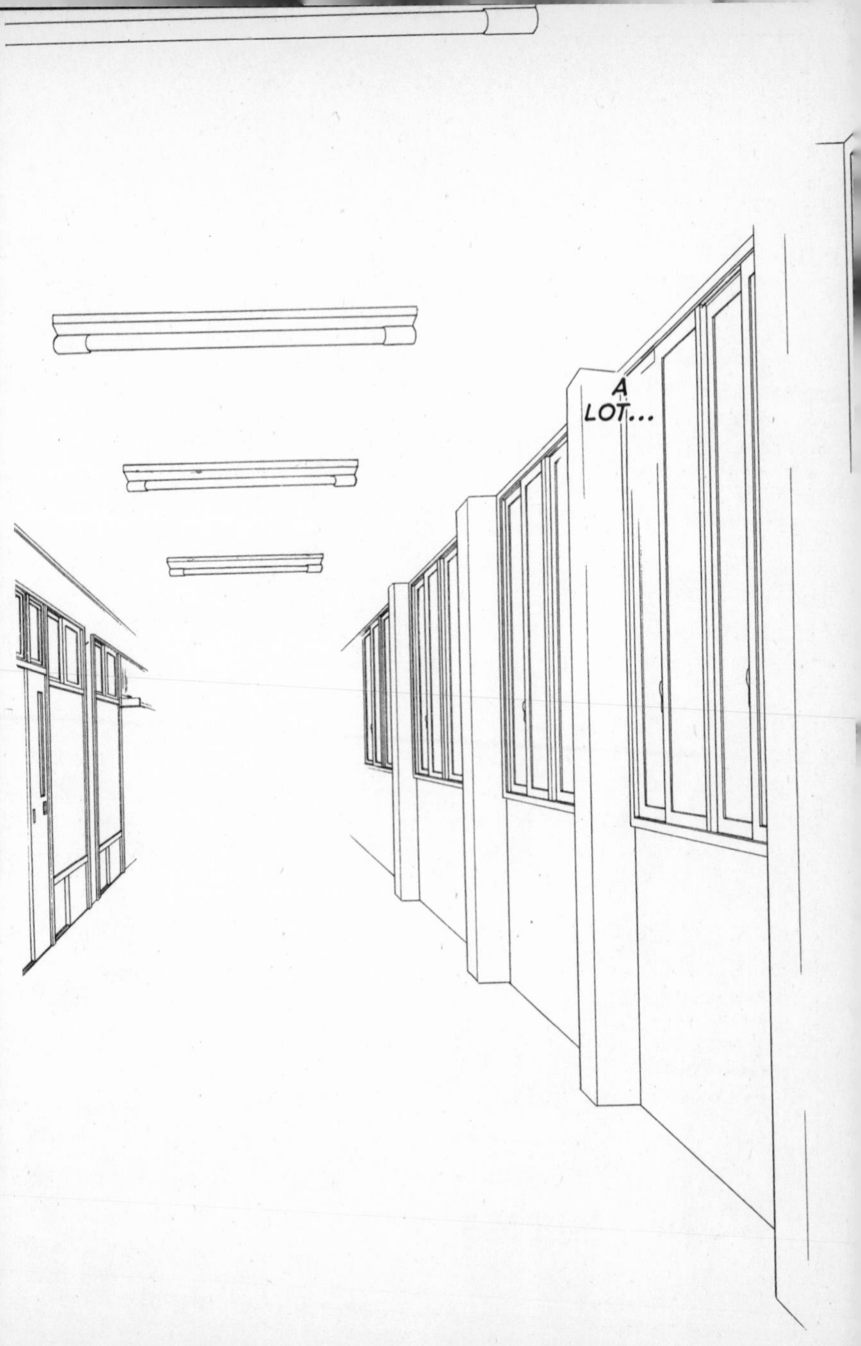
A LOT...

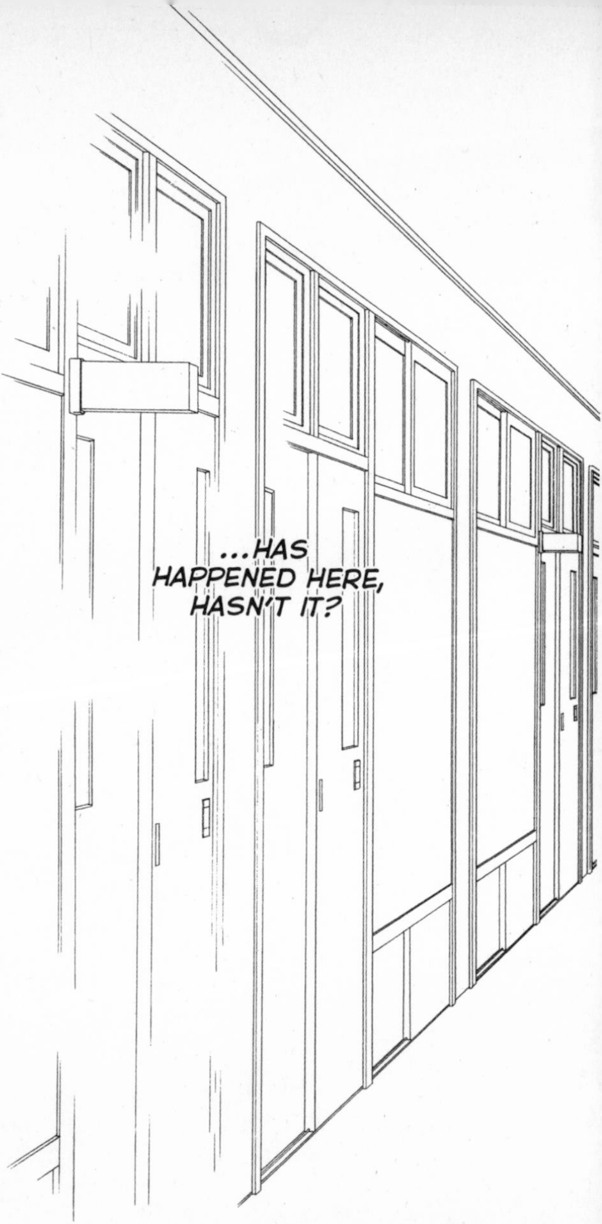
...HAS HAPPENED HERE, HASN'T IT?

3

The theme for the second half of this year will be physicality.

Ever since I started exercising and feeling healthier, I've gotten interested in the body.

With all of the plays and dancing and ballet and opera and the Olympics and K-1 I've seen, I've been noticing everyone's incredible muscles.

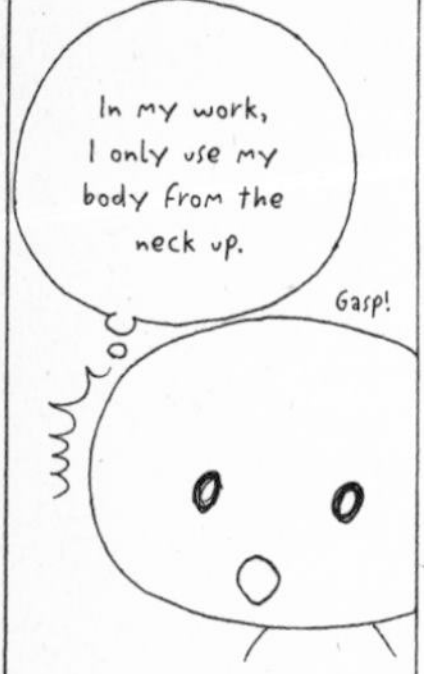
In my work, I only use my body from the neck up.
Gasp!

And so, I've started exercising. I've started seriously reading Yoshinori Kono's books, too!

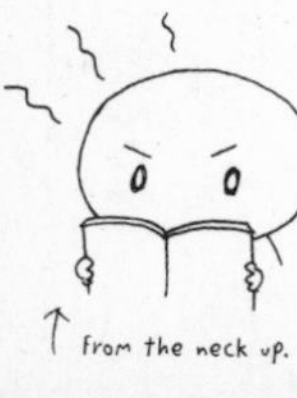
↑ From the neck up.

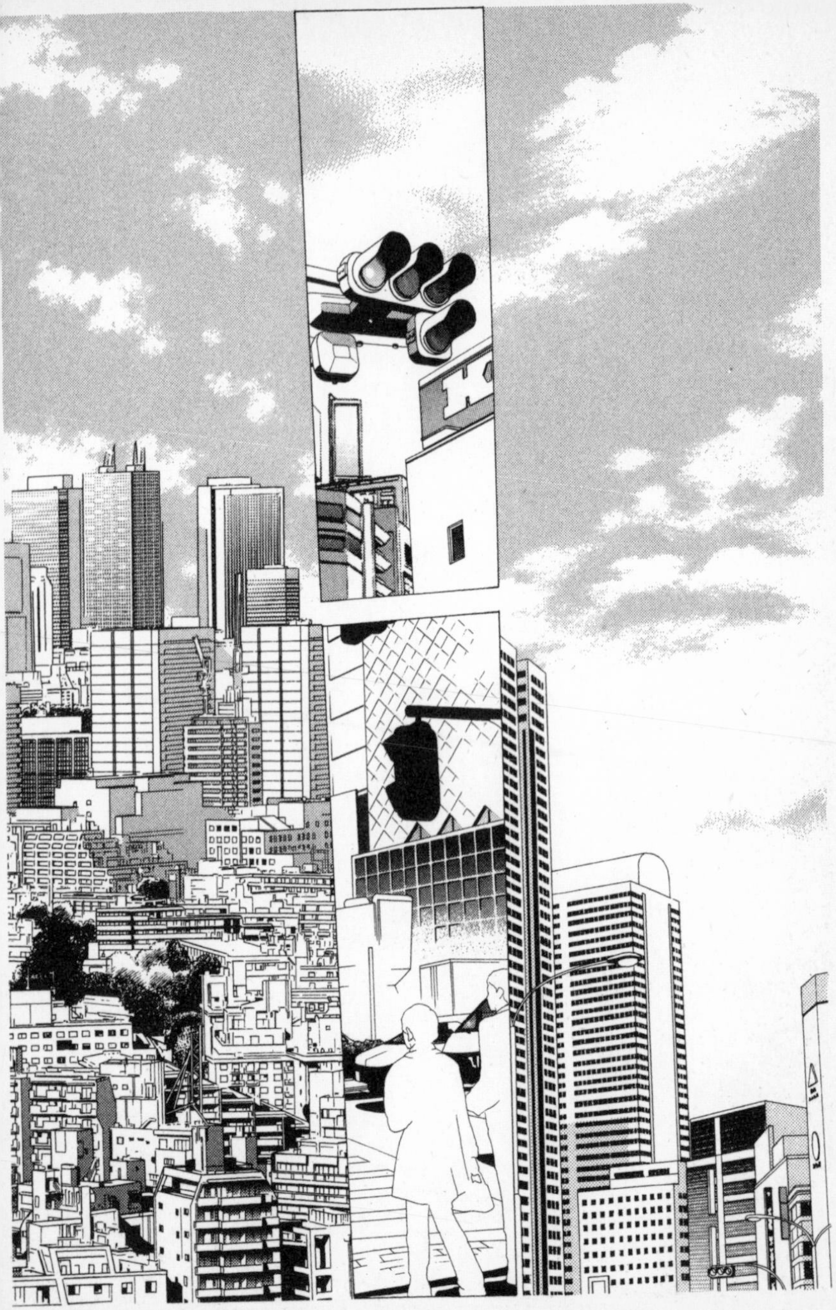

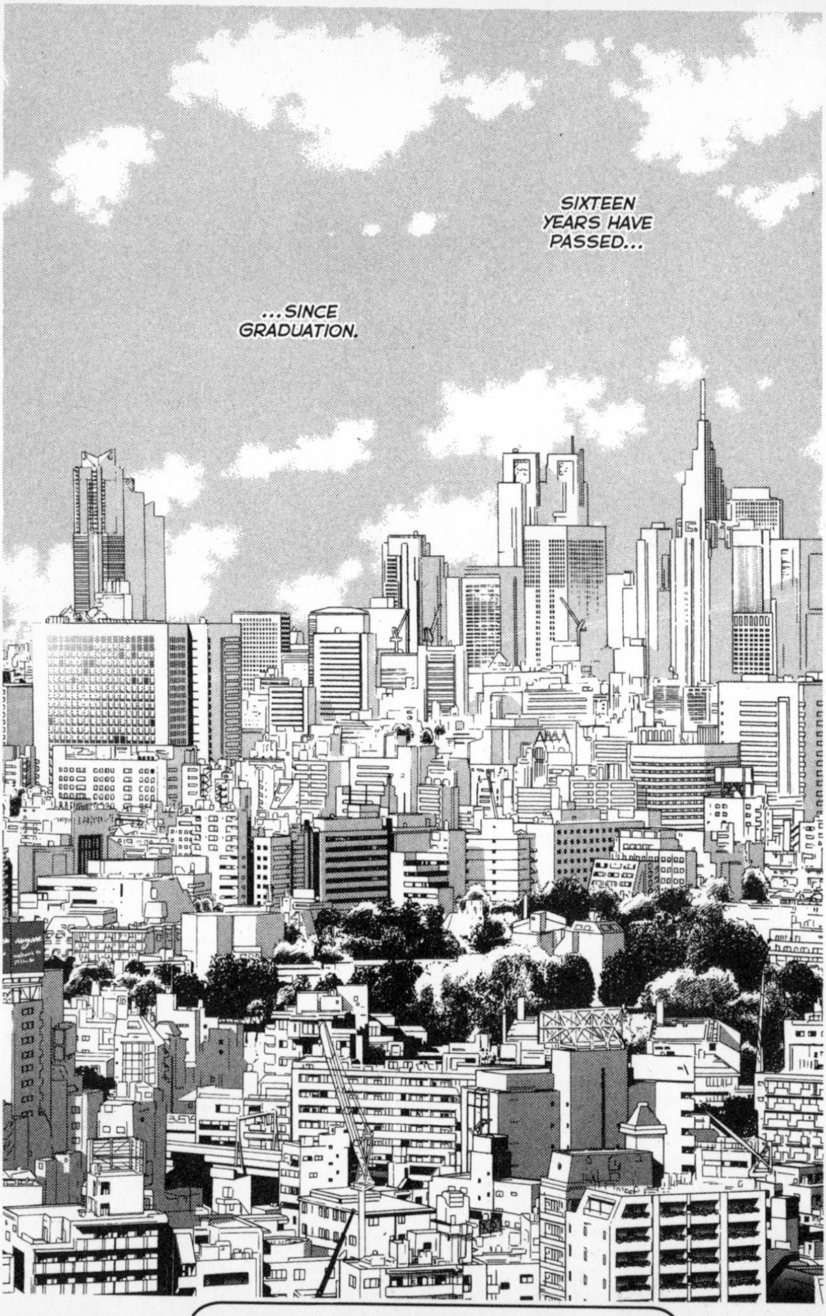
SIXTEEN YEARS HAVE PASSED...
...SINCE GRADUATION.

ACT 101 ★ SPRING AND MARCH / END

# kare kano

*his and her circumstances*

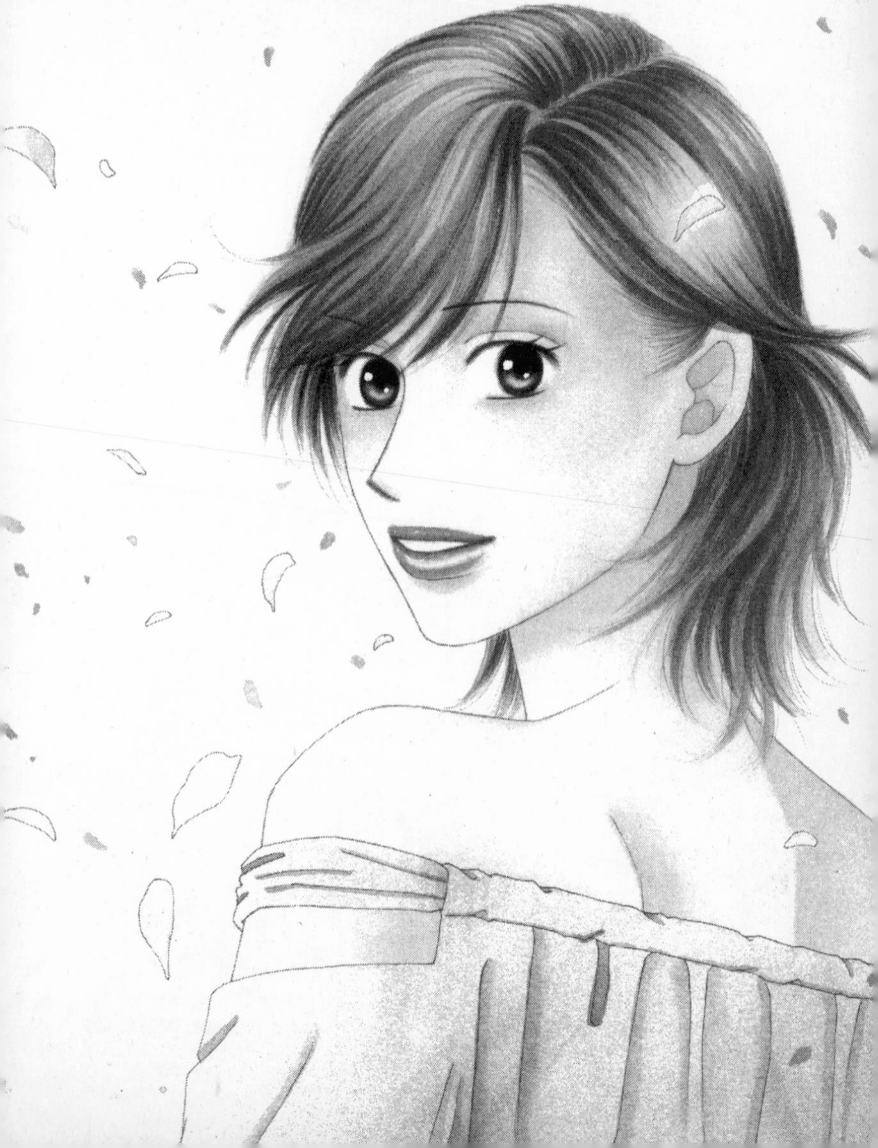

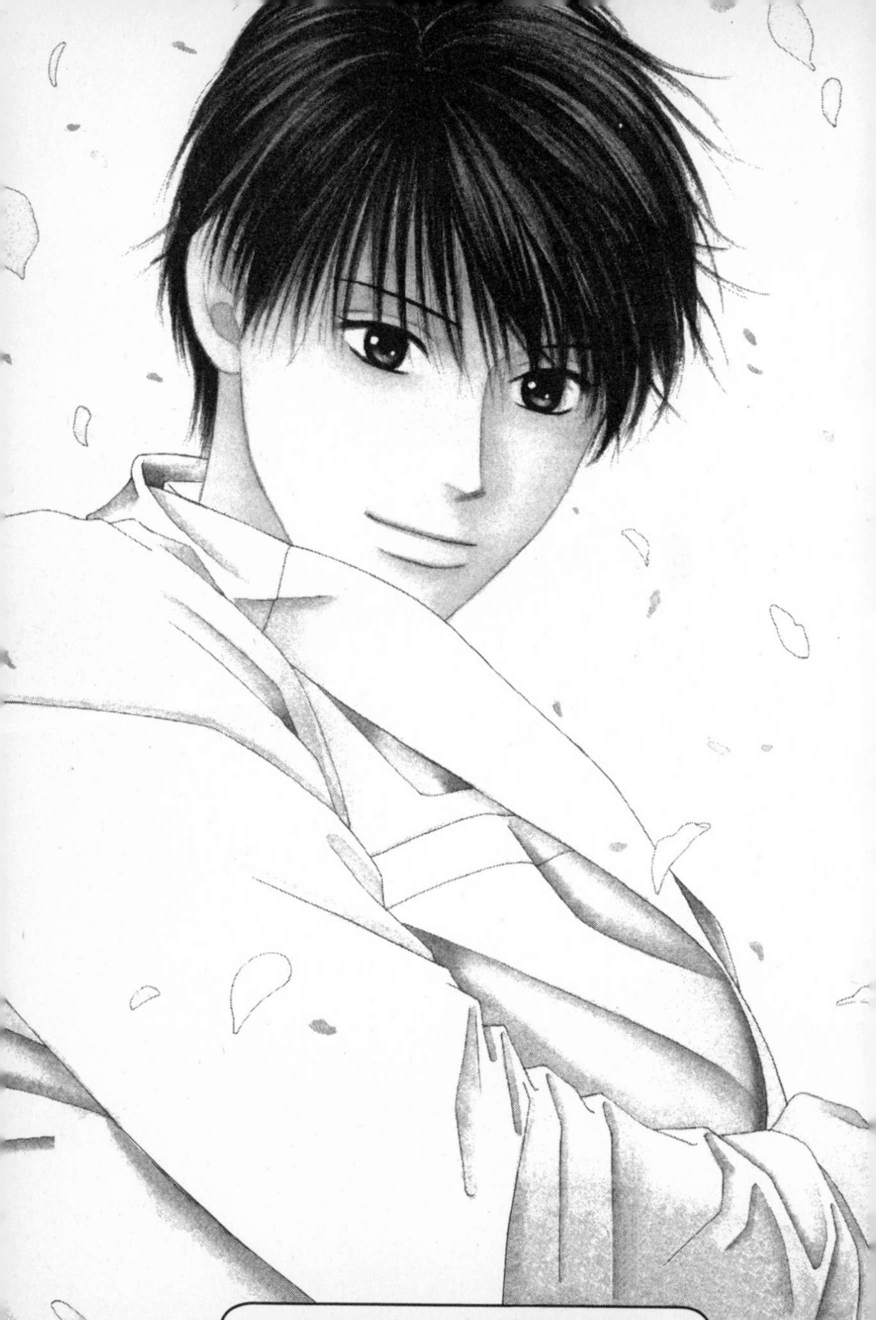

## FINAL ACT ★ NOTHING BETTER

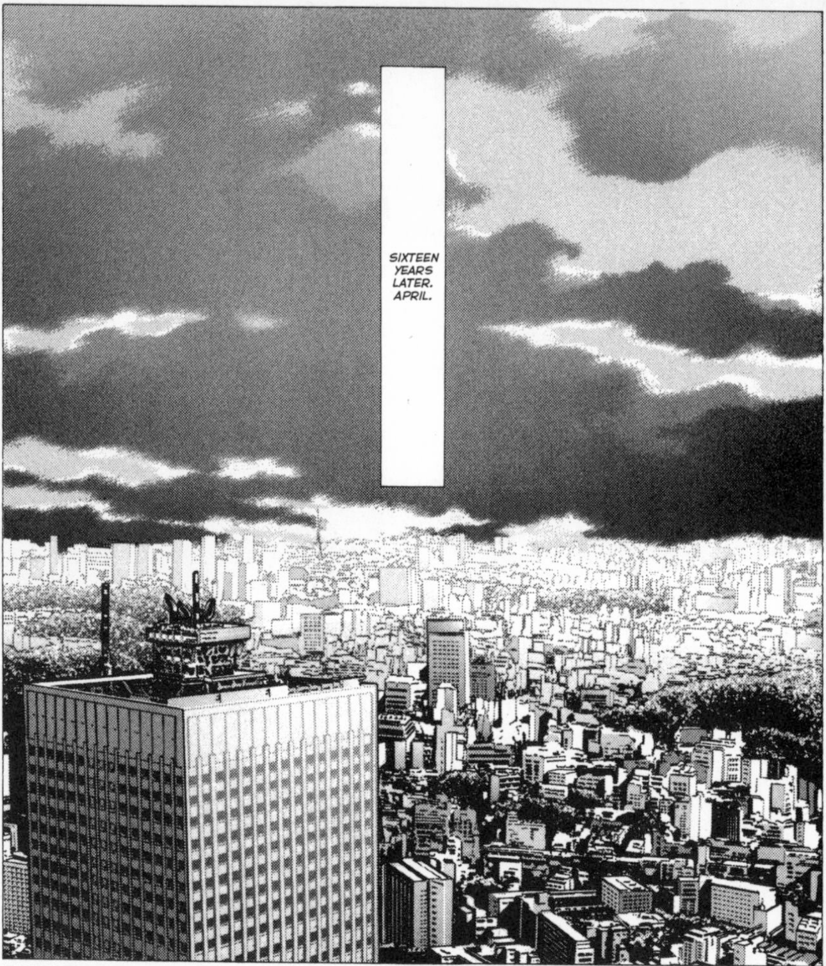
SIXTEEN YEARS LATER. APRIL.

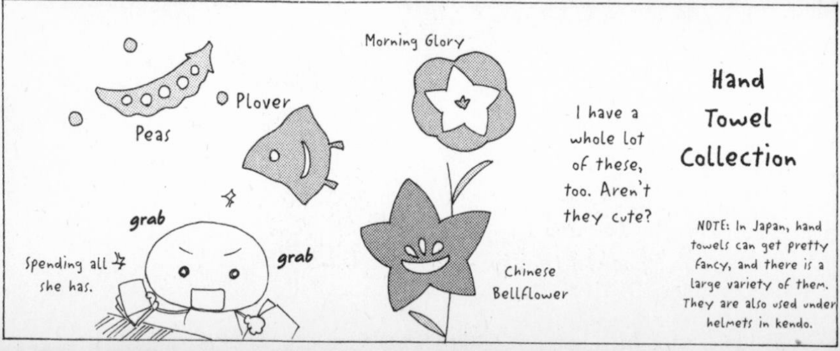
Hand Towel Collection
NOTE: In Japan, hand towels can get pretty fancy, and there is a large variety of them. They are also used under helmets in kendo.
I have a whole lot of these, too. Aren't they cute?
Morning Glory
Chinese Bellflower
Plover
Peas
grab
grab
Spending all she has.

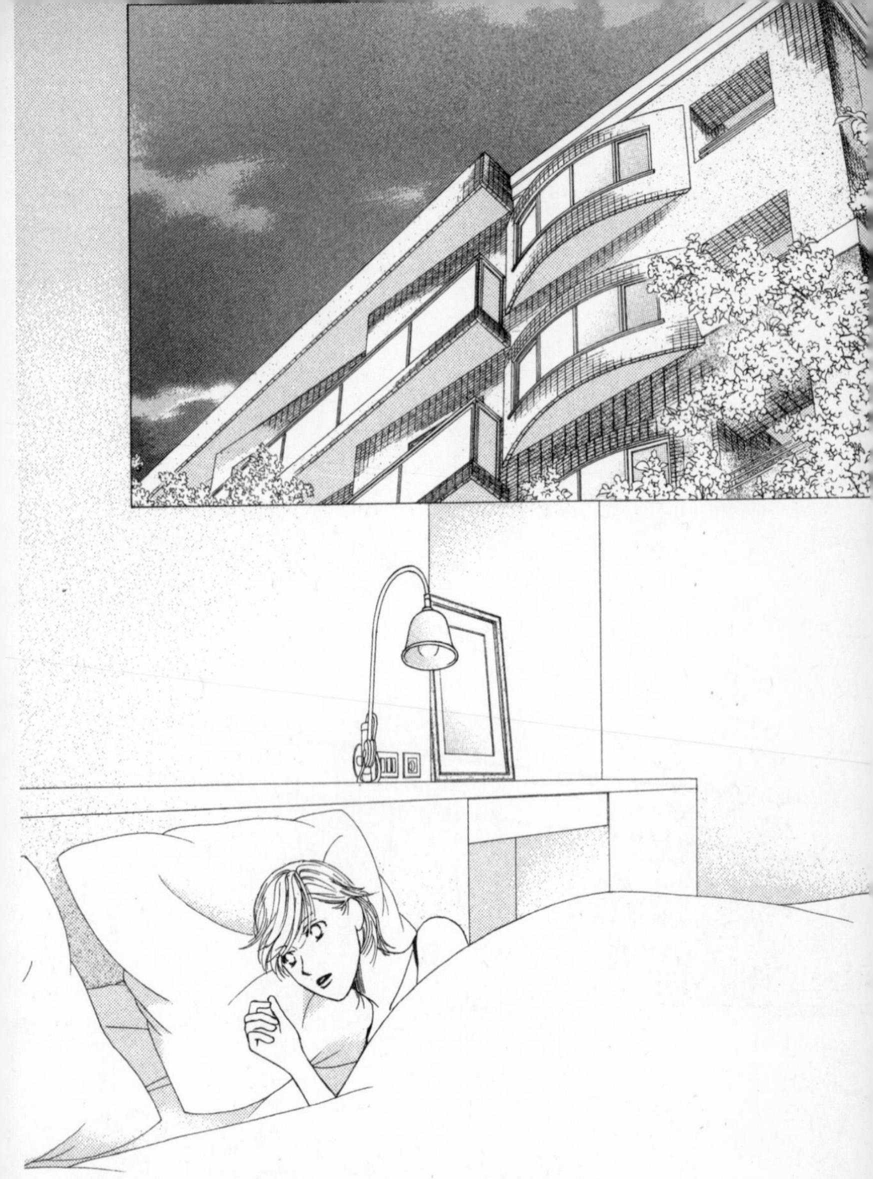

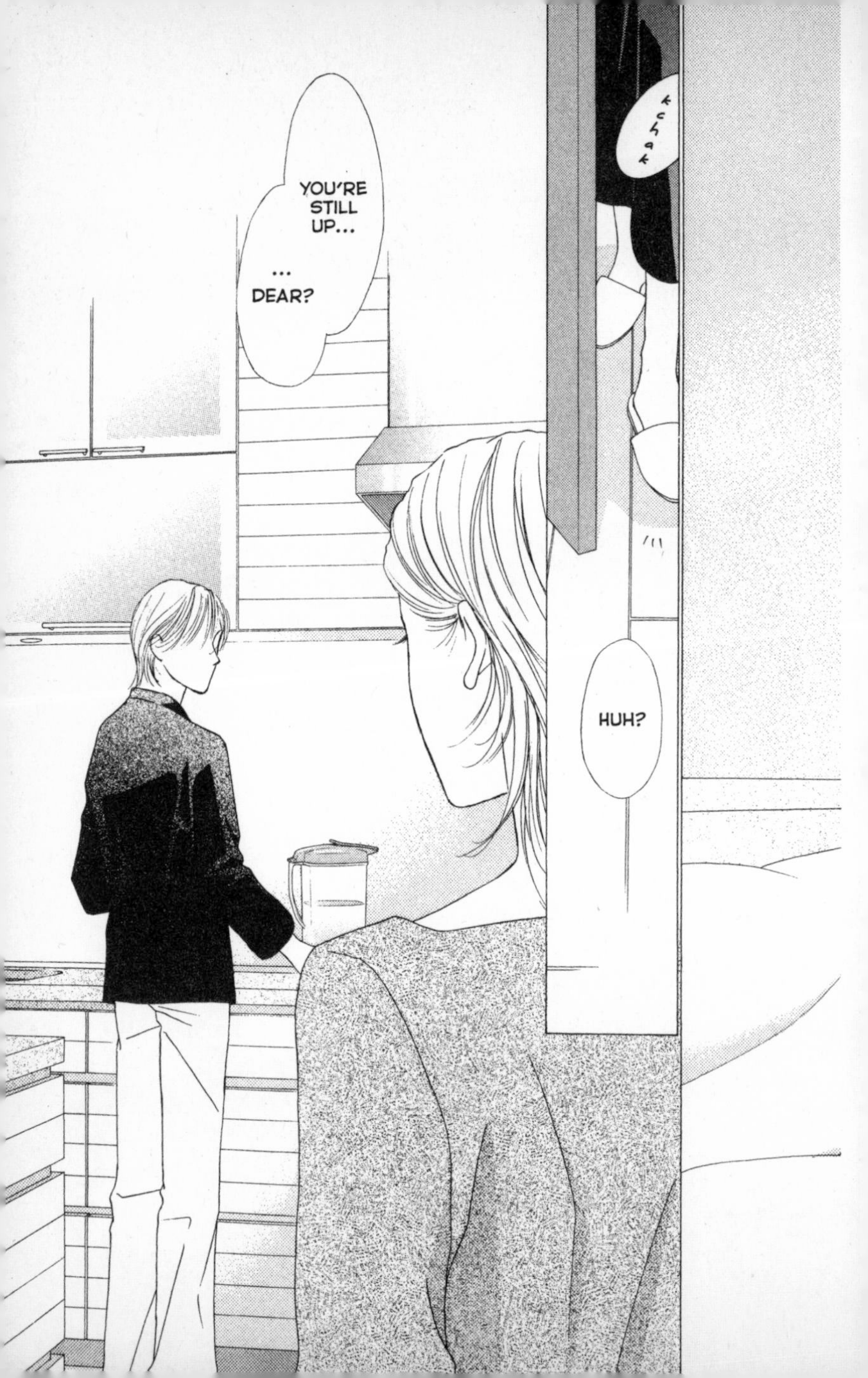
kchak
YOU'RE STILL UP...
...DEAR?
HUH?

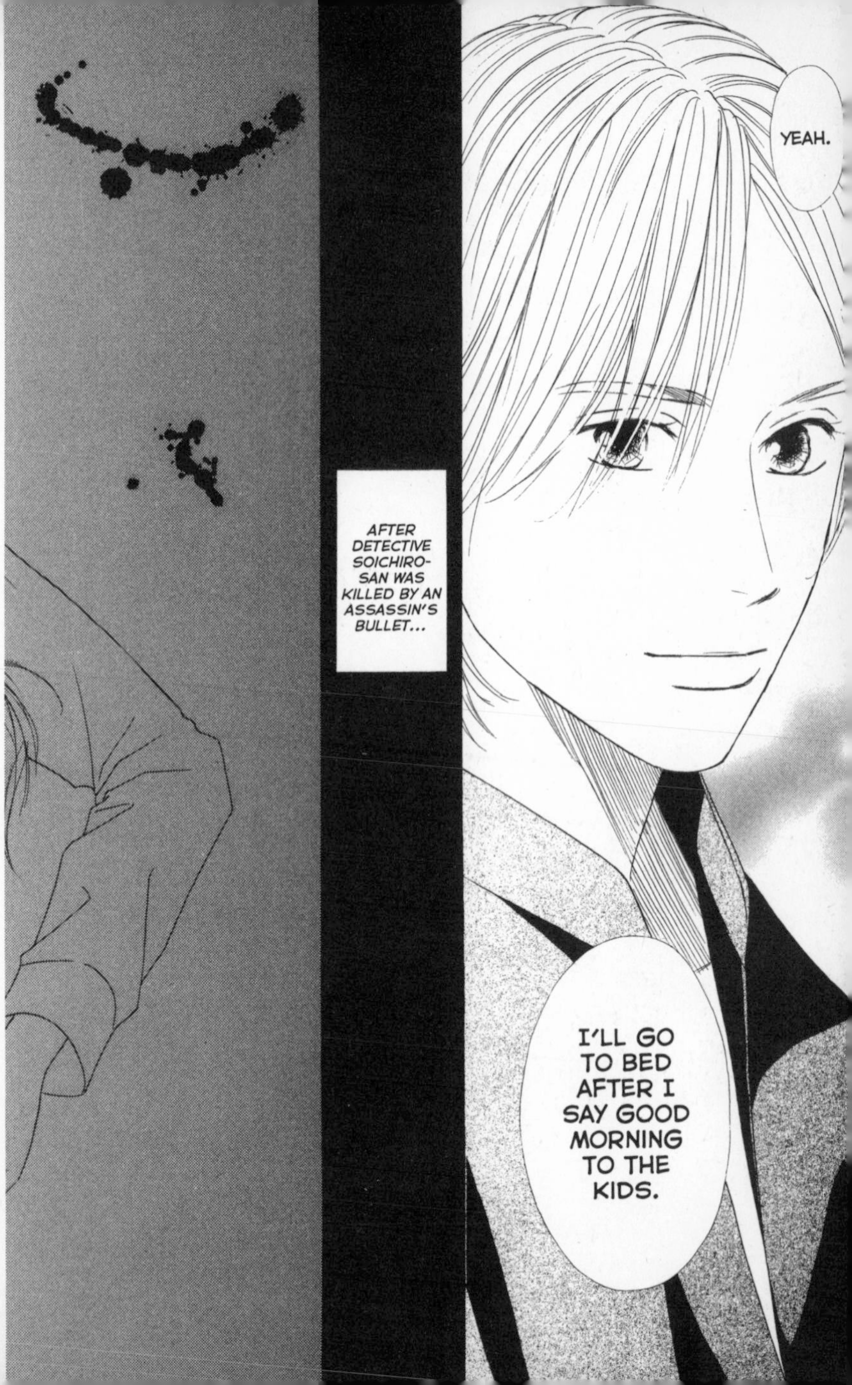
YEAH.
I'LL GO TO BED AFTER I SAY GOOD MORNING TO THE KIDS.
AFTER DETECTIVE SOICHIRO-SAN WAS KILLED BY AN ASSASSIN'S BULLET...

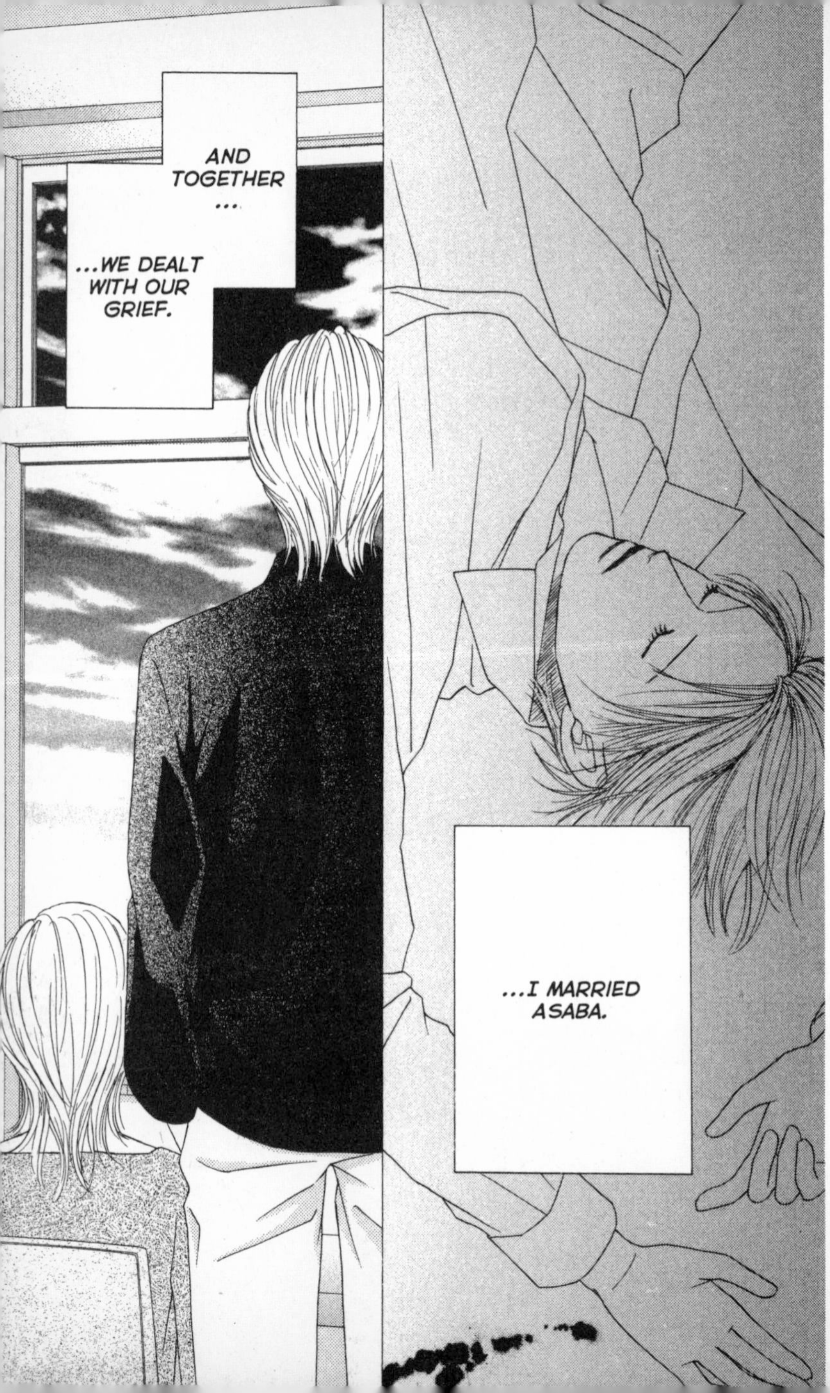
...I MARRIED ASABA.
AND TOGETHER ...
...WE DEALT WITH OUR GRIEF.

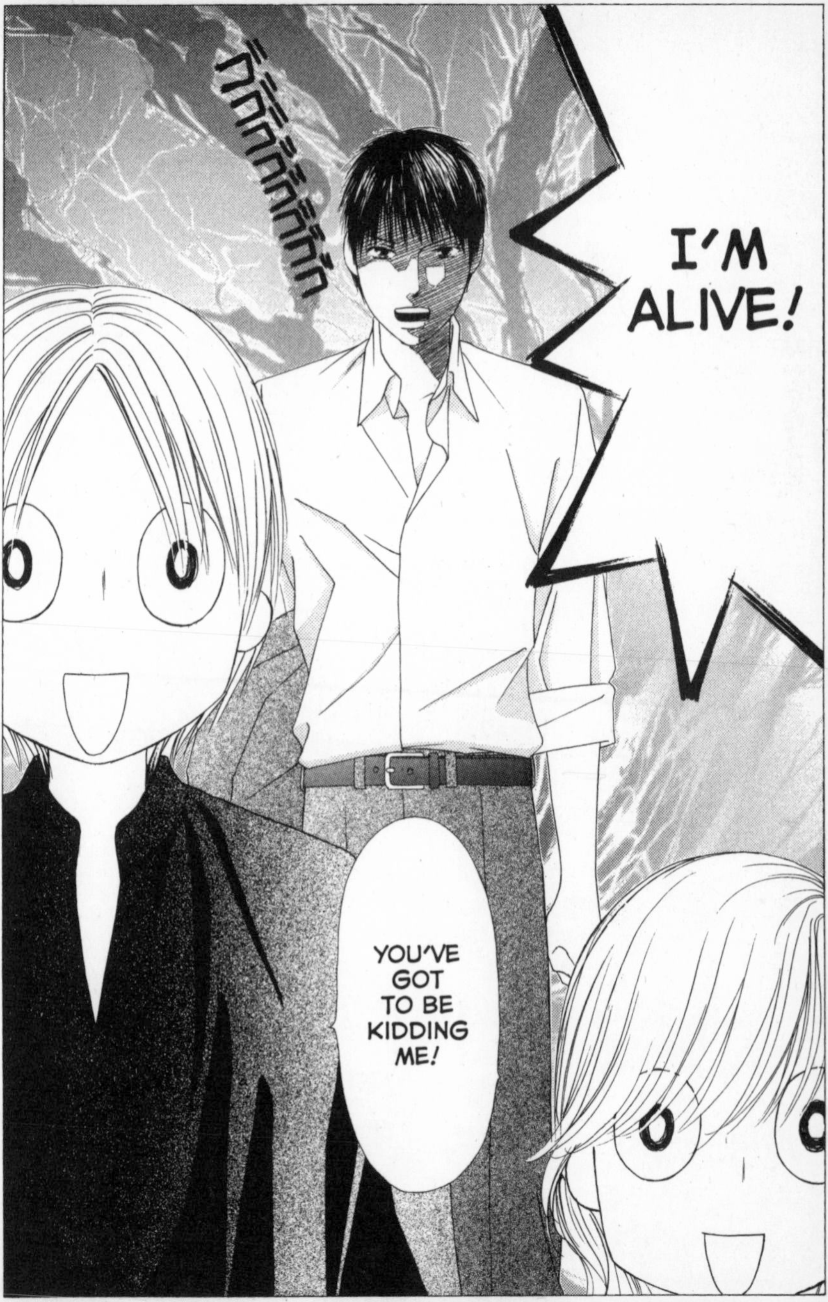
I'M ALIVE!
YOU'VE GOT TO BE KIDDING ME!

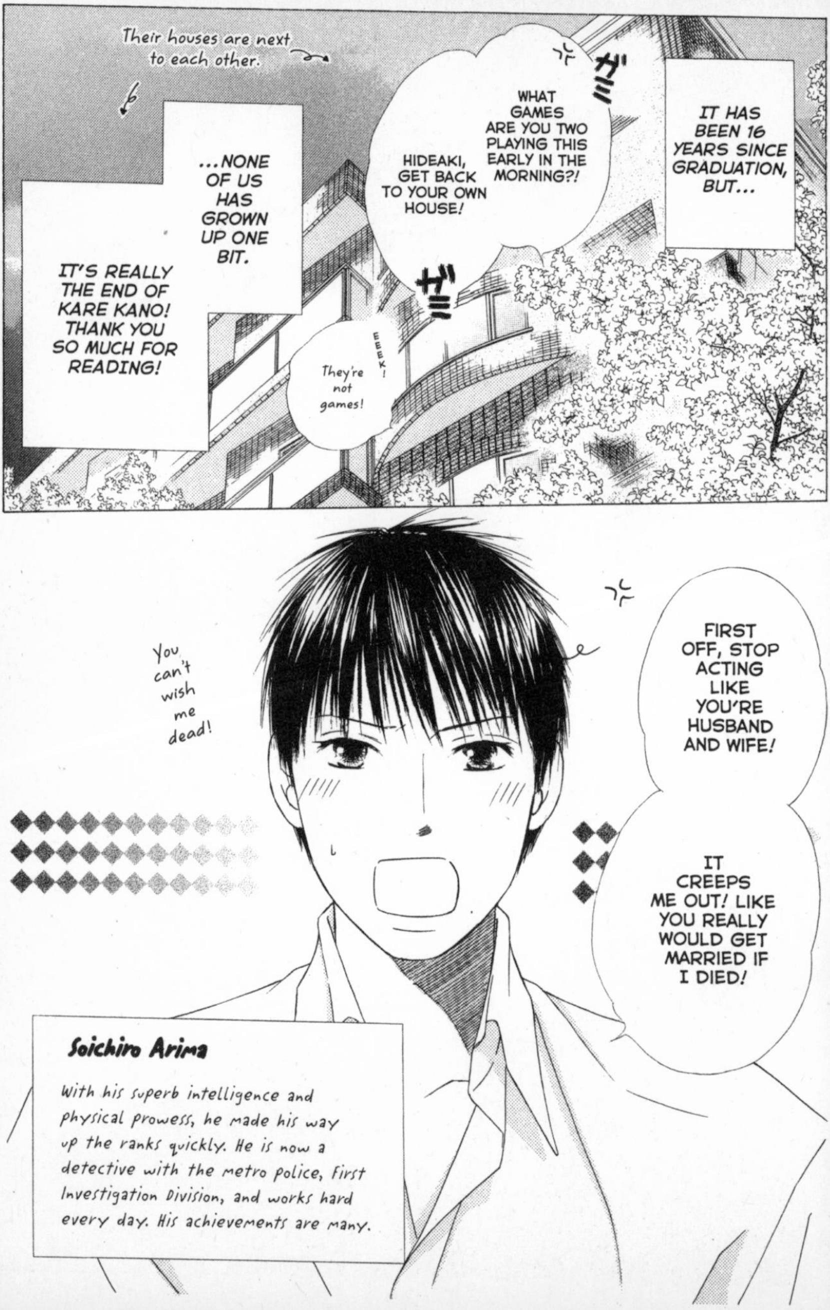
IT HAS BEEN 16 YEARS SINCE GRADUATION, BUT...
ガミ
WHAT GAMES ARE YOU TWO PLAYING THIS EARLY IN THE MORNING?!
HIDEAKI, GET BACK TO YOUR OWN HOUSE!
ガミ
Their houses are next to each other.
...NONE OF US HAS GROWN UP ONE BIT.
EEEK!
They're not games!
IT'S REALLY THE END OF KARE KANO! THANK YOU SO MUCH FOR READING!
FIRST OFF, STOP ACTING LIKE YOU'RE HUSBAND AND WIFE!
IT CREEPS ME OUT! LIKE YOU REALLY WOULD GET MARRIED IF I DIED!
You can't wish me dead!
Soichiro Arima
With his superb intelligence and physical prowess, he made his way up the ranks quickly. He is now a detective with the metro police, First Investigation Division, and works hard every day. His achievements are many.

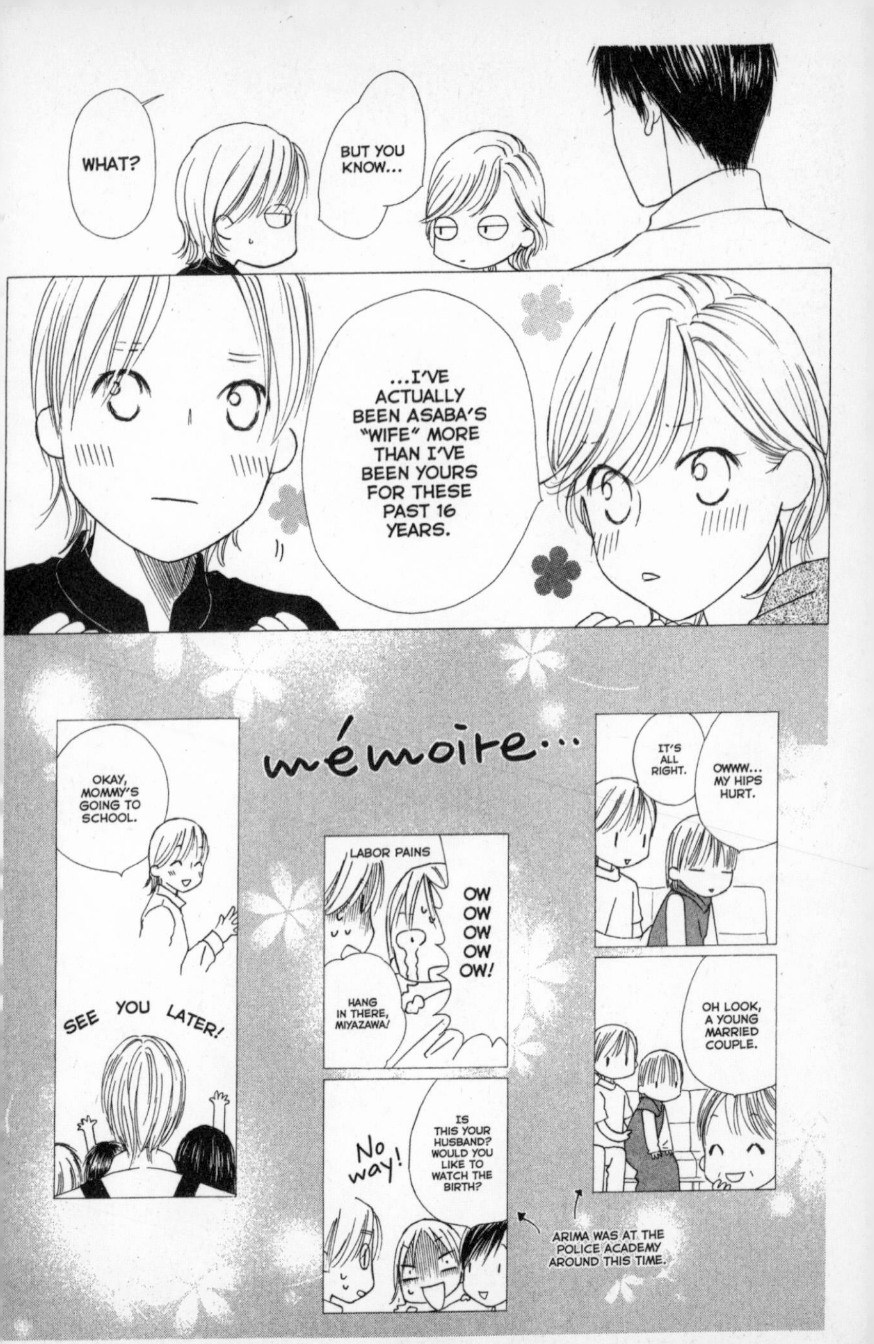
BUT YOU KNOW...
WHAT?
...I'VE ACTUALLY BEEN ASABA'S "WIFE" MORE THAN I'VE BEEN YOURS FOR THESE PAST 16 YEARS.
mémoire...
OWWW... MY HIPS HURT.
IT'S ALL RIGHT.
OH LOOK, A YOUNG MARRIED COUPLE.
ARIMA WAS AT THE POLICE ACADEMY AROUND THIS TIME.
OW OW OW OW OW!
LABOR PAINS
HANG IN THERE, MIYAZAWA!
IS THIS YOUR HUSBAND? WOULD YOU LIKE TO WATCH THE BIRTH?
No way!
OKAY, MOMMY'S GOING TO SCHOOL.
SEE YOU LATER!

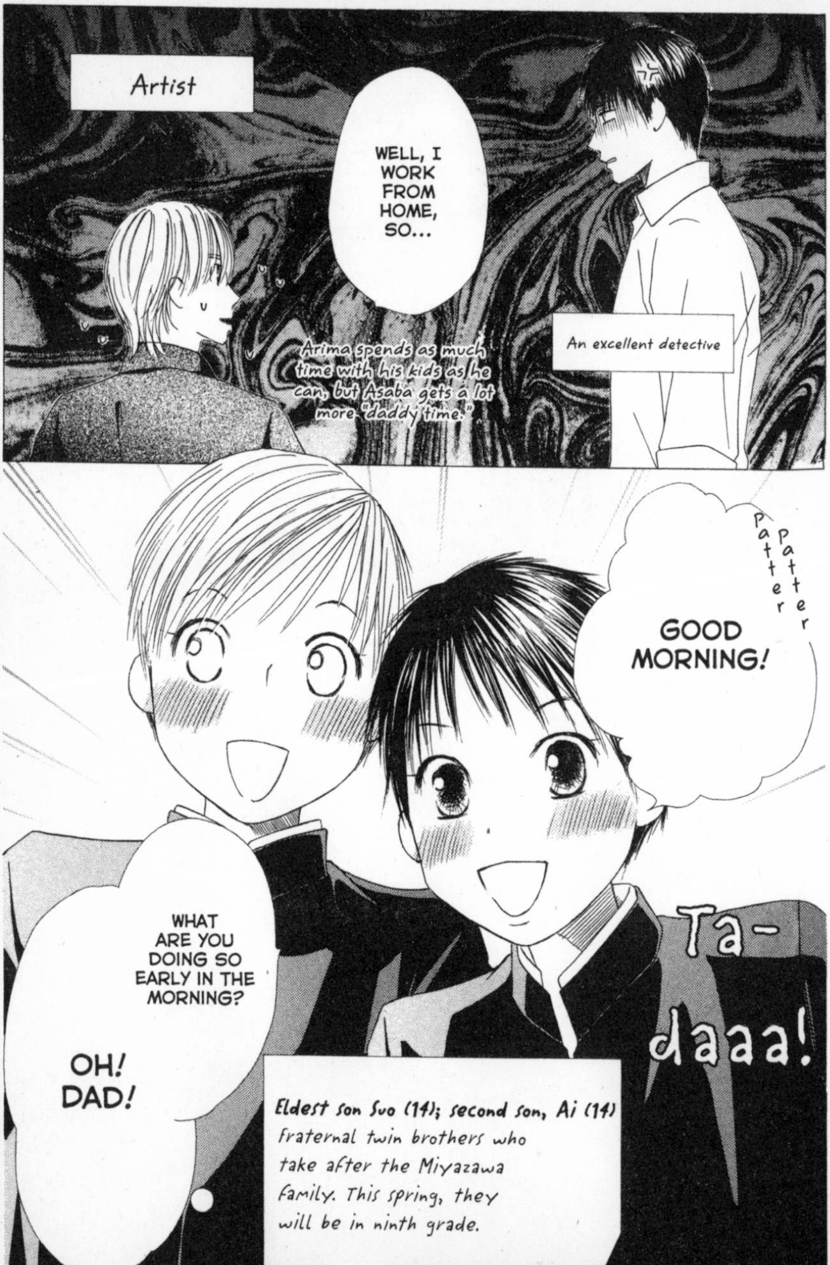
WELL, I WORK FROM HOME, SO...
Artist
An excellent detective
Arima spends as much time with his kids as he can, but Asaba gets a lot more "daddy time."
Patter patter
GOOD MORNING!
Ta-daaa!
WHAT ARE YOU DOING SO EARLY IN THE MORNING?
OH! DAD!
Eldest son Suo (14); second son, Ai (14)
Fraternal twin brothers who take after the Miyazawa family. This spring, they will be in ninth grade.

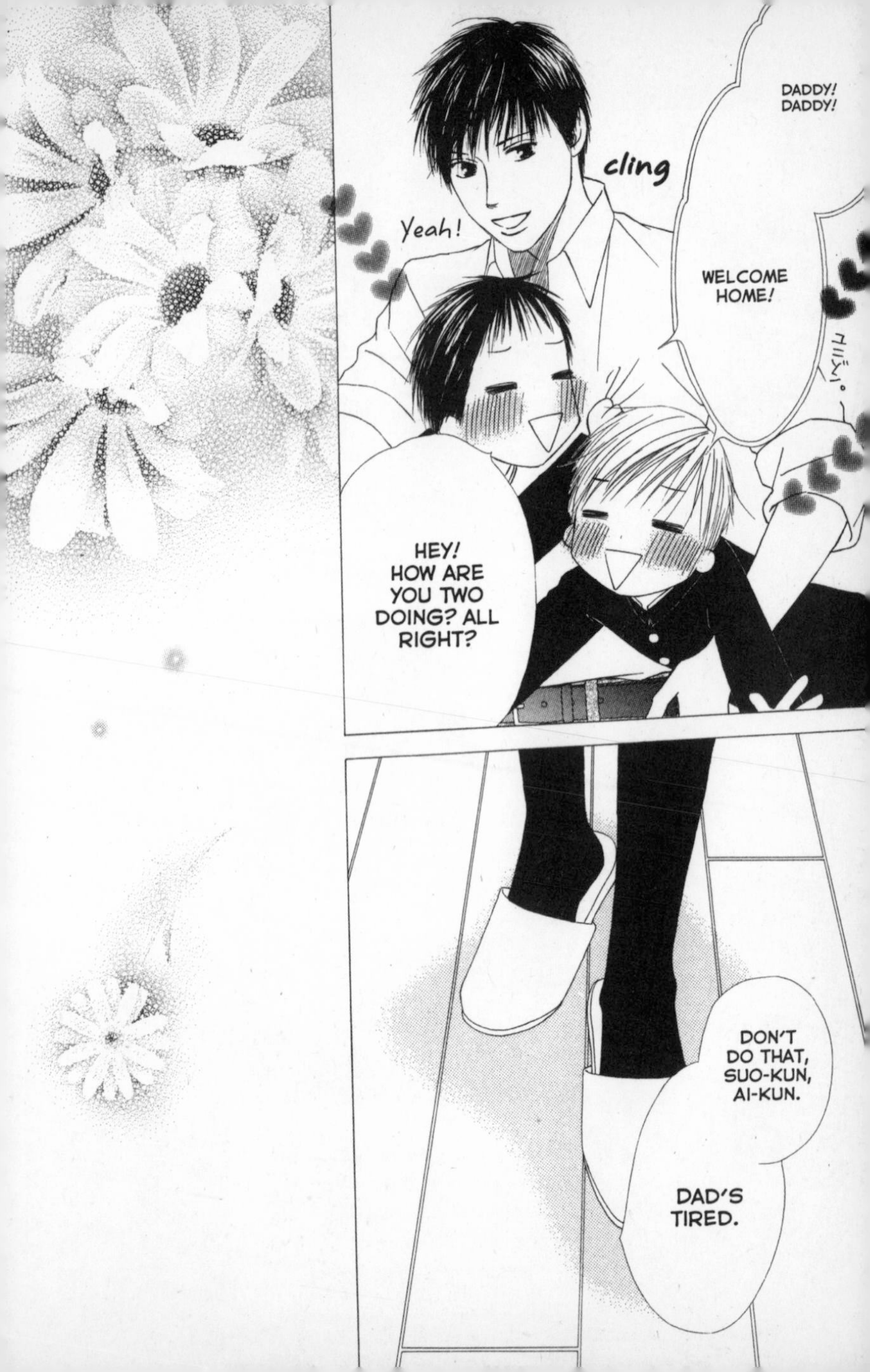
DADDY! DADDY!
WELCOME HOME!
cling
Yeah!
HEY! HOW ARE YOU TWO DOING? ALL RIGHT?
DON'T DO THAT, SUO-KUN, AI-KUN.
DAD'S TIRED.

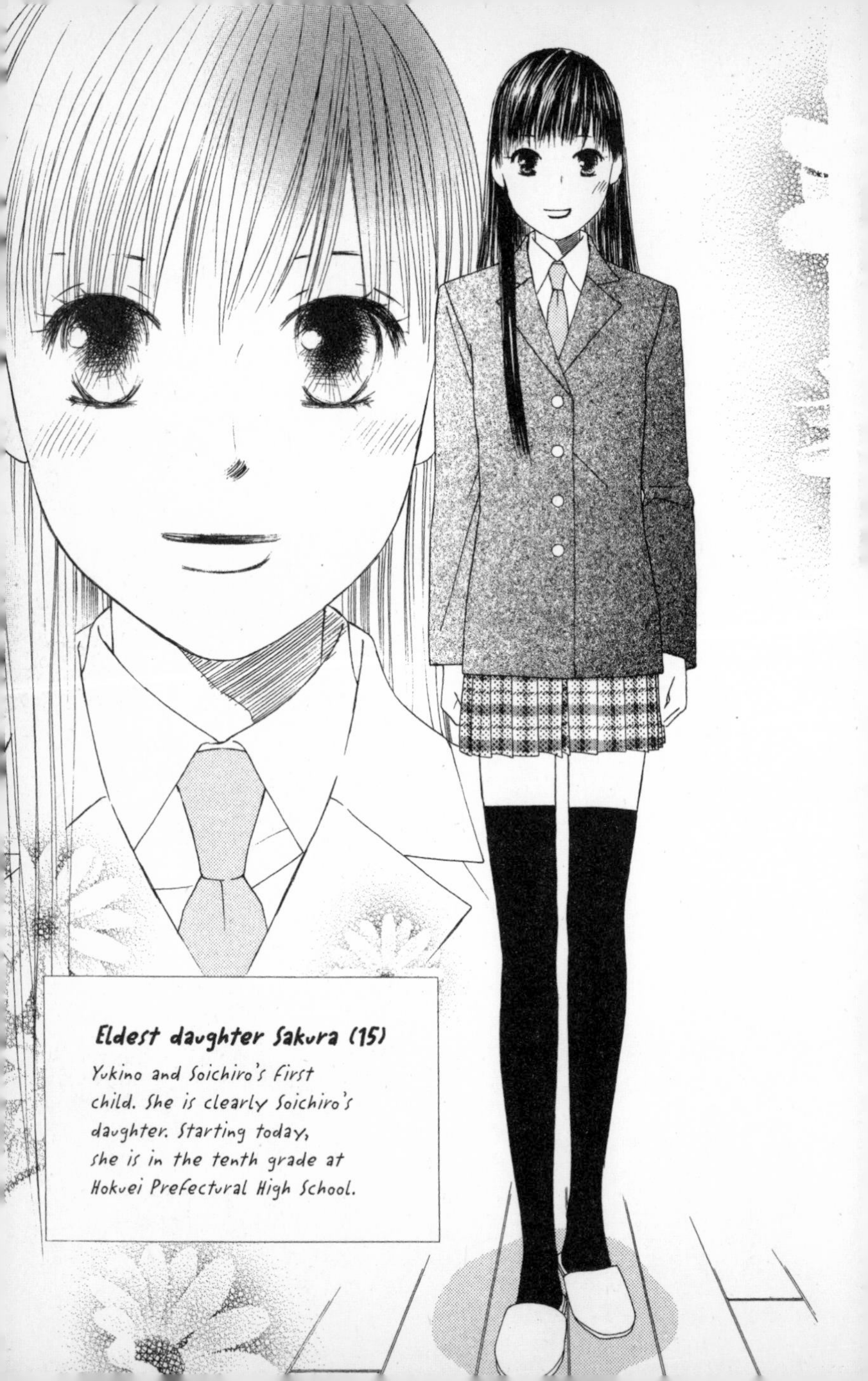
Eldest daughter Sakura (15)
Yukino and Soichiro's first child. She is clearly Soichiro's daughter. Starting today, she is in the tenth grade at Hokuei Prefectural High School.

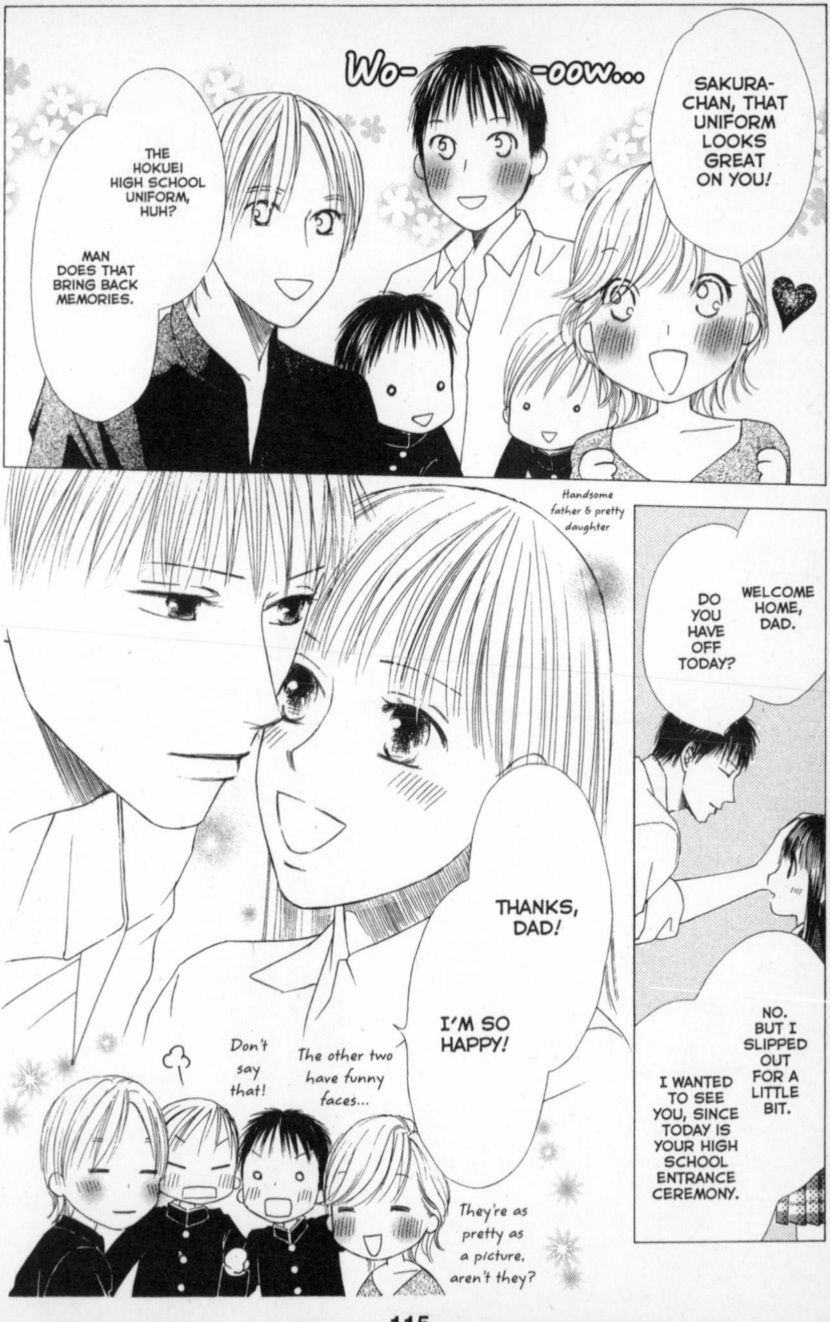
Wo- -oow...
SAKURA-CHAN, THAT UNIFORM LOOKS GREAT ON YOU!
THE HOKUEI HIGH SCHOOL UNIFORM, HUH?
MAN DOES THAT BRING BACK MEMORIES.
WELCOME HOME, DAD.
DO YOU HAVE OFF TODAY?
NO. BUT I SLIPPED OUT FOR A LITTLE BIT.
I WANTED TO SEE YOU, SINCE TODAY IS YOUR HIGH SCHOOL ENTRANCE CEREMONY.
Handsome father & pretty daughter
THANKS, DAD!
I'M SO HAPPY!
They're as pretty as a picture, aren't they?
The other two have funny faces...
Don't say that!

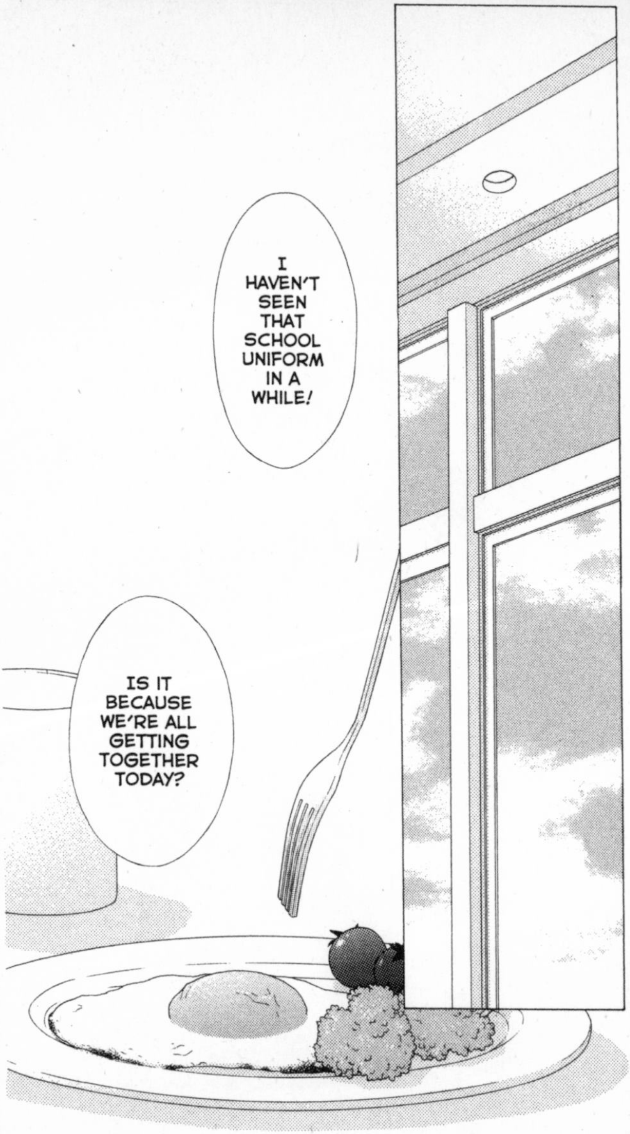
I HAVEN'T SEEN THAT SCHOOL UNIFORM IN A WHILE!
IS IT BECAUSE WE'RE ALL GETTING TOGETHER TODAY?

4

Korean Drama

**Jewel in the Palace**

It's broadcasting on NHK. But by the time this book is published, it will be over.

**This is seriously good!**

I usually forget to watch dramas, but I've been watching every single episode of this one from the very beginning!

I especially liked that scene in Episode 27 (I think ^^;; ) where Lady Han and Lady Choi have their last talk in the prison. It was an amazing scene, the first one to give me goose bumps in a long time!

I'm really amazed that dramas can be so amazing!

**Waaaah!**

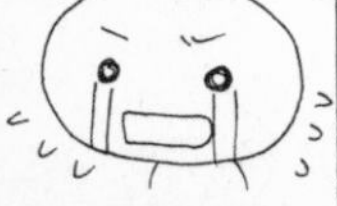

I want lots of people to watch it! Soon it will be on video, too!

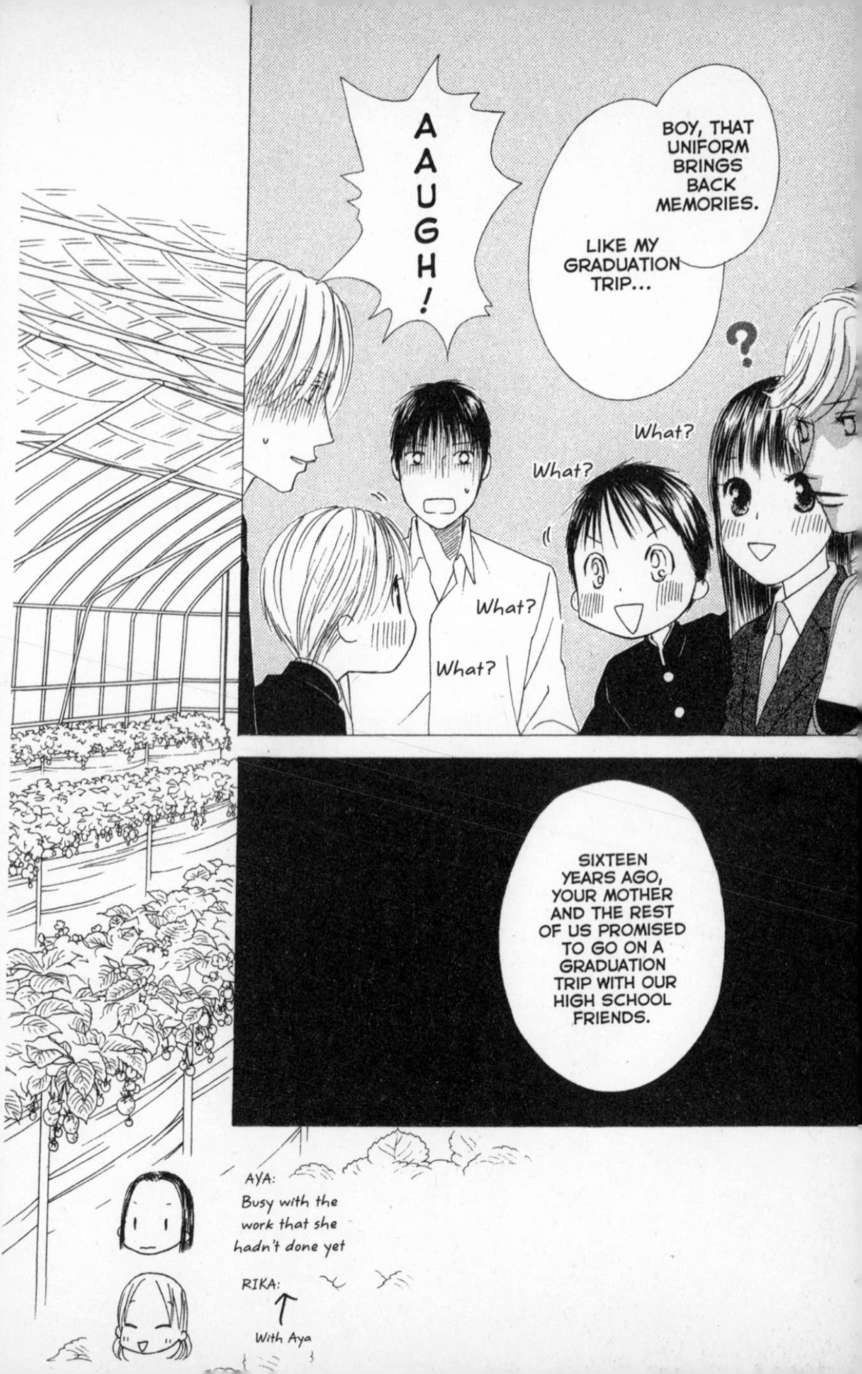
BOY, THAT UNIFORM BRINGS BACK MEMORIES.
LIKE MY GRADUATION TRIP...
?
AAUGH!
What?
What?
What?
What?
SIXTEEN YEARS AGO, YOUR MOTHER AND THE REST OF US PROMISED TO GO ON A GRADUATION TRIP WITH OUR HIGH SCHOOL FRIENDS.
AYA:
Busy with the work that she hadn't done yet
RIKA:
With Aya

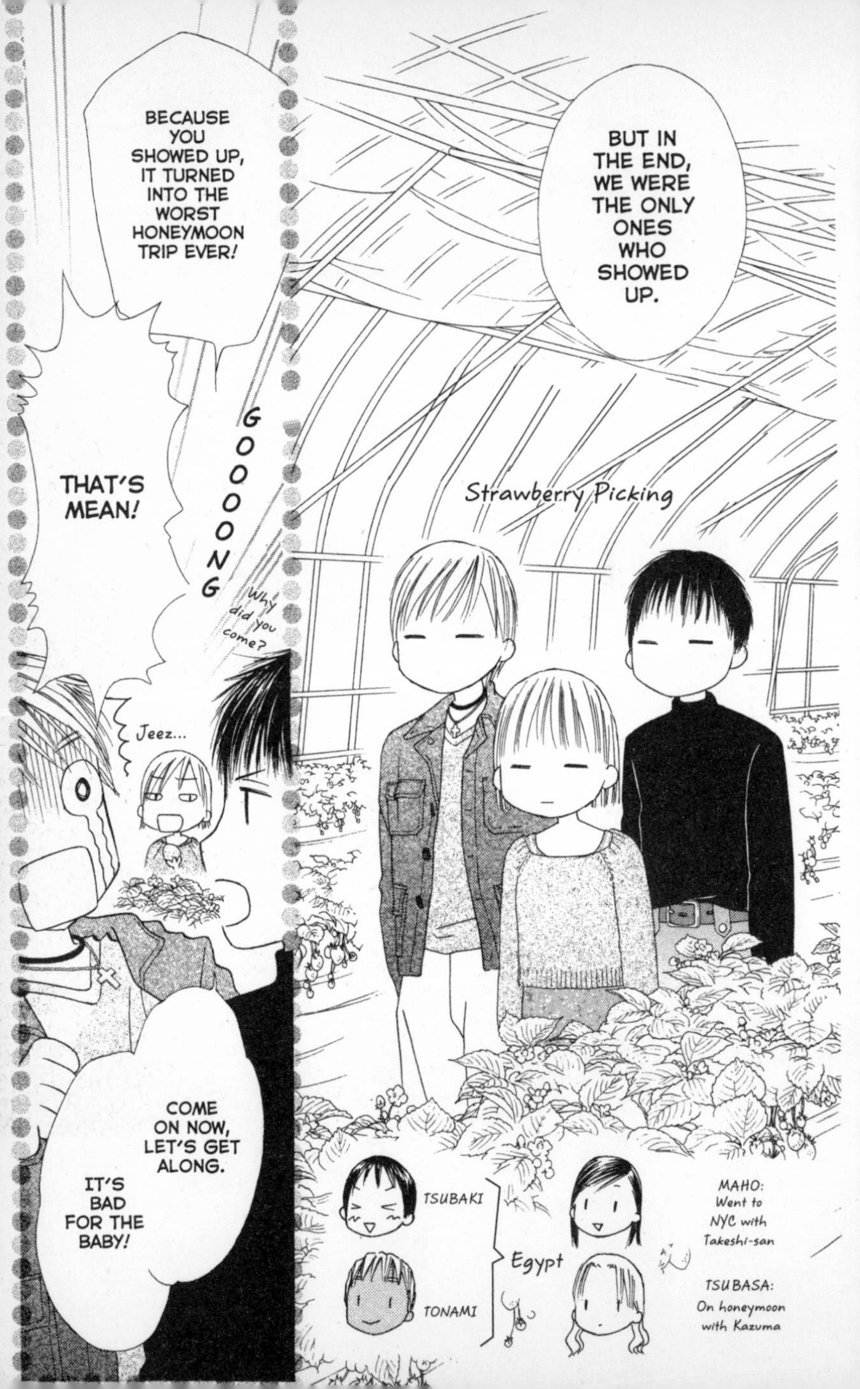
BUT IN THE END, WE WERE THE ONLY ONES WHO SHOWED UP.
Strawberry Picking
MAHO: Went to NYC with Takeshi-san
TSUBASA: On honeymoon with Kazuma
TSUBAKI
TONAMI
Egypt
BECAUSE YOU SHOWED UP, IT TURNED INTO THE WORST HONEYMOON TRIP EVER!
GOOOOONG
THAT'S MEAN!
Why did you come?
Jeez...
COME ON NOW, LET'S GET ALONG.
IT'S BAD FOR THE BABY!

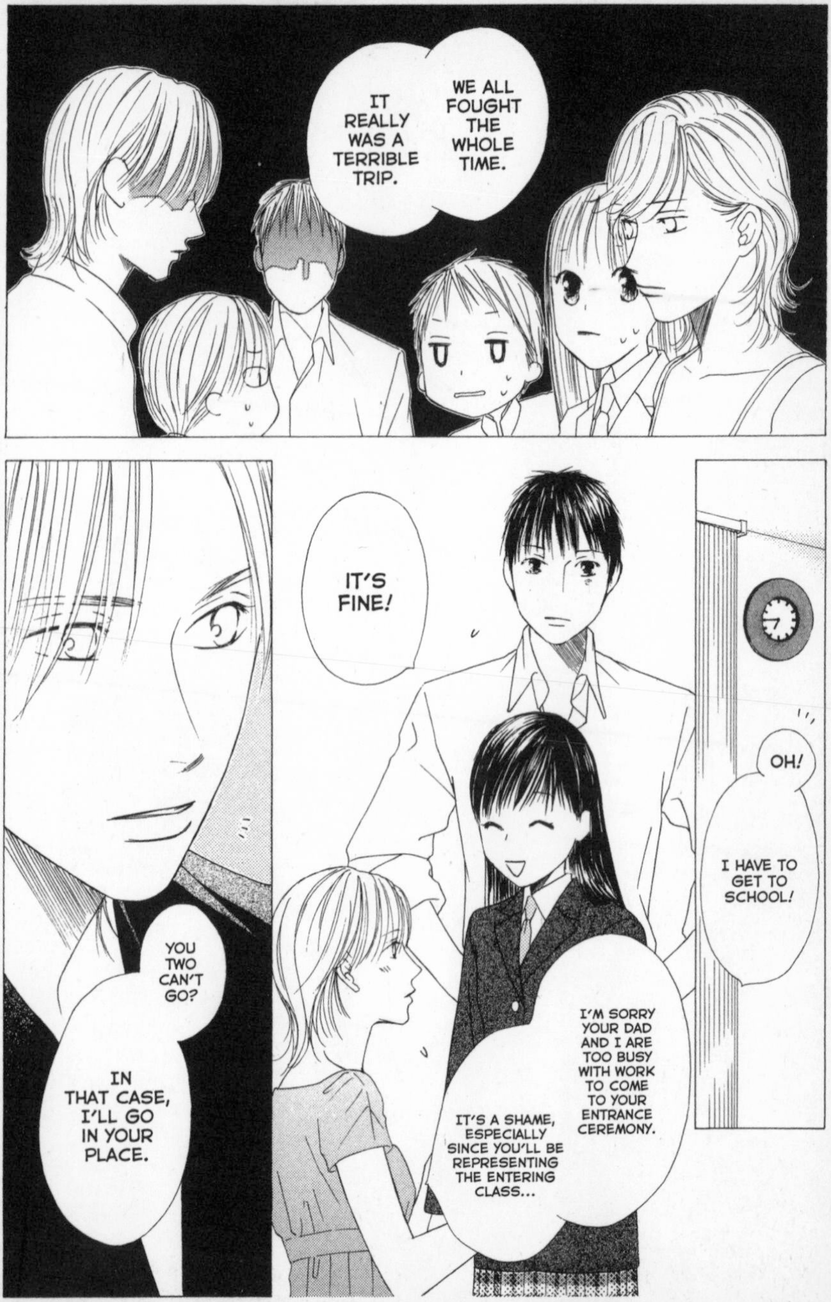
WE ALL FOUGHT THE WHOLE TIME.
IT REALLY WAS A TERRIBLE TRIP.
OH!
I HAVE TO GET TO SCHOOL!
IT'S FINE!
I'M SORRY YOUR DAD AND I ARE TOO BUSY WITH WORK TO COME TO YOUR ENTRANCE CEREMONY.
IT'S A SHAME, ESPECIALLY SINCE YOU'LL BE REPRESENTING THE ENTERING CLASS...
YOU TWO CAN'T GO?
IN THAT CASE, I'LL GO IN YOUR PLACE.

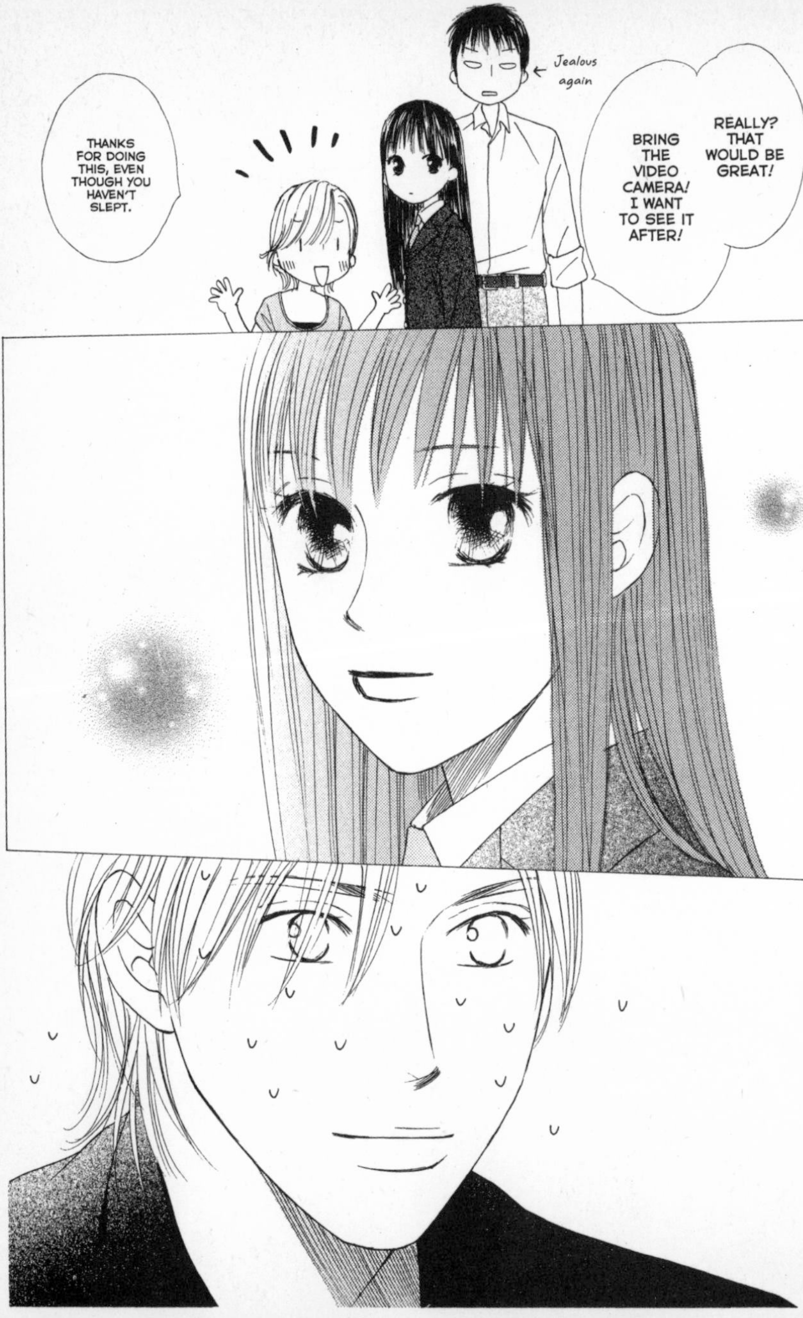
REALLY? THAT WOULD BE GREAT!
BRING THE VIDEO CAMERA! I WANT TO SEE IT AFTER!
Jealous again
THANKS FOR DOING THIS, EVEN THOUGH YOU HAVEN'T SLEPT.

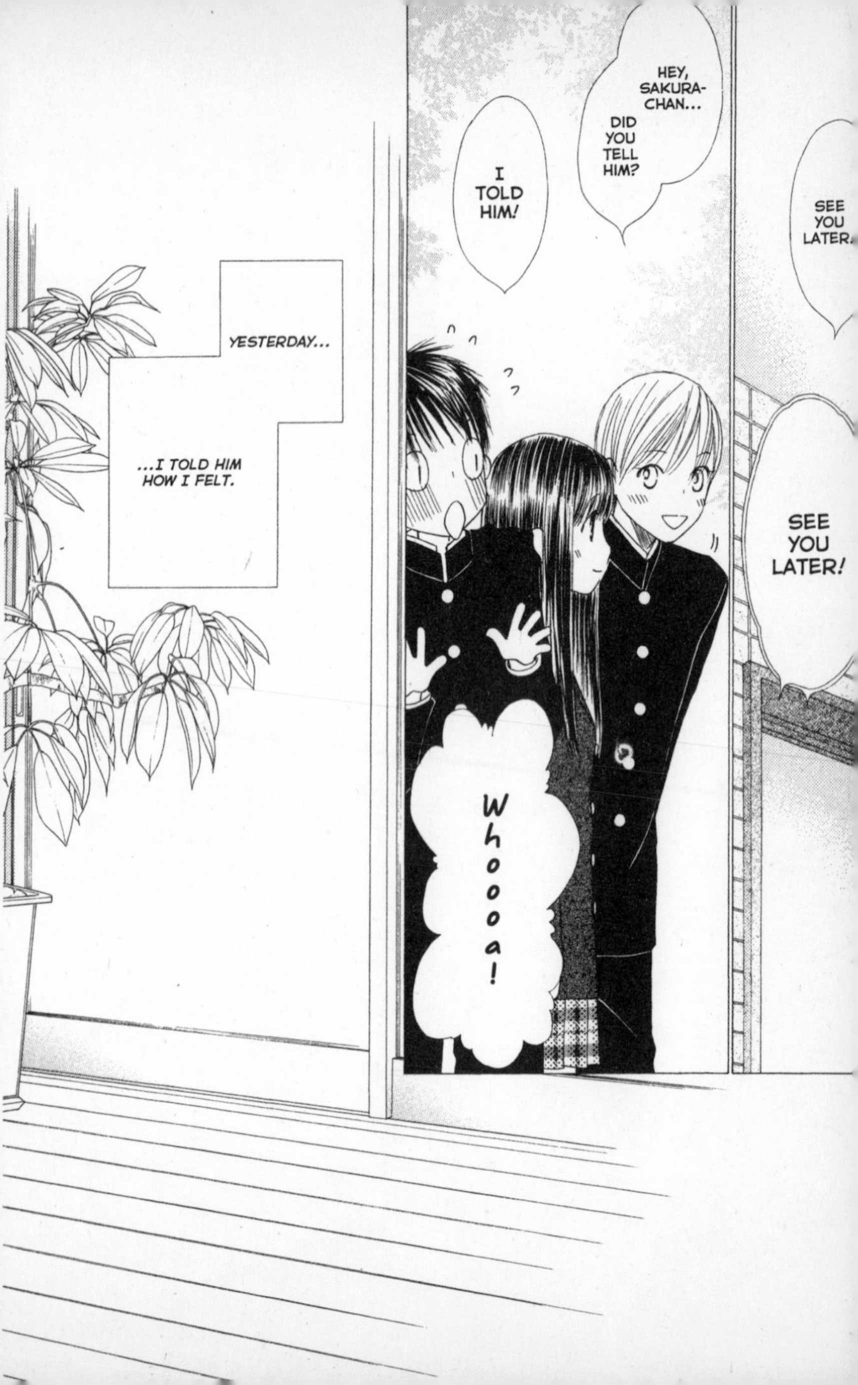
SEE YOU LATER.
HEY, SAKURA-CHAN...
DID YOU TELL HIM?
I TOLD HIM!
SEE YOU LATER!
Whoooa!
YESTERDAY...
...I TOLD HIM HOW I FELT.

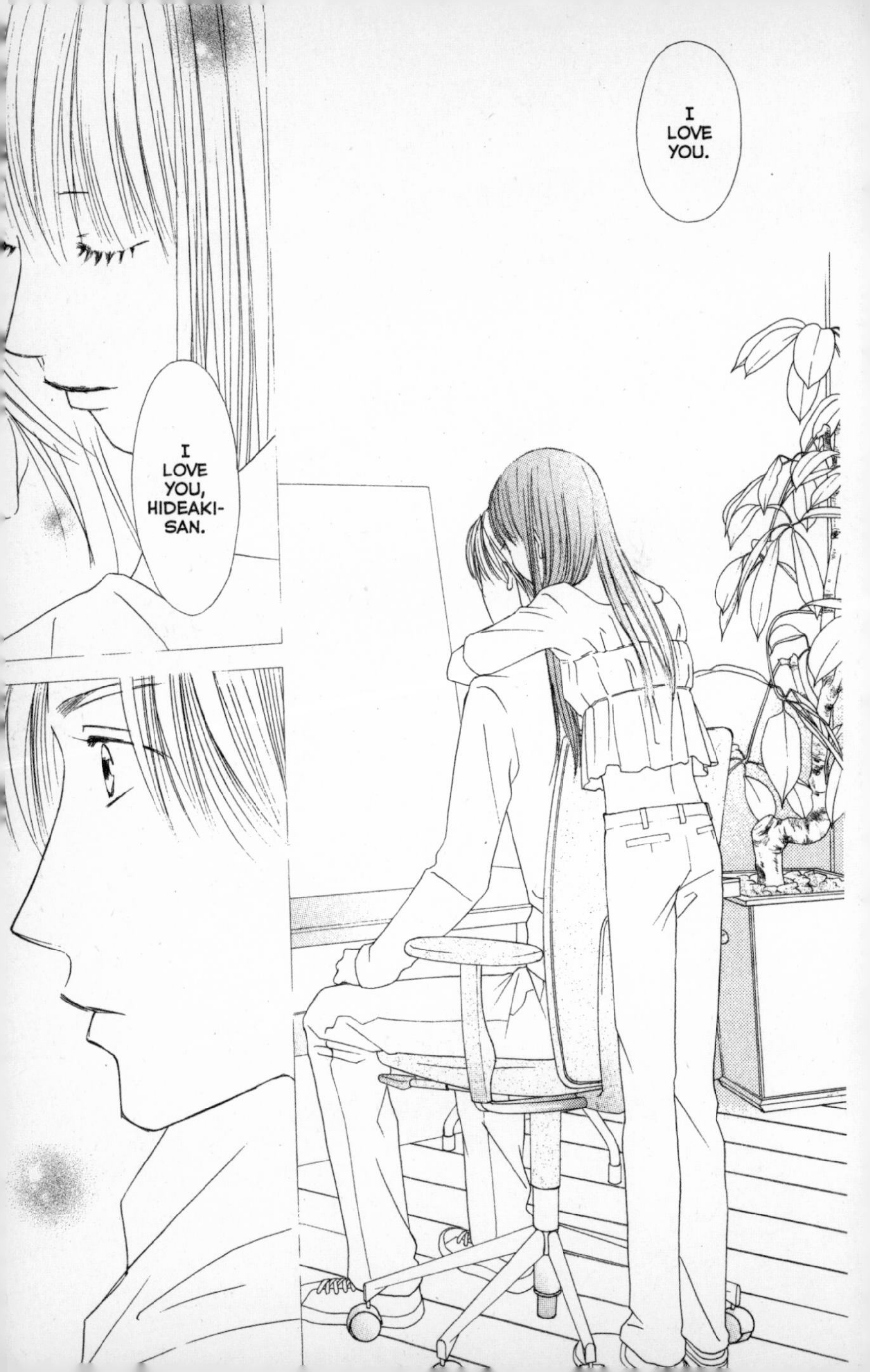
I LOVE YOU.
I LOVE YOU, HIDEAKI-SAN.

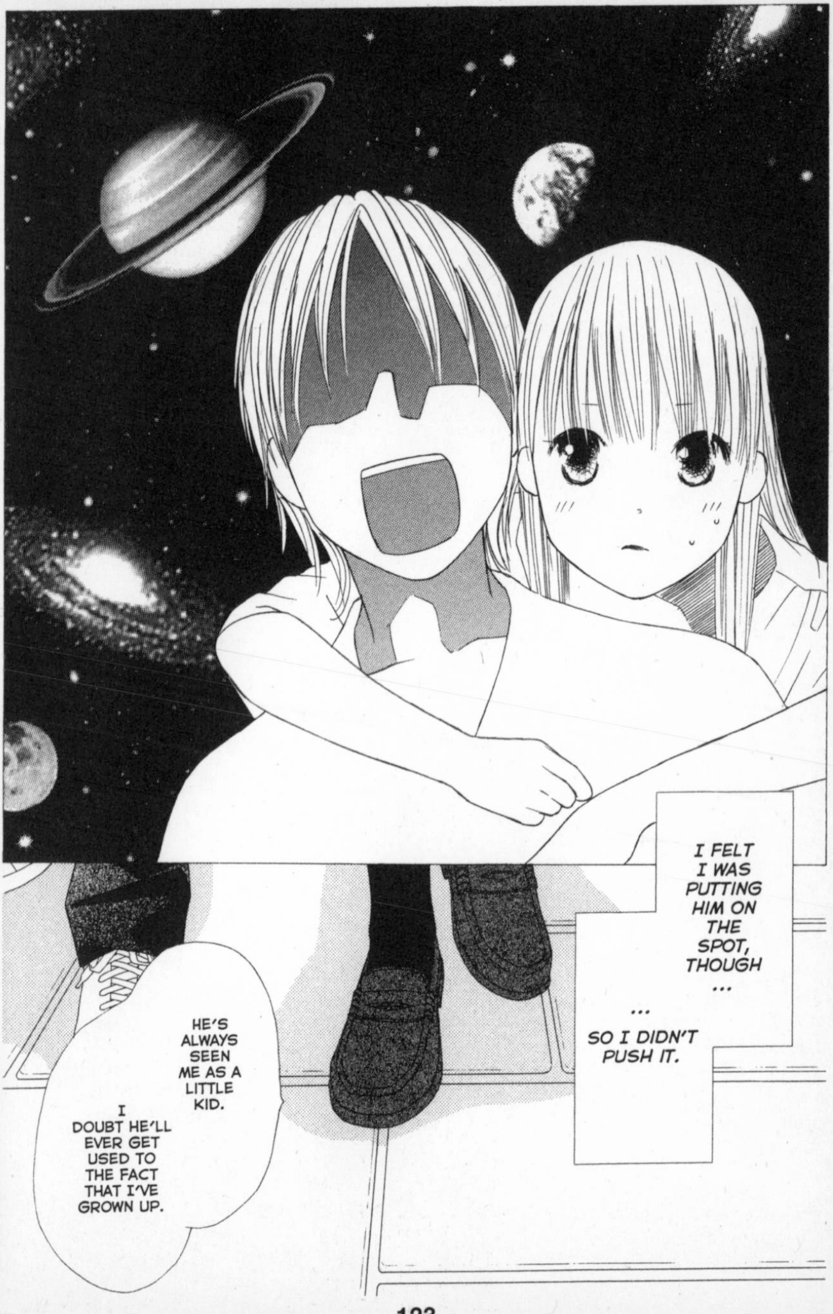
I FELT I WAS PUTTING HIM ON THE SPOT, THOUGH...
... SO I DIDN'T PUSH IT.
HE'S ALWAYS SEEN ME AS A LITTLE KID.
I DOUBT HE'LL EVER GET USED TO THE FACT THAT I'VE GROWN UP.

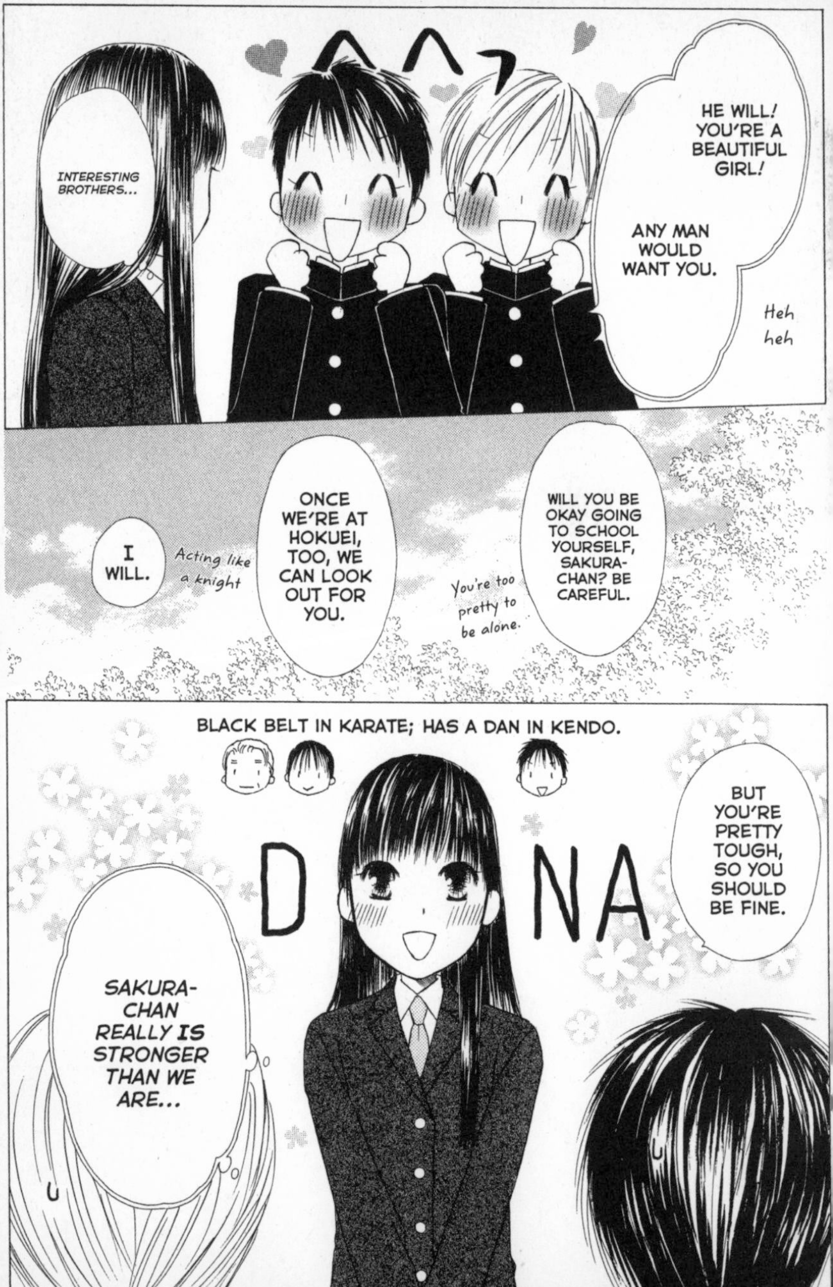
HE WILL! YOU'RE A BEAUTIFUL GIRL!
ANY MAN WOULD WANT YOU.
Heh heh
INTERESTING BROTHERS...
WILL YOU BE OKAY GOING TO SCHOOL YOURSELF, SAKURA-CHAN? BE CAREFUL.
You're too pretty to be alone.
ONCE WE'RE AT HOKUEI, TOO, WE CAN LOOK OUT FOR YOU.
Acting like a knight
I WILL.
BUT YOU'RE PRETTY TOUGH, SO YOU SHOULD BE FINE.
BLACK BELT IN KARATE; HAS A DAN IN KENDO.
D NA
SAKURA-CHAN REALLY IS STRONGER THAN WE ARE...

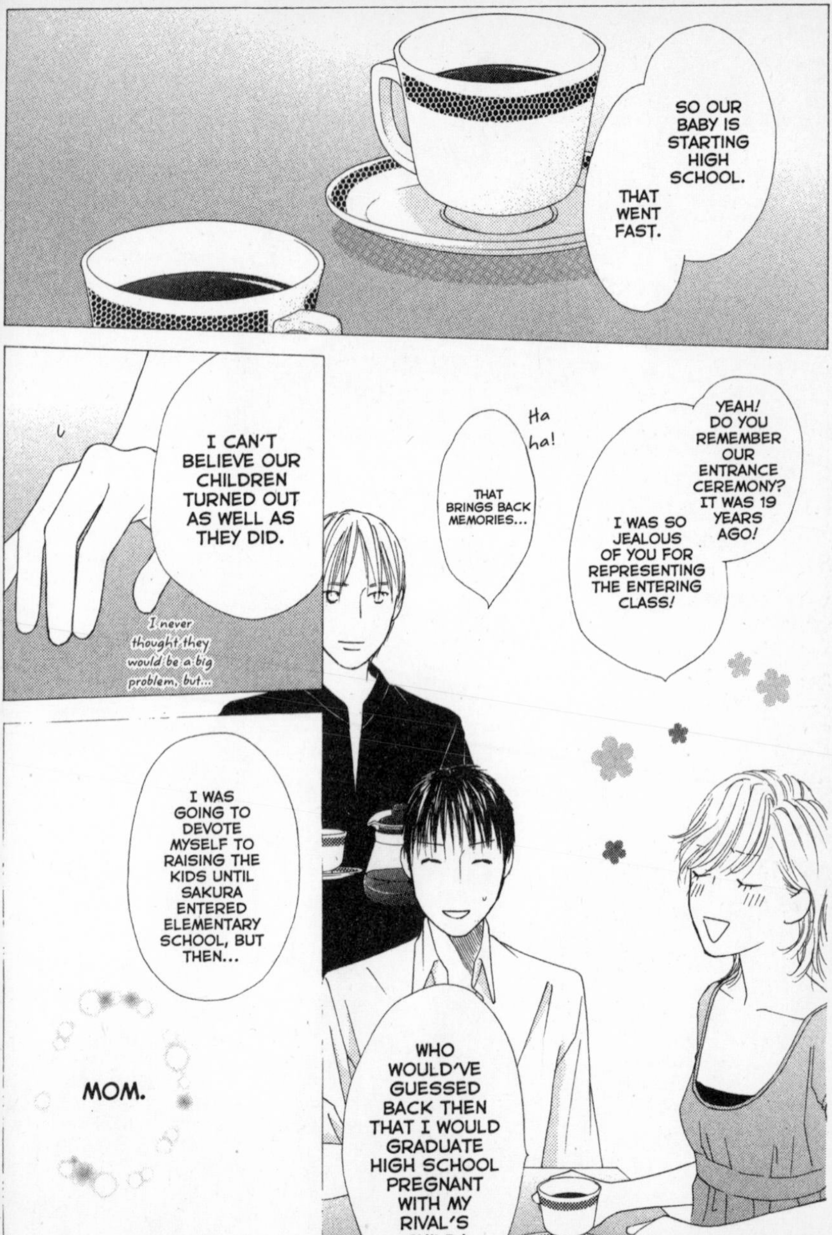
SO OUR BABY IS STARTING HIGH SCHOOL.
THAT WENT FAST.
YEAH! DO YOU REMEMBER OUR ENTRANCE CEREMONY? IT WAS 19 YEARS AGO!
I WAS SO JEALOUS OF YOU FOR REPRESENTING THE ENTERING CLASS!
Ha ha!
THAT BRINGS BACK MEMORIES...
WHO WOULD'VE GUESSED BACK THEN THAT I WOULD GRADUATE HIGH SCHOOL PREGNANT WITH MY RIVAL'S CHILD!
I CAN'T BELIEVE OUR CHILDREN TURNED OUT AS WELL AS THEY DID.
I never thought they would be a big problem, but...
I WAS GOING TO DEVOTE MYSELF TO RAISING THE KIDS UNTIL SAKURA ENTERED ELEMENTARY SCHOOL, BUT THEN...
MOM.

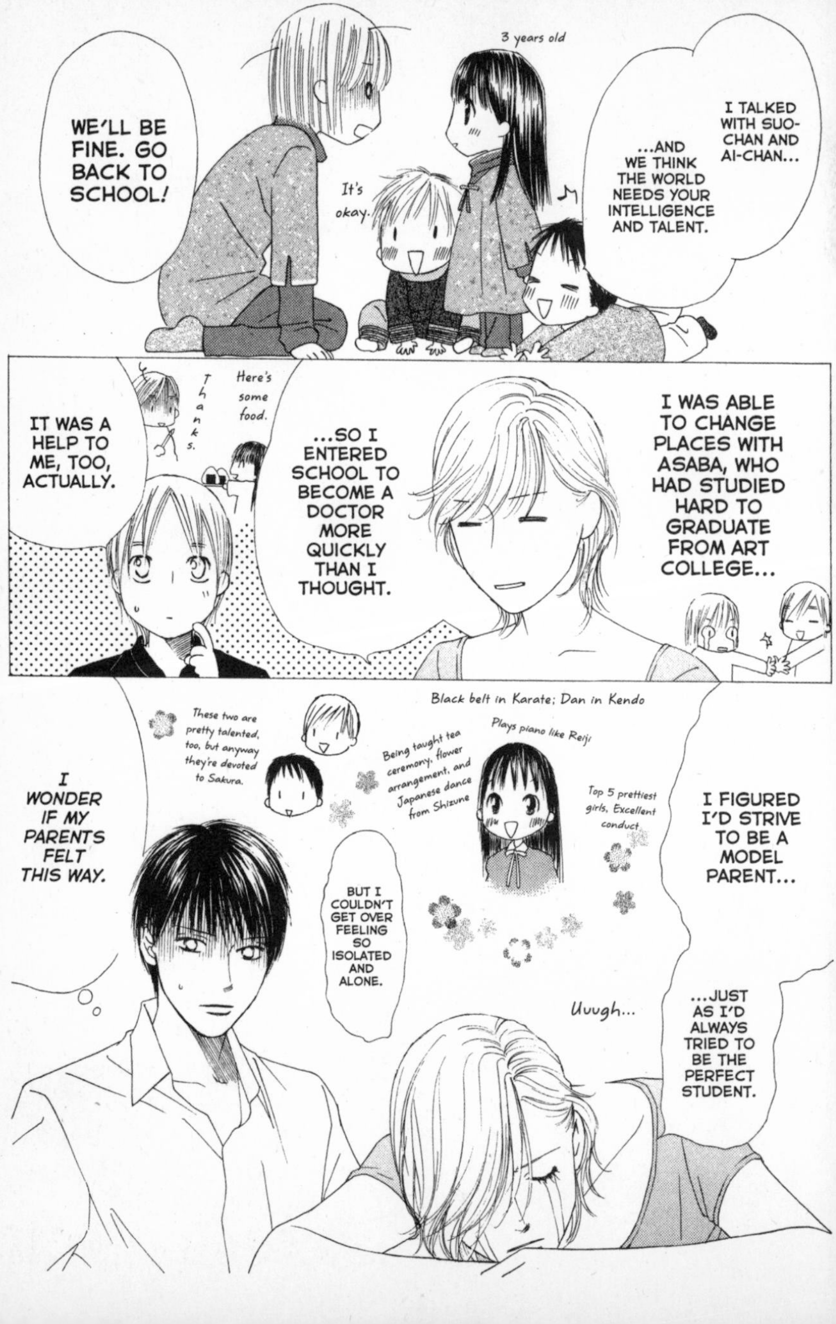
I TALKED WITH SUO-CHAN AND AI-CHAN...
...AND WE THINK THE WORLD NEEDS YOUR INTELLIGENCE AND TALENT.
3 years old
It's okay.
WE'LL BE FINE. GO BACK TO SCHOOL!
I WAS ABLE TO CHANGE PLACES WITH ASABA, WHO HAD STUDIED HARD TO GRADUATE FROM ART COLLEGE...
...SO I ENTERED SCHOOL TO BECOME A DOCTOR MORE QUICKLY THAN I THOUGHT.
Here's some food.
Thanks.
IT WAS A HELP TO ME, TOO, ACTUALLY.
I FIGURED I'D STRIVE TO BE A MODEL PARENT...
Black belt in Karate; Dan in Kendo
Plays piano like Reiji
Top 5 prettiest girls, Excellent conduct
Being taught tea ceremony, flower arrangement, and Japanese dance from Shizune
These two are pretty talented, too, but anyway they're devoted to Sakura.
...JUST AS I'D ALWAYS TRIED TO BE THE PERFECT STUDENT.
Uuugh...
BUT I COULDN'T GET OVER FEELING SO ISOLATED AND ALONE.
I WONDER IF MY PARENTS FELT THIS WAY.

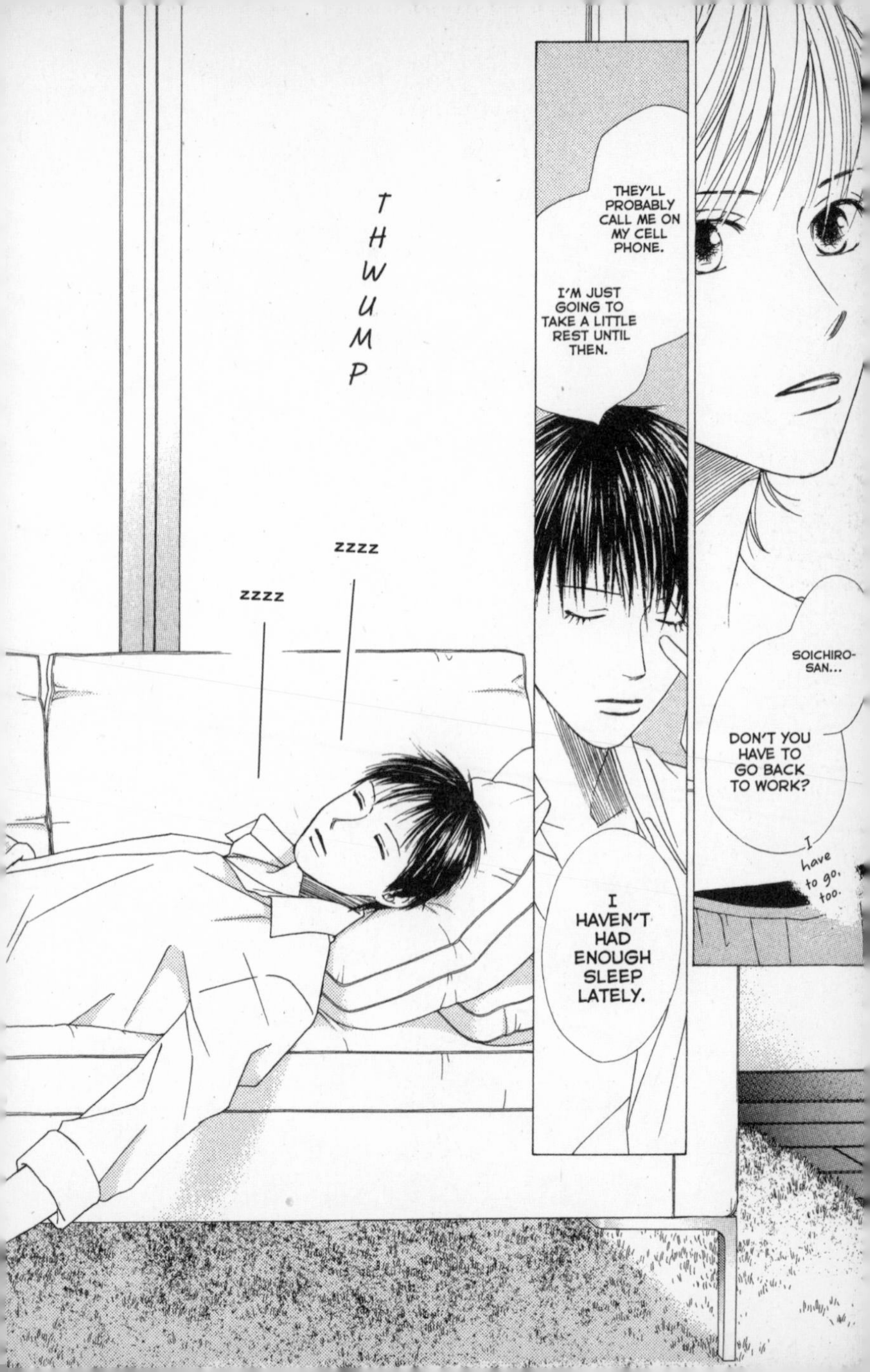
SOICHIRO-SAN...
DON'T YOU HAVE TO GO BACK TO WORK?
I have to go, too.
THEY'LL PROBABLY CALL ME ON MY CELL PHONE.
I'M JUST GOING TO TAKE A LITTLE REST UNTIL THEN.
I HAVEN'T HAD ENOUGH SLEEP LATELY.
THWUMP
zzzz
zzzz

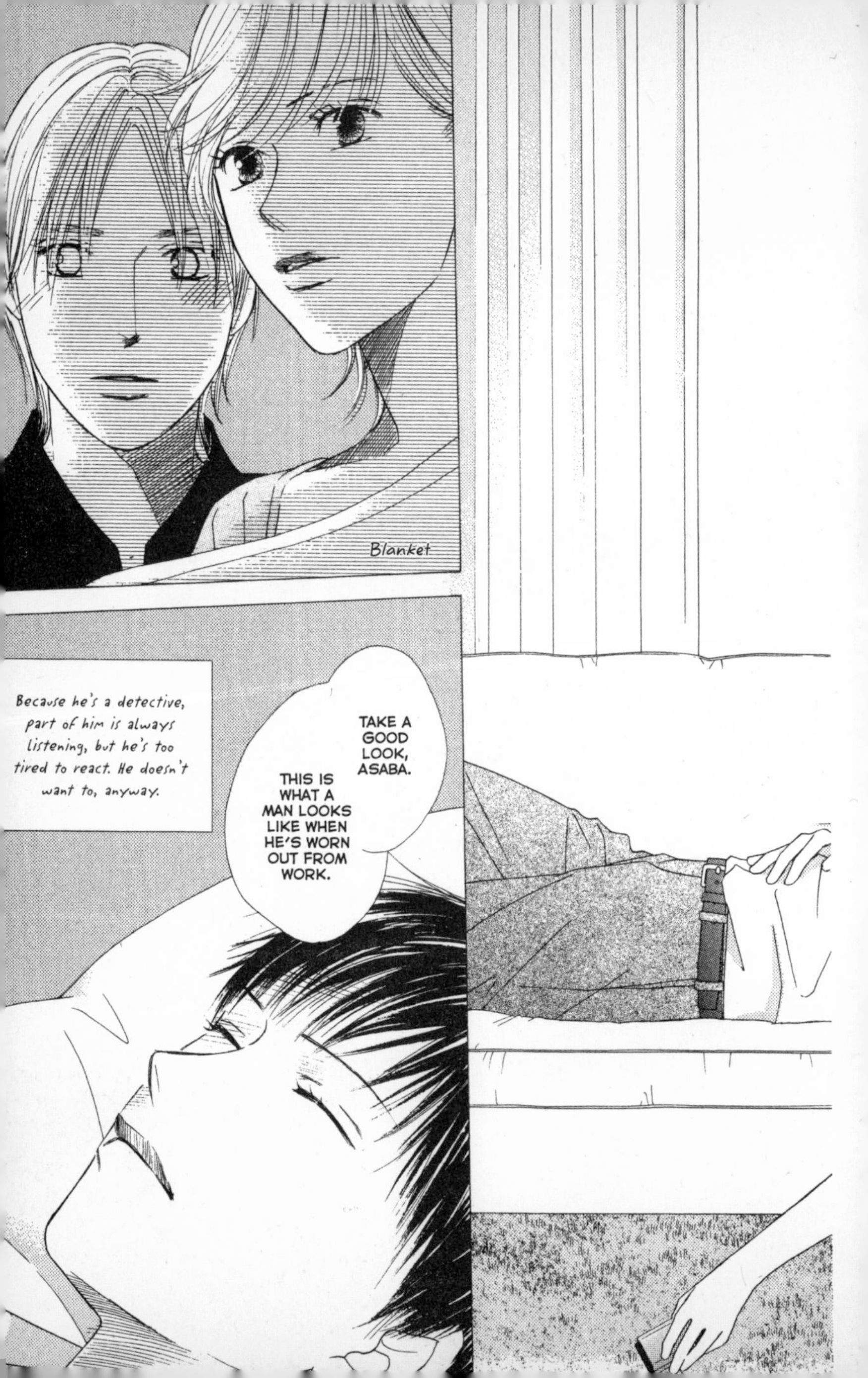
Blanket
TAKE A GOOD LOOK, ASABA. THIS IS WHAT A MAN LOOKS LIKE WHEN HE'S WORN OUT FROM WORK.
Because he's a detective, part of him is always listening, but he's too tired to react. He doesn't want to, anyway.

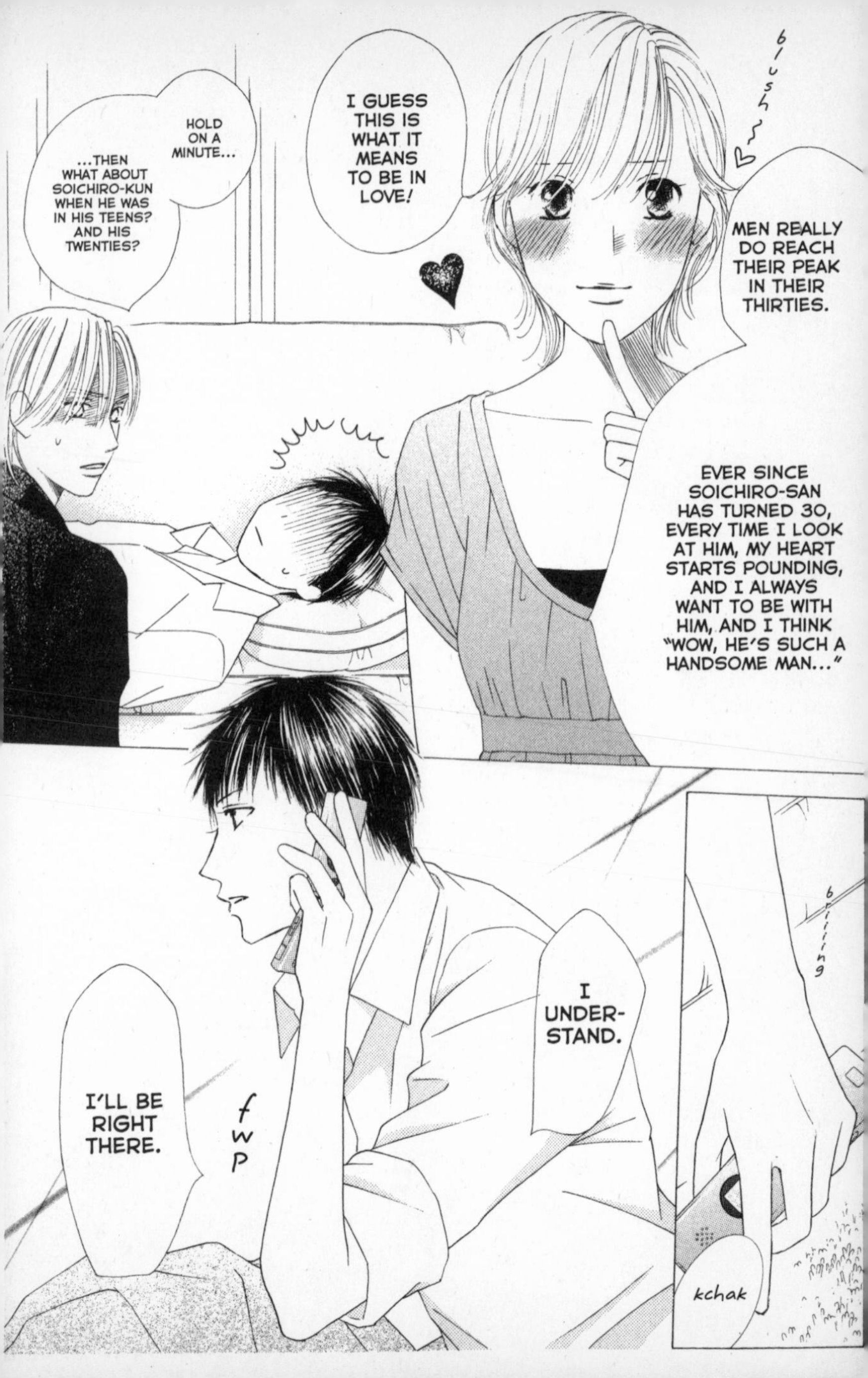
blush~~
MEN REALLY DO REACH THEIR PEAK IN THEIR THIRTIES.
EVER SINCE SOICHIRO-SAN HAS TURNED 30, EVERY TIME I LOOK AT HIM, MY HEART STARTS POUNDING, AND I ALWAYS WANT TO BE WITH HIM, AND I THINK "WOW, HE'S SUCH A HANDSOME MAN..."
I GUESS THIS IS WHAT IT MEANS TO BE IN LOVE!
HOLD ON A MINUTE...
...THEN WHAT ABOUT SOICHIRO-KUN WHEN HE WAS IN HIS TEENS? AND HIS TWENTIES?
briiiing
kchak
I UNDER-STAND.
fwp
I'LL BE RIGHT THERE.

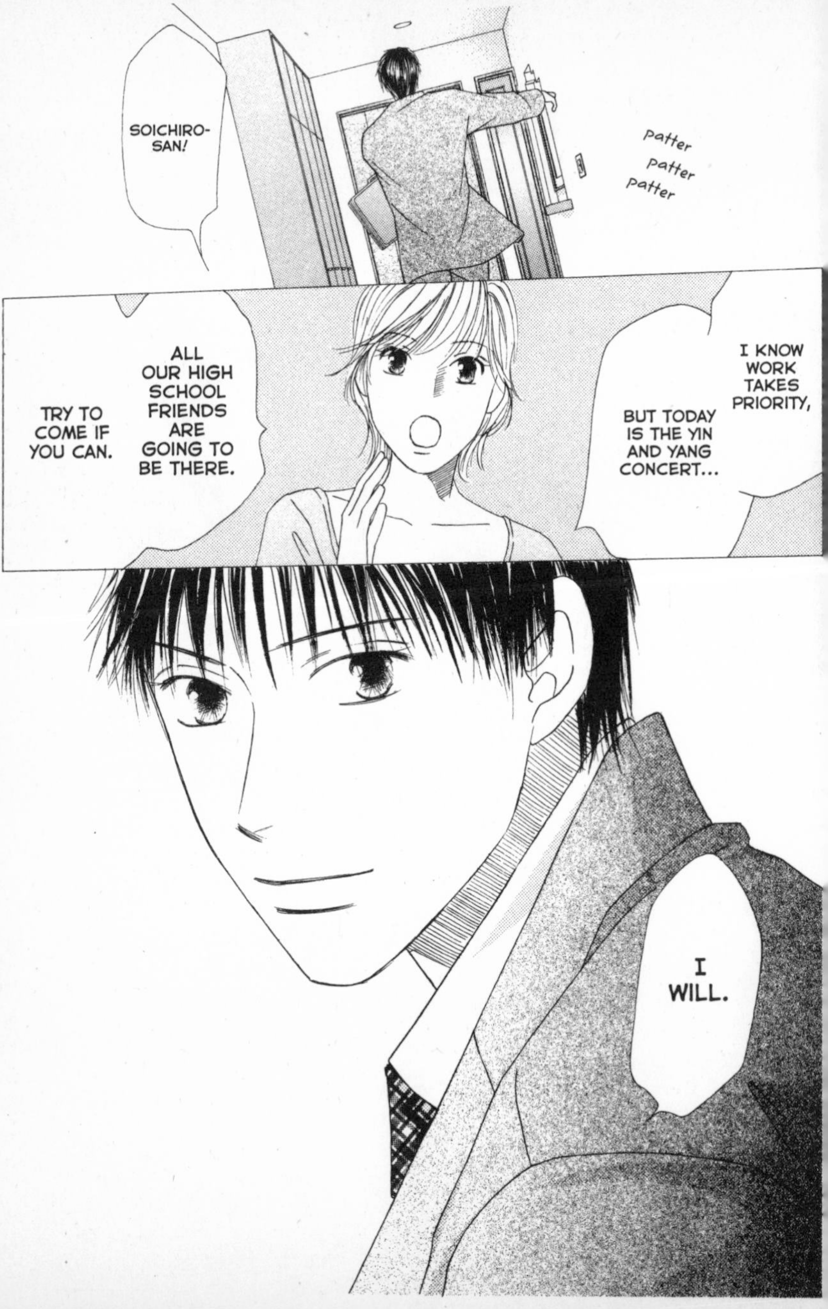
patter patter patter
SOICHIRO-SAN!
I KNOW WORK TAKES PRIORITY,
BUT TODAY IS THE YIN AND YANG CONCERT...
ALL OUR HIGH SCHOOL FRIENDS ARE GOING TO BE THERE.
TRY TO COME IF YOU CAN.
I WILL.

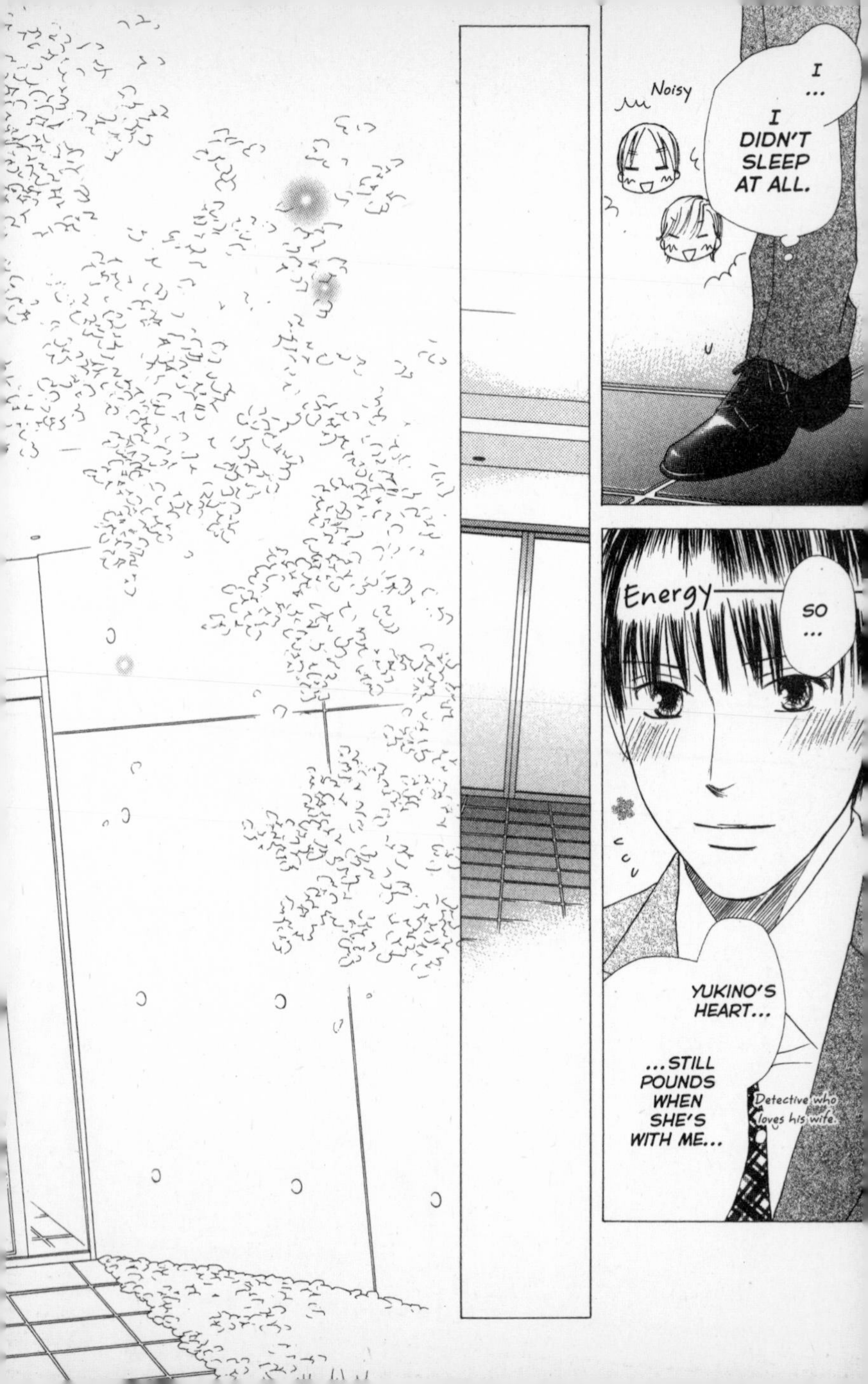
I
...
I DIDN'T SLEEP AT ALL.
Noisy
Energy
SO
...
YUKINO'S HEART...
...STILL POUNDS WHEN SHE'S WITH ME...
Detective who loves his wife.

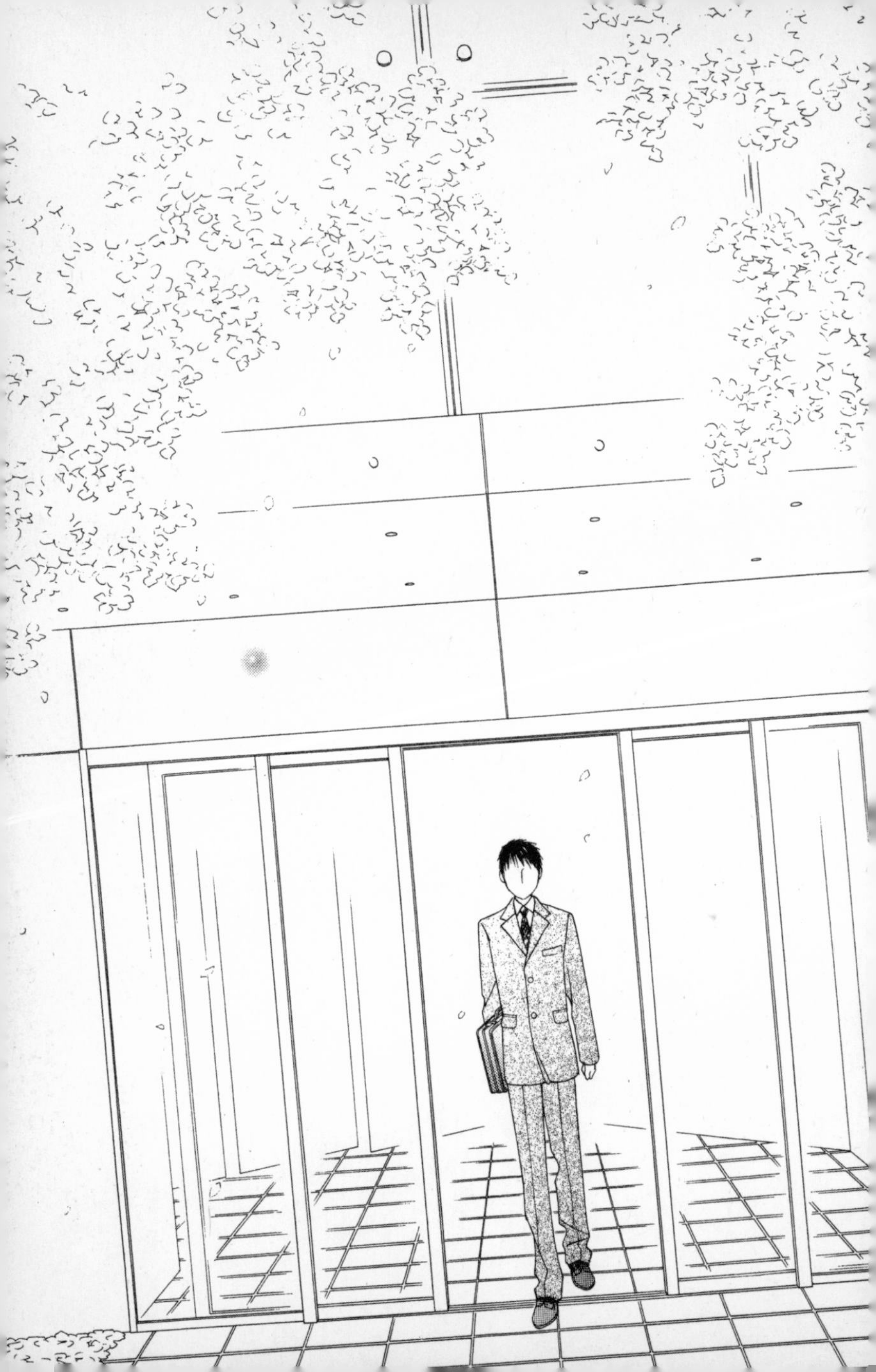

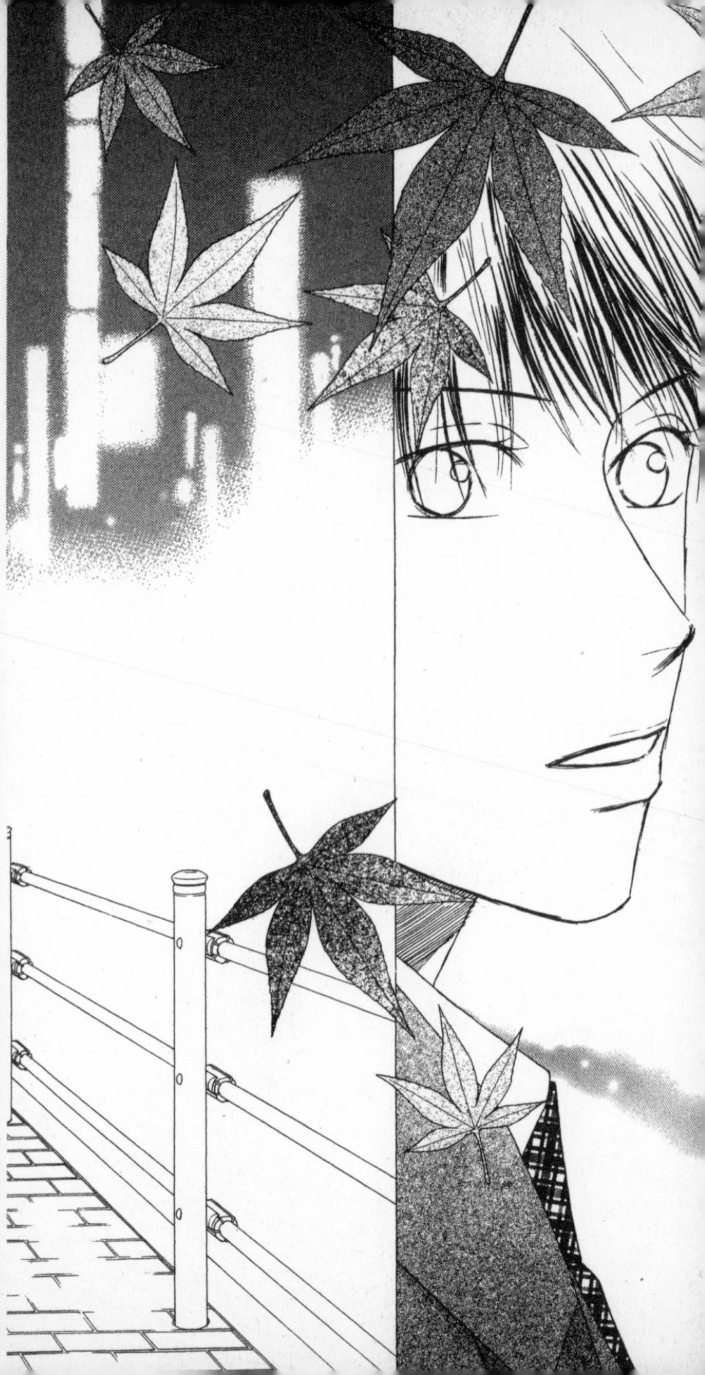

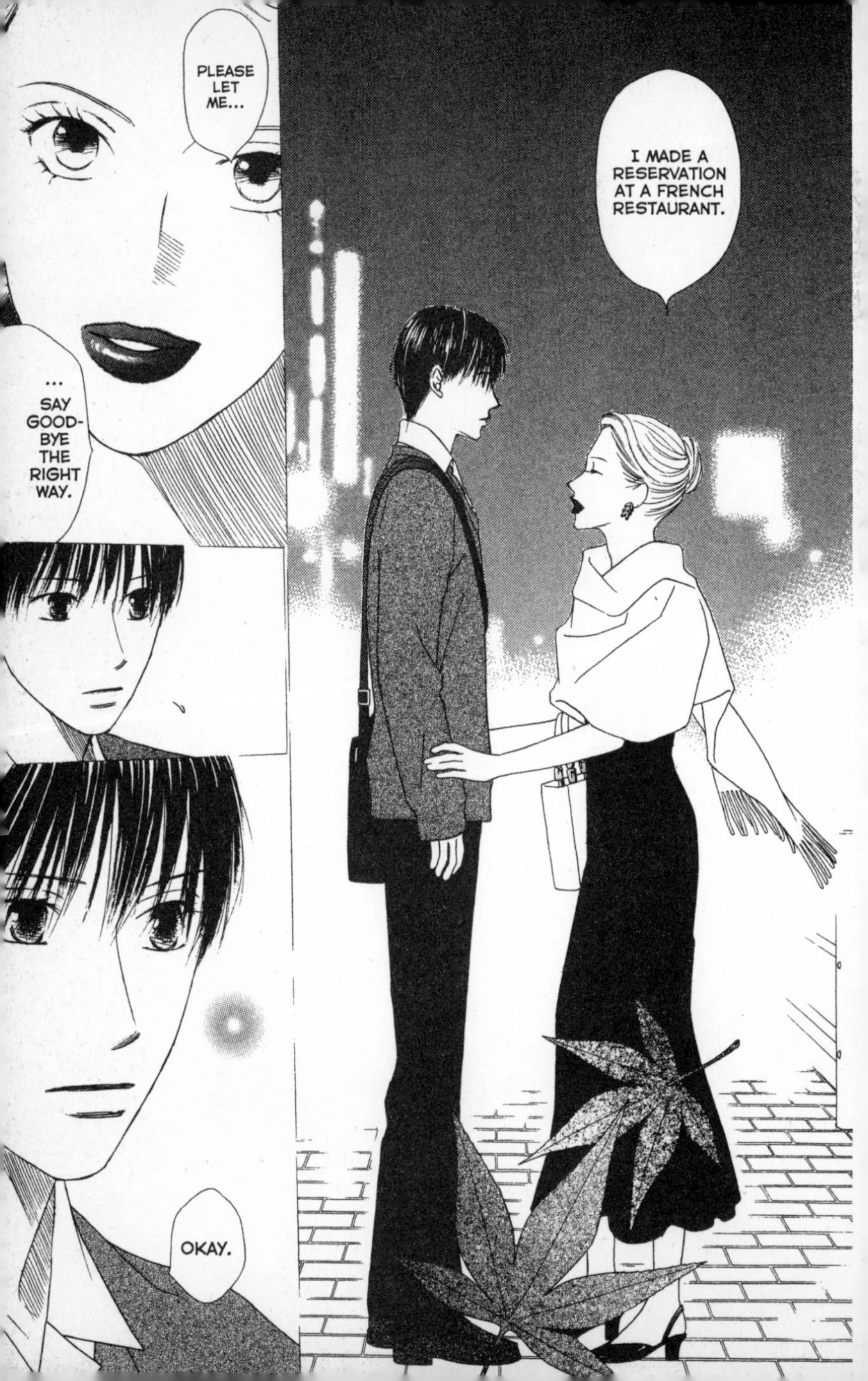
I MADE A RESERVATION AT A FRENCH RESTAURANT.
PLEASE LET ME...
... SAY GOOD-BYE THE RIGHT WAY.
OKAY.

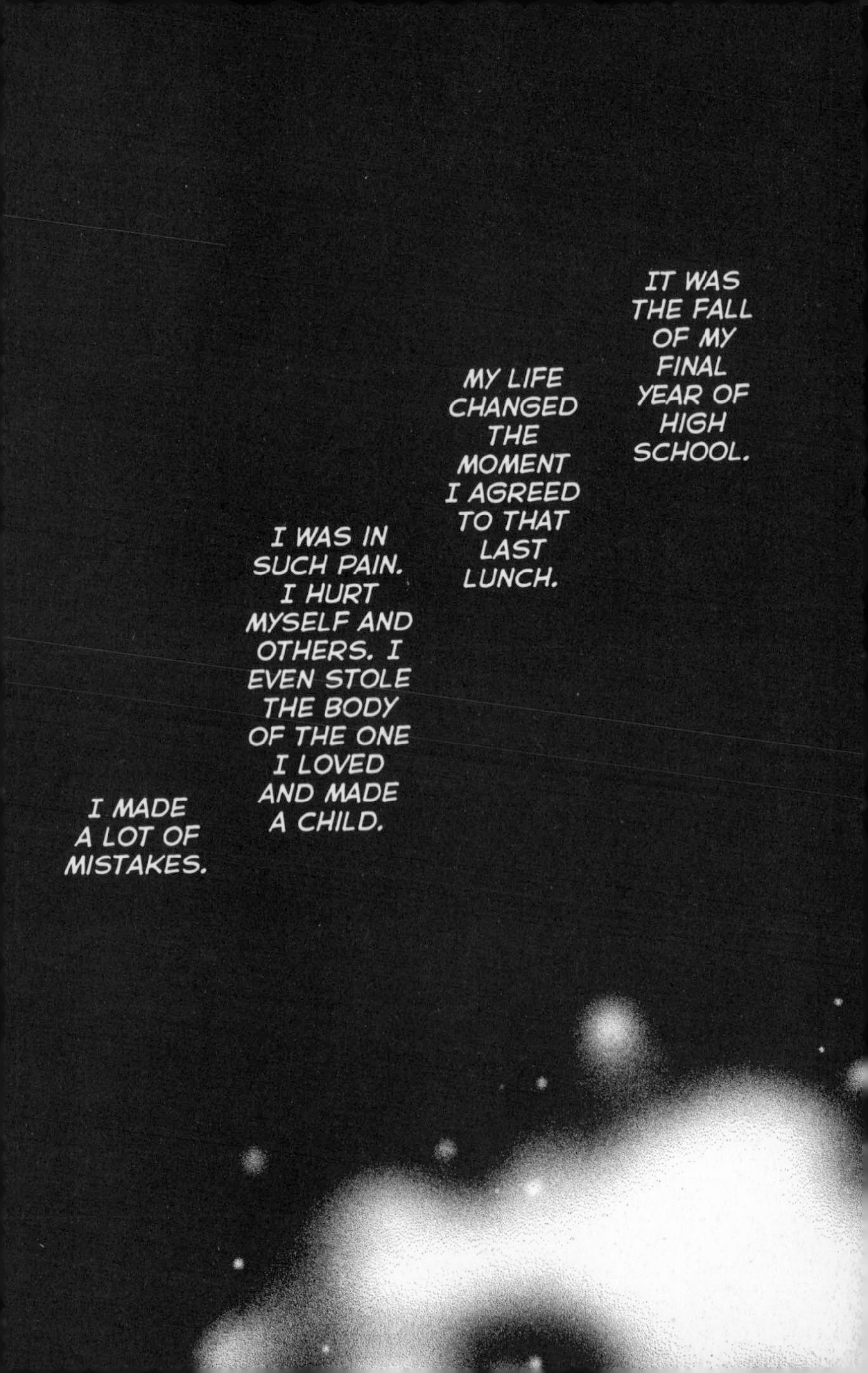
IT WAS THE FALL OF MY FINAL YEAR OF HIGH SCHOOL.
MY LIFE CHANGED THE MOMENT I AGREED TO THAT LAST LUNCH.
I WAS IN SUCH PAIN. I HURT MYSELF AND OTHERS. I EVEN STOLE THE BODY OF THE ONE I LOVED AND MADE A CHILD.
I MADE A LOT OF MISTAKES.

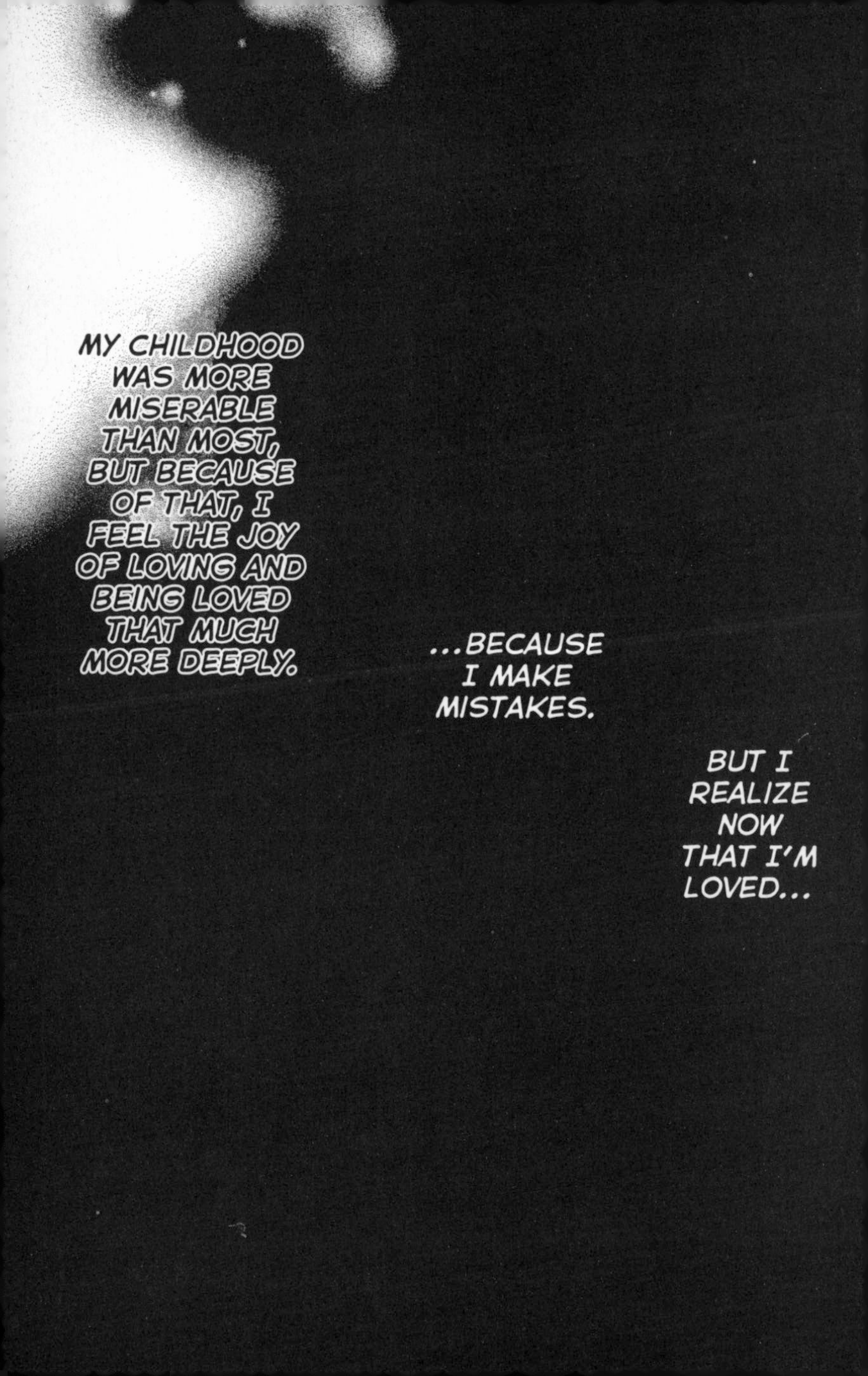
BUT I REALIZE NOW THAT I'M LOVED...
...BECAUSE I MAKE MISTAKES.
MY CHILDHOOD WAS MORE MISERABLE THAN MOST, BUT BECAUSE OF THAT, I FEEL THE JOY OF LOVING AND BEING LOVED THAT MUCH MORE DEEPLY.

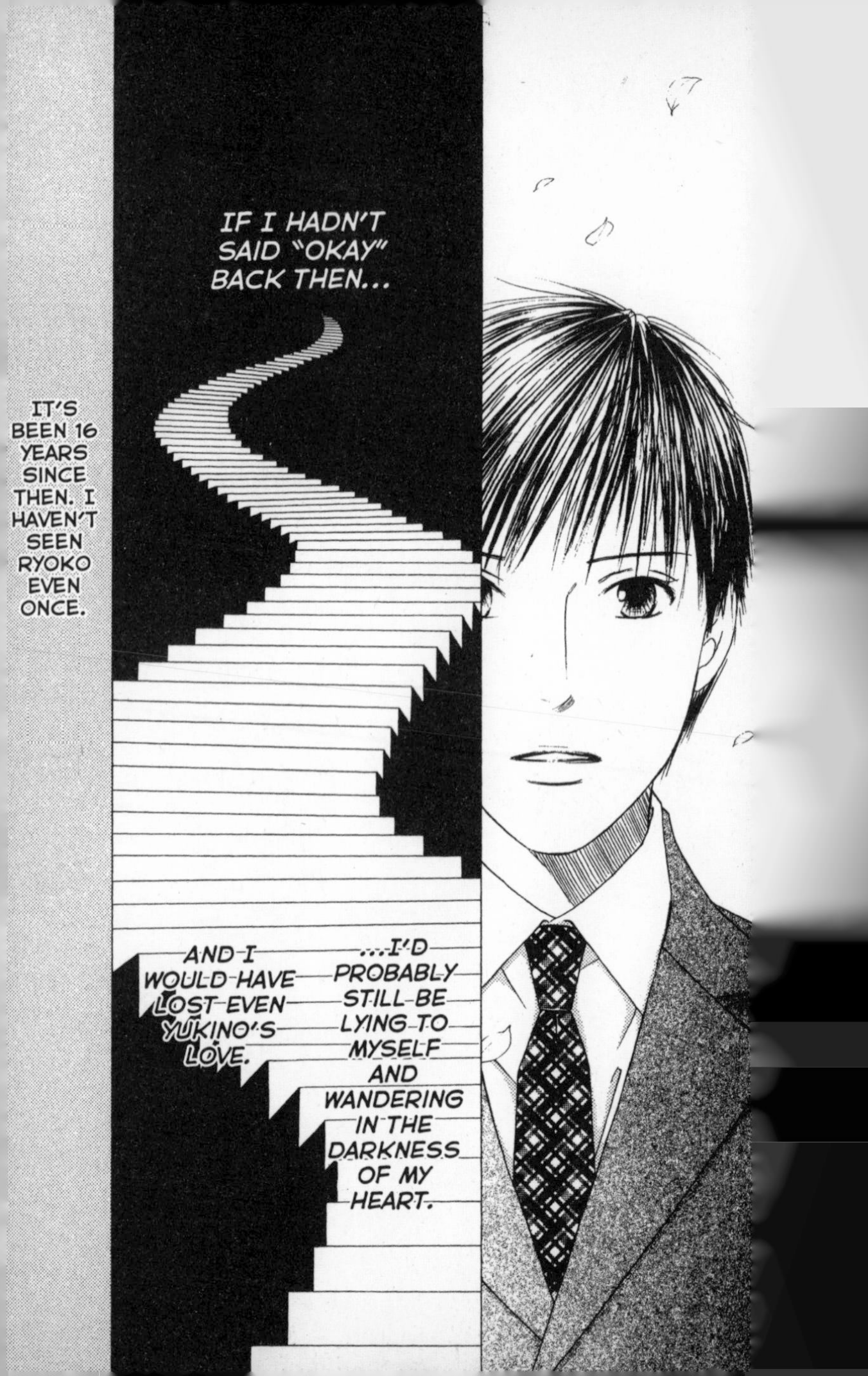
IF I HADN'T SAID "OKAY" BACK THEN...
...I'D PROBABLY STILL BE LYING TO MYSELF AND WANDERING IN THE DARKNESS OF MY HEART.
AND I WOULD HAVE LOST EVEN YUKINO'S LOVE.
IT'S BEEN 16 YEARS SINCE THEN. I HAVEN'T SEEN RYOKO EVEN ONCE.

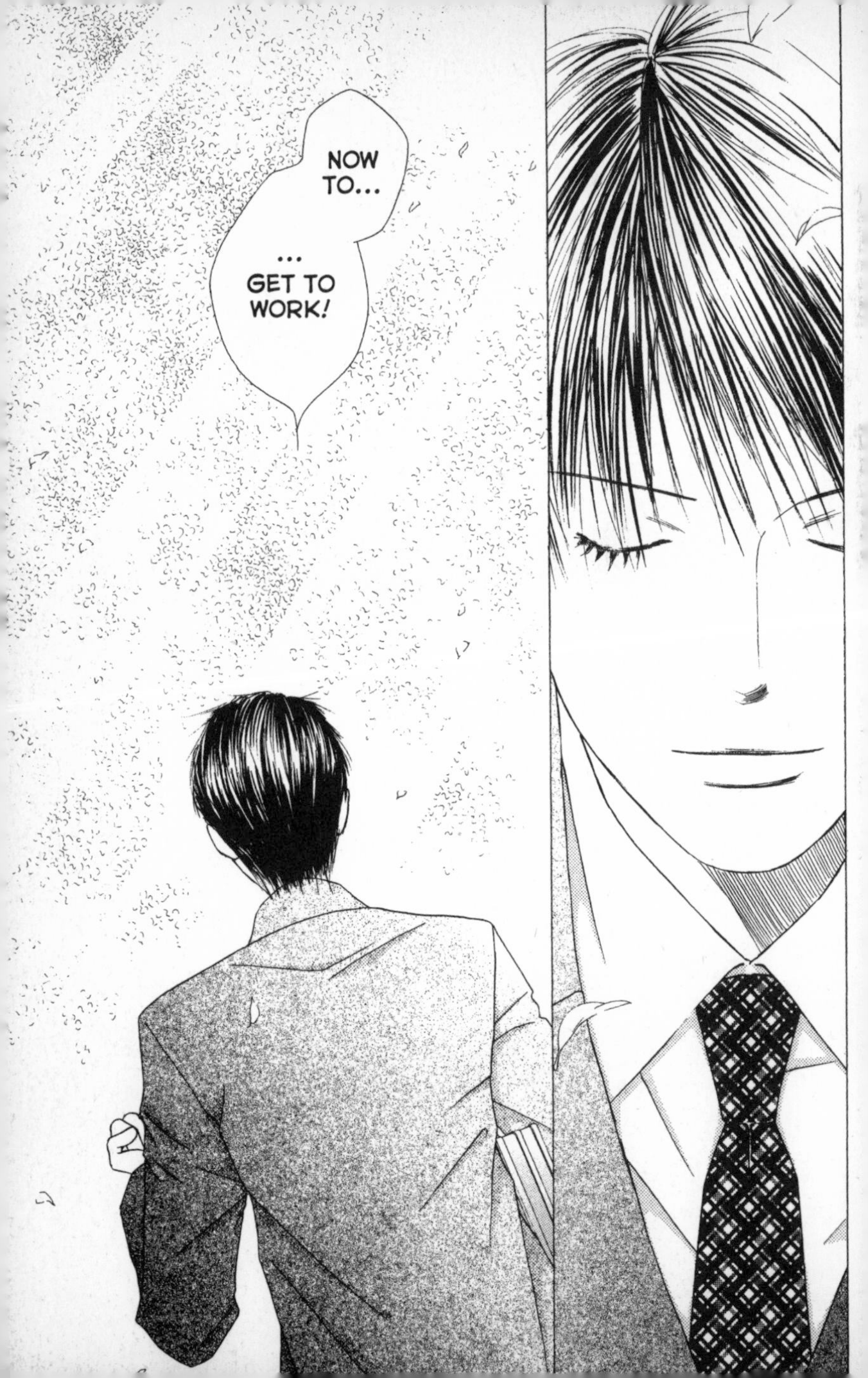
NOW TO...
... GET TO WORK!

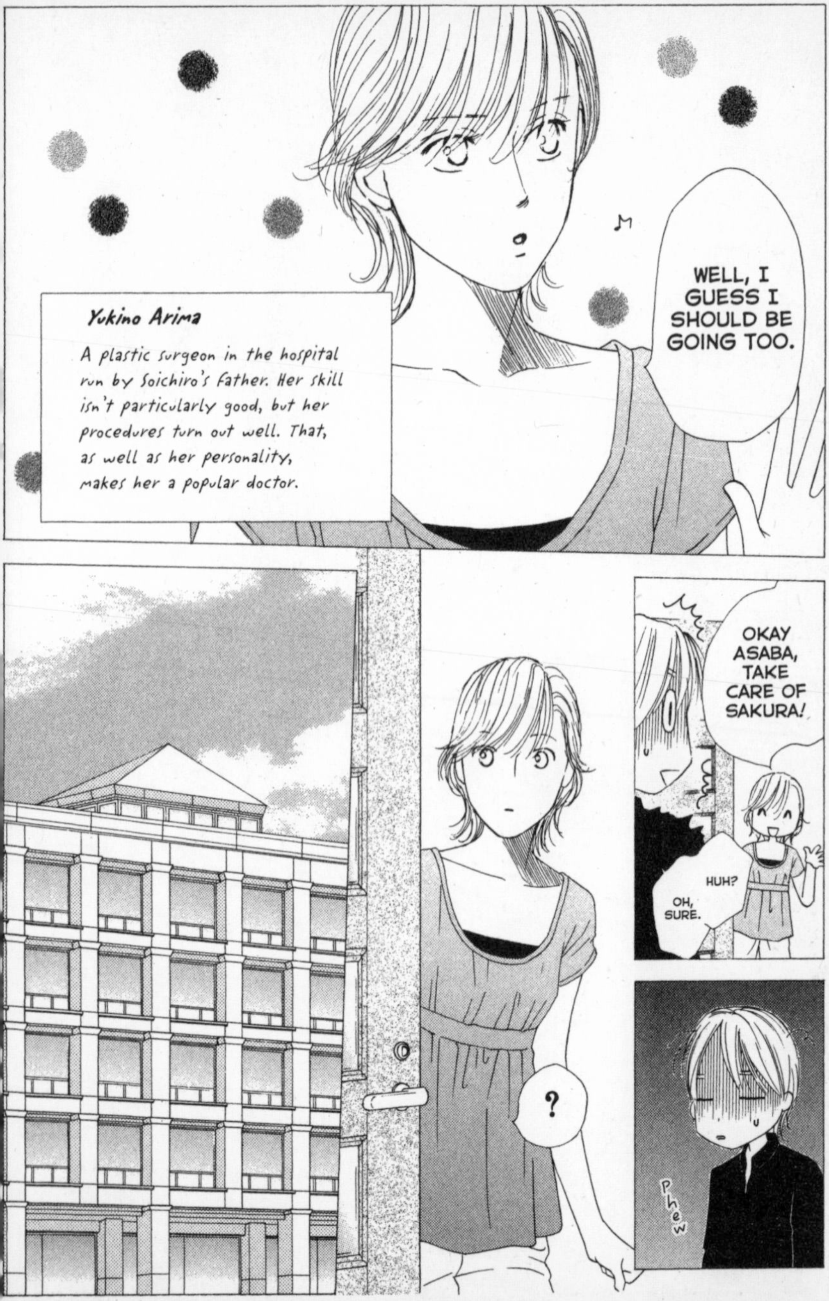
♪
WELL, I GUESS I SHOULD BE GOING TOO.
Yukino Arima
A plastic surgeon in the hospital run by Soichiro's father. Her skill isn't particularly good, but her procedures turn out well. That, as well as her personality, makes her a popular doctor.
OKAY ASABA, TAKE CARE OF SAKURA!
HUH?
OH, SURE.
Phew
?

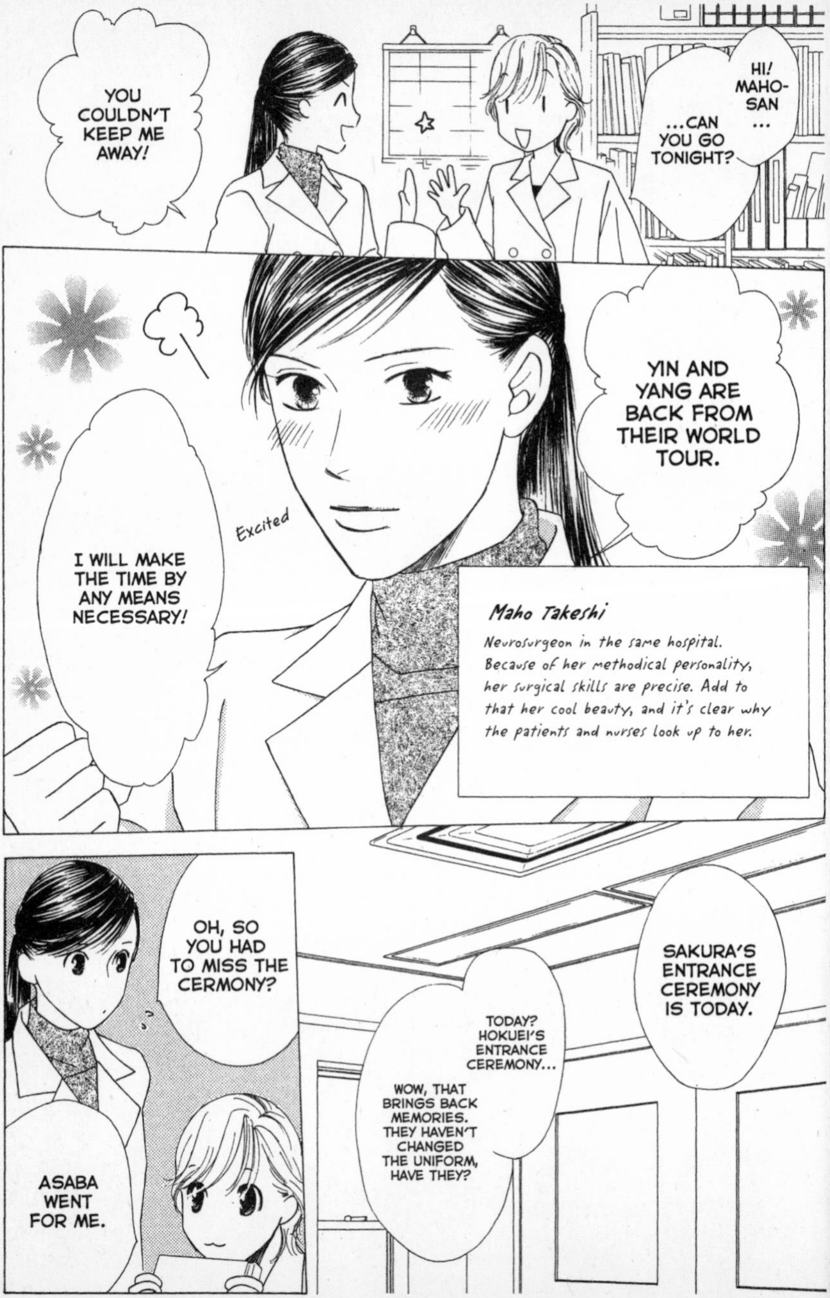
HI! MAHO-SAN...
...CAN YOU GO TONIGHT?
YOU COULDN'T KEEP ME AWAY!
YIN AND YANG ARE BACK FROM THEIR WORLD TOUR.
Excited
I WILL MAKE THE TIME BY ANY MEANS NECESSARY!
Maho Takeshi
Neurosurgeon in the same hospital. Because of her methodical personality, her surgical skills are precise. Add to that her cool beauty, and it's clear why the patients and nurses look up to her.
SAKURA'S ENTRANCE CEREMONY IS TODAY.
TODAY? HOKUEI'S ENTRANCE CEREMONY...
WOW, THAT BRINGS BACK MEMORIES. THEY HAVEN'T CHANGED THE UNIFORM, HAVE THEY?
OH, SO YOU HAD TO MISS THE CERMONY?
ASABA WENT FOR ME.

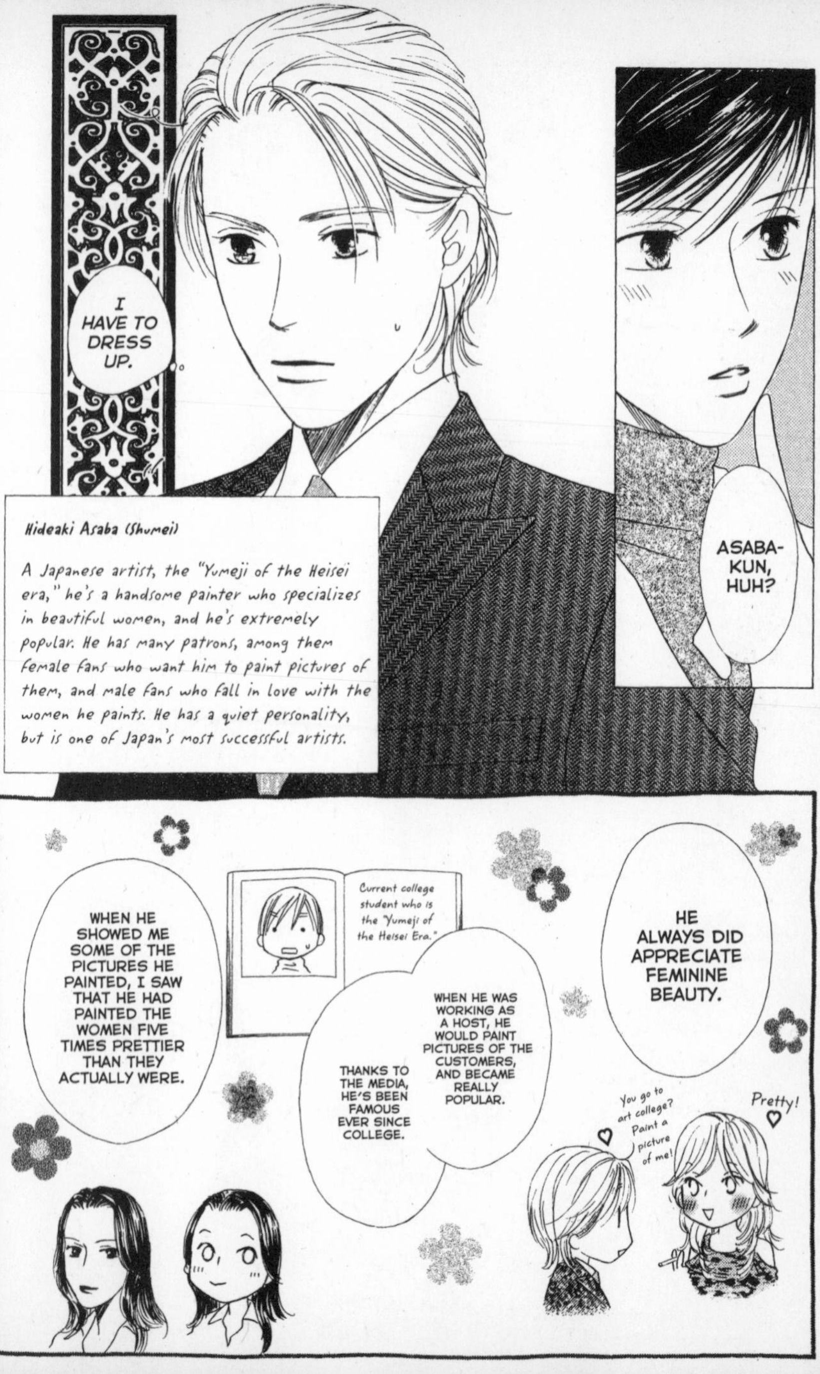
ASABA-KUN, HUH?
I HAVE TO DRESS UP.
Hideaki Asaba (Shumei)
A Japanese artist, the "Yumeji of the Heisei era," he's a handsome painter who specializes in beautiful women, and he's extremely popular. He has many patrons, among them female fans who want him to paint pictures of them, and male fans who fall in love with the women he paints. He has a quiet personality, but is one of Japan's most successful artists.
HE ALWAYS DID APPRECIATE FEMININE BEAUTY.
Pretty!
You go to art college? Paint a picture of me!
WHEN HE WAS WORKING AS A HOST, HE WOULD PAINT PICTURES OF THE CUSTOMERS, AND BECAME REALLY POPULAR.
THANKS TO THE MEDIA, HE'S BEEN FAMOUS EVER SINCE COLLEGE.
Current college student who is the "Yumeji of the Heisei Era."
WHEN HE SHOWED ME SOME OF THE PICTURES HE PAINTED, I SAW THAT HE HAD PAINTED THE WOMEN FIVE TIMES PRETTIER THAN THEY ACTUALLY WERE.

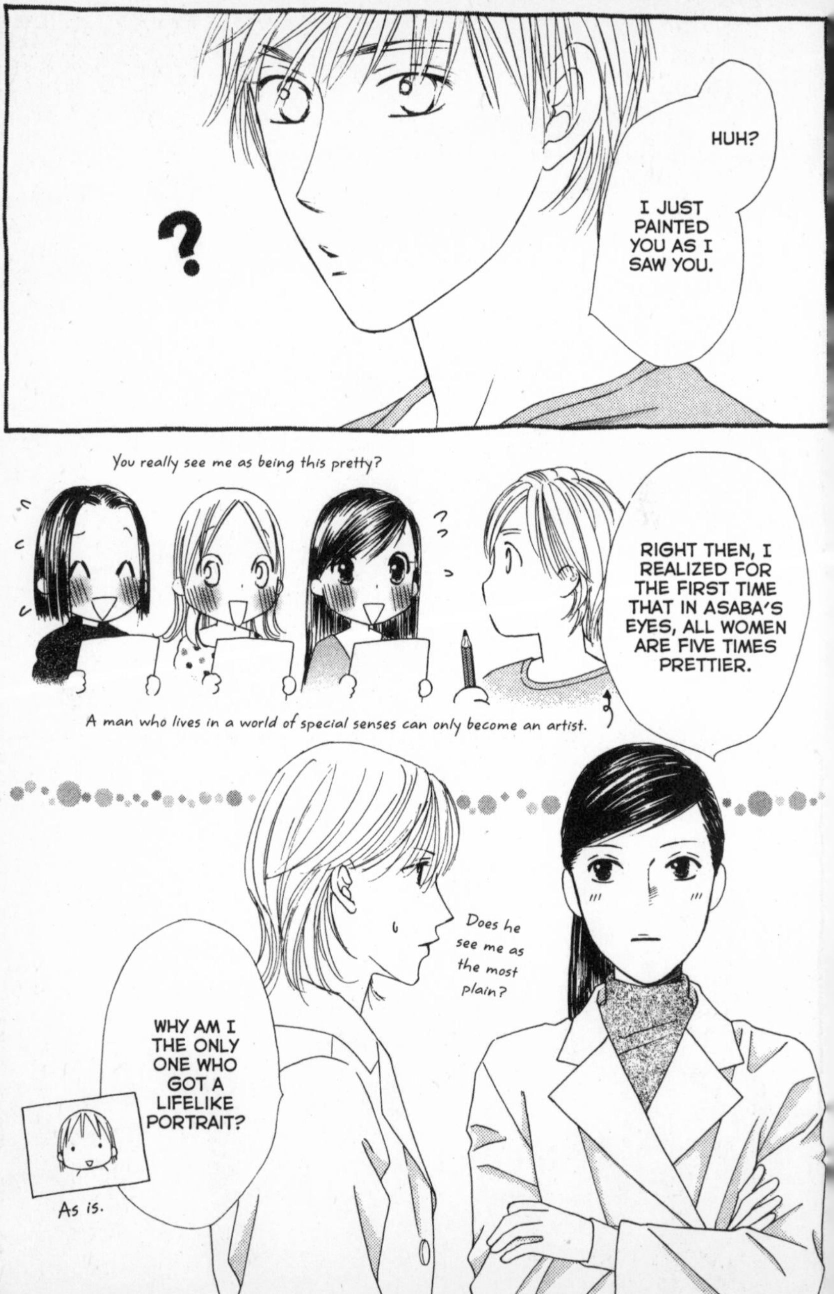
HUH?
I JUST PAINTED YOU AS I SAW YOU.
RIGHT THEN, I REALIZED FOR THE FIRST TIME THAT IN ASABA'S EYES, ALL WOMEN ARE FIVE TIMES PRETTIER.
You really see me as being this pretty?
A man who lives in a world of special senses can only become an artist.
Does he see me as the most plain?
WHY AM I THE ONLY ONE WHO GOT A LIFELIKE PORTRAIT?
As is.

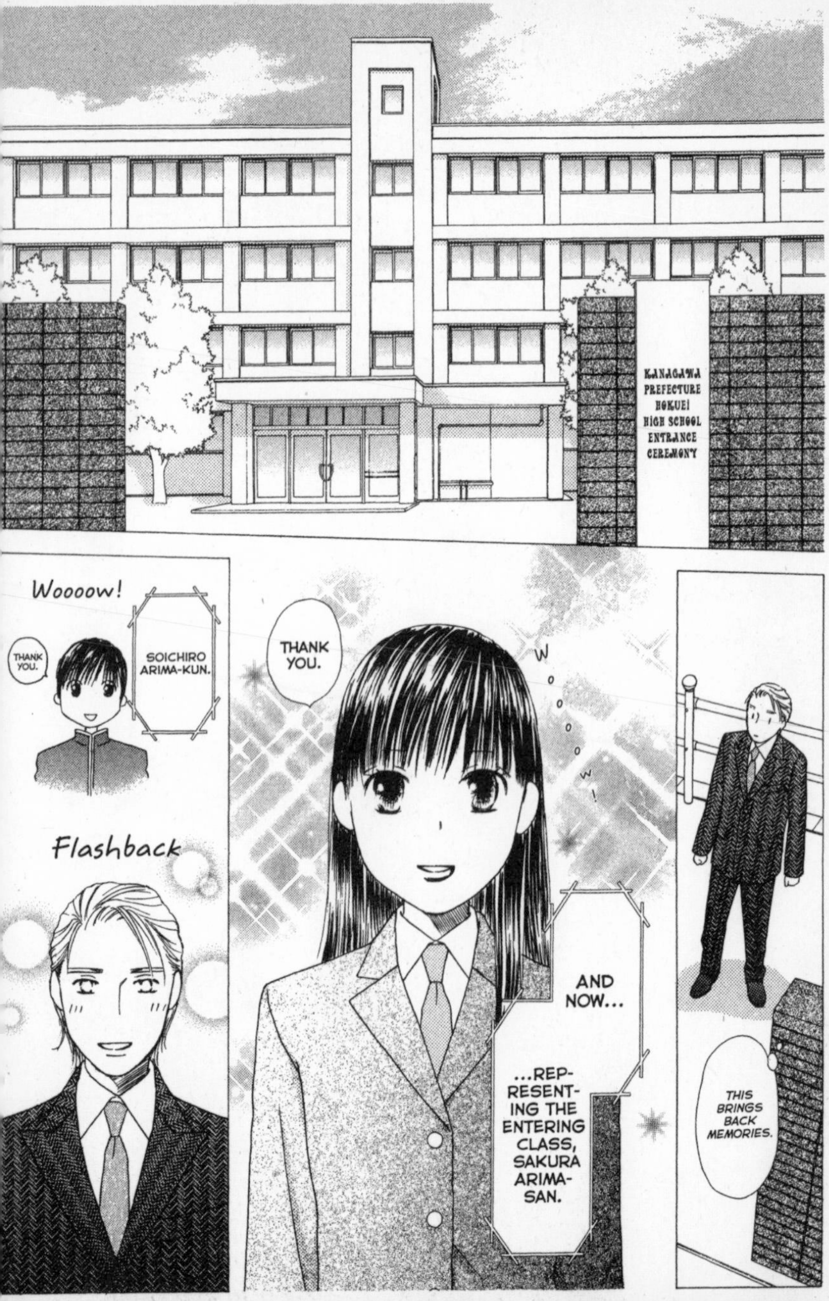
KANAGAWA PREFECTURE HOKUEI HIGH SCHOOL ENTRANCE CEREMONY
THIS BRINGS BACK MEMORIES.
Wooooow!
THANK YOU.
AND NOW...
...REPRESENTING THE ENTERING CLASS, SAKURA ARIMA-SAN.
SOICHIRO ARIMA-KUN.
Woooow!
THANK YOU.
Flashback

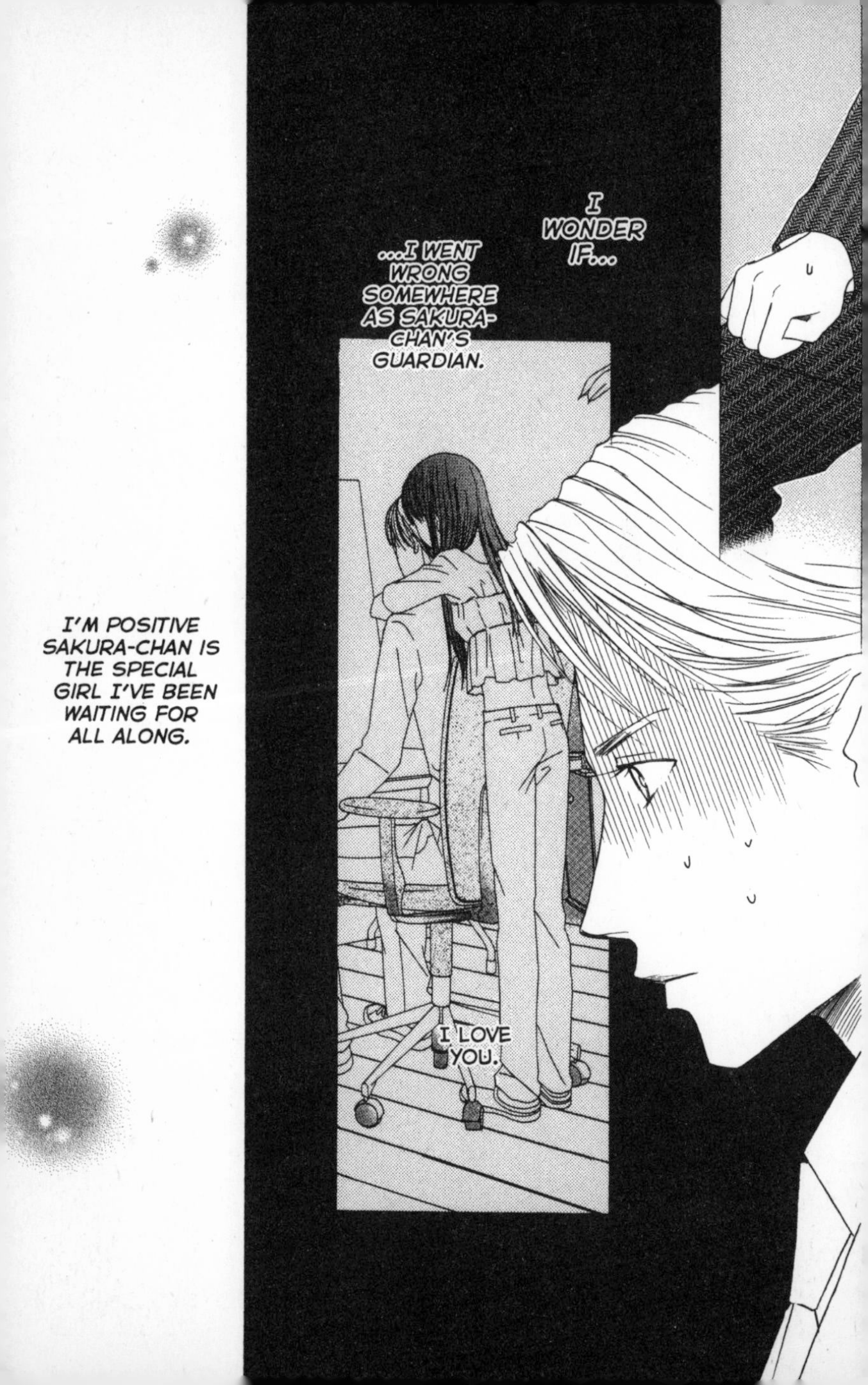
I WONDER IF...
...I WENT WRONG SOMEWHERE AS SAKURA-CHAN'S GUARDIAN.
I LOVE YOU.
I'M POSITIVE SAKURA-CHAN IS THE SPECIAL GIRL I'VE BEEN WAITING FOR ALL ALONG.

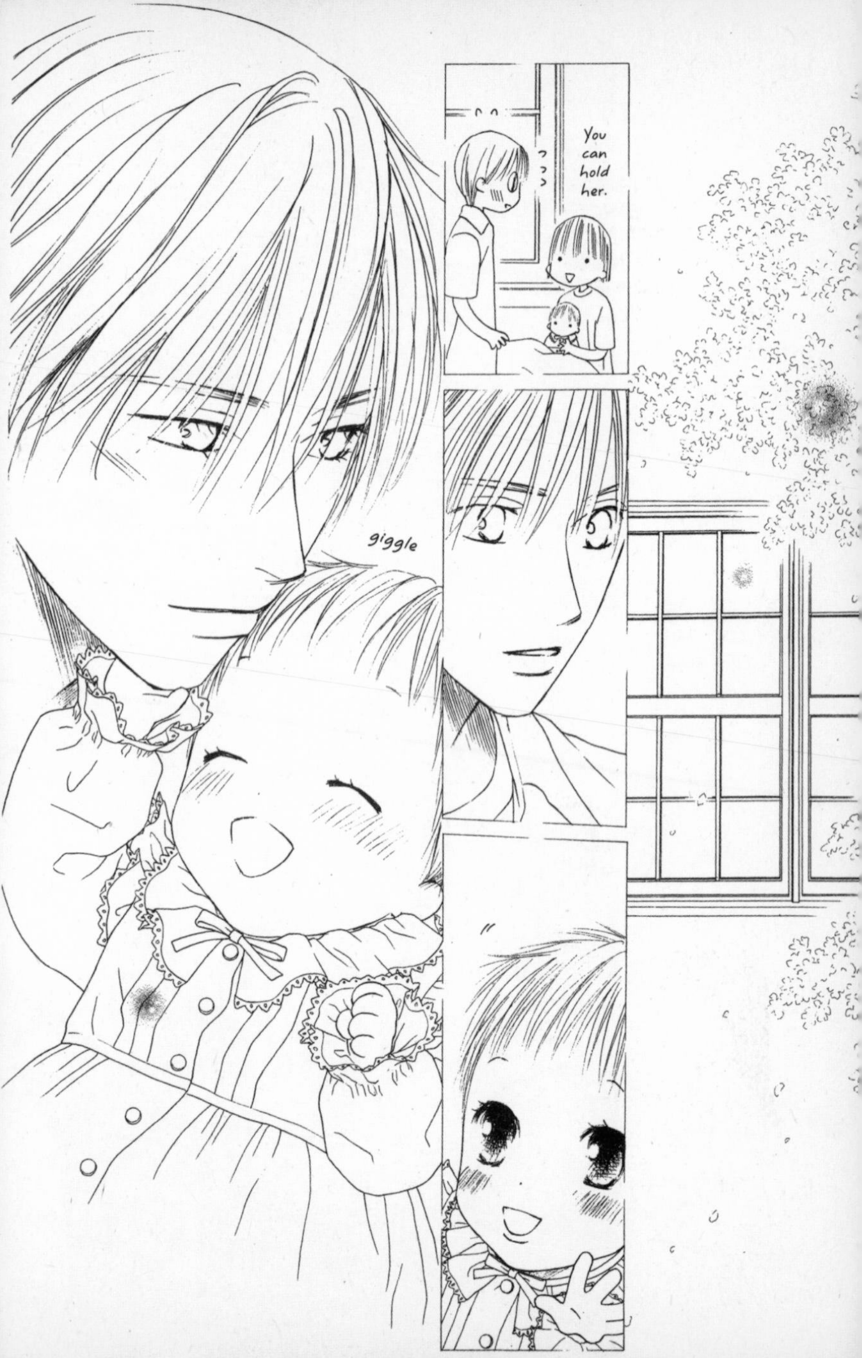
You can hold her.
giggle

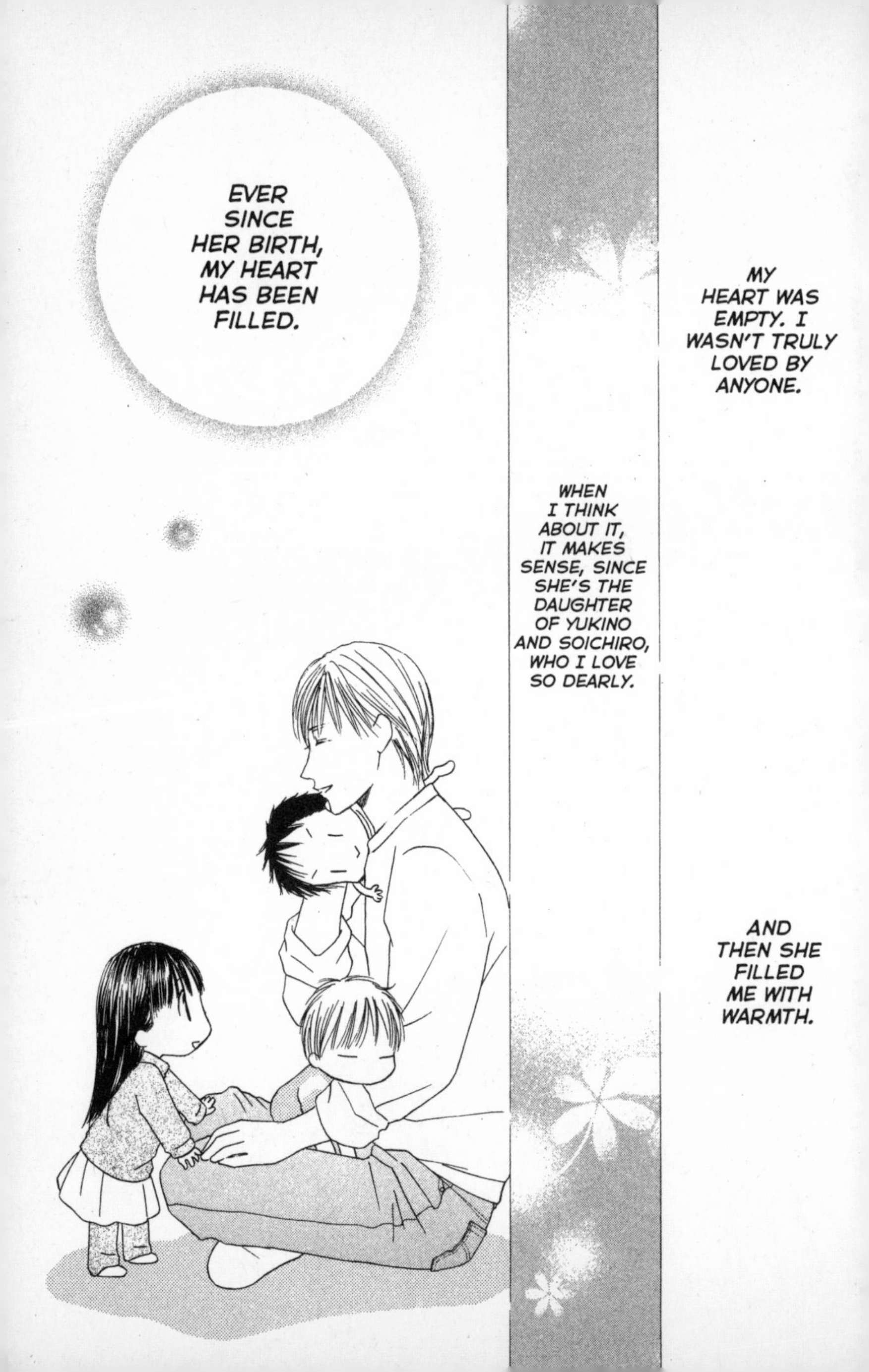
MY HEART WAS EMPTY. I WASN'T TRULY LOVED BY ANYONE.
WHEN I THINK ABOUT IT, IT MAKES SENSE, SINCE SHE'S THE DAUGHTER OF YUKINO AND SOICHIRO, WHO I LOVE SO DEARLY.
AND THEN SHE FILLED ME WITH WARMTH.
EVER SINCE HER BIRTH, MY HEART HAS BEEN FILLED.

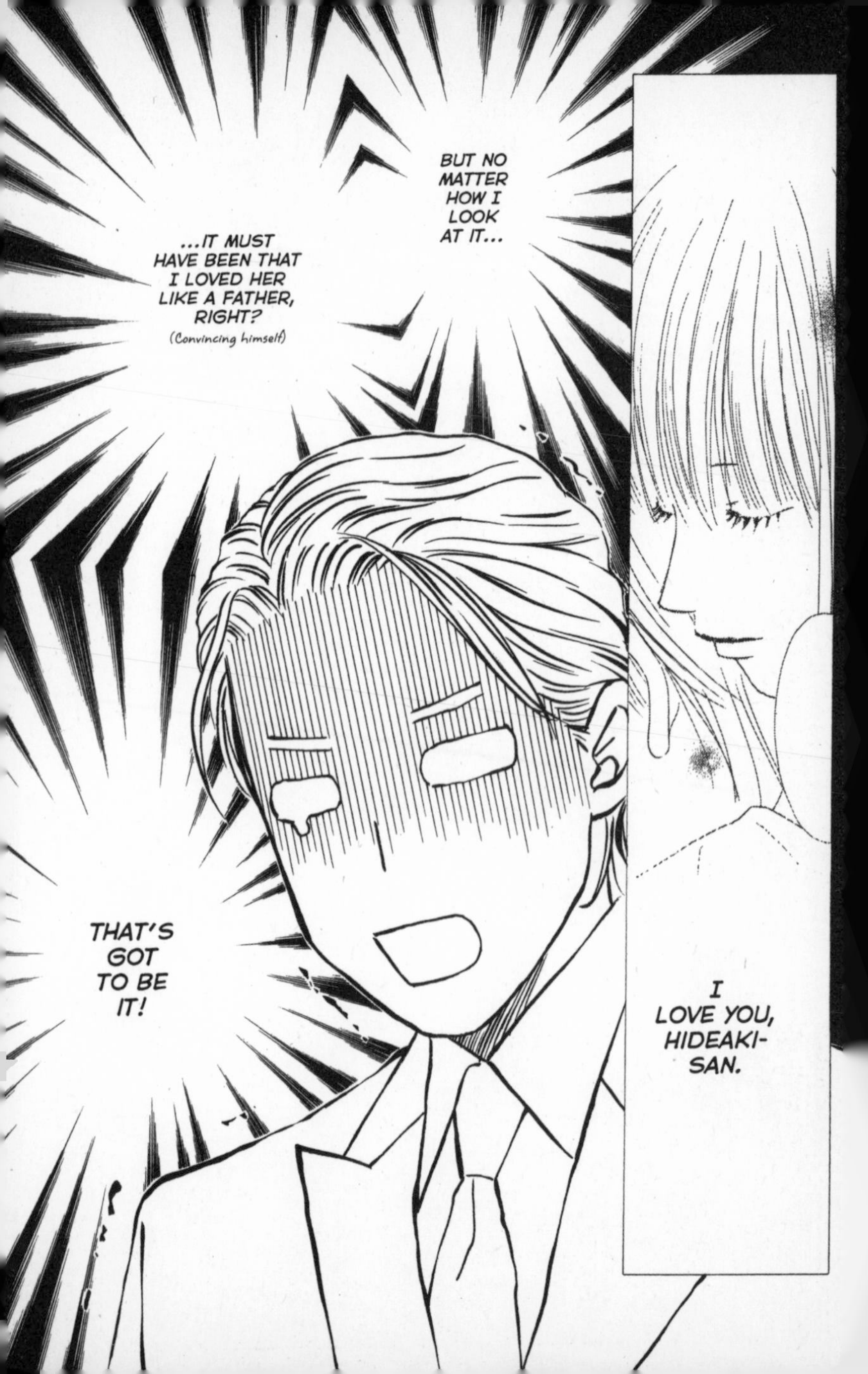
I LOVE YOU, HIDEAKI-SAN.
BUT NO MATTER HOW I LOOK AT IT...
...IT MUST HAVE BEEN THAT I LOVED HER LIKE A FATHER, RIGHT?
(Convincing himself)
THAT'S GOT TO BE IT!

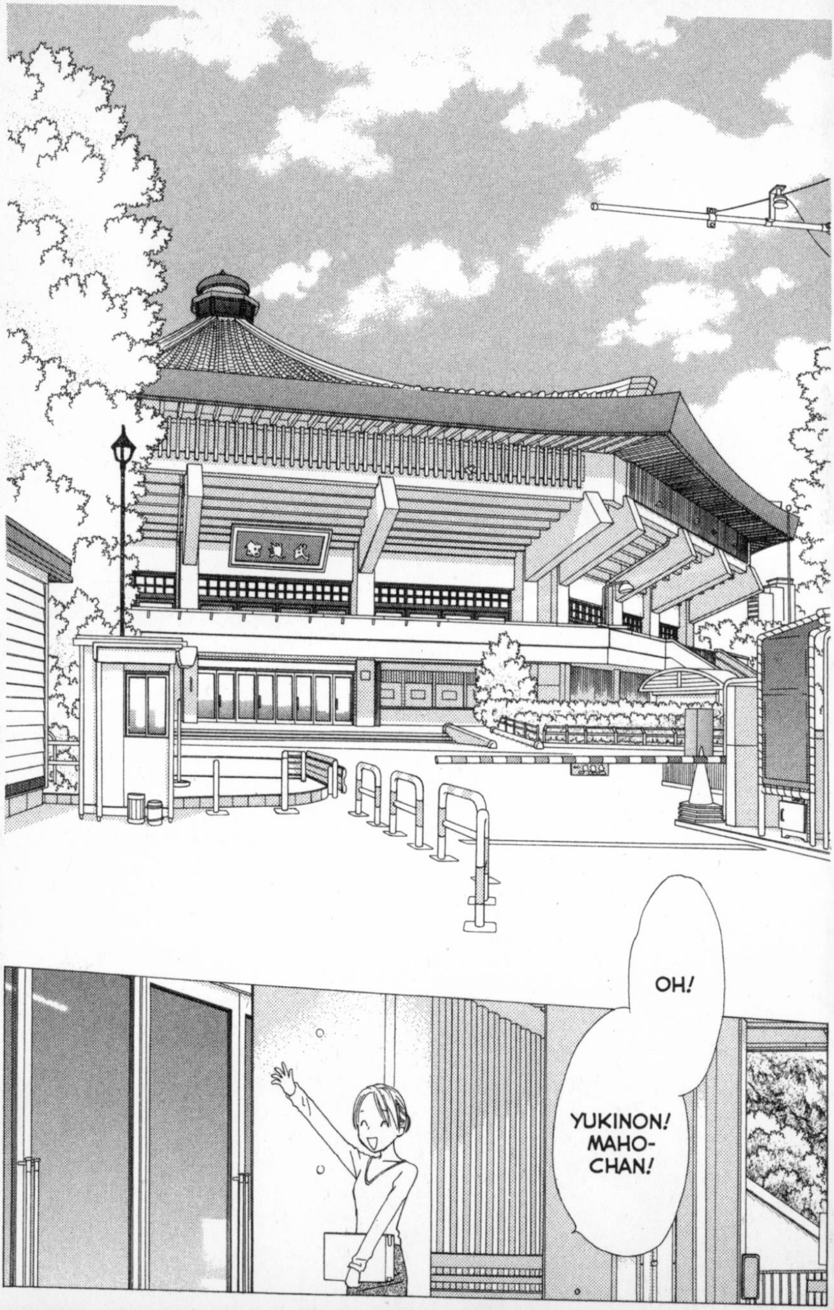
OH!
YUKINON! MAHO-CHAN!

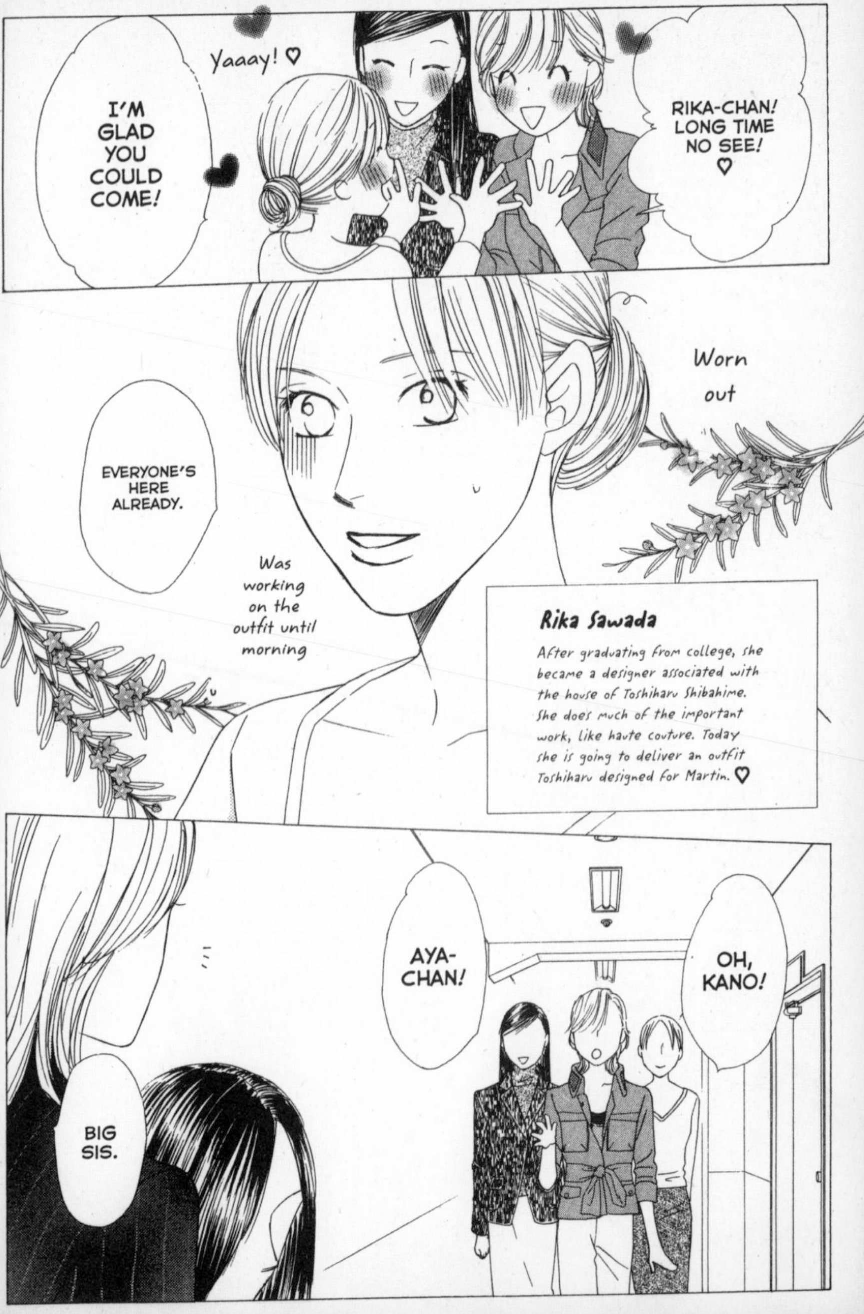
RIKA-CHAN! LONG TIME NO SEE! ♡
Yaaay! ♡
I'M GLAD YOU COULD COME!
Worn out
Rika Sawada
After graduating from college, she became a designer associated with the house of Toshiharu Shibahime. She does much of the important work, like haute couture. Today she is going to deliver an outfit Toshiharu designed for Martin. ♡
EVERYONE'S HERE ALREADY.
Was working on the outfit until morning
OH, KANO!
AYA-CHAN!
BIG SIS.

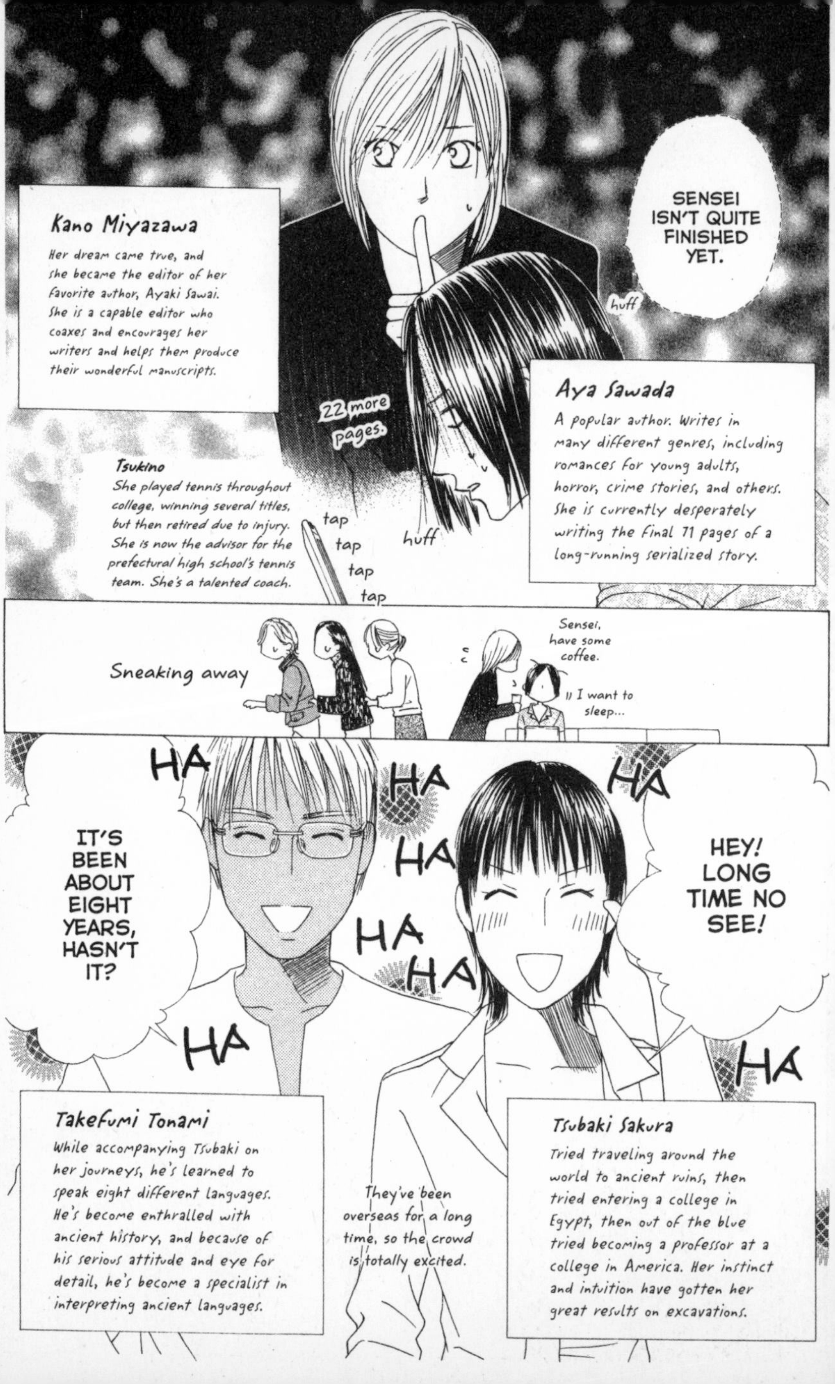
SENSEI ISN'T QUITE FINISHED YET.
huff
Kano Miyazawa
Her dream came true, and she became the editor of her favorite author, Ayaki Sawai. She is a capable editor who coaxes and encourages her writers and helps them produce their wonderful manuscripts.
Aya Sawada
A popular author. Writes in many different genres, including romances for young adults, horror, crime stories, and others. She is currently desperately writing the final 71 pages of a long-running serialized story.
22 more pages.
huff
tap
tap
tap
tap
Tsukino
She played tennis throughout college, winning several titles, but then retired due to injury. She is now the advisor for the prefectural high school's tennis team. She's a talented coach.
Sensei, have some coffee.
I want to sleep...
Sneaking away
HEY! LONG TIME NO SEE!
HA
HA
HA
HA
HA
HA
HA
HA
IT'S BEEN ABOUT EIGHT YEARS, HASN'T IT?
Tsubaki Sakura
Tried traveling around the world to ancient ruins, then tried entering a college in Egypt, then out of the blue tried becoming a professor at a college in America. Her instinct and intuition have gotten her great results on excavations.
They've been overseas for a long time, so the crowd is totally excited.
Takefumi Tonami
While accompanying Tsubaki on her journeys, he's learned to speak eight different languages. He's become enthralled with ancient history, and because of his serious attitude and eye for detail, he's become a specialist in interpreting ancient languages.

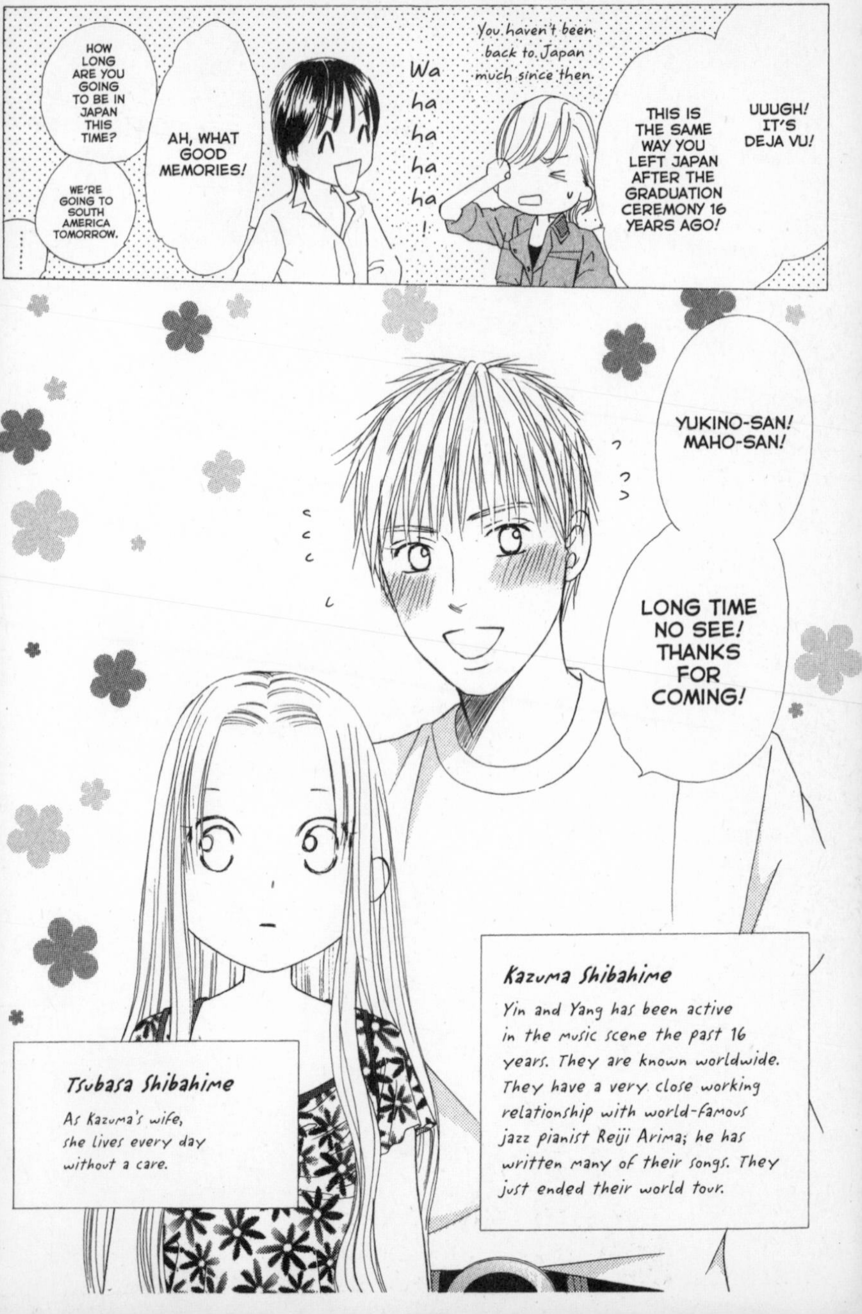
UUUGH! IT'S DEJA VU!
THIS IS THE SAME WAY YOU LEFT JAPAN AFTER THE GRADUATION CEREMONY 16 YEARS AGO!
You haven't been back to Japan much since then.
Wa ha ha ha ha!
AH, WHAT GOOD MEMORIES!
HOW LONG ARE YOU GOING TO BE IN JAPAN THIS TIME?
WE'RE GOING TO SOUTH AMERICA TOMORROW.
......
YUKINO-SAN! MAHO-SAN!
LONG TIME NO SEE! THANKS FOR COMING!
Kazuma Shibahime
Yin and Yang has been active in the music scene the past 16 years. They are known worldwide. They have a very close working relationship with world-famous jazz pianist Reiji Arima; he has written many of their songs. They just ended their world tour.
Tsubasa Shibahime
As Kazuma's wife, she lives every day without a care.

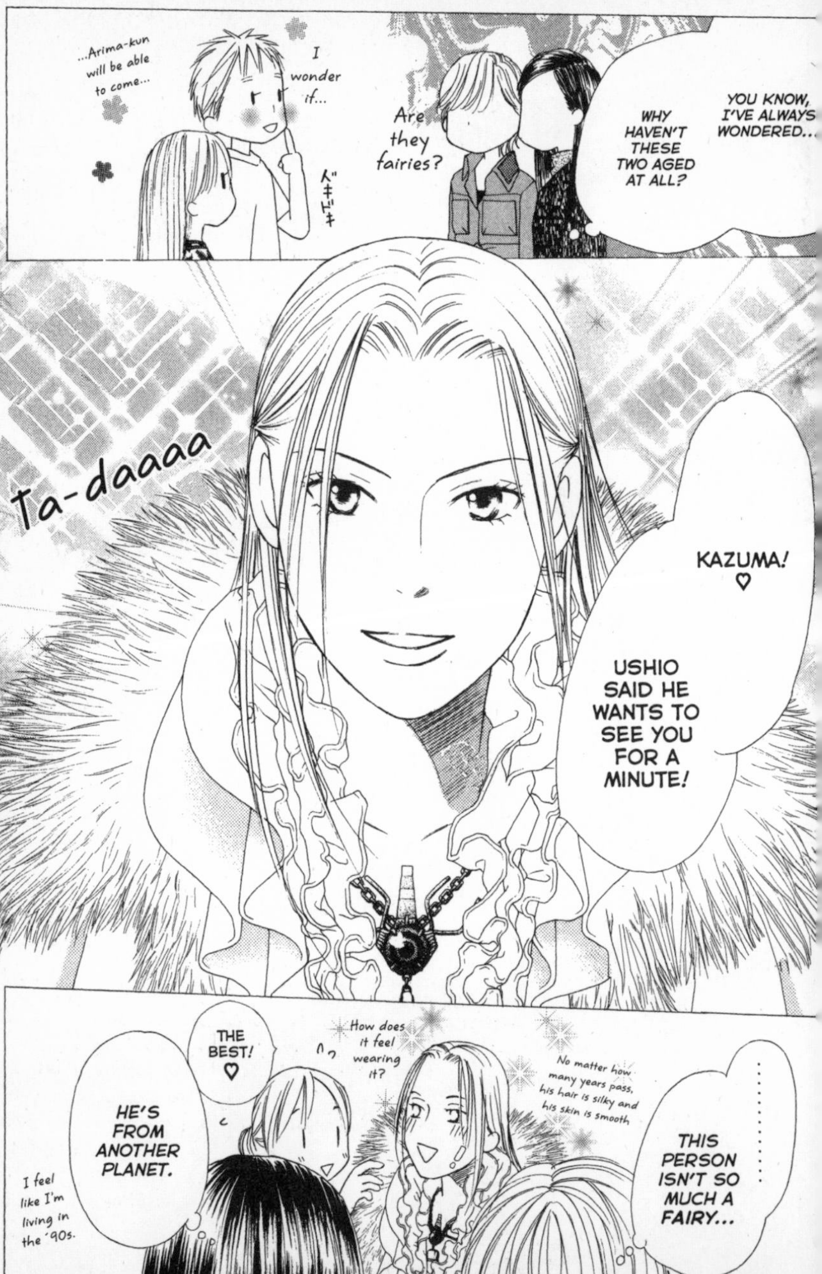

YOU KNOW, I'VE ALWAYS WONDERED...
WHY HAVEN'T THESE TWO AGED AT ALL?
Are they fairies?
I wonder if...
...Arima-kun will be able to come...
ドキドキ
KAZUMA! ♡
USHIO SAID HE WANTS TO SEE YOU FOR A MINUTE!
Ta-daaaa
......
THIS PERSON ISN'T SO MUCH A FAIRY...
No matter how many years pass, his hair is silky and his skin is smooth
How does it feel wearing it?
THE BEST! ♡
HE'S FROM ANOTHER PLANET.
I feel like I'm living in the '90s.

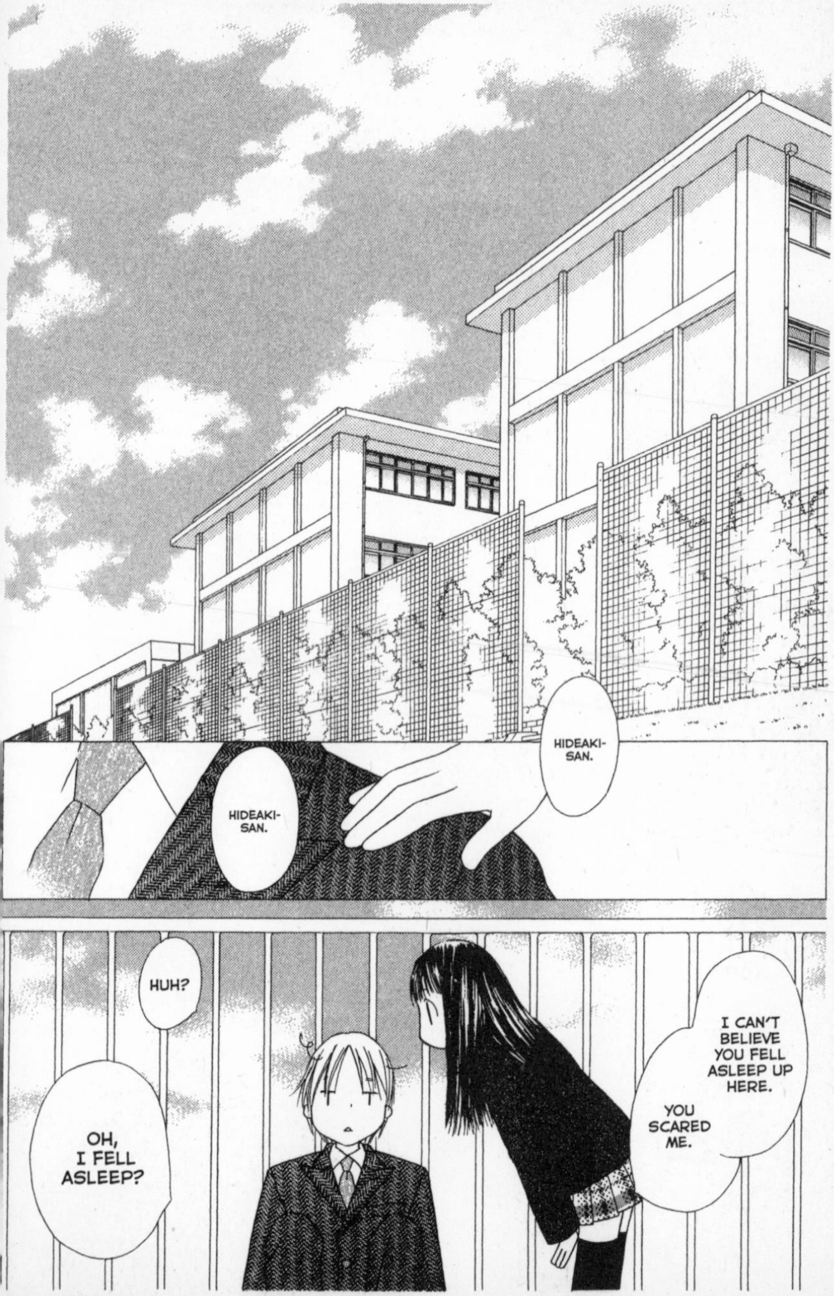
HIDEAKI-SAN.
HIDEAKI-SAN.
HUH?
I CAN'T BELIEVE YOU FELL ASLEEP UP HERE.
YOU SCARED ME.
OH, I FELL ASLEEP?

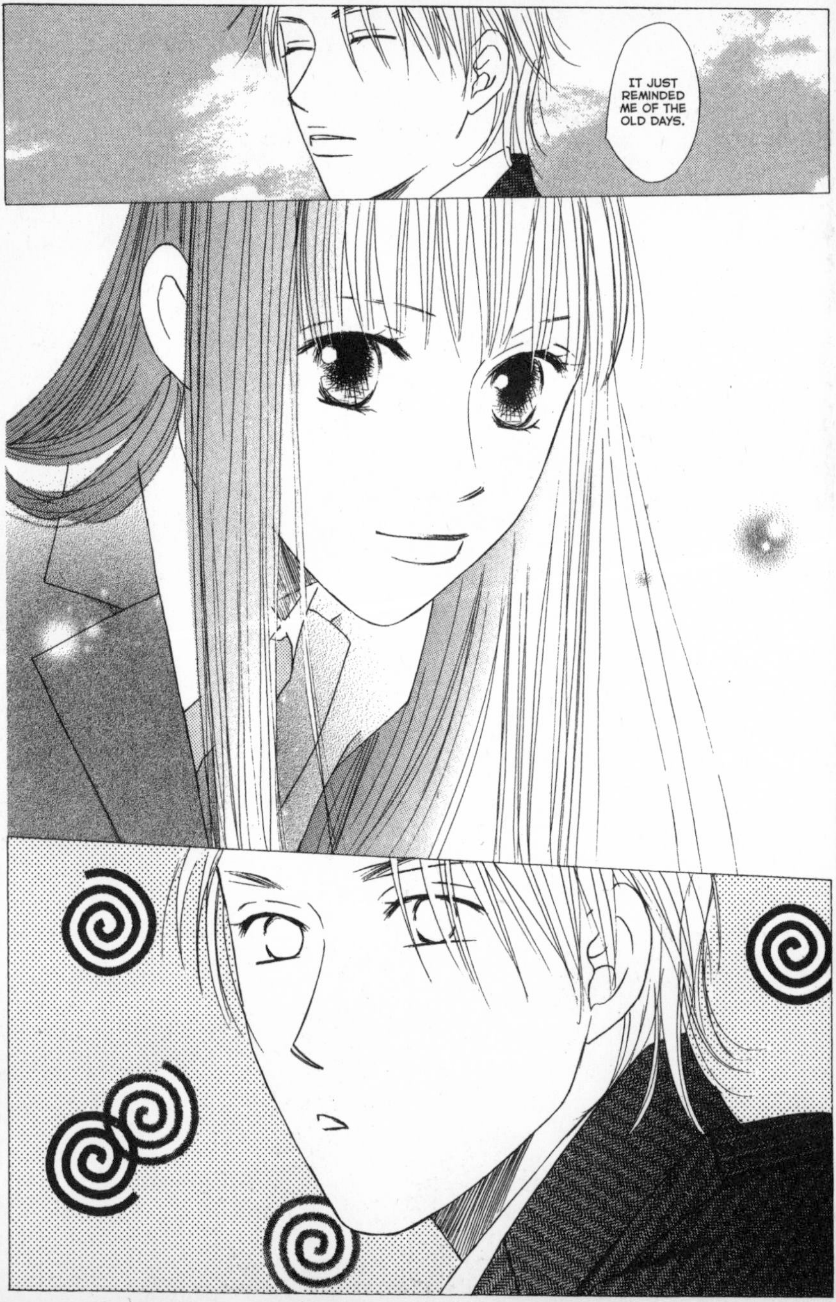
IT JUST REMINDED ME OF THE OLD DAYS.

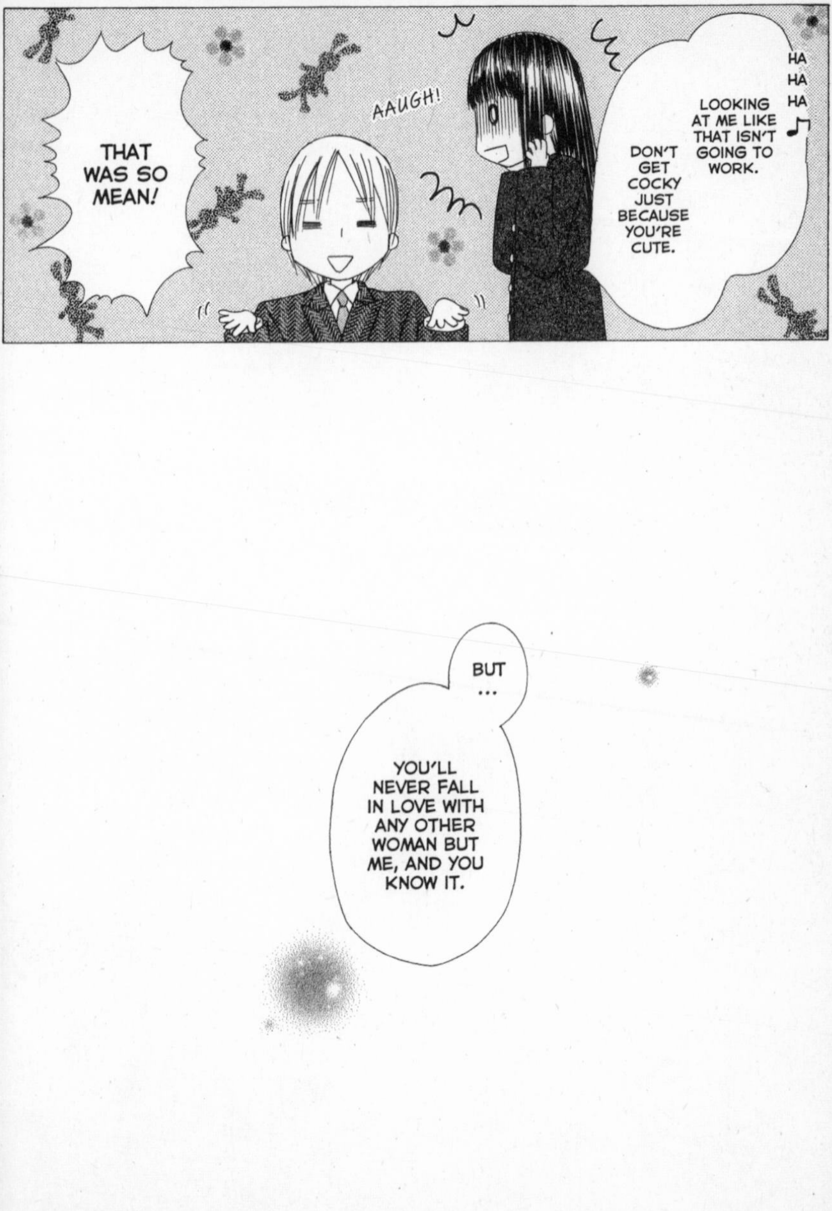
HA HA HA ♪
LOOKING AT ME LIKE THAT ISN'T GOING TO WORK.
DON'T GET COCKY JUST BECAUSE YOU'RE CUTE.
AAUGH!
THAT WAS SO MEAN!
BUT ...
YOU'LL NEVER FALL IN LOVE WITH ANY OTHER WOMAN BUT ME, AND YOU KNOW IT.

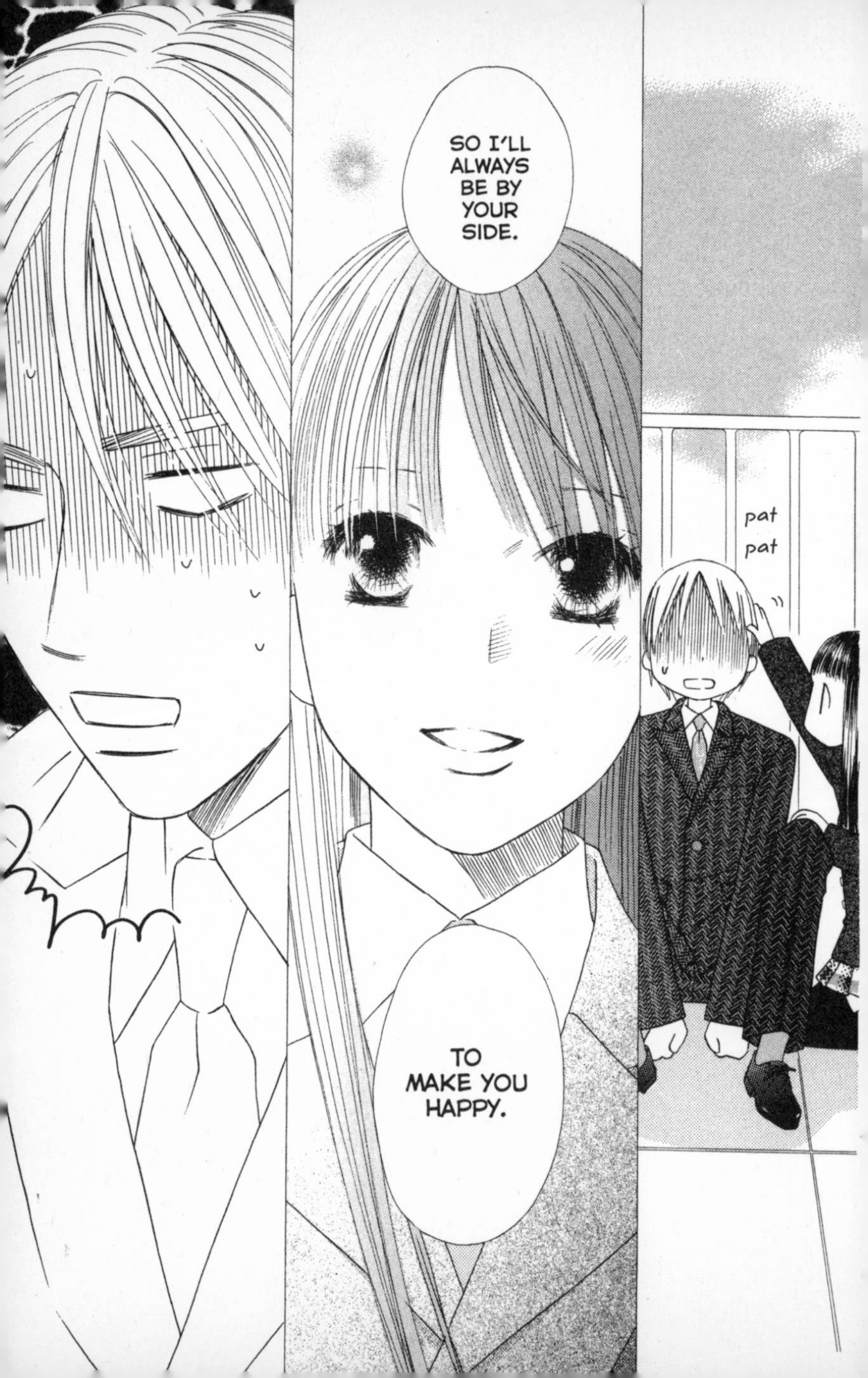
pat
pat
SO I'LL ALWAYS BE BY YOUR SIDE.
TO MAKE YOU HAPPY.

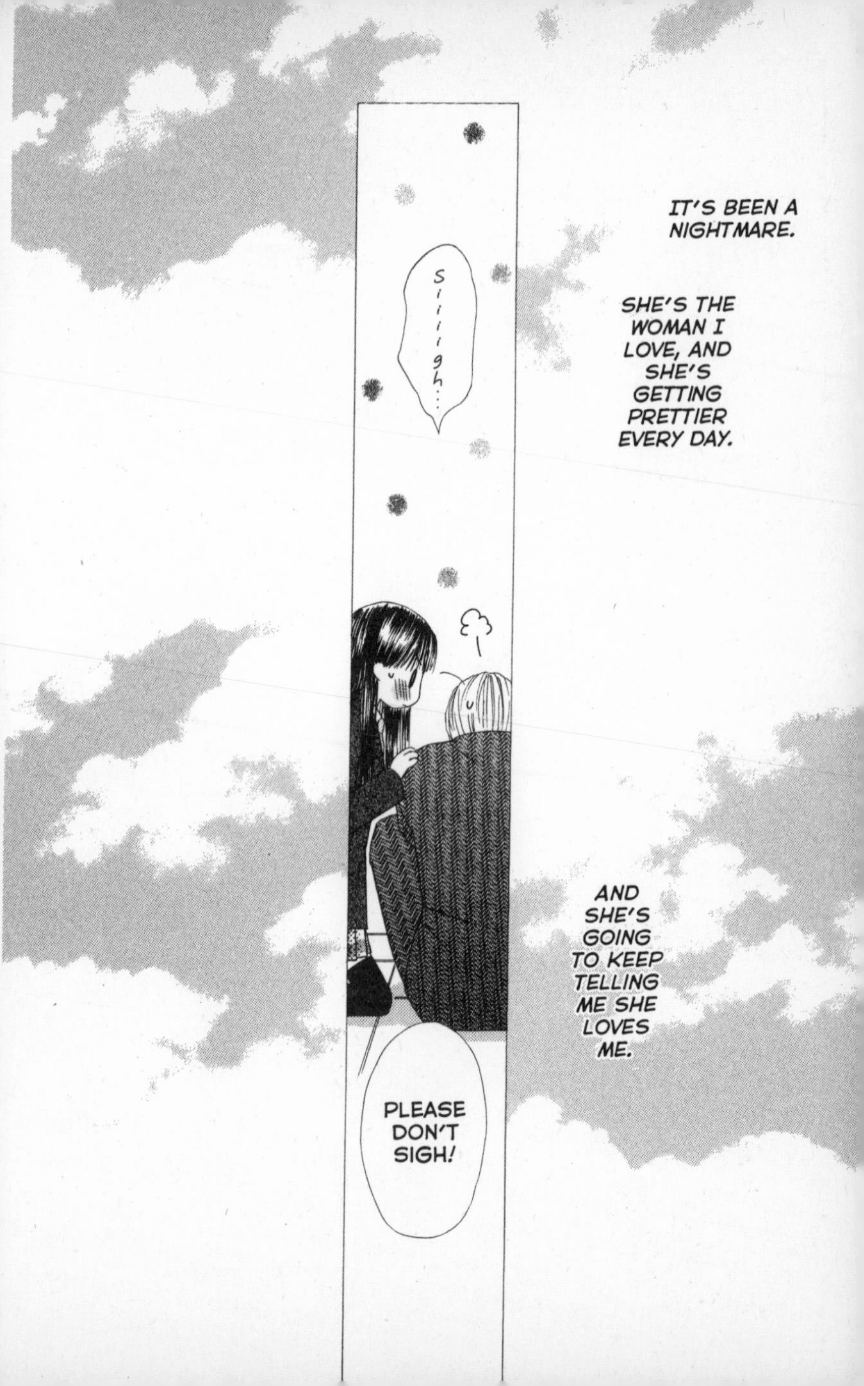
IT'S BEEN A NIGHTMARE.
SHE'S THE WOMAN I LOVE, AND SHE'S GETTING PRETTIER EVERY DAY.
Siiiigh...
AND SHE'S GOING TO KEEP TELLING ME SHE LOVES ME.
PLEASE DON'T SIGH!

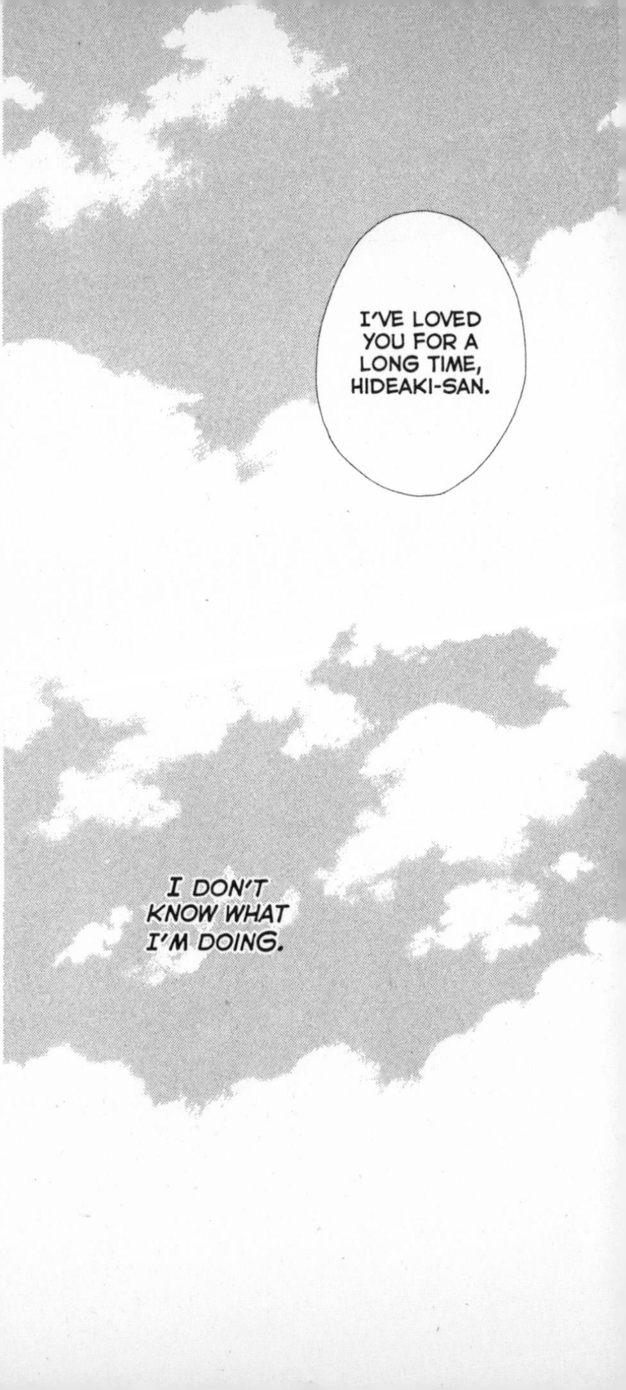
I'VE LOVED YOU FOR A LONG TIME, HIDEAKI-SAN.
I DON'T KNOW WHAT I'M DOING.

5

My last chat space.

Around the time I was drawing the last chapter, the editor who has been working with me for a looong time, ever since my debut manga, switched over to working for a different magazine.

And this year, I'll be putting the last entry in the *Kare Kano* diary I have been keeping for 10 years, almost since I started drawing the series.

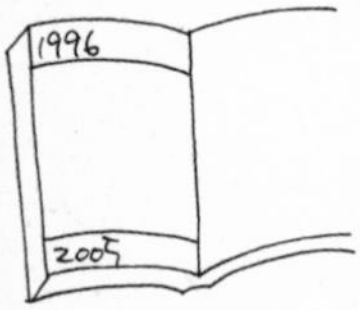
1996
2005

It turned out to be a big section, didn't it?

Well, this is the end to the first chapter of Tsuda's journey along the path of manga.

**Farewell!**

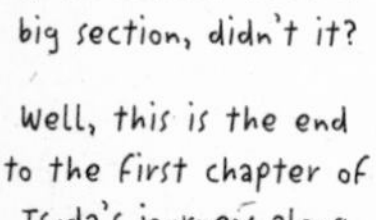

Masami Tsuda

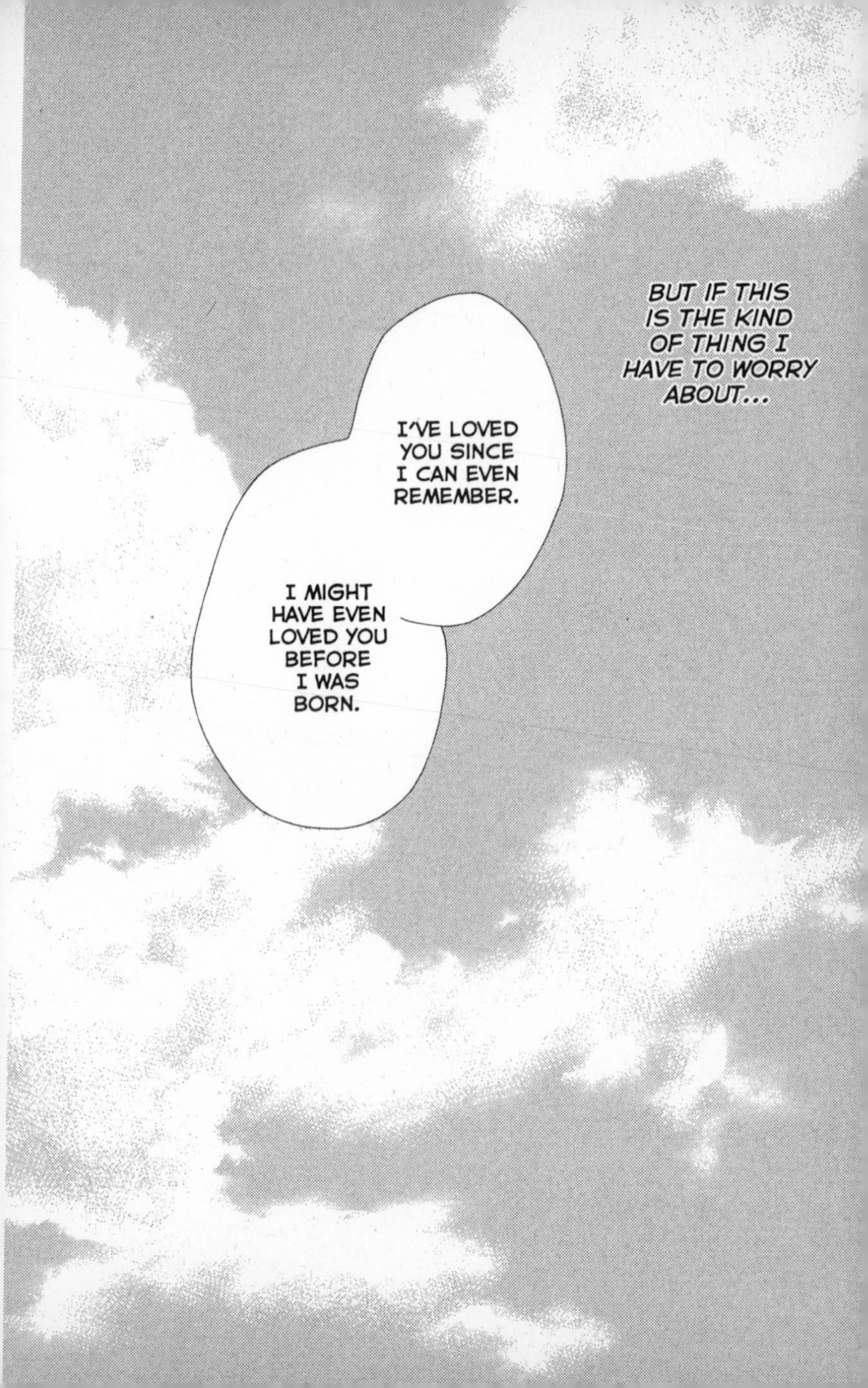
BUT IF THIS IS THE KIND OF THING I HAVE TO WORRY ABOUT...
I'VE LOVED YOU SINCE I CAN EVEN REMEMBER.
I MIGHT HAVE EVEN LOVED YOU BEFORE I WAS BORN.

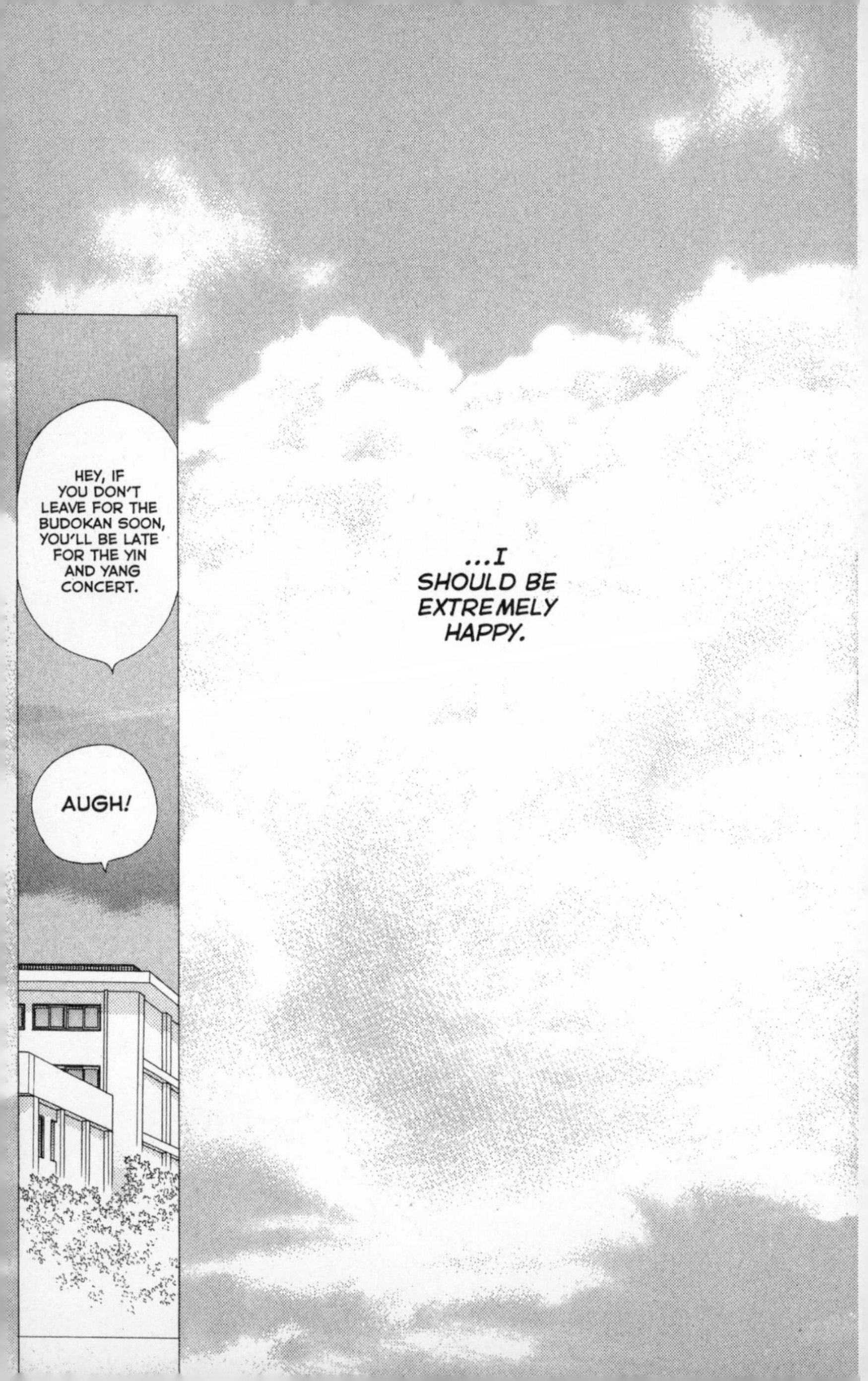
...I SHOULD BE EXTREMELY HAPPY.
HEY, IF YOU DON'T LEAVE FOR THE BUDOKAN SOON, YOU'LL BE LATE FOR THE YIN AND YANG CONCERT.
AUGH!

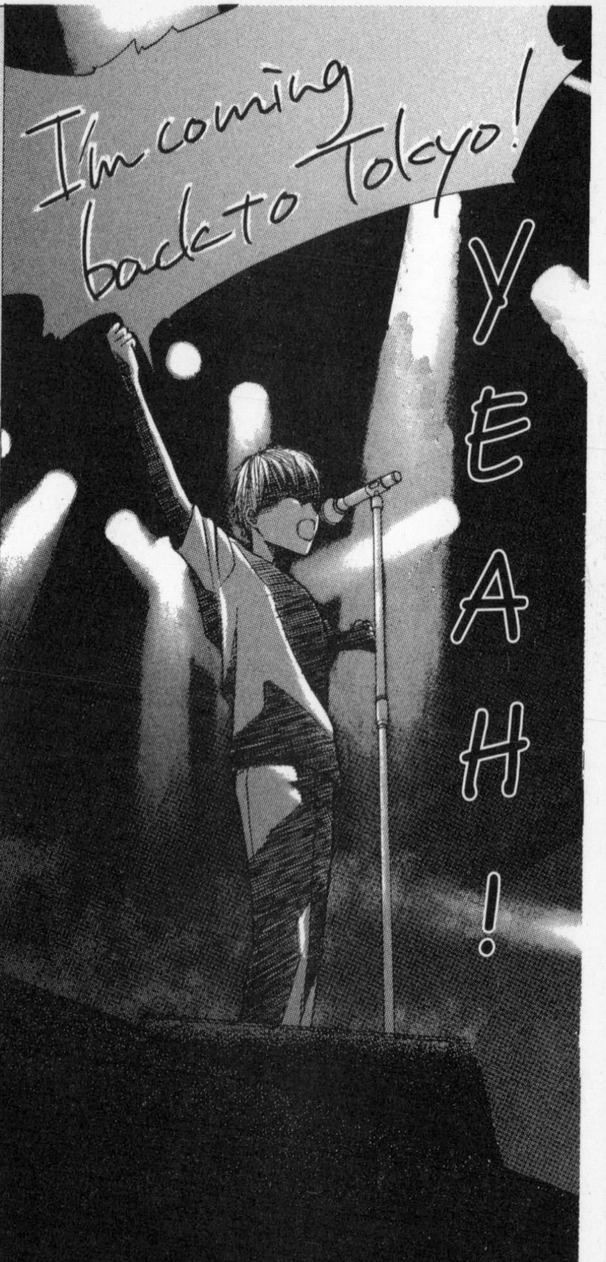
I'm coming back to Tokyo!
YEAH!
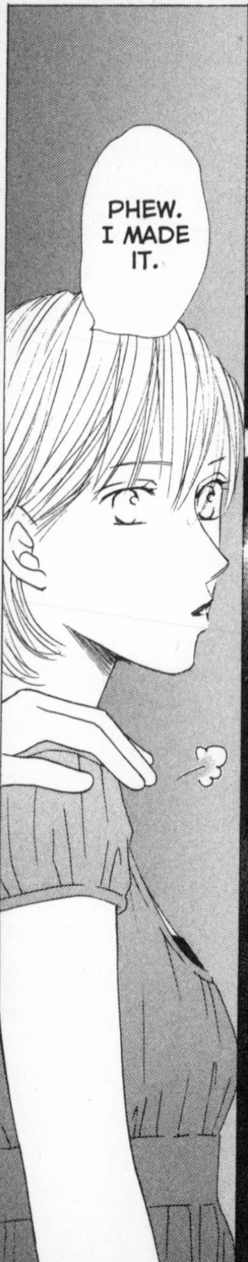
PHEW. I MADE IT.

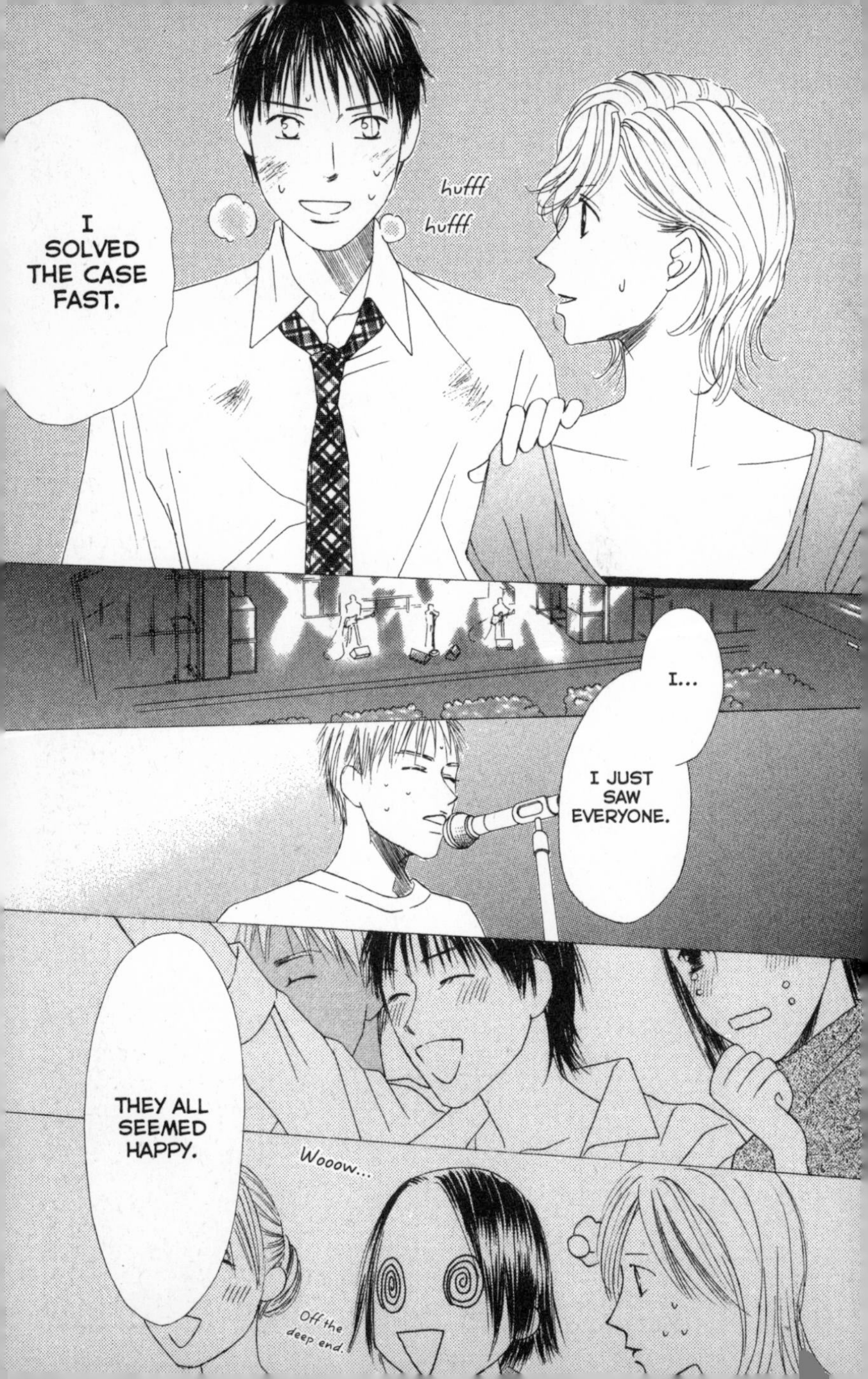
hufff
hufff
I SOLVED THE CASE FAST.
I...
I JUST SAW EVERYONE.
THEY ALL SEEMED HAPPY.
Wooow...
Off the deep end.

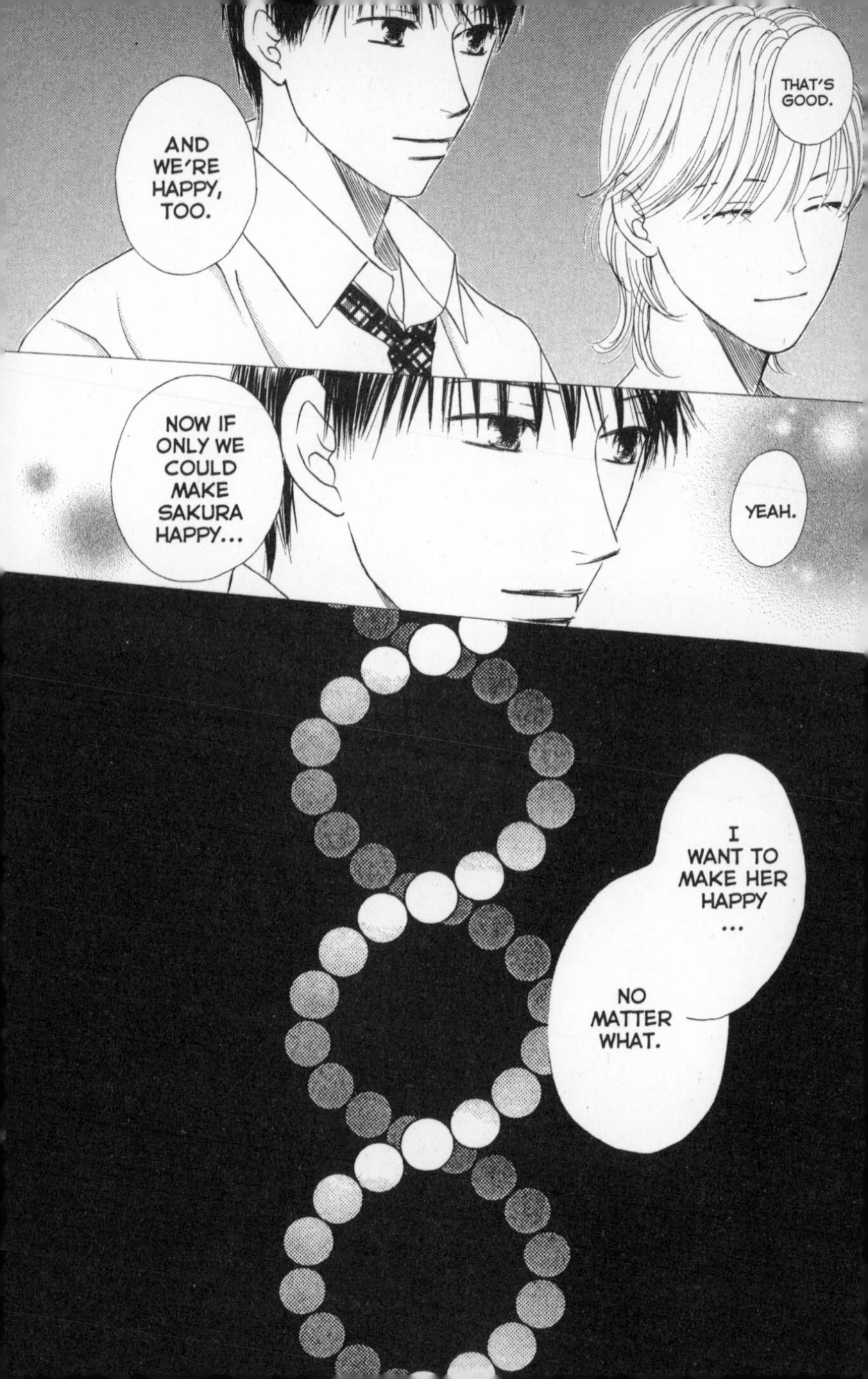
THAT'S GOOD.
AND WE'RE HAPPY, TOO.
YEAH.
NOW IF ONLY WE COULD MAKE SAKURA HAPPY...
I WANT TO MAKE HER HAPPY ...
NO MATTER WHAT.

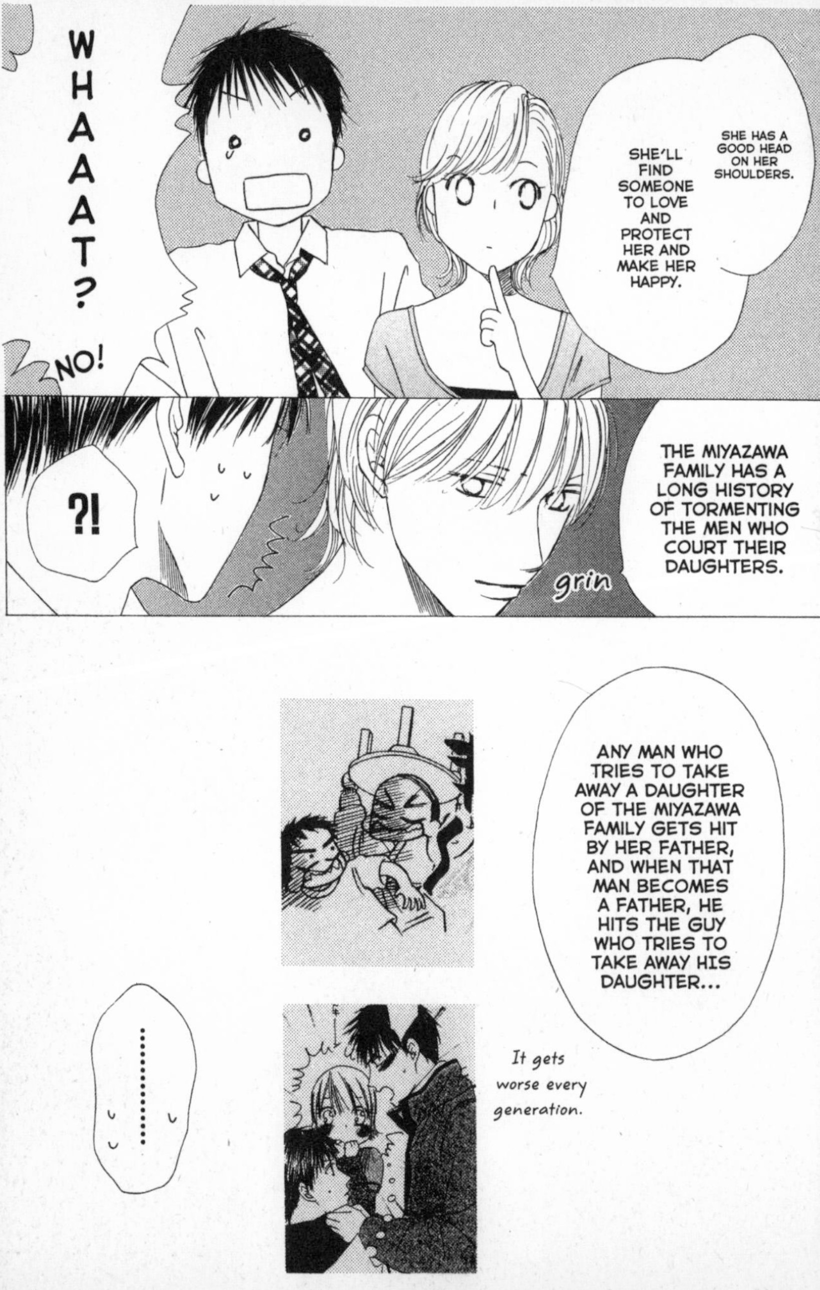
SHE HAS A GOOD HEAD ON HER SHOULDERS.
SHE'LL FIND SOMEONE TO LOVE AND PROTECT HER AND MAKE HER HAPPY.
WHAAAT?
NO!
THE MIYAZAWA FAMILY HAS A LONG HISTORY OF TORMENTING THE MEN WHO COURT THEIR DAUGHTERS.
grin
?!
ANY MAN WHO TRIES TO TAKE AWAY A DAUGHTER OF THE MIYAZAWA FAMILY GETS HIT BY HER FATHER, AND WHEN THAT MAN BECOMES A FATHER, HE HITS THE GUY WHO TRIES TO TAKE AWAY HIS DAUGHTER...
It gets worse every generation.
......

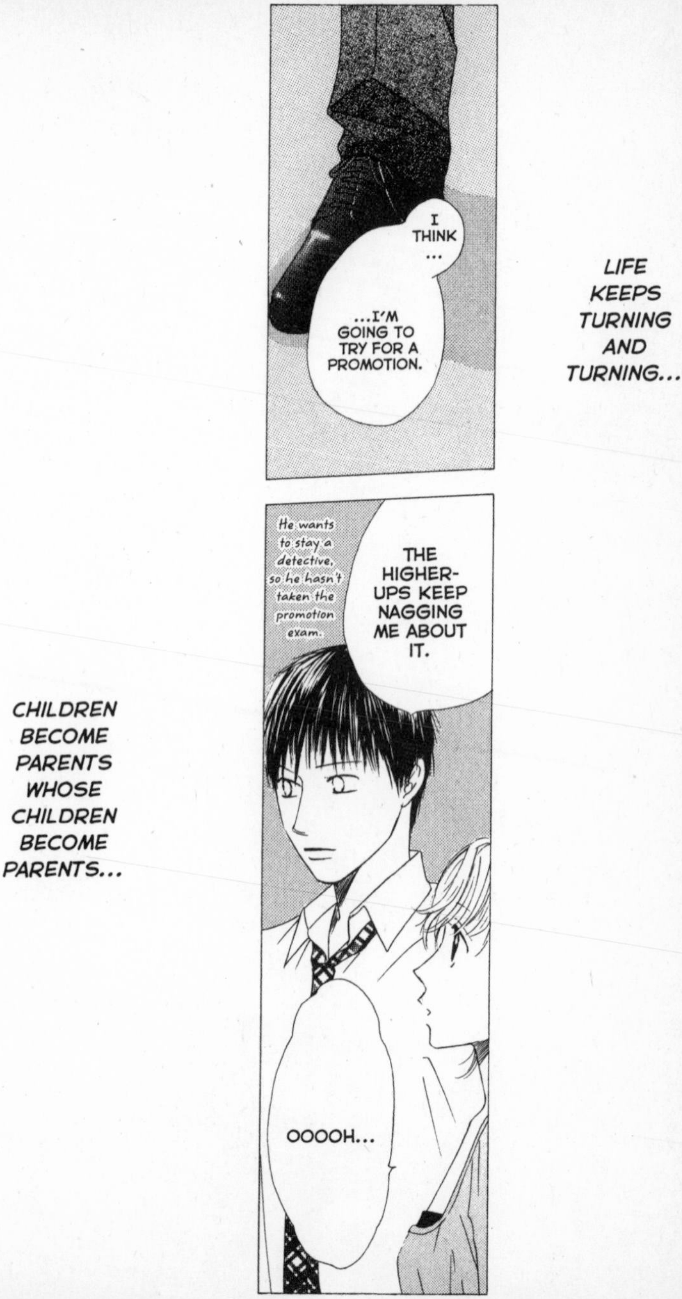
LIFE KEEPS TURNING AND TURNING...
I THINK ...
...I'M GOING TO TRY FOR A PROMOTION.
THE HIGHER-UPS KEEP NAGGING ME ABOUT IT.
He wants to stay a detective, so he hasn't taken the promotion exam.
OOOOH...
CHILDREN BECOME PARENTS WHOSE CHILDREN BECOME PARENTS...

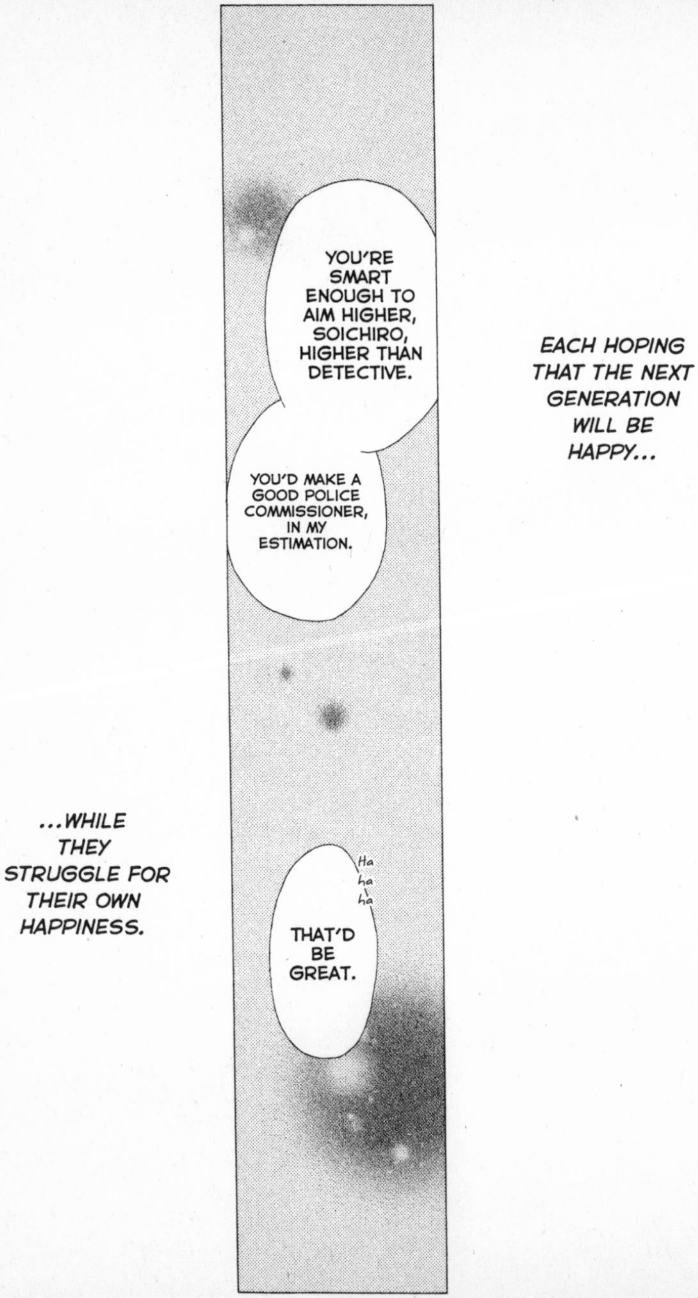
EACH HOPING THAT THE NEXT GENERATION WILL BE HAPPY...
YOU'RE SMART ENOUGH TO AIM HIGHER, SOICHIRO, HIGHER THAN DETECTIVE.
YOU'D MAKE A GOOD POLICE COMMISSIONER, IN MY ESTIMATION.
Ha ha ha
THAT'D BE GREAT.
...WHILE THEY STRUGGLE FOR THEIR OWN HAPPINESS.

LOVE, FRIENDSHIP, HATRED, ANGER, SUCCESS, DESPAIR,
EXALTATION, FRUSTRATION, TRUTH, LIES, HURT, SALVATION,
GREED, GENEROSITY, DEGRADATION, REBIRTH.

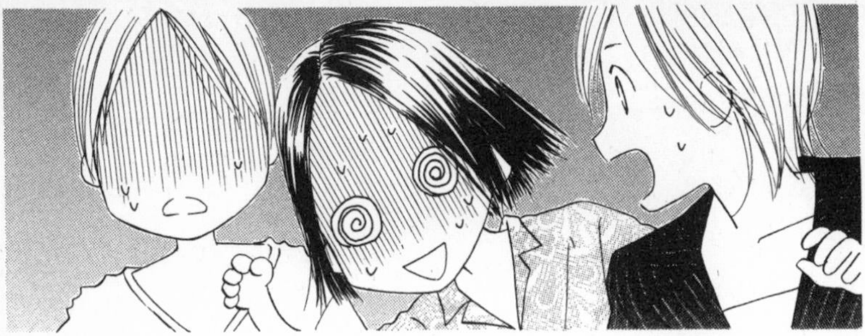

ALL OF THESE SPIRAL AROUND IN THIS WORLD.

WITHOUT KNOWING HOW MUCH TIME WE HAVE, WE FUMBLE...

...AND SWIM THROUGH LIFE'S MURKY WATERS.

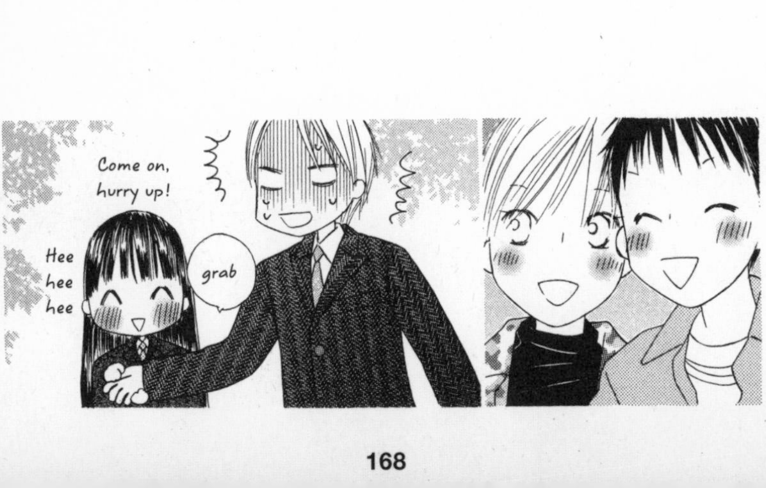
Come on, hurry up!
grab
Hee hee hee

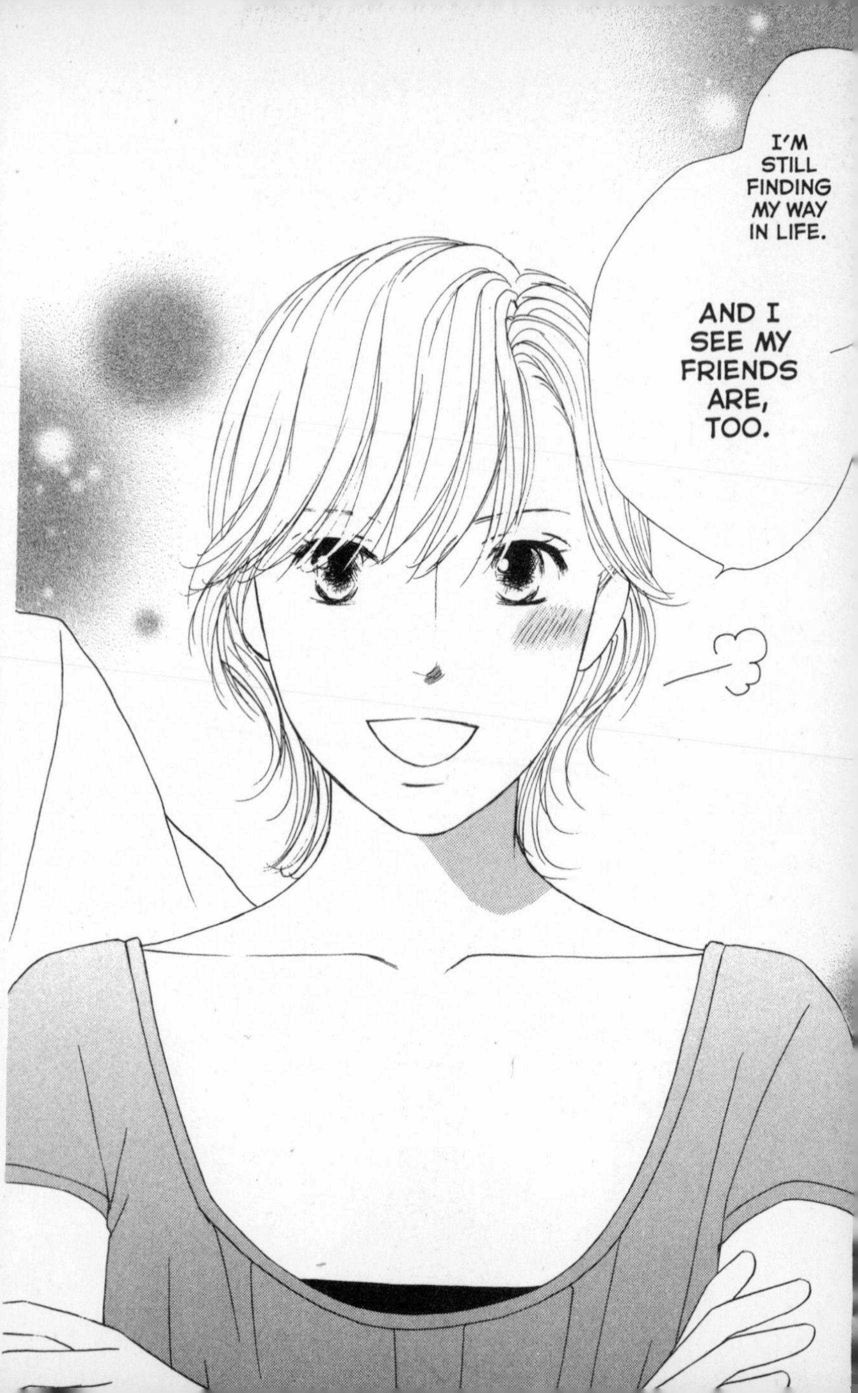
I'M STILL FINDING MY WAY IN LIFE.
AND I SEE MY FRIENDS ARE, TOO.

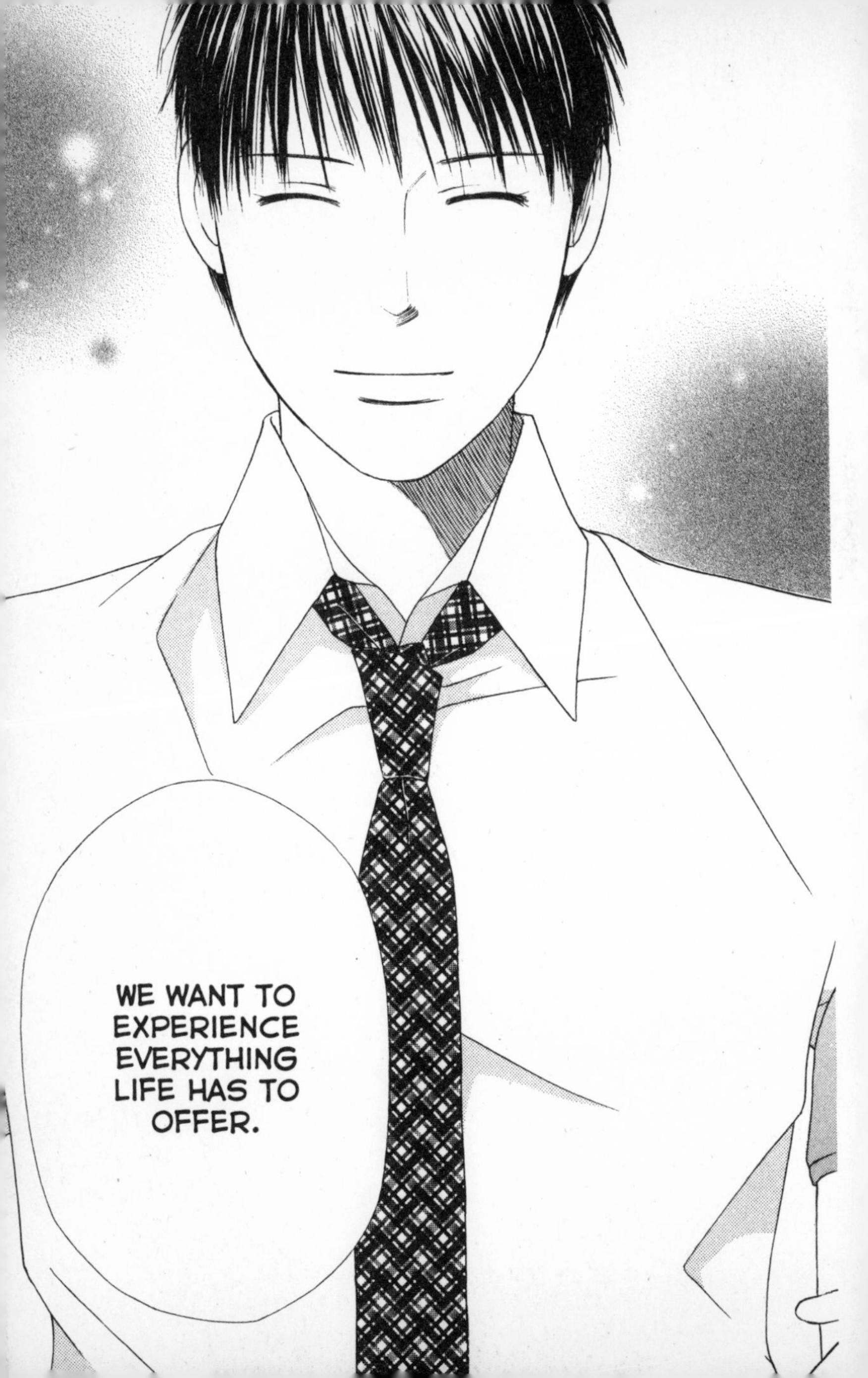
WE WANT TO EXPERIENCE EVERYTHING LIFE HAS TO OFFER.

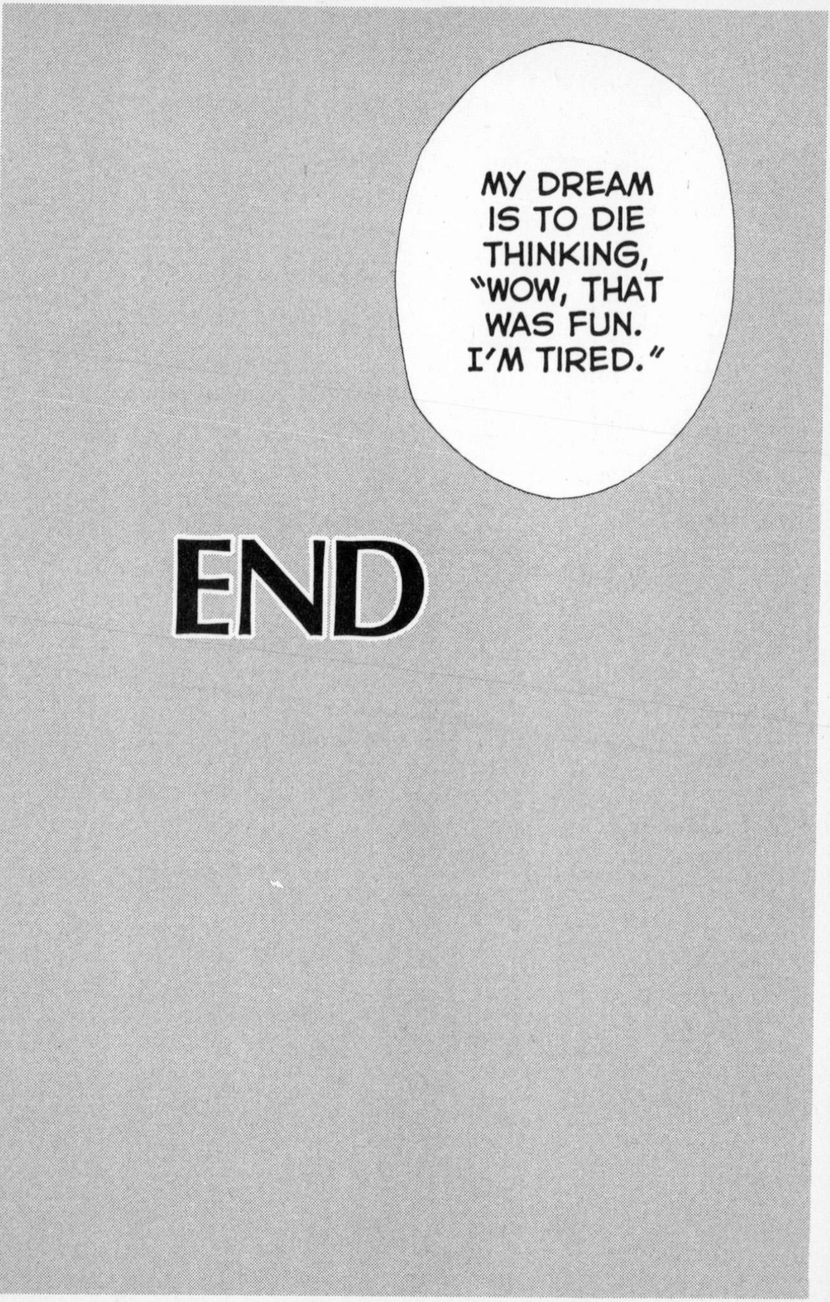
MY DREAM IS TO DIE THINKING, "WOW, THAT WAS FUN. I'M TIRED."
END

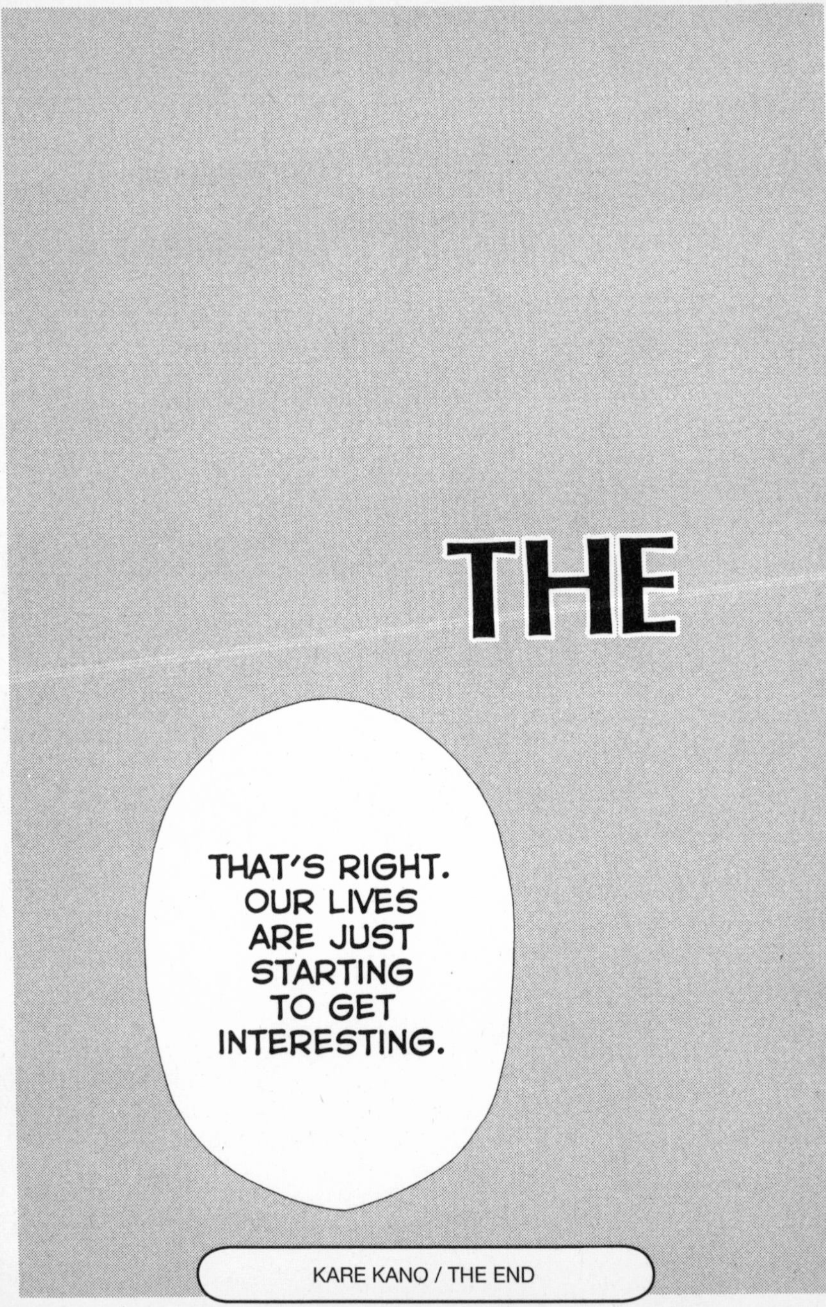
THE
THAT'S RIGHT. OUR LIVES ARE JUST STARTING TO GET INTERESTING.
KARE KANO / THE END

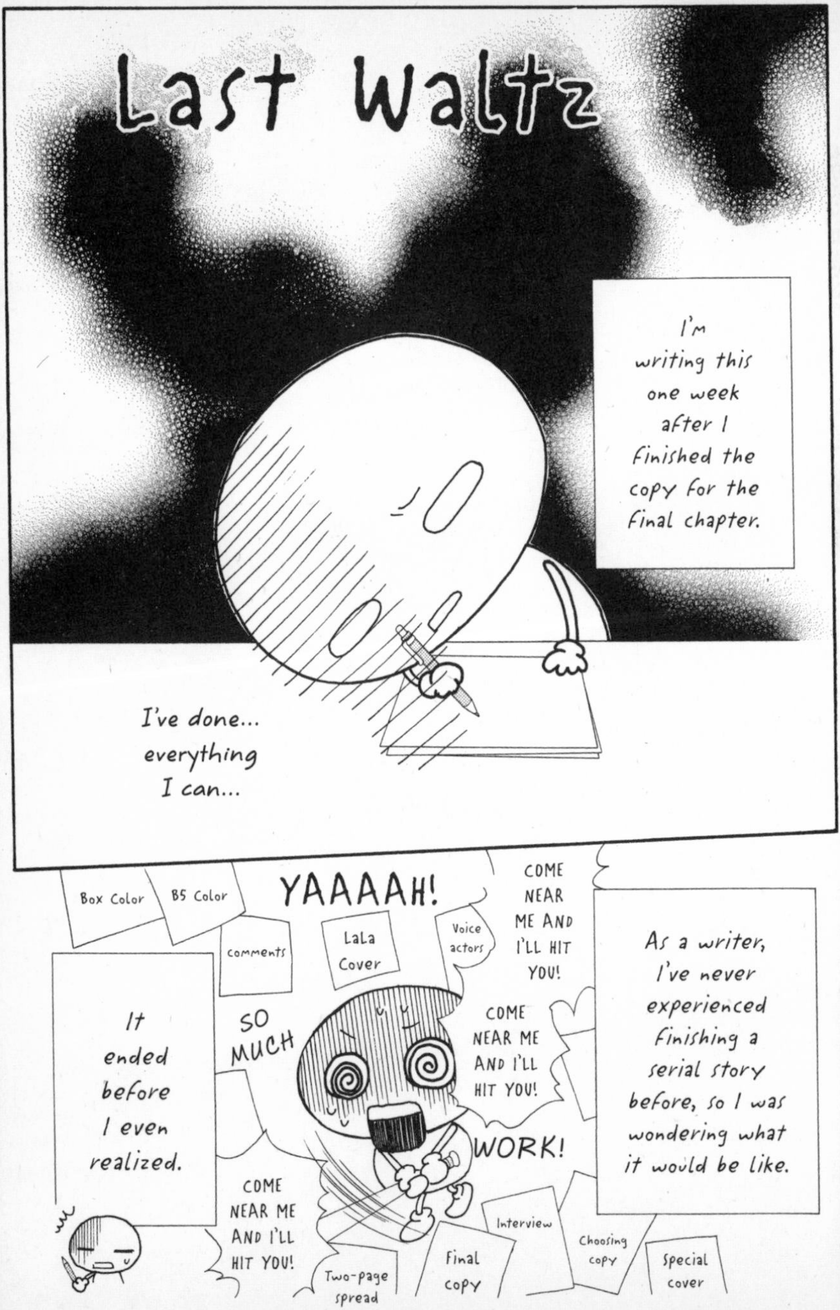
Last Waltz
I'm writing this one week after I finished the copy for the final chapter.
I've done... everything I can...
As a writer, I've never experienced finishing a serial story before, so I was wondering what it would be like.
COME NEAR ME AND I'LL HIT YOU!
YAAAAH!
Voice actors
LaLa Cover
B5 Color
Box Color
comments
COME NEAR ME AND I'LL HIT YOU!
SO MUCH
WORK!
It ended before I even realized.
Special cover
Choosing copy
Interview
Final copy
Two-page spread
COME NEAR ME AND I'LL HIT YOU!

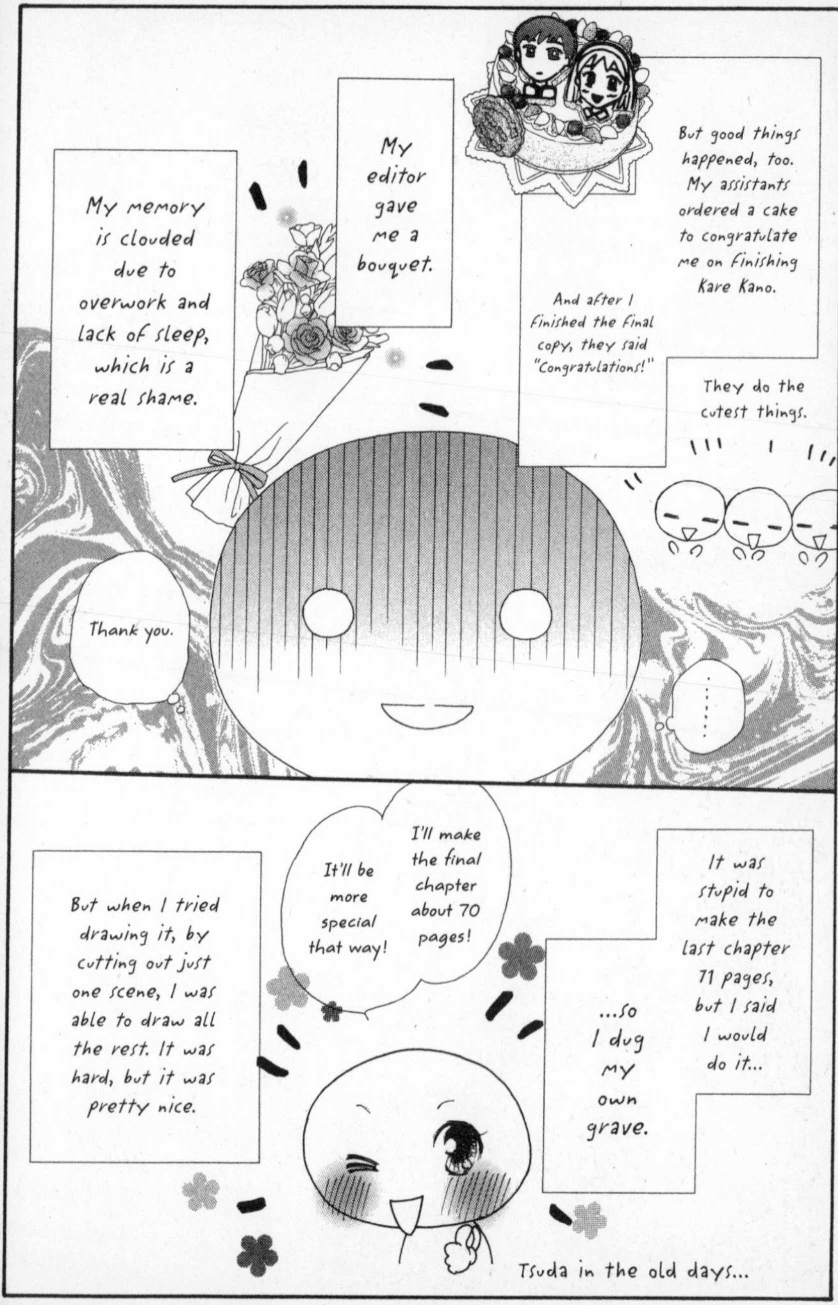
But good things happened, too. My assistants ordered a cake to congratulate me on finishing Kare Kano.
And after I finished the final copy, they said "Congratulations!"
They do the cutest things.
My editor gave me a bouquet.
My memory is clouded due to overwork and lack of sleep, which is a real shame.
Thank you.
......
It was stupid to make the last chapter 71 pages, but I said I would do it...
...so I dug my own grave.
I'll make the final chapter about 70 pages!
It'll be more special that way!
But when I tried drawing it, by cutting out just one scene, I was able to draw all the rest. It was hard, but it was pretty nice.
Tsuda in the old days...

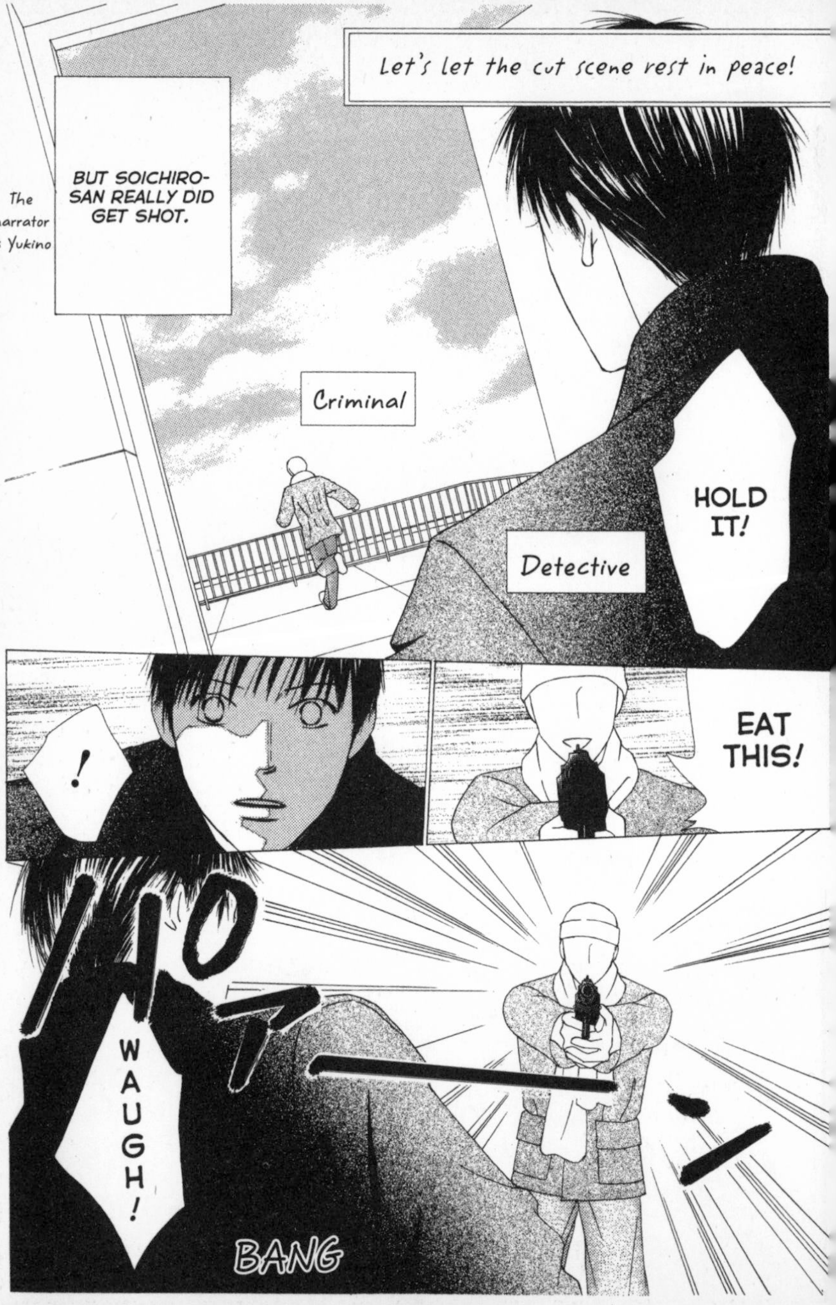
Let's let the cut scene rest in peace!
BUT SOICHIRO-SAN REALLY DID GET SHOT.
The narrator is Yukino
Criminal
HOLD IT!
Detective
EAT THIS!
!
WAUGH!
BANG

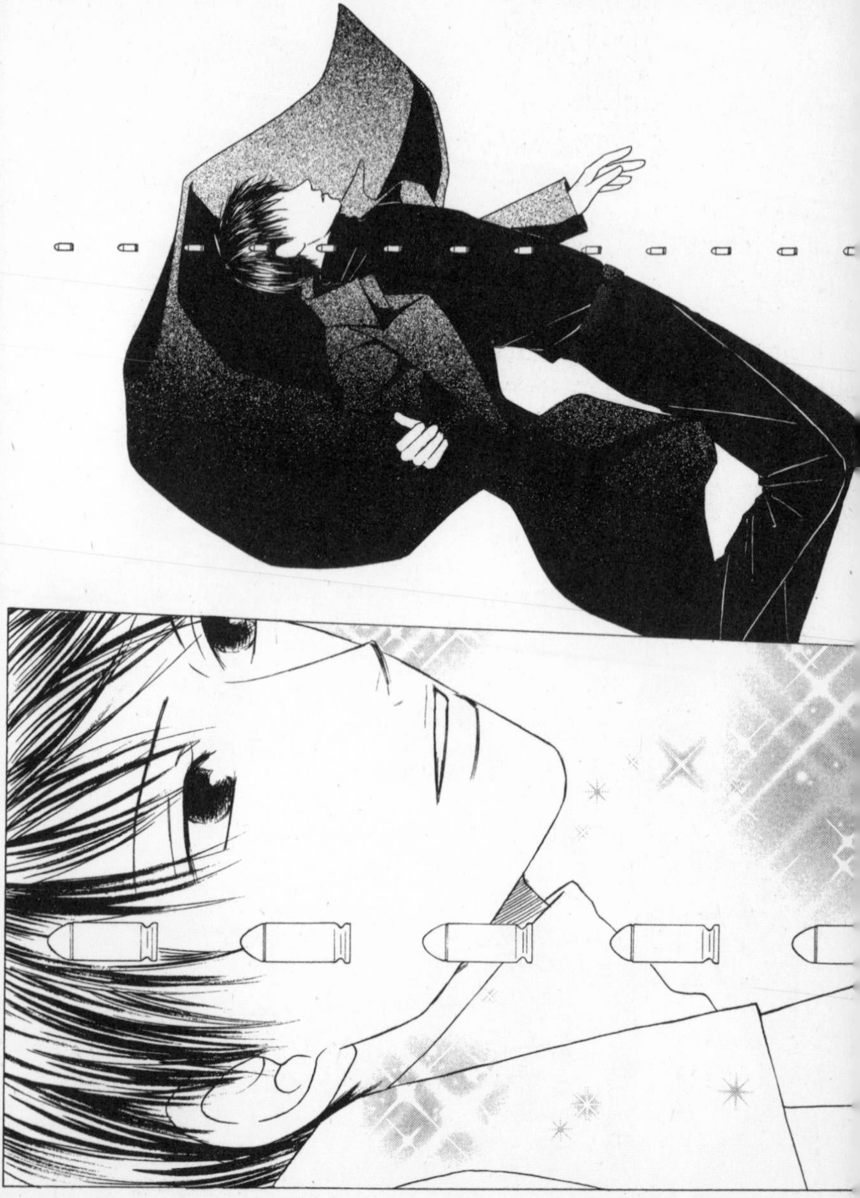

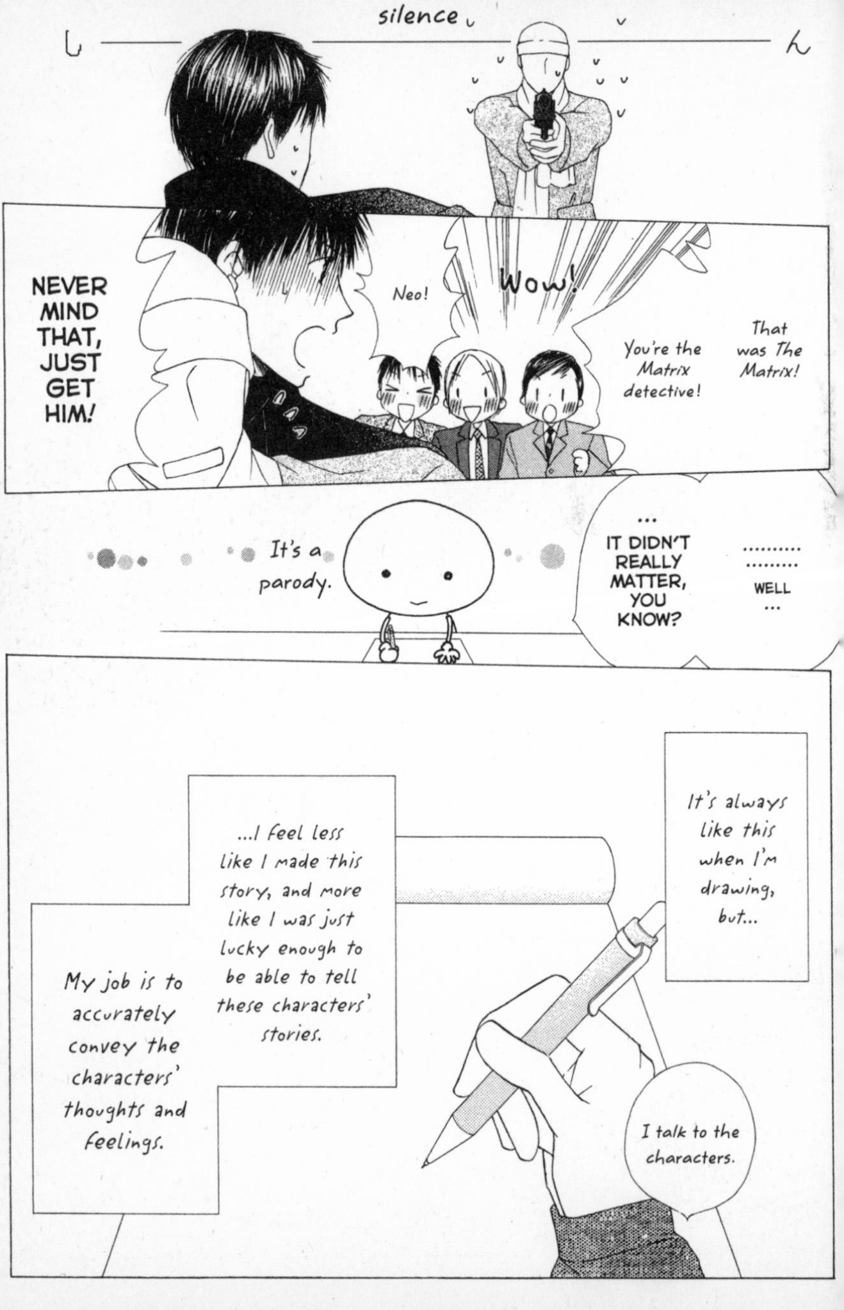
し silence ん
That was The Matrix!
You're the Matrix detective!
Wow!
Neo!
NEVER MIND THAT, JUST GET HIM!
.......... ......... WELL ...
... IT DIDN'T REALLY MATTER, YOU KNOW?
It's a parody.
It's always like this when I'm drawing, but...
I talk to the characters.
...I feel less like I made this story, and more like I was just lucky enough to be able to tell these characters' stories.
My job is to accurately convey the characters' thoughts and feelings.

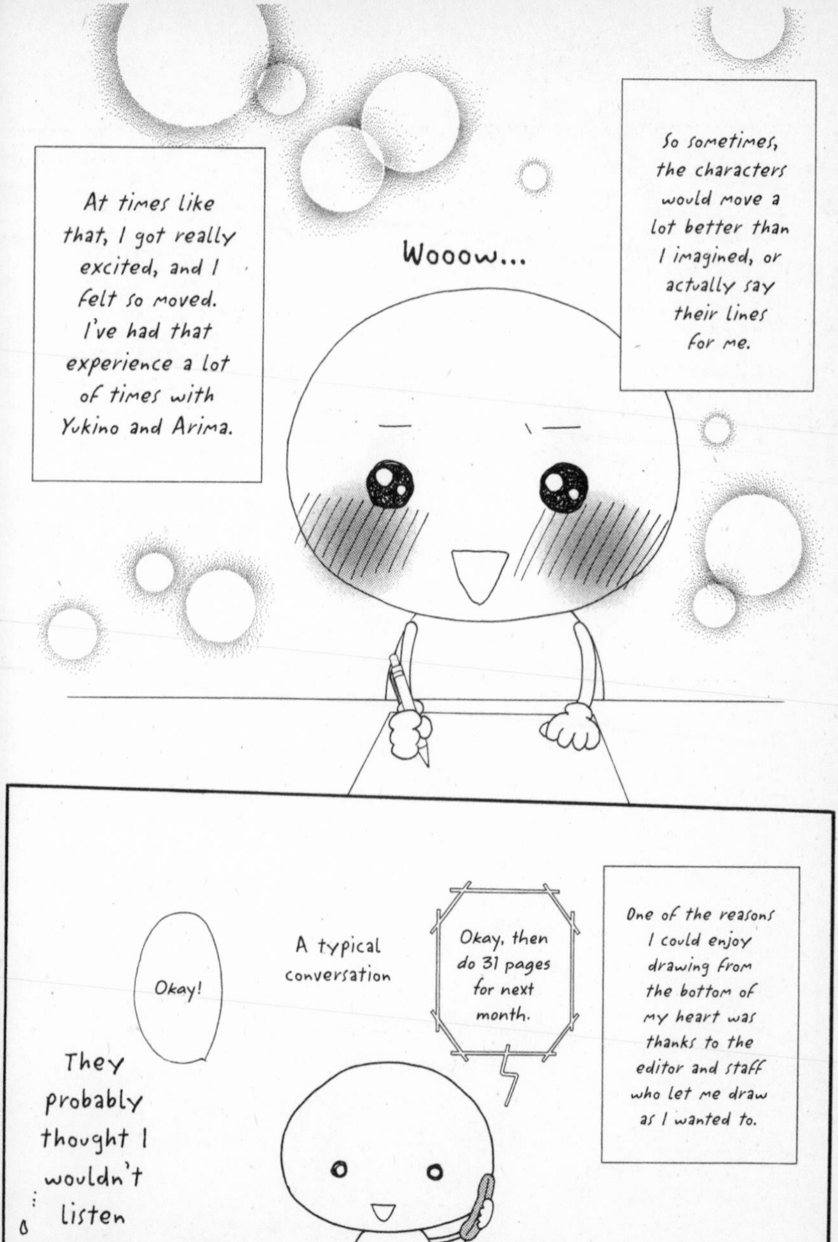

So sometimes, the characters would move a lot better than I imagined, or actually say their lines for me.
At times like that, I got really excited, and I felt so moved. I've had that experience a lot of times with Yukino and Arima.
Wooow...
One of the reasons I could enjoy drawing from the bottom of my heart was thanks to the editor and staff who let me draw as I wanted to.
Okay, then do 31 pages for next month.
A typical conversation
Okay!
They probably thought I wouldn't listen anyway.

They let me draw as I pleased for one reason only: my faithful readers.
Right now, I have about six cardboard boxes worth of *Kare Kano* goods that have piled up in my closet, and I'm coming up with a plan to send them to my readers! If you would like one of them, then please send me a letter with your thoughts on *Kare Kano*! You have a pretty good chance of getting something.
I'm glad I did my best.
I couldn't write back too often.

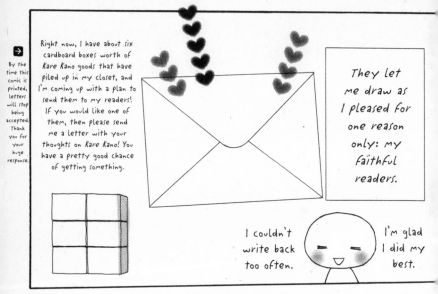

→ By the time this comic is printed, letters will stop being accepted. Thank you for your huge response.

I'll miss these characters. I spent nine years with them!

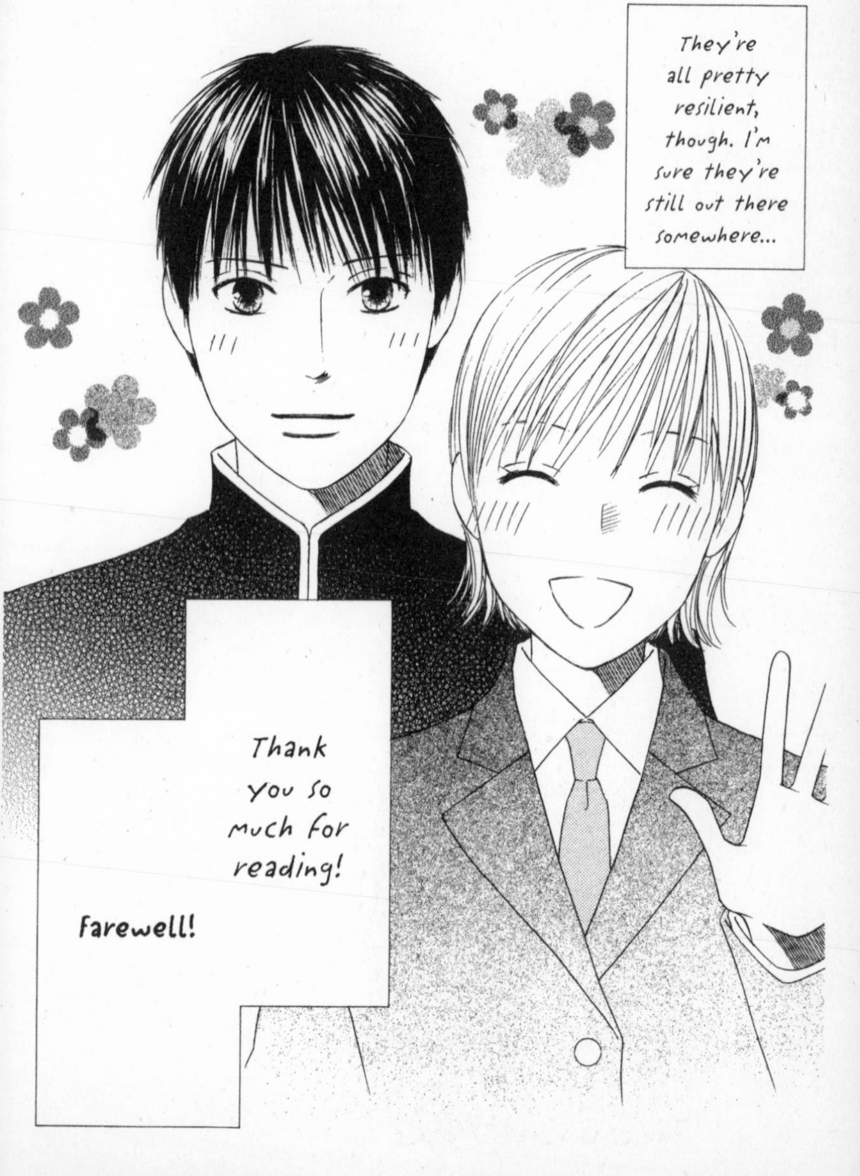
They're all pretty resilient, though. I'm sure they're still out there somewhere...
Thank you so much for reading!
Farewell!

LAST WALTZ / THE END

TO COMMEMORATE THE END OF KARE KANO...

# AUTOGRAPH COLLECTION!

There was an "autograph contest" that ran in Lala magazine, and I've collected some of the entries here! Thank you for the huge response! There were lots of memories, tears, and smiles.

TO ME, *KARE KANO* WILL NEVER DIE! IT'S THE BIBLE OF YOUTH! IT'S EVERYTHING IN LIFE! I REALLY LOVE IT!
(MARIE TAZAKI / TOKYO)

I'M WEAK, BUT *KARE KANO* GAVE ME A LOT OF COURAGE. IT'S THE MOST SPECIAL STORY TO ME. THIS SERIES HAS HELPED ME SO MUCH, AND IT WILL PROBABLY HELP ME EVEN MORE.
(FUMI / KANAGAWA)

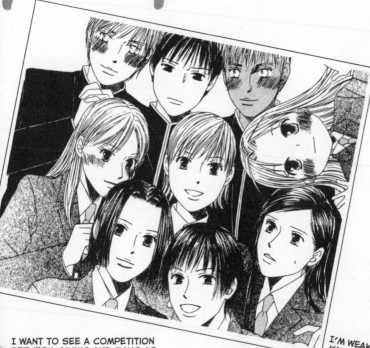

I WANT TO SEE A COMPETITION BETWEEN YUKINO AND MAHO AS FEMALE DOCTORS!
(SUNAO HOMATSU / HOKKAIDO)

I LOVE ALL OF THE CHARACTERS, WHO GREW NOT WITH RESPECT TO GETTING GOOD GRADES OR GROWING PHYSICALLY, BUT AS PEOPLE. THANK YOU SO MUCH, MS. TSUDA!
(SHEEP / TOCHIKI)

*KARE KANO* HAS TAUGHT ME SO MUCH. LOVE, FRIENDSHIP, FREEDOM, HONESTY, HOPE, HAPPINESS...I AM SO GRATEFUL THAT YOU MADE THIS STORY, AND THAT I COULD READ IT.
(IZUMI AOKI / GUNMA)

*KARE KANO* IS THE BIBLE OF MY HEART!
(KANATA / IWATE)

I CAN FEEL THE DEEP CONNECTIONS BETWEEN PEOPLE IN *KARE KANO*. IT'S A REAL HUMAN DRAMA! I WONDER IF I'VE GROWN, TOO? THANK YOU SO MUCH FOR MAKING SUCH A GREAT SERIES!
(KALEIDOSCOPE / MIYAGI)

I LOVE ARIMA-KUN--HE'S LIKE A PRINCE! I ALWAYS WISH HAPPINESS TO YUKINO-SAN AND ASAPIN (LOL)! I LOVE *KARE KANO*!
(GINTO / TOKYO)

I THINK THAT BECAUSE THEIR GIRLFRIEND/BOYFRIEND WAS A GOOD RIVAL, THEY WILL ALWAYS BE ABLE TO UNDERSTAND EACH OTHER. THEY'RE PRETTY YOUNG TO DETERMINE THEIR ENTIRE LIVES, BUT THERE'S NO WAY THEY CAN LET GO OF THE REAL THING EITHER.
(NEKO MIDORI / SAITAMA)

YUKINO KEEPS GOING NO MATTER WHAT HAPPENS. I WANT TO BE AS STRONG AS HER.
(IY / NIIGATA)

I HOPE MY HIGH SCHOOL LIFE IS AS GREAT AS IN *KARE KANO*!
(YUZUKO / IBARAKI)

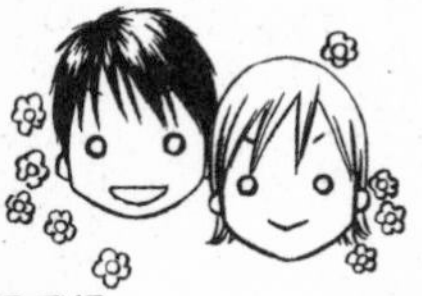

YOU'VE TAUGHT ME THE PRECIOUS FEELING OF LOVING ANOTHER. THANK YOU...I WISH YOU HAPPINESS.
( YUZU KASHIWAGI / OITA )

I WANT TO BE LIKE YUKINO-SAN. STAY JUST LIKE YOU ARE.
(NARUMIN / HYOGO)

HAPPY

THANK YOU FOR ALL THE EMOTIONS! YUKINON, SOICHIRO-KUN, PLEASE BE HAPPY!
(REI MIZUSHIRO / KANAGAWA)

It's a strange feeling, knowing that the story I've been writing in the middle of the night, sometimes anxiously and sometimes happily, was read by so many people, and touched so many people.

I hope that I have given back to all of you what you have given to me.

In the last part, I tried hard to finish in a way that would leave an impact. I wanted to leave this series without any regrets. Anyway, I did everything I could. I hope you liked it.

As a writer, I'm very happy to read in your letters that you worried about the characters as if they were real people.

Let's meet again if the chance arises.

Masami Tsuda

Please direct fan mail to:

Masami Tsuda

c/o Tokyopop editorial

5900 Wilshire Blvd.

Suite 2000

Los Angeles, CA 90036


Many thanks:


Editors    S. Taneoka

M. Tanzi


Staff    N. Shimizu

R. Ogawa

Y. Etou

R. Takahashi

E. Ouchi


The therapists at the massage parlor


AND   K. U

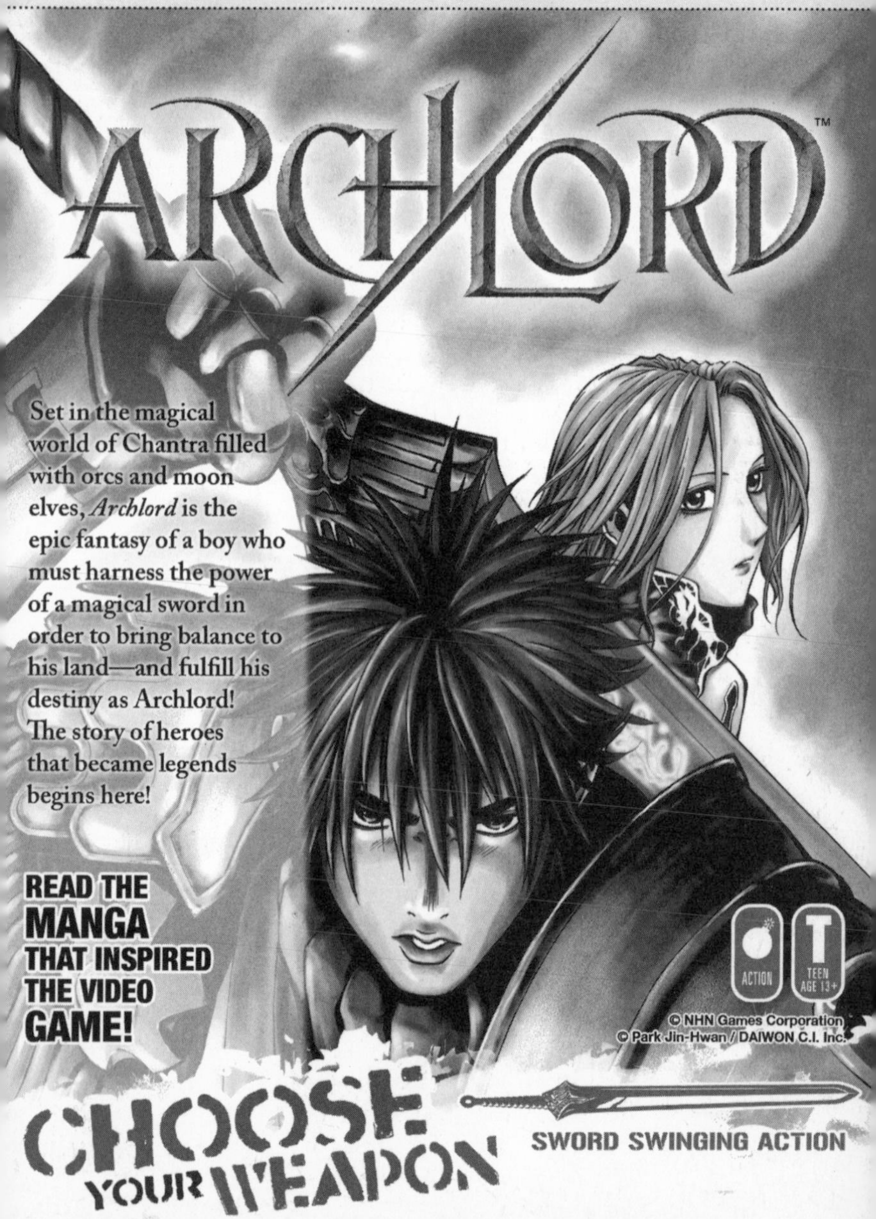
ARCHLORD™
Set in the magical world of Chantra filled with orcs and moon elves, *Archlord* is the epic fantasy of a boy who must harness the power of a magical sword in order to bring balance to his land—and fulfill his destiny as Archlord! The story of heroes that became legends begins here!
READ THE MANGA THAT INSPIRED THE VIDEO GAME!
ACTION
T
TEEN AGE 13+
© NHN Games Corporation
© Park Jin-Hwan / DAIWON C.I. Inc.
CHOOSE YOUR WEAPON
SWORD SWINGING ACTION

FOR MORE INFORMATION VISIT: WWW.TOKYOPOP.COM

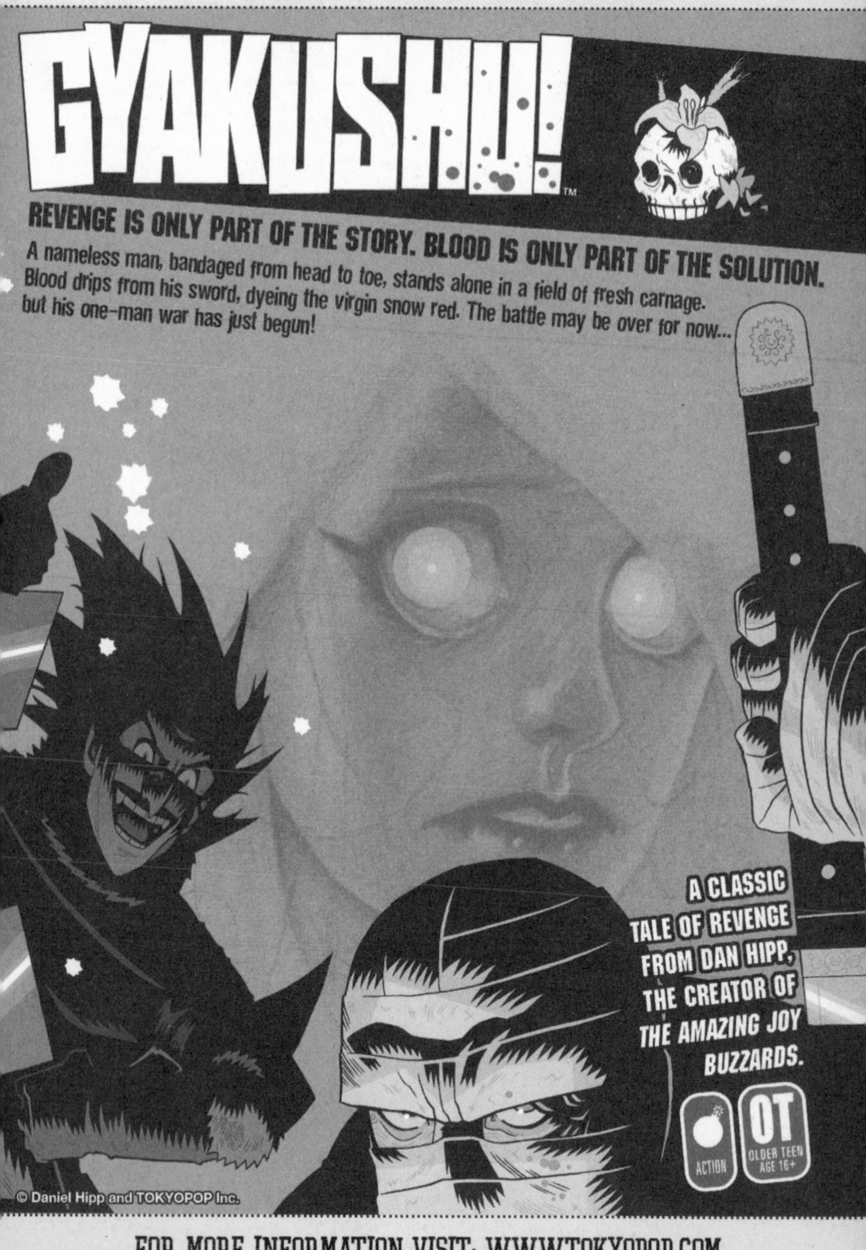
GYAKUSHU!™
REVENGE IS ONLY PART OF THE STORY. BLOOD IS ONLY PART OF THE SOLUTION.
A nameless man, bandaged from head to toe, stands alone in a field of fresh carnage. Blood drips from his sword, dyeing the virgin snow red. The battle may be over for now... but his one-man war has just begun!
A CLASSIC TALE OF REVENGE FROM DAN HIPP, THE CREATOR OF THE AMAZING JOY BUZZARDS.
ACTION
OT OLDER TEEN AGE 16+
© Daniel Hipp and TOKYOPOP Inc.